SO-DLS-882

KENT AARON REYNOLDS, Ph.D. (2007) in Hebrew and Semitic Studies, University of Wisconsin-Madison, is a Postdoctoral Fellow at Union Theological Seminary in NY. He was previously a research fellow at the Hebrew University of Jerusalem.

Torah as Teacher

Supplements

to

Vetus Testamentum

VOLUME 137

Torah as Teacher

The Exemplary Torah Student in Psalm 119

by

Kent Aaron Reynolds

BRILL

LEIDEN • BOSTON
2010

This book is printed on acid-free paper.

Library of Congress Cataloging-in-Publication Data

Reynolds, Kent Aaron.
  Torah as teacher : the exemplary Torah student in Psalm 119 / by Kent Aaron Reynolds.
    p. cm. — (Supplements to Vetus Testamentum ; v. 137)
    Includes bibliographical references and index.
    ISBN 978-90-04-18268-4 (hardback : alk. paper) 1. Bible. O.T. Psalms CXIX—Criticism, interpretation, etc. I. Title. II. Series.

  BS1450119th .R49 2010
  223'.2066—dc22

                                                                    2010005651

ISSN 0083-5889
ISBN 978 90 04 18268 4

Mixed Sources
Productgroep uit goed beheerde bossen
en andere gecontroleerde bronnen.
www.fsc.org Cert no. CU-COC-803902
© 1996 Forest Stewardship Council

PRINTED IN THE NETHERLANDS

for my parents

Don and Cheryl

who have always loved me without any conditions

CONTENTS

ACKNOWLEDGMENTS

Many people have made this book possible, and I am grateful to them. My *Doktorvater* Professor Michael V. Fox, who consistently models sensible scholarship, offered invaluable guidance and at the same time urged me to think for myself. Professor Hans Barstad's editorial instructions improved the book in numerous ways. Professor Cynthia Miller gave me helpful comments and suggestions, especially in linguistic matters. Dr. Jonathan W. Schofer taught me a great deal about the field of Rabbinics and helped me think beyond the boundaries of traditional biblical scholarship. Professors Rachel Brenner, Gilead Morhag, and Simone Schweber provided help from their perspective as experts in Hebrew literature and pedagogy. My friends Dr. Michael Lyons, Dr. D. Andrew Teeter, and Dr. William Tooman made helpful suggestions and encouraged me along the way. Karla Prigge commented on the work at different stages and often provided insightful comments. Wendy Widder and Suzanna Smith served as copy editors. Of course, any errors or shortcomings are my own.

In addition to the above individuals, the George L. Mosse Foundation provided financial support that made some of the research possible. Several librarians, whose names I do not know, have provided their assistance with some of my seemingly strange requests, most importantly in the interlibrary loan department at the University of Wisconsin–Madison, the Jewish Reading Room at the National Library of Israel, and the library of the École Biblique in Jerusalem.

ABBREVIATIONS

ABD	*Anchor Bible Dictionary*
AGJU	Arbeiten zur Geschichte des antiken Judentums und des Urchristentums
ASV	American Standard Version
BASOR	*Bulletin of the American Schools of Oriental Research*
BBE	The Bible in Basic English
BEThL	Bibliotheca Ephemeridum theologicarum Lovaniensium
BHL	*Biblia Hebraica Leningradensia*
BHS	*Biblia Hebraica Stuttgartensia*
Bib	*Biblica*
BJS	Brown Judaic Studies
BKAT	Biblischer Kommentar Altes Testament
BZAR	Beihefte zur Zeitschrift für altorientalische und biblische Rechtsgeschichte
BZAW	Beihefte zur Zeitschrift für die alttestamentliche Wissenschaft
CBR	*Currents in Biblical Research*
CBQ	*Catholic Biblical Quarterly*
CBQMS	Catholic Biblical Quarterly Monograph Series
DBY	The Darby Bible
Deissler	Alfons Deissler, *Psalm 119 und seine Theologie*
DJD	Discoveries in the Judaean Desert
Ehrlich	Arnold B. Ehrlich, *Die Psalmen*
ESV	English Standard Version
EvTh	*Evangelische Theologie*
FAT	Forschungen zum Alten Testament
FRLANT	*Forschungen zur Religion und Literatur des Alten und Neuen Testaments*
FOTL	Forms of the Old Testament Literature
GKC	*Gesenius' Hebrew Grammar*. Edited by E. Kautzsch. Translated by A. E. Cowley.
GNV	Geneva Bible
Ha-Keter	The "Ha-Keter" edition of *Miqra'ot Gedolot*. This abbreviation refers to the second Psalms volume unless otherwise specified.

HALOT	*Hebrew and Aramaic Lexicon of the Old Testament*
HAR	*Hebrew Annual Review*
HAT	Handbuch zum Alten Testament
HBS	Herders biblische Studien
HKAT	Handkommentar zum Alten Testament
HSM	Harvard Semitic Monographs
HThKAT	Herders theologischer Kommentar zum Alten Testament
HTR	*Harvard Theological Review*
HUCA	*Hebrew Union College Annual*
IBHS	*An Introduction to Biblical Hebrew Syntax* by Bruce Waltke and Michael O'Connor
ICC	International Critical Commentary
Int	*Interpretation*
JBL	*Journal of Biblical Literature*
JBQ	*Jewish Bible Quarterly*
JETS	*Journal of the Evangelical Theological Society*
JJS	*Journal of Jewish Studies*
JM	*A Grammar of Biblical Hebrew* by Paul Joüon and Takamitsu Muraoka
JNES	*Journal of Near Eastern Studies*
JNSL	*Journal of Northwest Semitic Languages*
JPS	The Jewish Publication Society 1917 translation of the Hebrew Bible
JSJSup	Supplements to *Journal for the Study of Judaism*
JSOT	*Journal for the Study of the Old Testament*
JSOTSup	Journal for the Study of the Old Testament: Supplement Series
JSS	*Journal of Semitic Studies*
KJV	King James Version
NASB	New American Standard Bible
NEB	Neue Echter Bibel
NET	New English Translation
NIV	New International Version
NKJ	New King James Version
NLT	New Living Translation
NRSV	New Revised Standard Version
OBO	Orbis biblicus et orientalis
OED	*Oxford English Dictionary*
OTE	*Old Testament Essays*
OTL	Old Testament Library

OtSt	*Oudtestamentische Studiën*
RB	*Revue biblique*
RevQ	*Revue de Qumran*
RGG	*Religion in Geschichte und Gegenwart*
RSV	Revised Standard Version
SBTS	Sources for Biblical and Theological Study
ST	*Studia theologica*
ThPh	*Theologie und Philosophie*
TLOT	*Theological Lexicon of the Old Testament* Jenni & Westermann
TNK	The Jewish Publication Society 1985 translation of the Hebrew Bible
TRE	*Theologische Realenzyklopädie*
UF	*Ugarit-Forschungen*
VT	*Vetus Testamentum*
VTSup	Supplements to *Vetus Testamentum*
WMANT	Wissenschaftliche Monographien zum Alten und Neuen Testament
YLT	Young's Literal Translation
ZAR	*Zeitschrift für altorientalische und biblische Rechtsgeschichte*
ZAW	*Zeitschrift für die alttestamentliche Wissenschaft*
ZThK	*Zeitschrift für Theologie und Kirche*

Grammatical and Technical Terms

D	Piel
Dp	Pual
DSS	Dead Sea Scrolls
G	Qal
H	Hiphil
inf.	Infinitive
LBH	Late Biblical Hebrew
LXX	Septuagint
MSS	Manuscripts
MT	Masoretic Text
N	Niphal
pl.	Plural
sing.	Singular
k	*Ketib*, (e.g., v. 147k)

TRANSLATION

א

1 Happy are those whose way is blameless—
  the ones who walk in the Torah of YHWH.
2 Happy are the ones who keep his stipulations;
  they seek him wholeheartedly.
3 Also they do not do iniquity;
  they walk in his ways.
4 You yourself appointed your precepts,
  in order that [everyone] should observe [them] carefully.
5 O, that my ways would be established,
  in order to observe your statutes!
6 Then I would not be ashamed,
  when I gaze at all your commandments.
7 I will praise you with an upright heart,
  when I learn your righteous regulations.
8 I will observe your statutes;
  do not forsake me completely.

ב

9 How shall a lad purify his path?
  By keeping it according to your word.
10 I sought you with all my heart;
  do not cause me to stray from your commandments.
11 I hid your word (אמרה) in my heart,
  so that I would not sin against you.
12 Blessed are you, O YHWH;
  teach me your statutes.
13 I recounted with my lips
  all the regulations of your mouth.
14 In the way of your stipulations I delight
  like [one delights] over all wealth.
15 I will muse on your precepts,
  and I will gaze at your paths.
16 I will delight myself in your statutes;
  I will not forget your word.

גּ

17 Deal [well] with your servant so that I may live,
　　and I will observe your word.
18 Open my eyes that I may gaze on
　　miracles from your Torah.
19 I am a temporary resident in the land;
　　do not hide your commandments from me.
20 My soul is ground down from longing
　　for your regulations all the time.
21 You have rebuked the accursed insolent ones—
　　the ones who go astray from your commandments.
22 Remove from me reproach and contempt,
　　for I keep your stipulations.
23 Also princes sit and speak against me;
　　your servant will muse on your statutes.
24 Also your stipulations are my delight—
　　the men of my counsel.

ד

25 My soul clings to the dust;
　　give me life according to your word.
26 I recounted my ways, and you answered me.
　　Teach me your statutes.
27 Give me insight in the way of your precepts,
　　and I will muse on your miracles.
28 My soul drips from anguish;
　　establish me according to your word.
29 Remove the way of deception from me,
　　and grace me [with] your Torah.
30 I have chosen the way of faithfulness;
　　I set your regulations [continually before me].
31 I cling to your stipulations;
　　O YHWH, do not shame me.
32 I will run in the way of your commandments,
　　for you expand my heart.

ה

33 Teach me, O YHWH, the way of your statutes,
　　and I will keep it—עֵקֶב.

34 Give me insight, and I will keep your Torah.
    I will observe it wholeheartedly.
35 Make me walk in the path of your commandments,
    for in it I take delight.
36 Incline my heart to your stipulations
    and not to extortion.
37 Turn my eyes away from seeing worthlessness;
    give me life in your path.
38 Establish your word (אמרה) for your servant,
    which [leads] to fear of you.
39 Make my reproach, which I fear, pass away,
    for your regulations are good.
40 Behold, I long for your precepts;
    give me life by your righteousness.

ו

41 Let your mercy come to me—O YHWH—
    your salvation according to your word (אמרה).
42 I will give the one who reproaches me an answer,
    for I trust in your word.
43 Do not completely withhold a word of truth from my mouth,
    because I hope for your justice.
44 I will observe your Torah continually—
    forever and ever.
45 I will walk about in a broad place,
    for I seek your precepts.
46 I will speak your stipulations in front of kings,
    and I will not be ashamed
47 I will take delight in your commandments,
    which I love.
48 I will lift up my hands to your commandments, which I love,
    and I will muse on your statutes

ז

49 Remember the word for your servant,
    on which you made me hope.
50 This is my comfort in my affliction,
    because your word (אמרה) gives me life.
51 The insolent mock me greatly,
    but I have not turned aside from your Torah.

52 I remember your regulations of old,
      O YHWH, and I take comfort.
53 Dread has seized me because of the wicked—
      the ones who abandon your Torah.
54 Your statutes have become songs for me
      in my temporary dwelling.
55 In the night I remember your name, O YHWH,
      that I may observe your Torah.
56 This belongs to me,
      because I keep your precepts.

ח

57 YHWH is my portion;
      I promise to observe your words.
58 I entreat your favor wholeheartedly;
      give me grace according to your word (אמרה).
59 I have considered my ways,
      so that I might turn my feet to your stipulations.
60 I hurried—and did not delay—
      to observe your commandments.
61 The cords of the wicked surrounded me,
      but I did not forget your Torah.
62 In the middle of the night I will arise to praise you
      about your righteous regulations.
63 I am a companion to all who fear you—
      to the ones who observe your precepts.
64 Your mercy fills the earth, O YHWH;
      teach me your statutes.

ט

65 You have acted well toward your servant,
      O YHWH, according to your word.
66 Teach me discretion and knowledge,
      for I believe your commandments.
67 Before I was afflicted, I strayed,
      but now I observe your word (אמרה).
68 You are good and the one who causes good things;
      teach me your statutes.

69 The insolent have smeared me with falsehood;
  but I will keep your precepts wholeheartedly.
70 Their heart is dull with fat,
  but I take delight in your Torah.
71 It was good for me to be afflicted,
  in order that I might learn your statutes.
72 Better for me is Torah of your mouth
  than hoards of gold and silver.

י

73 Your hands made me and established me;
  give me insight so I can learn your commandments.
74 The ones who fear you see me and rejoice,
  because I hope for your word.
75 I know, O YHWH, that your regulations are righteous,
  and you afflicted me in faithfulness.
76 Let your mercy comfort me,
  according to your word (אמרה) for your servant.
77 Let your compassion come to me that I might live,
  because your Torah is my delight.
78 Let the insolent be ashamed for they twist me with deception.
  I will muse on your precepts.
79 The ones who fear you will turn to me—
  the ones who know your stipulations.
80 Let my heart be blameless in your statutes,
  so that I will not be ashamed.

כ

81 My soul fails for your salvation;
  I hope for your word.
82 My eyes fail for your word (אמרה),
  saying "When will you comfort me?"
83 Though I am like a wineskin in smoke,
  I do not forget your statutes.
84 How many are the days of your servant?
  How long until you execute judgment on the ones who oppress
  me?
85 The insolent dig pits for me,
  which are not according to your Torah.

86   All your commandments are faithful.
        They oppress me with deception; help me!
87   They almost consumed me in the land,
        but I did not abandon your precepts.
88   Give me life according to your mercy,
        and I will observe the stipulations of your mouth.

ל

89   Forever, O YHWH,
        your word is established in the heavens.
90   Your faithfulness [endures] for generations.
        You founded the earth, and it stood.
91   According to your regulations they stand today,
        because all are your servants.
92   If your Torah had not been my delight,
        then I would have perished in my affliction.
93   I will never forget your precepts,
        for by them you give me life.
94   I am yours—save me,
        for I have sought your precepts.
95   The wicked wait for me in order to destroy me;
        I will consider your stipulations.
96   I have seen a limit for everything;
        your commandment is very expansive.

מ

97   How I love your Torah!
        All day it is my musing.
98   Your commandment makes me wiser than my enemies,
        for it is mine forever.
99   I have more discretion than all my teachers,
        for your stipulations are my musings.
100   I have more insight than elders,
        for I keep your precepts.
101   I restrain my feet from every wicked path,
        so that I might observe your word.
102   I do not turn away from your regulations,
        because you yourself instruct me.

103 How much smoother is your word (אמרה) to my palate
     than honey to my mouth.
104 I consider your precepts;
     therefore, I hate every path of deception.

נ

105 Your word is a lamp for my foot
     and a light for my path.
106 I have sworn—and I will do it—
     to observe your righteous regulations.
107 I am greatly oppressed;
     O YHWH, give me life according to your word.
108 Let the offerings of my mouth be pleasing, O YHWH,
     and teach me your regulations.
109 My life is continually in my hand,
     but I have not forgotten your Torah.
110 The wicked set a snare for me,
     but from your precepts I have not erred.
111 I possess your stipulations forever,
     for they are the joy of my heart.
112 I have inclined my heart to do your statutes
     forever—עקב.

ס

113 I hate divided things,
     but I love your Torah.
114 You are my hiding place and shield;
     I hope for your word.
115 Turn away from me, O evildoers,
     and I will keep the commandments of my God.
116 Support me according to your word (אמרה), and I will live.
     And do not let me be ashamed of my hope.
117 Support me so I will be delivered,
     and I will gaze at your statutes continually.
118 You have tossed aside all those who stray from your statutes,
     because their deceitfulness is deception.
119 You put an end to all the wicked of the land—the dross;
     therefore, I love your stipulations.

120   My flesh bristles with dread of you,
         and I fear your regulations.

ע

121   I have done justice and righteousness;
         do not turn me over to my oppressors.
122   Be a guarantee of goodness for your servant;
         do not let the insolent oppress me.
123   My eyes fail for your salvation
         and for your righteous word (אמרה).
124   Deal with your servant according to your mercy,
         and teach me your statutes.
125   I am your servant—give me insight,
         so that I may know your stipulations.
126   It is time for YHWH to act,
         [because] they have broken your Torah.
127   Therefore I love your commandments
         more than gold—even fine gold.
128   Therefore I walk straight by all the precepts of everything;
         I hate every path of deception.

פ

129   Your stipulations are miraculous;
         therefore, my soul keeps them.
130   The opening of your words gives light,
         giving insight to the callow.
131   I opened my mouth and panted,
         because I longed for your commandments.
132   Turn to me and give me grace,
         according to the justice of those who love your name.
133   Establish my steps in your word (אמרה);
         do not let any wickedness rule over me.
134   Redeem me from the oppression of men,
         so that I can observe your precepts.
135   Cause your face to shine on your servant,
         and teach me your statutes.
136   My eyes run with streams of water,
         because they do not observe your Torah.

צ

137 You are righteous, O YHWH,
        and your regulations are upright.
138 You appointed righteousness in your stipulations
        and great faithfulness.
139 My zeal silences me,
        for my enemies forget your words.
140 Your word (אמרה) is completely refined,
        and your servant loves it.
141 I am insignificant and despised,
        but I do not forget your precepts.
142 Your righteousness is righteous forever,
        and your Torah is true.
143 Trouble and distress find me;
        but your commandments are my delight.
144 Your stipulations are righteous forever;
        give me insight that I may live.

ק

145 I call out wholeheartedly—answer me, YHWH,
        so that I can keep your statutes.
146 I called you—deliver me
        so that I can observe your stipulations.
147 I arose in the twilight and cried out;
        I hope for your word.
148 My eyes anticipated the night watches
        to muse on your word (אמרה).
149 Hear my voice according to your mercy;
        O YHWH, give me life according to your justice.
150 The ones who pursue schemes draw near,
        but they are far from your Torah.
151 You are near, YHWH,
        and all of your commandments are true.
152 I had knowledge from your stipulations beforehand,
        for you founded them forever.

ר

153 Look at my affliction and deliver me,
    for I have not forgotten your Torah.
154 Argue my case and redeem me;
    give me life according to your word (אמרה).
155 Salvation is far from the wicked,
    because they have not sought your statutes.
156 Your compassions are numerous, O YHWH;
    give me life according to your regulations.
157 My pursuers and my enemies are numerous,
    but I have not strayed from your stipulations.
158 I have seen the treacherous ones, and I was disgusted—
    those who do not observe your word (אמרה).
159 Look, for I love your precepts;
    O YHWH, give me life according to your mercy.
160 The beginning of your word is true,
    and all of your righteous justice endures forever.

ש

161 Princes pursued me for no reason,
    yet my heart trembles at your word.
162 I rejoice over your word (אמרה)
    like one finding great plunder.
163 I hate and loath deception;
    I love your Torah.
164 I praise you seven times a day
    on account of your righteous regulations.
165 There is great peace for the ones who love your Torah,
    and there is no stumbling block for them.
166 I hope for your salvation, O YHWH,
    and I do your commandments.
167 My soul observes your stipulations,
    and I love them very much.
168 I observe your precepts and stipulations,
    because all my ways are before you.

ת

169 Let my cry come before you, O YHWH;
    give me insight according to your word.

170   Let my supplication come before you;
         deliver me according to your word (אמרה).
171   My lips will bubble praise
         when you teach me your statutes.
172   My tongue repeats your word (אמרה),
         because all of your commandments are righteous.
173   Let your hand help me,
         because I choose your precepts.
174   I long for your salvation, O YHWH,
         and your Torah is my delight.
175   Let my soul live, that it may praise you;
         and let your justice help me.
176   I have gone astray like a perishing sheep; seek your servant,
         because I have not forgotten your commandments.

CHAPTER ONE

INTRODUCTION

Bernhard Duhm begins his brief comments on Ps 119 with complete disdain:

> What sort of purpose the author had in view during the composition of these 176 verses, I do not know. In any case, this "psalm" is the most empty product that has ever darkened a piece of paper.[1]

Forty years later, in the commentary by Artur Weiser, Ps 119 fares only slightly better: "The psalm is a many-coloured mosaic of thoughts which are often repeated in a wearisome fashion."[2] Is Ps 119 merely empty, wearisome repetition for the sake of filling out the acrostic format? Can Ps 119 truly be summarized "with welcome brevity" in a short hymn as Weiser claims?[3]

1.1. INTRODUCTION

The claim of this study is that Ps 119 contains a striking message, which cannot be summarized in a short hymn, and that previous studies have failed to recognize a central rhetorical aim in the psalm. This oversight has negatively affected interpretation both of individual verses and of the psalm as a whole. As a result the contribution of Ps 119 to the Psalter and to the development of Judaism has not been adequately described. What is the striking message? In the following

---

[1] "Was der Autor bei der Abfassung dieser 176 Verse für einen Zweck im Auge gehabt hat, weiss ich nicht. Jedenfalls ist dieser „Psalm" das inhaltsloseste Produkt, das jemals Papier schwarz gemacht hat." Bernhard Duhm, *Die Psalmen*, 2d ed., Kurzer Hand-Kommentar zum Alten Testament, ed. D. Karl Marti, vol. 14 (Tübingen: J. C. B. Mohr, 1922), 427.

[2] Artur Weiser, *The Psalms*, OTL, trans. Herbert Hartwell (Philadelphia: Westminster Press, 1962), 739. On the same page Weiser also states that this psalm "is a particularly artificial product of religious poetry." The English edition quoted here is based primarily on the fourth German edition (1955); the first edition appeared in 1939 exactly forty years after Duhm's commentary.

[3] "Wohl dennen, die da wandeln vor Gott in Heiligkeit" by Cornelius Becker. This is a short poem of four stanzas based on Ps 119 that was published in the late 1500's and popularized by its inclusion in many German hymnals.

paragraphs, I give a précis of the message and an overview of how this study proceeds.[4]

Psalm 119 teaches that the righteous should internalize Torah to the point that it is character forming. Instead of admonishing the reader to study and obey Torah, the author portrays someone who does so. By means of the portrayal, the author creates—in the persona of the speaker—a model for the reader to follow. The speaker loves Torah, clings to it, yearns to understand it. He is not obeying God's law simply to avoid punishment; he rejoices and delights in his obedience. Thus, the speaker models the message. He is completely immersed in Torah—both the observance and the study of Torah.

Torah study does not enjoy preeminence within the Hebrew Bible; instead Torah observance does. However, Torah study is the definitive religious activity of Rabbinic Judaism. This difference indicates that a dramatic shift took place in the conception of Torah. The emphasis on Torah study in Ps 119 is unique within the Hebrew Bible and contributes to the shift in the conception of Torah, especially its function in the life of the righteous. This shift, combined with Ps 119's expansive praise of Torah raises the question: "What is Torah in Psalm 119?"

The conception of Torah in Ps 119 is not merely the five books of Moses. Torah includes rules that govern the universe (vv. 89–91); the justice that God will eventually visit upon the wicked (v. 84); and any instruction from God for humanity. Torah also includes stipulations about how God should act. Because these stipulations are self-imposed, they are trustworthy promises, which are comforting for God's servants. Any commandment, statute, precept, regulation, or stipulation is Torah, but Torah is not merely a collection of laws and rules. The rules and promises logically imply certain things, and the implications are also Torah. The rules and implications reveal what God desires, and this in turn teaches something about what God is like—something about God's character. All of these notions are a single, unified entity, because they are from the mouth of God. This expansive, inclusive conception of Torah in Ps 119 is a step towards the multi-faceted conception of Torah in Rabbinic Judaism.

---

[4] Since this is a précis, there are many unsubstantiated claims and no footnotes in what follows. I provide the argumentation and citations in the body of the work.

The heart of my study is to describe the portrayal of the exemplary Torah student (chapter 3) and to explore the conception of Torah (chapter 4). These two emphases in the psalm are mutually reinforcing. For example, portraying the speaker's intense longing for Torah would have less rhetorical effect if the conception of Torah could be limited to a specific text. Since the portrayal of the speaker is a central rhetorical aim of Ps 119, much of the psalm is about the function of Torah rather than its essence. The emphasis on the character-shaping function of Torah must be taken into account in a coherent description of Ps 119's conception of Torah, and this consideration dictates the relative order of chapters 3 and 4. An essential foundation for the discussion is an examination of poetics, which I begin in the following section and continue in the final section of this chapter by addressing the question of the psalm's genre.

The discussion of poetics continues in chapter 2, where I argue that the use of traditional religious language is a constitutive literary feature of the psalm. More specifically, as the speaker in Ps 119 addresses God, the words that come from his mouth sound like the words of Torah itself. For example, the speaker uses the language of the Priestly Blessing. Previous studies of Ps 119 have discussed this constitutive feature of the psalm but have failed to provide a cohesive explanation of it. I argue that the author uses this traditional religious language to characterize the speaker as someone who has internalized Torah so completely that it shapes his speech. Because the words are traditional, they resonate with the beliefs of the pious, and this resonance increases the rhetorical effectiveness of the psalm.

Separating the discussions of chapters 2 and 3 is necessary for a sound methodology, but there are overlaps between the discussions. For example, I discuss "enemies" in chapter 2 as evidence that the author uses traditional religious language, but I do not explain why the author uses the motif. In chapter 3, I argue that the author uses "enemies" as a means to portray the exemplary Torah student in antagonistic situations, which contributes to his characterization. Thus in chapter 2, I describe *what* the author is doing, and in chapter 3, *why* he is doing it.

Finally in chapter 5, I explore the place of Ps 119 in its literary and historical contexts. Typically in biblical studies, the discussion of historical context provides a foundation for further study, but this cannot be the first step in the case of Ps 119, due to the lack of evidence. Thus, the question that I address in chapter 5 is how to relate the conclusions of chapters 3 and 4—especially the conception of Torah—to the Psalter, the Hebrew Bible as a whole, and to the history of the development of Judaism.[5]

1.2. Poetics

A discussion of the poetics of Ps 119 is essential, since the poem is a carefully crafted work. The two most prominent literary features of Ps 119 are the acrostic format and the use of the number eight. There are eight verses for each letter of the alphabet. The first eight verses begin with the first letter of the alphabet—א. The next eight verses (vv. 9–16) begin with the second letter of the alphabet—ב. This pattern continues for each of the twenty-two letters of the alphabet, resulting in twenty-two stanzas of eight verses for a total of 176 verses. Throughout this massive acrostic poem the author uses eight terms for Torah, and none of the eight terms for Torah occurs at the beginning of any verse as a part of the acrostic framework.[6] The eight terms are תורה "Torah"; עדות "stipulations"; פקודים "precepts"; חקים "statutes"; מצות "commandments"; משפטים "regulations"; אמרה "word"; and דבר "word."[7]

1.2.1. The Relationship between Form and Function

No one can seriously deny that the artistic form of Ps 119 is important and that the author took great care in the construction of the poem; nevertheless, specifying how the form contributes to the message is a difficult and subjective enterprise. For example, many scholars claim that the acrostic format contributes to the following message: God's word is complete or perfect (תמם). That is, it runs "from A to Z." Connecting the idea of completeness with the alphabet is not a modern

---

[5] The discussion in chapters 1–5 assumes the commentary, which begins on p. 185.

[6] Will Soll describes these two features of Ps 119 as "the two axes" around which the author constructed his poem. Will Soll, *Psalm 119: Matrix, Form, and Setting*, CBQMS, vol. 23 (Washington, D.C.: Catholic Biblical Association, 1991), 1.

[7] I use these glosses consistently with the exception of few cases where different nuances of the Hebrew terms are emphasized. Such cases are limited to the two terms משפטים and אמרה, and I note these cases as necessary. I discuss the meaning of the eight terms and the relationships between them in chapter 4.

invention as the following quote illustrates: "'The whole of Israel has transgressed your Torah.' It does not say here 'against your Torah' but simply 'your Torah' because they transgressed it from *aleph* to *taw*."[8]

Regarding the repetition of the number eight, Zenger comments that the pattern 7 + 1 is reminiscent of the pattern of feast days (Lev 9:1), the dedication of the temple under Solomon (1 Kgs 8:66), and especially the reading and explanation of Torah under the direction of Ezra, which lasted for eight days.[9] "And day by day, from the first day to the last day, he read from the book of the law of God (בספר תורת האלהים). They kept the festival seven days; and on the eighth day there was a solemn assembly..." (Neh 8:18 NRSV). Although it is impossible to prove that the author was alluding to these texts, this explanation for the use of the number eight seems reasonable.

In addition to the above comments on the 7 + 1 pattern, the following claims about how the form contributes to the meaning are listed by Erich Zenger:[10] (1) the use of all the letters of the alphabet and the eightfold repetition indicates the completeness and abundance of God's word; (2) the eight-fold acrostic framework combined with the distribution of the eight different Torah terms indicates the unshakeable order that God's word creates; (3) the use of an acrostic possibly indicates that the author of Ps 119 assumed that Torah was a written text; (4) the petitions in the psalm indicate that the world in which human beings live is chaotic; (5) the recitation of the psalm indicates an invoking of the orderliness of God's word. I doubt that the data can support all of these conclusions, and the following paragraph illustrates the difficulty.

---

[8] 3 Enoch 44:9. Translation by P. Alexander in *The Old Testament Pseudepigrapha*, ed. James Charlesworth, vol. 1 (Garden City, NY: Doubleday, 1983), 296.

[9] Erich Zenger, "Torafrömmigkeit: Beobachtungen zum Poetischen und Theologischen Profil von Psalm 119," in *Freiheit und Recht: Festschrift für Frank Crüsemann zum 65. Geburtstag*, ed. Christof Hardmeier, Rainer Kessler, and Andreas Ruwe (Gütersloh: Verlagshaus Chr. Kaiser, 2003) 385–86. Deissler made a similar observation, see p. 72. Freedman suggests that "the selection of the number eight may result from the notion that the eight acts of creation in Genesis 1 reflect the perfection of the universe as crafted by God, and the resulting correspondences between the law as the perfect expression and the universe as the perfect creation of the same God." David Noel Freedman, *Psalm 119: The Exaltation of Torah* (Winona Lake, IN: Eisenbrauns, 1999), 78.

[10] Zenger, "Torafrömmigkeit," 385. I use his list since it is one of the most recently published articles, and he draws insights from earlier studies.

Several scholars claim that the structure of Ps 119 can be associated with a claim about orderliness. The acrostic is orderly. The author's use of eight is orderly; he uses eight verses for each letter of the alphabet as well as eight different terms for God's word. Soll argues that there is a further pattern: "one Torah word for each line."[11] If this were true, it might provide additional evidence to support Zenger's fifth claim that God's word brings structure to the world. However, not every verse contains one of the eight terms. Soll is forced to emend the Masoretic Text in four verses (vv. 3, 37, 90, and 122), since none of the eight terms occurs in these verses.[12] Zenger, arguing for Torah as the "comprehensive ordering structure of the world," says, "that there are a few lines, in which no Torah term stands, and that analogously in a few lines two Torah terms are used, is from my point of view not an argument *against* the programmatic meaning of the 176 examples, but rather directly *for* this function."[13] Freedman makes a different claim about the order: "The two poles of the poem's framework, then, are order (the acrostic format) and (apparent) chaos (the distribution of the key words)."[14] The psalmist broke the plan of having one Torah term in every verse in order to indicate that the world is not orderly, and he used the acrostic format to argue that God's word creates order in the midst of chaos.[15]

---

[11] Soll, *Psalm 119: Matrix, Form, and Setting*, 52. Soll states that the limitation of one Torah term per line that the author imposed on himself is the true source of the monotony in Ps 119 rather than the acrostic format (p. 55). It is noteworthy that Soll, who argues for the aesthetic value of the acrostic format (pp. 5–30), finds the repetition of the Torah terms monotonous.

[12] It would be even more orderly if every stanza used each of the eight terms one time—not only one Torah term per line, but also a different Torah term in each of the eight lines of every stanza. The Briggs attempt to emend and rearrange the text with this goal. Charles A. and Emilie G. Briggs, *The Psalms*, in ICC, 2 Vols. (Edinburgh: T & T Clark, 1906).

[13] Zenger, arguing for Torah as the "umfassende Ordungsstruktur der Welt," says, "daß es einige Zeilen gibt, in denen kein Torabegriff steht, und daß dann analog in einigen Zeilen zwei Torabegriffe verwendet werden, ist m.E. kein Argument *gegen* die programmatische Bedeutung der 176 Belege, sondern gerade *für* diese Funktion. Erich Zenger, "Torafrömmigkeit," 388–89. Yet something must be changed in order to arrive at the number 176; the Torah terms occur 177 times in the psalm. Zenger emends v. 168.

[14] Freedman, *Psalm 119: The Exaltation of Torah*, 93.

[15] Freedman's analysis extends far beyond the acrostic form. He presents numerous tables with an impressive collection of data: syllable counts, distribution of the Torah terms, the relationship between cola (stichs) and accents, and more. It seems rather odd to me that an author would arrange all of the data with the goal of indicating that the world is chaotic. Once the author chose to use an acrostic format and eight

The examples above demonstrate the difficulty in correlating aesthetics with meaning, even for Ps 119. Soll, Freedman, and Zenger draw different conclusions from the same evidence. One author's argument for emending the text is that the poem should be orderly. The same data are another author's evidence that the world lacks order. This is not to say that the form and structure should be ignored, but any significance attributed to the formal features should be corroborated with some other evidence.

1.2.2. *Structure or Progression in Addition to the Acrostic Form*

More recent scholars respond to the sort of disdain that Duhm expressed by attempting to show a progression of thought in Ps 119 or to discern a secondary structure in addition to the acrostic format.[16] Presumably, a thematic progression or some additional structuring device would show that Ps 119 is not an "empty product" as Duhm labels it. I agree that Ps 119 is not an empty product, but the arguments for a secondary structure are largely unconvincing.[17] For example, Zenger states that the middle stanzas (vv. 81–88 and vv. 89–96) form "the dramatic center of the psalm."[18] True, these verses are close to the center of the psalm mathematically speaking, but he does not show that they are the *dramatic* center.[19] The themes that Zenger describes to support this claim occur elsewhere in the psalm, and whatever tension that exists is not reduced in the stanzas following the so-called climax. Soll argues

---

different terms for Torah, it seems likely that many of the other phenomena that Freedman sees in Ps 119 would occur coincidently.

[16] A particularly thorough example is the monograph by Pierre Auffret, *Mais tu élargiras mon cœr: Nouvelle etude structurelle du psaume 119*, in BZAW, vol. 359. (Berlin: Walter de Gruyter, 2006).

[17] There are a few exceptions to this negative evaluation; see the following paragraphs. However, in several cases my evaluation is that the Rorschach principle comes into play; that is, authors have found a structure simply because they were looking for a structure.

[18] "… das dramatische Zentrum des Psalms." Zenger, "Torafrömmigkeit," 392.

[19] Karin Finsterbusch also believes that the ל stanza (she uses the label "strophe") is the middle of the poem, but she does not provide argumentation. She views the structure as follows: stanzas 1 and 2 constitute a prologue that provides the standard or norm for the poem; stanza 22 constitutes a conclusion; and stanza 12 is the central section that includes a cosmic perspective of Torah. The remaining stanzas are therefore in two blocks of material, one preceding the central stanza (3–11) and one following the central stanza (13–21). These two blocks comprise 9 stanzas each. Karin Finsterbusch, "Multiperspektivität als Programm: Das betende Ich und die Tora in Psalm 119," in *Was ist der Mensch, dass du seiner gedenkst? (Psalm 8,5)*, Festschrift für Bernd Janowski zum 65. Geburtstag (Neukirchen-Vluyn: Neukirchener, 2008), 94.

that the "movement" of Ps 119 follows the sequence of an individual
lament not once, "but rather recapitulates the sequence several times
in different ways in the course of an exceptionally long prayer."[20] It is
not at all clear that the psalm follows the sequence of an individual
lament. In any case, whatever sequence Soll finds is altered and thus
does not amount to a recapitulation.

Whybray identifies a series of keywords in Ps 119.[21] He lists the
following repetition of words in close proximity: לבב/לב (vv. 7, 10);
לב (vv. 32, 34); חרף (vv. 39, 42); למד (vv. 71, 73); ארץ (vv. 87, 90);
על כן (vv. 128, 129). What is noteworthy about these repetitions is
that they link adjacent stanzas. The first occurrence is near the end of
a stanza, and the repetition is near the beginning of the next stanza.
For example, the second to last verse of the כ stanza (v. 87) and the
second verse of the ל stanza (v. 90) both contain the word ארץ, which
functions to stitch the stanzas together. Although the stanzas are not
all linked by a repeated keyword, Whybray lists too many examples of
this phenomenon to ignore.[22] The stitch-words reinforce the structure
that is established by the acrostic form, but the repeated words alone
would not shape the stanzas.

Marcus Nodder also notes that the author used a particular word in
the first verse of a stanza and then repeated that word in the seventh
verse.[23] This phenomenon occurs in the following verses: ארח (vv. 9,
15); עבדך (vv. 17, 23); דבק (vv. 25, 31) זכר (vv. 49, 55); שמר (vv. 57,
63); כלה (vv. 81, 87); מה (vv. 97, 103); אהבתי (vv. 113, 119); ראה
(imv.; vv. 153, 159). It is not clear why he placed the repetition in the
seventh verse (second to last) instead of the eighth verse (last). Nodder
thinks that the verses are couplets; presumably, he means one should
read vv. 15 and 16 as a couplet that closes the stanza. However, there
is no formal reason that these verses (or the other examples, such as

---

[20] Soll, *Psalm 119: Matrix, Form, and Setting*, 71.

[21] Roger N. Whybray, "Psalm 119: Profile of a Psalmist," in *Wisdom, You Are My Sister*, ed. Michael L. Barré, CBQMS, vol. 29 (Washington: Catholic Biblical Association, 1997), 31–43.

[22] Whybray believes that the links he identifies demonstrate that the author intended to produce a coherent literary work. However, Whybray concludes his article by stating that "the author has been only partially successful... the immense difficulties presented by the literary medium that he had imposed on himself seem ultimately to have defeated him, or at least to have impaired his grand plan." Whybray, "Psalm 119: Profile of a Psalmist," 42–43.

[23] Marcus Nodder, "What is the Relationship between the Different Stanzas of Psalm 119?" *Churchman* 119 (2005): 328.

vv. 23 and 24; or vv. 63 and 64; etc.) form a couplet. In any case, these repetitions can only be identified because the acrostic shapes the stanzas.

Similar to the repetition of individual words is the repetition of themes in close proximity. This sort of linking based on thematic connections is plausible, although identifying such connections is admittedly subjective.[24] Verse 76 includes the ideas of mercy (חסד) and comfort (נחם), and v. 77 mentions compassion (רחם). The idea of shame (בוש) occurs in vv. 78 and 80. In close proximity the reader will notice these connections, and it seems reasonable that a particular idea sparked an association for the author. In his discussion of proverbs, Michael Fox calls such connections "associative sequences."[25] Associative sequences do have an impact on interpretation, especially of individual verses, but they do not necessarily amount to a structuring principle.

1.3. Genre

Scholars classify Ps 119 into several different genres. It has been classified as a psalm of mixed form, a psalm of individual lament, a wisdom psalm, and a Torah psalm. Some studies classify Ps 119 as both a Torah psalm and a wisdom psalm. For example, Schmitt includes it under the heading "Weisheitspsalm," and within the same section he states that it is thematically grouped with the so called "Torapsalmen."[26] The lack of consensus demonstrates that Ps 119 cannot be easily classified, and the question of its genre poses a problem for interpretation.

---

[24] Various commentators have noted connections; for example, Ehrlich repeatedly comments that an idea is related to the previous verse or verses, using phrases such as "hängt eng zusammen" and "in Bezug auf das Vorherg." Ehrlich, passim.

[25] "When one thought gives rise to another or one word evokes a related one, the result is an associative sequence. An 'editor' (or 'compiler') writes down one proverb he knows, and this makes him think of another on the same theme, and since it is on the same theme, it is likely to use similar wording. This process is prominent in the series of righteousness-wickedness antitheses in Prov 10:1–15:33, in the string of sayings on divine control in 16:1–9, and in the reflections on kingship in 16:10–15." Michael V. Fox, *Proverbs 10–31 A New Translation with Introduction and Commentary*, The Anchor Yale Bible, vol. 18B. (New Haven: Yale University Press, 2009), 480.

[26] Hans-Christoph Schmitt, *Arbeitsbuch zum Alten Testament* (Göttingen: Vandenhoeck & Ruprecht, 2005), 424.

1.3.1. *A Lament Psalm?*

Various scholars note that Ps 119 uses genre elements found in lament psalms. Gunkel states that the most commonly used form in Ps 119 was borrowed from laments, and he lists more than forty verses in Ps 119 that contain petitions.[27] Mowinckel also notes the influence of lament formulas in Ps 119.[28] Will Soll provides the most thorough arguments that Ps 119 is a lament psalm and devotes a chapter of his book to defend this claim.[29] Soll claims that over ninety verses contain a formula or motif taken from the lament genre.[30] He concludes that Ps 119 is an individual lament of an exiled Davidic king, specifically Jehoiachin, who is praying for the restoration of his kingdom.[31] Soll's conclusion reaches far beyond what the evidence can support, and there are methodological problems with his argument. Soll adopts the methods of form criticism, which deal with the "preliterary phase of the story."[32] But there is no evidence that Ps 119 had a "preliterary phase." On the contrary, the eightfold acrostic format demonstrates that it is a literary work without an oral prehistory. Gunkel himself argued that Ps 25 and Lam 3—laments that use an acrostic framework—"show how far the [lament] genre has been removed from its 'life setting.'" The same would be true for other acrostics, which "could only have been composed for written form to please the eyes…"[33] Soll identifies Ps 119 as an individual lament with an acrostic framework and then

---

[27] Hermann Gunkel, *An Introduction to the Psalms: The Genres of the Religious Lyric of Israel*, trans. James D. Nogalski (Macon, GA: Mercer University Press, 1998), 157.

[28] Sigmund Mowinckel, *The Psalms in Israel's Worship*, trans. by D. R. Ap-Thomas (New York: Abingdon Press, 1962), 2:78.

[29] Soll, *Psalm 119: Matrix, Form, and Setting*, 59–86 [chap. 3].

[30] Soll, *Psalm 119: Matrix, Form, and Setting*, 70.

[31] Soll, *Psalm 119: Matrix, Form, and Setting*, 152–54.

[32] Gene M. Tucker, *Form Criticism of the Old Testament*, Guides to Biblical Scholarship (Philadelphia: Fortress Press, 1971), v.

[33] Gunkel, *An Introduction to the Psalms*, 128. Gunkel's commentary on the Psalms first appeared in 1926, but his contribution to the study of form criticism had already had a significant influence on the field of biblical studies through his various articles, especially in *RGG*. Since Gunkel's time, the methodology of form criticism has evolved in various ways, but it is interesting that Gunkel's cautionary notes often adumbrate excesses or errors that took place in the decades following his work. In my opinion, if these cautions had been heeded, many banal applications of form criticism could have been avoided. For recent studies on the methodology see the essays in *The Changing Face of Form Criticism for the Twenty-First Century*, ed. Marvin A. Sweeney and Ehud Ben Zvi (Grand Rapids: Eerdmans, 2003) and Carol A. Newsom, "Spying out the Land: A Report from Genology," in *Seeking Out the Wisdom of the Ancients: Essays*

proceeds to describe a *Sitz im Leben*, precisely what Gunkel argued was impossible. Soll's description of the *Sitz im Leben* has not been widely accepted—and rightly so—but his analysis of Ps 119 as a lament psalm has been adopted in some important works.[34]

Since Soll's classification has received some approval, it deserves further discussion, and even if his incredible claim about Jehoiachin is set aside, the question remains: Does the use of genre elements of lament psalms mean that Ps 119 is a lament? The answer is unequivocally, no. The use of a genre element is not sufficient evidence to classify a text within any particular genre. Qohelet, for example, imitates features of royal inscriptions, but the use is ironic.[35] In chapter 2, I discuss the use of various genre elements in Ps 119, including various features of lament psalms. It does not follow that Ps 119 is a lament psalm.

There are several reasons why Ps 119 should not be classified as a lament. First, individual lament psalms begin with an address to God—often the name "YHWH" used as a vocative. "Passages where the psalm does not begin with the summons deviate so strongly from the normal style that the song should not be designated as an individual complaint song in the strict sense, even if it otherwise uses the motifs of the genre."[36] The first two verses of Ps 119 begin with macarisms ("Happy are those…" אשרי). The third verse provides further information about the people named in vv. 1 and 2.[37] Soll recognizes that Ps 119 does not begin with an address to God, but he argues that Gunkel's criteria are "too definitive and rigid."[38] However *defining* a genre, which is Gunkel's goal, should be definitive.

Secondly, the elements of lament psalms that do occur in Ps 119 are not arranged in a recognizable order. The general structure of lament psalms outlined by Gunkel remains undisputed and includes the following elements: (1) address to God, (2) general complaint, (3) petition or plea for help, (4) imprecation or complaint about enemies,

---

Offered to Honor Michael V. Fox on the Occasion of His Sixty-fifth Birthday, ed. Ronald L. Troxel et al., 437–50, (Winona Lake, IN: Eisenbrauns, 2005).

[34] Freedman says, "Soll has shown persuasively that the psalm is an individual lament." Freedman, *Psalm 119: The Exaltation of Torah*, 93. See also Erich Zenger, "Torafrömmigkeit."

[35] Michael V. Fox, *A Time to Tear Down and A Time to Build Up* (Grand Rapids: Eerdmans, 1999), 179.

[36] Gunkel, *Introduction to the Psalms*, 152.

[37] I discuss the introductory character of vv. 1–3 at the beginning of chapter 3.

[38] Soll, *Psalm 119: Matrix, Form, and Setting*, 71.

(5) affirmation of confidence in God, (6) protest of innocence or confession of sins, (7) acknowledgement of God's help, and (8) thanksgiving or praise.[39] A certain progression is an important feature of
individual laments, even if the order is not rigid. For example, laments
can contain both imprecations and thanksgiving. The thanksgiving is
generally at the end of the lament, providing the psalmist's response
to God's deliverance. Placing the element of thanksgiving prior to the
imprecation would make little sense. The lack of a specific arrangement
in Ps 119 may not be conclusive. Nevertheless, it is evidence that argues
against identifying Ps 119 as an individual lament.[40]

Finally, Ps 119 contains elements borrowed from other genres.
Mowinckel argues that the formal elements in some psalms disinte-
grate, and he gives Ps 119 as an example. "In a late psalm like Ps 119
prayer and lament and hymnal motives so intermingle as to make the
interpreters feel at a loss with regard to the character and purpose of
the psalm."[41] Despite Mowinckel's lack of appreciation for Ps 119 and
its purpose, he does recognize that Ps 119 borrows from various types
of psalms and does not limit it to a particular type.

Soll is correct that Ps 119 contains elements or traits of traditional
lament psalms, but identifying Ps 119 as an individual lament distorts the picture. These features are redeployed by the author in his
portrayal of the exemplary Torah student. Because the formal elements
of laments are used for a different purpose in Ps 119, their presence
does not support Soll's claim that Ps 119 is an individual lament. The
goal of interpretation should be to explain the purpose that the various genre elements serve, an explanation that I provide in chapters 3
and 4.

1.3.2. A Wisdom Psalm?

Avi Hurvitz argues convincingly that Ps 119 uses wisdom locutions,
that is, words or phrases that are characteristic of wisdom literature.[42]

---

[39] Gunkel, *An Introduction to the Psalms*, 152–98. See also Claus Westermann,
Praise and Lament in the Psalms, trans. Keith Crim and Richard N. Soulen (Atlanta:
John Knox, 1981).

[40] See the above comments regarding Soll's claim that Ps 119 recapitulates a
sequence multiple times, p. 20.

[41] Mowinckel, *The Psalms in Israel's Worship*, 2:77.

[42] Avi Hurvitz, "Wisdom Vocabulary in the Hebrew Psalter: A Contribution to the
Study of 'Wisdom Psalms,'" *VT* 38 (1988): 41–51. See also Avi Hurvitz, שקיעי חכמה

Beyond the phraseology, the psalm also has conceptual connections with wisdom literature; for example, a sharp contrast between the righteous and the wicked, an association between piety and intellectual pursuits, various tropes, and the like.[43] Borrowed locutions and motifs do not prove that Ps 119 is a wisdom psalm; Fox points out that the avoidance of terms for wisdom "seems intended to distance the poem from Wisdom ideology in favor of a Torah-centered doctrine."[44]

Identifying which psalms belong to the category of "wisdom psalm" is still a matter of debate. Kuntz argues that there are "*bona fide* wisdom poems" in the Psalter, which can be identified by their use of "stylistic features, typical vocabulary, and motifs that regularly inhabit Proverbs, Job, and Ecclesiastes."[45] Kuntz is correct that there is a group of psalms that exhibit these characteristics, but they do not praise wisdom. Instead they appropriate the vocabulary and concepts of wisdom in order to promote piety. It is wise to fear God (Pss 111, 112), to trust in God not in wealth or power (Pss 37, 49), to confess sin (Pss 32, 51, 90), to recognize that the wicked will ultimately be judged despite their apparent success (Ps 73), and to walk in Torah (Pss 1, 119). If wisdom psalms are defined as a group of psalms that argue it is wise to be pious, then Ps 119 can be included in the group.[46] However, the label "wisdom psalm" only communicates half of the story, and assigning Ps 119 to the group can only be done on the basis of inference, since the psalm never explicitly states that it is wise to be pious.

בספר תהלים [*Wisdom Language in Biblical Psalmody* (Hebrew)] (Jerusalem: Magnes Press, 1991).

[43] I provide a summary of the evidence listed by Hurvitz in addition to the other conceptual connections in the following chapter, pp. 50–52.

[44] Michael V. Fox, *Proverbs 10–31*, 955.

[45] J. Kenneth Kuntz, "Reclaiming Biblical Wisdom Psalms: A Response to Crenshaw," *CBR* 1 (2003): 145–54. This article is part of an ongoing debate about whether "wisdom psalm" is a helpful category. See the bibliography on Crenshaw and Kuntz.

[46] The fact that "wisdom psalms" is identified as a genre illustrates the idiosyncrasies of Psalms scholarship and the study of genres. (See the previous footnote.) Wisdom literature is a widespread phenomenon in the ancient world—widespread both geographically and chronologically. The texts of wisdom literature employ a wide variety of genres, but by another definition wisdom literature itself can be labeled a genre. "If the word [wisdom] is not used too loosely (as it sometimes is, for example, when applied to Esther or the Joseph story), it is an appropriate label for a fairly cohesive genre." Michael V. Fox, *Proverbs 1–9 A New Translation with Introduction and Commentary*, The Anchor Bible, vol. 18A, (New York: Doubleday, 2000), 17.

1.3.3. A Torah Psalm?

Psalms 1, 19b and 119 have been labeled "Torah Psalms," but they do not constitute a genre, since similar subject matter does not equal genre. Furthermore, if Ps 119 did not exist, it is very doubtful that Ps 1 and Ps 19b would be classified together.[47] Psalm 1 is about a person, and Ps 19b is about God's self-disclosure. Their respective emphases are quite different. Psalm 119 combines both emphases, but this overlap in subject matter does not warrant the creation of an otherwise unattested genre.

If genre classification is to be of any value, then the genre must be established without reference to the text being studied. Doing otherwise results in a viciously circular argument. For example, the characteristics of lament psalms can be established without reference to Ps 3. Once the characteristics are established, it is then beneficial for exegesis to identify Ps 3 as a lament psalm. Since the category "Torah psalm" can only be described by including all three examples (1, 19b, and 119), the label contributes nothing to the discussion of their respective genres.

Mays notes that Pss 1, 19b, and 119 "do not fit easily into any of the accepted genres," but they do have a function in shaping the Psalter.[48] He argues that Pss 1, 19b, and 119 (together with verses in other psalms) are part of the final redactional layer of the book of Psalms. In reference to Ps 119 specifically he states,

> Within the acrostic structure the poetic lines form a generic montage of elements drawn from the principal types of psalms. The elements of the hymn, the thanksgiving, the lament, the song of confidence, and the didactic poem are used.... All this generic diversity is held together as though the one who addresses God through the psalm were himself in

---

[47] Although the word "Torah" does not occur in Ps 111, Erich Zenger calls it a Torah psalm: "Ps 111 is a Torah psalm—and yet does not exhibit (like its nearest relatives Ps 19 and 119 [do]) the word 'tōrā'. Instead it uses the word *berīt* 'covenant' (which is lacking in Ps 19 and 119)." "Ps 111 ist ein Tora-Psalm—und bietet doch nicht (wie seine nächsten Verwandten Ps 19 und 119) das Wort »tōrā«. Stattdessen verwendet er das Wort *berīt* »Bund« (das in Ps 19 und 119 fehlt)." Frank-Lothar Hossfeld and Erich Zenger, *Psalmen 101–150*, HThKAT (Freiburg: Herder, 2008), 231. See also Zenger's article "Dimensionen der Tora-Weisheit in der Psalmenkomposition Ps 111–112," in *Die Weisheit—Ursprünge und Rezeption; Festschrift für Karl Löning zum 65. Geburtstag*, (Münster: Aschendorff, 2003), 37–58. Even if Zenger is correct in his assessment, his argument is about the subject matter or content of the psalm. Adding Ps 111 to the list, does not affect my argument that these psalms do not constitute a genre.

[48] James L. Mays, "The Place of the Torah-Psalms in the Psalter," *JBL* 106 (1987): 3.

his trust and experience the life setting of it all. This combination of psalmic genres into speech with which the servant of the Lord speaks to God is a clue to the way the rest of the psalms are viewed. They are all particular cases of the way a servant addressed his divine Lord, themselves fragments of a larger whole brought together in Ps 119.[49]

Several of the psalms that Mays groups together with Pss 1, 19b, and 119 as part of the final shaping of the Psalter are the same chapters discussed above as wisdom psalms.[50] "They all belong to the last stratum of the collection or have been developed by Torah interests."[51] The combined message of these psalms is that God has given instruction and the righteous study and obey it. Because they study and obey God's instruction, they will be successful. In other words, it is wise to be pious. Defined in May's terms, "Torah psalms" can be a useful rubric for referring to a group of related psalms, but the psalms in question do not constitute a genre.

1.3.4. An Anthological Psalm?

One of Alfons Deissler's important contributions to the study of Ps 119 was to explore and describe the psalm's use of diverse motifs and locutions, which he labels an "anthological style." His discussion is related to the question of Ps 119's genre, in part due to the similarities between "anthological" and the label *Mischgattung* that has been applied to Ps 119.[52] Deissler recognizes that the label *Mischgattung* contributes little to the explanation of Ps 119: "One can designate this negative fact [that it does not match the other *Psalmengattungen*] with the title „Mischgattung," but something positive and above all a deeper understanding of what the psalm conveys is not thereby revealed."[53]

---

[49] Mays, "The Place of the Torah-Psalms in the Psalter," 7.

[50] Mays lists Pss 18, 25, 33, 78, 89, 93, 94, 99, 103, 105, 111, 112, 147, and 148.

[51] Mays, "The Place of the Torah-Psalms in the Psalter," 8.

[52] Although various commentators since Gunkel have attributed him with classifying Ps 119 as a *Mischgattung*, that is technically incorrect. Gunkel did not identify Ps 119 as an exemplar of this supposed genre. See Gunkel, *An Introduction to the Psalms*, 306.

[53] "Diese negative Tatsache [that it does not match the other *Psalmengattungen*] kann man mit dem Titel „Mischgattung" bezeichnen, aber etwas Positives und vor allem das tiefere Verständis des Psalmes Förderndes wird damit nicht ausgesagt." Deissler, 268. The rubric *Mischgattung* identifies a problem not a solution, and the fact that some authors use this label is illustrative of a more widespread problem in Psalms research, specifically that "genre" and "*Gattung*" are used in various ways by different scholars. See the discussion above regarding form criticism and its applicability for Ps 119 beginning on p. 22.

By "anthological," Deissler does not mean that Ps 119 is a random pastiche or collage, instead he is referring to a style of writing that is characteristic of post-exilic biblical texts.[54] According to Deissler this writing style is a precursor to the biblical interpretation found in *midrashim* and *pesharim*. Other examples of the style are Ben Sira, Jubilees, Wisdom of Solomon, and the sectarian writings found at Qumran. It is true that Deissler is painting "anthological style" with a very broad brush at this point, but in fairness, the section containing these examples is part of his introduction.[55]

According to Deissler, an author writing in this anthological style borrows words, phrases, and motifs from earlier Scripture, and the meaning of the antecedent text affects the interpretation of the borrowing text (in this case Ps 119). The problem is that Deissler does not have a precise methodology for establishing the nature of relationship between texts, and he was quickly criticized by Klaus Koch for this methodological problem.[56] Koch is correct that Deissler's methodology was not careful. Nevertheless, the literary features that Deissler describes as "an anthological style" are constitutive features of Ps 119.

1.3.5. *Conclusion*

The problem of identifying Ps 119's genre remains. Fowler notes that genres emerge, evolve, mutate, and then new genres emerge, and in light of this observation perhaps Ps 119 is an example of a transitional stage. Fowler identifies three phases in the development of genres and states that the third phase "occurs when an author uses a secondary form in a radically new way."[57] It is possible that the author of Ps 119 uses a genre in such a radical way that it is difficult to classify. Yet this possibility does not solve the problem, because Ps 119 is not a transition from any single genre. The genre elements, phraseology, and

---

[54] The section where Deissler introduces the topic is entitled "On the question of an 'anthological' biblical style" ("Zur Frage eines „anthologischen" biblischen Stil"), which is different than simply saying Ps 119 is an anthology. Deissler, 19–31.

[55] I return to this point in chapter 5, especially in the section on Judaism.

[56] Klaus Koch, "Review of Alfons Deissler Psalm 119 (118) und seine Theologie," *Theologische Literaturzeitung* 83 (1958): 186–87.

[57] Alastair Fowler, "The Life and Death of Literary Forms," *New Literary History* 2 (1971): 212. The third phase does not necessarily occur for every genre.

motifs are borrowed from a variety of genres rather than a particular one.[58]

One must come to the conclusion, along with various scholars, that Ps 119 is *sui generis*.[59] But this is not to say that a discussion of genre elements used in Ps 119 is dispensable. On the one hand, recognizing the elements of lament psalms, wisdom terminology, tropes, and *topoi* in Ps 119 is an essential step in understanding the psalm correctly. On the other hand, identifying the genre of Ps 119 based on these diverse elements, without explaining how the elements function and contribute to the psalm, leads to misunderstanding. Any coherent and comprehensive explanation of Ps 119 must account for the data that Deissler describes with the rubric "anthological." In the following chapter, I describe the phenomenon as the use of traditional religious language. Although I am studying the same literary features as Deissler, my explanation is different since I am not arguing for a relationship between specific texts.

---

[58] K. C. Hanson posits a historical development of acrostics that results in an acrostic genre, and it may be possible to correlate his thesis with Fowler's description of how new genres emerge. Hanson argues that the acrostic format was first an aesthetic or poetic device, but over time authors began to write acrostics merely for the sake of completing the acrostic. If this definition of "genre" is accepted, then this answers the question of Ps 119's genre. But this is an atypical definition of "genre," since genres are not typically defined based on a single, formal feature. K. C. Hanson, "Alphabetic Acrostics: A Form Critical Study," Ph.D. diss., Claremont Graduate School, 1984.

[59] "Le Ps. 119 est *sui generis*, et il est faux d'y déceler un mélange de genres, ou même de parler à son sujet d'un genre mixte. Certes l'on retrouve dans le Ps. 119 des expressions propres au style des «lamentations», mais elles sont fort en minorité par rapport aux expressions que j'ai mentionnées." J. P. M. van der Ploeg, "Le Psaume 119 et la Sagesse," in *La Sagesse de l'Ancien Testament*, ed. Hemchand Gossai (Paris: Gembloux, 1979), 85. I agree that Ps. 119 is *sui generis*, but I disagree that the "lamentations" are not essential to the message of Ps. 119. Regardless of whether or not they are in the minority, they contribute to the psalm's message, and I discuss that contribution in chapter 3.

"Ps 119 ist kein 'Mischgedicht,' sondern eine Größe 'sui generis,' das Produkt eines Schriftstellers, also keine Gattung mehr.... Ps 119 handelt nicht ausschließlich vom Gesetz, sondern entfaltet eine erstaunliche Fülle von Theologumena—in oft recht allgemeiner Weise. Der Psalmist will zwar nicht alles über Gott und Mensch sagen, aber doch vieles." Hans-Peter Mathys, *Dichter und Beter: Theologen aus spätalttestamentlicher Zeit*, Orbis Biblicus et Orientalis, vol. 132 (Freiburg/Schweiz: Universitätsverlag, 1994), 283.

"Psalm 119 represents a category of its own in among the religious expressions included in the Psalter." "מזמור קיט מיצג חטיבה בפני עצמה בין התעודות הדתיות". "מקומו של מזמור קיט בתולדות דת" ,Yehoshua Amir, "הכללות בספר תהילים." "עיונים במקרא ספר זכרון ליהושע מאיר גריץ" ,in ,ישראל" ["The Place of Psalm 119 in the religion of Israel" in *Studies in scripture: a volume in memory of Joshua Meir Grintz* (Hebrew)] (Tel Aviv: Hakibbutz Hamuchad Publishing, 1982), 57.

CHAPTER TWO

THE USE OF TRADITIONAL RELIGIOUS LANGUAGE

אם שגה אדם בדברי תורה, דברי תורה משגים אותו
מדרש תהלים מזמור ז

2.1. INTRODUCTION

Viewed in isolation, many verses in Psalm 119 are difficult or impossible to interpret correctly; however, when viewed in light of themes, tropes, or *topoi* that the author borrows from elsewhere, the meaning becomes more clear. Psalm 119:19b illustrates the phenomenon:

Ps 119:19b   אל תסתר ממני מצותיך   *Do not hide your commandments from me.*

What does this mean? Surely the author of Ps 119, who wrote an extended poem about Torah, knew the commandments. Thus, in what sense could they be hidden? Rashi solves the problem by adding the word נפלאות (miracles): "Do not hide from me the miracles of your commandments which are hidden."[1] His interpretation of v. 19 draws from v. 18, which reads: "Open my eyes that I may see miracles (נפלאות) from your Torah." Thus, Rashi has some contextual support, but his solution masks an essential feature of the verse, namely the *topos* found in the following petitions:

Ps 27:9a   אל תסתר פניך ממני   *Do not hide your face from me.*
Ps 69:18a   ואל תסתר פניך מעבדך   *Do not hide your face from your servant.*
Ps 102:3a   אל תסתר פניך ממני   *Do not hide your face from me.*
Ps 143:7b   אל תסתר פניך ממני   *Do not hide your face from me.*

It is appropriate to label this phrase a *topos*, since it is a literary convention used by various biblical authors in the composition of their own texts.[2] In some instances a *topos* may be a metaphor, for example,

---

[1] ואל תסתר ממני נפלאות מצותיך הנעלמים Ha-Keter, 164.
[2] For a discussion of *topos* as a technical term see O. B. Hardison Jr. and Ernst H. Behler, "Topos," in *The New Princeton Encyclopedia of Poetry and Poetics*. The *topos* is common, cf. Gen 4:14; Isa 54:8; Jer 33:5; Ezek 39:23; Mic 3:4; Ps 10:11; 13:2; Job

"the world as a stage." In the case of "God hiding his face" the *topos* incorporates a figure of speech, specifically the anthropomorphism of God's face; however, the *topos* is not limited to the figure of speech. In addition to the anthropomorphism the *topos* includes the element of displeasure.[3] Near the end of Deuteronomy, God predicts that the people of Israel will break the covenant and follow other gods. God then says "My anger will burn against them on that day, and I will abandon them, and I will hide my face from them [יועזבתים והסתרתי פני מהם]" (Deut 31:17).

Psalm 119:19b adapts and appropriates the *topos* by substituting "commandments" (מצות) in place of the anthropomorphism. The substitution implies that the act of giving Torah is an instance of God acting favorably towards humanity—or if God withheld his word, an instance of his displeasure. Other passages also teach that God withholds his word as a sign of his displeasure. Amos 8:11 prophesies that a famine is coming—not of bread and water but a lack of God's word.[4] Jeremiah 23:25–40 teaches that God will forsake the people in response to false prophecy, and according to Jeremiah when God forsakes the people they will have no word from him. Part of the judgment declared by Ezekiel was that prophets will lack visions, priests will lack instruction, and elders will lack counsel (Ezek. 7:26).[5] Conceptually,

---

13:24. These verses are only a sampling; for a detailed study of the phrase see Samuel E. Balentine, *The Hidden God: The Hiding of the Face of God in the Old Testament.* Oxford Theological Monographs, ed. James Barr et al. (Oxford: Oxford University Press, 1983).

[3] Balentine (*The Hidden God*, v) notes that in laments the supplicants are protesting that they have done nothing to deserve God's punishment. This is a valid point, but the protests indicate that the supplicants perceive God's displeasure. Even if the perception is wrong, the feeling of God's displeasure is still poignant. Groenewald states that uncertainty about God's presence is at the heart of the lament psalms; Alphonso Groenewald, "'And Please, Do Not Hide Your Face from Your Servant' (Ps 69:18a): The Image of the 'Hidden God,'" in *Vom Ausdruck zum Inhalt, Vom Inhalt zum Ausdruck*, Festschrift der Schülerinnen und Schüler für Theodor Seidl, ed. Maria Häusl and David Volgger, Arbeiten zu Text und Sprache im Alten Testament, vol. 75 (St. Ottilien: Eos Verlag, 2005), 135. For another discussion of this phrase see R. E. Friedman, "The Biblical Expression *mastir panim*," *HAR* 1 (1977): 139–47; for more general or theological discussions see the footnotes below.

[4] Jörg Jeremias, *The Book of Amos*, OTL, trans. Douglas W. Stott (Louisville: Westminster John Knox, 1998), 151; Francis I. Andersen and David Noel Freedman, *Amos: A New Translation with Introduction and Commentary*, The Anchor Bible, vol. 24A (New York: Doubleday, 1989), 824–25.

[5] These passages are part of a larger motif about God's self-disclosure that is often discussed under the rubrics of "transcendence" or "immanence." See for example, R. E. Friedman, *The Hidden Face of God* (New York: Harper Collins, 1997); R. E.

the teaching that God demonstrates his goodness by revealing his will is not unique to Ps 119, but the substitution in Ps 119:19b results in a unique locution.

Identifying the use of a *topos* in Ps 119:19 is essential for understanding the meaning of the verse, and there are many other verses throughout the psalm that use a "conventionalized element." Recognizing these elements is necessary to understand how Ps 119 communicates its message, and the purpose of this chapter is to identify and describe them. Since the elements are diverse, I use the phrase "traditional religious language" as a general label. By "traditional" I simply mean that the author used preexisting material. It is religious, because it includes declarations of devotion to God's word, petitions addressed to God, praise of God's instruction, and claims of fealty to Torah. In what follows, I argue that the use of traditional religious language is a constitutive literary feature of Ps 119.

There are similarities between the following discussion and a wide variety of studies that deal with allusions, citations, influence, inner-biblical interpretation, or echoes.[6] I avoid these terms because they are used, especially in biblical studies, to describe the relationships between texts, and I am not arguing here for specific textual relationships.[7] Another frequently used term is "intertextuality," which was originally coined to describe interrelated signifying practices.[8]

Friedman, "The Hiding of the Face: An Essay on the Literary Unity of Biblical Narrative," in *Judaic Perspectives on Ancient Israel*, ed. Jacob Neusner et al., 207–22 (Philadelphia: Fortress Press, 1987); Lothar Perlitt, "Die Verborgenheit Gottes," in *Probleme biblischer Theologie*. Festschrift für Gerhard von Rod zum 70. Geburtstag (Munich: Chr. Kaiser Verlag, 1971), 367–82; Joseph Reindl, *Das Angesicht Gottes im Sprachgebrauch des Alten Testaments*, Erfurter Theologische Studien, vol. 25 (Leipzig: St. Benno Verlag, 1970); Hans-Jürgen Hermisson, "Der verborgene Gott im Buch Jesaja," in *Studien zu Prophetie und Weisheit*, FAT, vol. 23, ed. Bernd Janowski und Hermann Spieckermann, 105–16 (Tübingen: Mohr Siebeck, 1998).

[6] See the bibliography on Ben-Porat, Bloom, Charlesworth, Nogalski, Plett, Schultz, and Sommer for representative examples.

[7] For the most part it is not possible to demonstrate a relationship between Ps 119 and other texts; however, see the discussion of this topic in chapter 5.

[8] See Julia Kristeva, *Revolution in Poetic Language*, trans. Margaret Waller (New York: Columbia University Press, 1984), 60: "If one grants that every signifying practice is a field of transpositions of various signifying systems (an intertextuality), one then understands that its 'place' of enunciation and its denoted 'object' are never single, complete, and identical to themselves, but always plural, shattered, capable of being tabulated." See also Julia Kristeva, "Word, Dialogue, and Novel," in *Desire in Language: A Semiotic Approach to Literature and Art*, ed. Leon S. Roudiez, trans. Thomas Gora, Alice Jardine, and Leon S. Roudiez, 64–91 (New York: Columbia University Press, 1980): "The addressee, however, is included within a book's discursive

This term has too many possible connotations to be helpful for my
study, especially since it has been appropriated by biblical scholars
and applied to a wide variety of literary phenomena.[9] In this chapter I identify the use of traditional religious language and argue that
recognizing it is essential for understanding Ps 119. In the following
chapter I explain how the traditional religious language contributes to
the rhetoric of the psalm.

2.2. The Language of Piety

The substitution discussed above ("commandments" in place of "God's
face") is only one of many substitutions throughout the psalm. In the
traditional religious expressions, God himself is typically the object of
the verb, but in Ps 119 the object of the verb is Torah. When God is
the object of the verb, the expressions indicate piety.[10] These expressions of piety, in which Torah is substituted for God as the object of
piety, show that the phrase "Torah piety" describes a salient character-

---

universe only as discourse itself. He thus fuses with this other discourse, this other
book, in relation to which the writer has written his own text. Hence horizontal axis
(subject-addressee) and vertical axis (text-context) coincide, bringing to light an
important fact: each word (text) is an intersection of words (texts) where at least one
other word (text) can be read.... Any text is construed as a mosaic of quotations;
any text is the absorption and transformation of another. The notion of *intertextuality* replaces that of intersubjectivity, and poetic language is read as at least *double*"
(65–66, italics original). Other studies include Jacques Derrida, "Living On: Border
Lines," in *Deconstruction and Criticism*, ed. Harold Bloom et al., trans. James Hulbert,
75–176 (New York: Seabury Press, 1979); and Roland Barthes, "Theory of the Text," in
Untying the Text: A Post-Structuralist Reader, ed. R. Young, 31–47 (Boston: Routledge
& Kegan Paul, 1981).

[9] This is not to say that biblical scholars are unaware of what they are doing. See
for example, James D. Nogalski, "Intertextuality and the Twelve," in *Forming Prophetic
Literature. Essays on Isaiah and the Twelve in Honor of John D. W. Watts*, JSOTSup
235, ed. James W. Watts and Paul House, 102–24 (Sheffield: Sheffield Academic Press,
1996), who deliberately defines "intertextuality" in contrast to Julia Kristeva. My discussion in this chapter is perhaps closest to Michael Fishbane who states that "...new
texts may imbed, reuse, or otherwise allude to precursor materials—both as strategy
for meaning-making, and for establishing the authority of a given innovation. Put in
a nutshell, I would say that intertextuality is a form that literary creativity takes when
innovation is grounded in tradition." "Types of Biblical Intertextuality," in *Congress
Volume. Oslo 1998*, ed. A. Lemaire and M. Sæbø, 39–44, VTSup 80 (Leiden: Brill,
2000), 39.

[10] I am using the term "piety" here in the sense of devotion and reverence for God.

istic of Ps 119.[11] The focus of the following paragraphs is to discuss the substitutions as a surface feature of the text—a feature which demonstrates that Ps 119 uses traditional religious language.[12]

2.2.1. *Clinging to Torah*—דבק

In v. 31 the speaker states that he has clung (דבק) to God's stipulations (עדות); this verse substitutes "stipulations" in place of God himself. "Clinging to God" figures commitment to God and thus the exclusion of other gods.[13] In Deut 4:3–4 those who "clung to YHWH" (דבק) were not destroyed like those who followed Baal Peor, and in Deut 10:20 the people are commanded, "You shall fear YHWH your God,

---

[11] For a recent article see Erich Zenger, "Torafrömmigkeit: Beobachtungen Zum Poetischen und Theologischen Profil von Psalm 119." in *Freiheit und Recht: Festschrift für Frank Crüsemann zum 65. Geburtstag*, ed. Christof Hardmeier, Rainer Kessler, and Andreas Ruwe, 380–96. (Gütersloh: Verlagshaus Chr. Kaiser, 2003). In earlier scholarship the concept of "Torah piety" was interrelated with "legal piety" (*Gesetzesfrömmigkeit*), a word which critical scholars, most famously Wellhausen, used to describe the lifeless religion of Judaism that arose after the more pristine and lively religion of ancient Israel. Wellhausen states that the written Torah is what distinguishes Judaism from ancient Israel, and with an allusion to Jeremiah condemns it: "The water which in old times rose from a spring, the Epigoni stored up in cisterns." Julius Wellhausen, *Prolegomena to the History of Ancient Israel* (Gloucester, MA: Peter Smith, 1973), 410. Of course Wellhausen was influenced by the contrast between "law and gospel" that can be traced through Luther back into the New Testament and perhaps even into Greek translations of "Torah" that predate the New Testament. The literature on this is vast; see for example *RGG*, s.v., "Gesetz," for a brief discussion of *Gesetzesfrömmigkeit*. See also Klaus Koch, "Gesetz I," in *TRE*. For a discussion of this topic in Deuteronomy, see Georg Braulik, "Gesetz als Evangelium," *ZThK* 79 (1982): 127–60. For a more recent discussion with special attention to Ps 119 and the LXX, see Frank Austermann, *Von der Tora zum Nomos: Untersuchungen zur Übersetzungsweise und Interpretation im Septuaginta-Psalter*, Mitteilungen des Septuaginta-Unternehmens, vol. 27 (Göttingen: Vandenhoeck & Ruprecht, 2003).

[12] The following paragraphs must be viewed in light of the related sections of chapter 3, in which I discuss the implications of the material presented here, as well as the commentary where I discuss other details of interpretation.

[13] Jenni notes that the expression may connote either "love" or "obedient faithfulness," but deciding between these options is not critical since the two connotations are interrelated, TLOT, 325. See below (p. 38), "Loving Torah." Moran translates Deut 11:22 and 30:20 with "to be loyal"; see William Moran, "The Ancient Near Eastern Background of the Love of God in Deuteronomy," *CBQ* 25 (1963): 78. Amos Hakham compares "clinging to God" with the metaphor of "walking in God's ways" (see Ps 119:1), and he cites 2 Sam 20:8 as a *mashal* in support of his argument. "All the men of Israel turned from following after David and went after Sheba the son of Bichri, but the men of Judah followed their king (lit. "clung to their king") from the Jordan unto Jerusalem" ויעל כל איש ישראל מאחרי דוד אחרי שבע בכרי ואיש יהודה דבקו במלכם מן הירדן ועד ירושלם. Amos Hakham. ספר תהלים בדעת מקרא [*Psalms* in *Da'at Mikra* (Hebrew)] (Jerusalem: Mossad HaRav Kook, 1990), 388.

serve him, and cling to him." The people are promised that God will
drive away their enemies if they will "carefully keep all these commandments which I command you to do—to love the LORD your
God, to walk in all His ways, and to cling to him" (לדבקה בו Deut
11:22). The verb occurs five times in Deuteronomy with YHWH as
the grammatical object (Deut 4:4; 10:20; 11:22; 13:5; 30:20), and the
trope of clinging to God is repeated in various places throughout the
Former Prophets. Joshua 22:5 exhorts, "Be very careful to do the commandment and the instruction which Moses, the servant of YHWH,
commanded you, to love YHWH your God, and to walk in all of his
ways, and to keep his commandments, and to cling to him (לדבקה
בו), and to serve him with all of your heart and with all of your soul."
In 2 Kgs 18:6, Hezekiah is praised for clinging (דבק) to YHWH and
obeying his commandments. The traditional trope of clinging to God
is appropriated by the author of Ps 119 and modified by substituting
God's word in place of God himself.

2.2.2. Trusting in Torah—בטח

Throughout the Hebrew Bible God's people are commanded to trust
(בטח) only in God. Trusting in anything or anyone other than God
himself is portrayed as a kind of betrayal, while trusting in God is
praised as the proper and reasonable course of action.[14] For example, in Deuteronomy the children of Israel are described as trusting
in their fortified cities—a misplaced trust that will bring curses upon
them (Deut 28:52). In the narrative of 2 Kgs 18 (// Isa 36) one of the
important questions is whether or not Hezekiah will trust God. When
he does put his trust in God, he is delivered. Trusting God is also a
common theme in the book of Psalms; for example, Ps 118:8 states that
it is better to take refuge in the Lord than to trust in humanity (טוב
לחסות ביהוה מבטח באדם). The word בטח occurs more than forty

---

[14] "...no other entity [except YHWH] can be an ultimate object of trust. This
restriction applies to almost all texts in which *bṭḥ* occurs; it is thus an eminently
theological term,..." TLOT, 229. Similarly, "the people of God are called on again
and again to place their hope in God alone." Hans-Joachim Kraus, *Theology of the
Psalms*, trans. Keith Crim, (Minneapolis: Augsburg Publishing, 1986), 53. This quote
from Kraus could just as easily have been included in the following section related to
the word יחל, and in fact, Kraus himself notes that the concepts of "hope" and "trust"
are interrelated. Furthermore, it is not only these two themes that are interrelated;
"trust" is also related to "believing," which is related to "fearing," which is related to
"loving," and so on.

times in the book of Psalms usually with God as the object.[15] However, the speaker in Ps 119:42 declares that he has trusted in God's word (בטחתי בדברך)—another example in which the psalmist uses traditional religious language and substitutes God's word for God himself.

2.2.3. Hoping in Torah—יחל

"Waiting" or "hoping" (יחל) on the Lord is conceptually related to trusting, and it is also a common motif in the Psalms.[16] In Ps 38:16 the psalmist declares "I hope in you, O YHWH," and in Ps 130:7 the psalmist exhorts Israel to hope in God because he is merciful. "In the Psalms 'to wait' [יחל] means not giving up, not growing tired, ... The hope of those who wait is based on the conviction that Yahweh is gracious."[17] Twice in the Psalms the object of hope is God's kindness (or "loyalty" חסד 33:18 and 147:11). Unlike "trust" (בטח), hoping on God's word is not unique. Psalm 130:5 states, "I wait for YHWH, my soul waits, and I hope for his word" (קויתי יהוה קותה נפשי ולדברו הוחלתי).[18] In Ps 119 this verb occurs six times, and the object is either God's justice (משפט v. 43) or his word (דבר vv. 49, 74, 81, 114, 147).

2.2.4. Believing in Torah—אמן

Believing (האמן) in God is also commended throughout the Hebrew Bible, and a lack of faith in God or believing in some substitute for God is condemned.[19] The contrast between belief and doubt is stark

---

[15] Many of the contexts outside the Psalter where this word occurs are either prayers or songs; TLOT, 228.

[16] See the previous section on "trust" and the related notes. Westermann claims that this verb in Ps 119 refers generally to the attitude of the pious. TLOT, 541. "Hope" in the Hebrew Bible is often grounded in a belief of that God will be faithful to his covenant. RGG, s.v. "Hoffnung." However, the notion of covenant is glaringly absent from Ps. 119; see chapter 4, p. 129. In Christian theology the discussions of "hope" are often related to an eschatological hope, and this can be related to the hope of ultimate judgment in the Hebrew Bible. See Walther Zimmerli, Der Mensch und seine Hoffnung im Alten Testament (Göttingen: Vandenhoeck & Ruprecht, 1968).

[17] Hans-Joachim Kraus, The Theology of the Psalms, 158.

[18] In Job 32:11, Job declares, "I waited for your words" (הוחלתי לדבריכם), but this is a different use of the word יחל. The nuance of "hope" is not in play, unless there is irony involved. See also Job 32:16.

[19] One of the most discussed topics in Old Testament theology is "faith." In part, this is due to the centrality of "faith" in Christian theology, but it is also due to the broad semantic range of the word itself, which can be used with a variety of nuances. See the articles in ABD, s.v. "faith"; RGG, s.v. "Glaube"; and Klaus Haacker, "Glaube

in Ps 106, which is a psalm that summarizes the history of Israel. Just after recounting the story of the miracle at the Red Sea (vv. 7–11), the psalmist states "and they believed his words (ויאמינו בדבריו) and sang his praise" (v. 12). However, in only a short time they forgot what happened at the Red Sea (v. 21). Subsequently, they did not believe his word (לא האמינו לדברו v. 24), and therefore they did not obey him. To believe someone's word implies that the person is reliable, and believing someone's word is a common idiom in the Hebrew Bible. In Ps 119:66 the speaker declares, "I believe your commandments" (במצותיך האמנתי), and this is the only example in the Hebrew Bible in which commandments (מצות) is the object of belief.[20]

2.2.5. Loving Torah—אהב

Loving God is an important expression of piety in the Hebrew Bible, and it is closely related to obedience.[21] Deuteronomy juxtaposes loving God and obeying his commandments in various ways.[22] In some cases the verbs of loving and obeying are syntactically coordinate. "You shall

---

II," in *TRE*. As already mentioned, I do not discuss the implications of the traditional religious language in this chapter; see the related discussions in chapters 3 and 4.

[20] This verse is "difficult to classify," according to the article in *TRE*. However, in light of all the other substitutions that I discuss in this chapter, the classification becomes less of an issue. It is simply one example of many in which the author substitutes God's word in place of God himself. "Schwieriger einzuordnen ist Ps 119,66 wo *he'emin* sich of die Gebote bezieht." Klaus Haacker, "Glaube II," in *TRE*.

[21] The theme of love in the Hebrew Bible has been discussed extensively; the following articles provide valuable summaries: *ABD*, s.v. "love"; *TLOT*, s.v. אהב; and Horst Seebaß, "Liebe II," in *TRE*. Scholars have noted that directives to love God occur in the context of a covenant and thus the notion includes the concept of loyalty, a concept that is emphasized in treaties between a king and his subjects. See for example, Moran, "The Ancient Near Eastern Background of the Love of God in Deuteronomy." Weinfeld notes, "Although love between God and Israel involves also affection and emotion…, the practical meaning of the command of love is loyalty and obedience,…" Moshe Weinfeld, *Deuteronomy 1–11. A New Translation with Introduction and Commentary*, AB, vol. 5. (New York: Doubleday, 1991), 351.

[22] Hermann Spieckermann explores the conception of love in Deuteronomy and its historical development in his article "Mit der Liebe im Wort: Ein Beitrag zur Theologie des Deuteronomiums," in *Liebe und Gebot: Studien zum Deuteronomium*, Festschift zum 70. Geburtstag von Lothar Perlitt, ed. Reinhard G. Kratz and Hermann Spieckermann, 190–205 (Göttingen: Vandenhoeck & Ruprecht, 2000). Spieckermann argues that many of the psalms predate Deuteronomy, but that the theology of the Psalter did not have a great influence on Deuteronomy. Instead, the marriage metaphor in the prophetic corpus, especially Hosea, influenced the expressions in Deuteronomy. There is much more to say about this theme, but the discussion here is only intended to show that "loving God" was one expression of piety with which the author of Ps 119 was familiar.

love YHWH your God, and you shall observe his service, his statutes, his regulations..." (Deut 11:1). In other cases "loving" is syntactically subordinate to obeying: obey my commandments "...in order to love YHWH your God" (לאהבה את יהוה אלהיכם Deut 11:13). In Deuteronomy God himself serves as the object of affection, but in Ps 119 the author substitutes God's word as the object of affection and portrays the speaker expressing his love for God's Torah (תורה vv. 97, 113, 163, 165), commandments (מצות vv. 47, 48, 127), word (דבר v. 140), precepts (פקודים v. 159), and stipulations (עדות vv. 119, 167). These are the only verses in the Hebrew Bible where any of these synonyms for God's word are the object of the verb "to love" (אהב).[23] The closest parallels are the verses in Deuteronomy that juxtapose loving God and keeping his commandments. For example, God shows mercy "to those who love me and keep my commandments" (Deut 5:10; cf. also Deut 7:9; 30:16; and Exod 20:6).

2.2.6. Fearing Torah—ירא

Fearing God and keeping his commandments are also juxtaposed in Deuteronomy.[24] "You shall fear YHWH your God, in order to keep his statutes and his commandments, which I am commanding you" (Deut 6:2). It would also be possible to translate the first part of the verse: "You shall fear YHWH your God by keeping his statutes...." The function of the infinitive לשמר is open to at least two interpretations. Keeping the commandment can either be (1) a demonstration of one's fear for God, namely logically subsequent, or (2) a means by which one fears God, and perhaps the two options are not mutually

---

[23] In reference to Ps 119 Horst Seebaß says, "Verständlicherweise sagt man auch 'seine Gebote Leben'...doch wohl kaum im gleichen Sinn." Horst Seebaß, "Liebe II," in *TRE*. However he neither discusses why it is "understandable" for one to love the commandments nor does he discuss the difference in the sense between loving God and loving his commandments.

[24] Like the theme of loving God, the theme of fearing God has been carefully studied, and it includes slightly different nuances in the different corpora of the Hebrew Bible. Vernon Kooy notes that in Deuteronomy it always has the theophany at Horeb [Sinai] as its backdrop. "The Fear and Love of God in Deuteronomy," in *Grace upon Grace*, ed. James I. Cook, (Grand Rapids: Eerdmans, 1975), 107. Kooy also notes many of the connections between fear, love, obedience, trust, and the like. This network of relationships expands the conception of piety in Deuteronomy; similarly, this network of relationships in Ps 119 expands the conception of Torah piety. I discuss these themes and relationships further in chapter 3; see the subsection entitled "The Language of Devotion."

exclusive but complementary. In Deut 14:23 the children of Israel are
told to eat their tithe offerings "in order to learn to fear YHWH your
God." In Ps 119:120 the speaker declares that he fears (ירא) God's
regulations (משפטים). Verse 120 is the only place in the Hebrew Bible
that משפט is the object of the verb "to fear."[25] Fearing God is a traditional expression of piety, and Ps 119 substitutes "regulations" as the
object of fear.

2.2.7. Seeking Torah—דרש

In the introduction to Ps 119, the author identifies the type of people he
is describing as those who seek God wholeheartedly (בכל לב ידרשוהו
Ps 119:2). The speaker identifies himself as one who has done this,
"I have sought you with my whole heart" (בכל לבי דרשתיך v. 10).
Seeking God or God's will is a relatively common motif in the Hebrew
Bible, and the action can be directed either to God himself or to one
of his representatives.[26] In Exod 18:15 Moses explains he was listening
to the people's problems all day long because they were coming to him
(i.e., Moses) to inquire of God (לדרש אלהים). Psalm 119:2 and 10 are
similar to Deut 4:29, where Moses exhorts the exiles that they will find
God "when (or "if") you seek him with your whole heart" (כי תדרשנו
בכל לבבך).[27] In this case, one can see the phenomenon of substitution
within the psalm itself. In vv. 45 and 94 the author substitutes God's
precepts in place of God (כי פקודיך דרשתי), and v. 155 declares that
the wicked are far from salvation because they have not sought God's
statutes (כי חקיך לא דרשו).

---

[25] Both Isaiah and Ezra (Isa 66:2, 5; Ezra 9:4) describe a group of people who "trem-
ble (חרד) at God's word." See Joseph Blenkinsopp, *A History of Prophecy in Israel*
(Philadelphia: Westminster, 1984), 250–51; and H. G. M. Williamson, "The Concept
of Israel in Transition," in *The World of Ancient Israel: Sociological, Anthropological,
and Political Perspectives*, ed. R. E. Clements (Cambridge: Cambridge University
Press, 1989), 152.

[26] The range of meaning for "seeking" (דרש) is quite broad in the Hebrew Bible,
and scholars have studied it at length. Given the nature of the term, it is quite important for this study; however, my purpose in this section is only to note the substitution
of Torah in place of God. For further discussion, see the sections on Torah study in
chapters 3 and 4.

[27] In critical scholarship, the true referent cannot be Moses, but I am adopting the
terms of the narrative world here.

2.2.8. *Setting Torah Before Me*

Recognizing the repeated substitution of Torah in place of God helps to explain verses in Ps 119 that otherwise pose difficulties for interpretation. Verse 30 contains the phrase שויתי משפטיך, which is enigmatic because it is incomplete. Regardless of how this phrase is interpreted, something must be supplied to complete the syntax.[28] Many translations (JPS, KJV, NASB, RSV) supply the phrase "before me" in order to complete the syntax of v. 30, thus "I have set your regulations [before me]." This solution is based on Ps 16:8 which reads, "I have set YHWH before me continually" (שויתי יהוה לנגדי תמיד).[29] Since the author substitutes Torah in place of God himself in so many other verses in the chapter, the substitution here is plausible.[30]

2.2.9. *Raising My Hands to Torah*

Another substitution occurs in v. 48, and the result is a unique expression: "I raise my hands to your commandments which I love." Raising one's hands is a gesture of prayer and should be directed to God as Ps 88:10 shows: "I have called on you, O YHWH, every day; I have stretched out my hands to you." Lamentations 3:41 indicates that the physical act of lifting up the hands symbolizes an attitude, since the

---

[28] The verb שוה can mean (1) "to place/set" or (2) "to be equal." The second meaning in D is therefore "to make equal" or "to compare." But in either case the valency of the verb in D is the same in an English verb "to place/set"; that is, it requires two arguments. Using only one argument (e.g., *"I set the glass.") results in an ungrammatical sentence. Reading the verb as G rather than D simply raises a different set of problems. Some commentators emend the verb from שויתי to אויתי. See, e.g., Hermann Gunkel, *Die Psalmen*, HKAT (Göttingen: Vandenhoeck & Ruprecht, 1926), 520.

[29] The interpretation follows Radaq. Ha-Keter, 165. Ibn Ezra interprets this verse using Prov 3:15, which states that no valuables can compare with the preciousness of wisdom (לא ישוו בה), but this does not solve the grammatical problem. I include both words from Ps 16:8 (לנגדי תמיד) in my translation of this verse: "I set your regulations [continually before me]." It is interesting that Hakham follows this interpretation for the verse, but he mentions neither any other commentators nor Ps 16. He simply states, "I have placed your stipulations before my eyes..." שמתי לנגד עיני את משפטיך, והם לי כתמרורים לדרך התמונה שבחרתי Amos Hakham, ספר תהלים בדעת מקרא [*Psalms in Da'at Mikra* (Hebrew)] (Jerusalem: Mossad HaRav Kook, 1990) 388. Many modern commentators mention Ps 16; e.g., Frank-Lothar Hossfeld and Erich Zenger, *Psalmen 101–150*. HThKAT (Freiburg: Herder, 2008) 347.

[30] I am not necessarily arguing that the author of Ps 119 was alluding to Ps 16:8 specifically, although this seems to be the simplest explanation. I discuss the implications of this interpretation in chapter 3; see the section beginning on p. 72.

verse juxtaposes lifting up the hands with lifting up the heart.[31] Various scholars emend Ps 119:48 based on a repetition of words from v. 47. The repeated phrase is vertically aligned in the center of the following table:

47	ואשתעשע	במצותיך אשר אהבתי:
48	־ואשא־כפי אל	מצותיך אשר אהבתי	ואשיחה בחקיך:

Since the words מצותיך אשר אהבתי occur in both vv. 47 and 48, commentators delete these words from v. 48 as a vertical dittography.[32] This emendation solves a theological problem, specifically praying to the commandments would be unacceptable. The beginning of v. 48 then reads: ואשא כפי אל, which is incomplete, so commentators also add the second person suffix (אליך), resulting in "I will lift my hands to you." This is a tidy solution—too tidy in my view. In light of all the other examples of substituting God's word in place of God, this example in v. 48 should not be emended on the basis of a conjecture.

The examples listed above support the claim that the author of Ps 119 borrowed from traditional religious language. It is neither possible nor necessary to demonstrate that the author of Ps 119 borrows from specific texts; however, because many of the above verses cannot be understood without recognizing the borrowed themes or locutions, those elements must have existed before the writing of Ps 119. In my opinion, Ps 119 was composed later than much of the Hebrew Bible, and the simplest explanation of the data is that the author of Ps 119 was using texts.[33] In any case, the psalm is composed by using locutions that occur elsewhere in the Hebrew Bible as expressions of piety.

---

[31] The text of Lam 3:41 in the MT is corrupt in some way, but despite the text critical problem it is clear that the physical action of lifting one's hands was symbolic for an attitude. See also Ps 63:5 and Lam 2:19. In Ps 28:2, the psalmist lifts up his hands in prayer toward the holy sanctuary (אל דביר קדשך). Since God dwells in the holy of holies, the psalmist is lifting up his hands to God himself.

[32] Deissler, 148. See also Yehoshua Amir, "מקומו של מזמור קיט בתולדות דת ישראל", in עיונים במקרא ספר זכרון ליהושע מאיר גריץ ["The Place of Psalm 119 in the religion of Israel," in Studies in scripture: a volume in memory of Joshua Meir Grintz (Hebrew)] (Tel Aviv: Hakibbutz Hamuchad Publishing, 1982), 66; and Gunkel, Die Psalmen, 522. Zenger says that this is possible but not a necessary interpretation. "Es ist denkbar, dass der Relativsatz « die ich liebe » durch Dittographie (vgl. v 47b) in den Text kam, aber zwingend ist dies nicht." Hossfeld and Zenger, Psalmen 101–150, 348.

[33] I discuss the question of texts further in chapter 5, see the discussion beginning on p. 163.

2.3. The Language of Lament

As noted in the section on genre, lament psalms are a well-established group of psalms that are identified by several different criteria.[34] I refer to the criteria here as genre elements or, more specifically, elements of lament psalms. The elements may be purely formal, but they are most often a combination of formal features and content or subject matter. For example, in lament psalms the petition is generally an imperative or jussive (formal feature) addressed to God, requesting deliverance, support, help, and the like (content). Because petitions, the motif of enemies, and claims of innocence are so frequent in Ps 119 and because these three elements occur elsewhere in lament psalms, I group them here and adduce them as evidence that the author used traditional religious language.[35]

2.3.1. Petitions

One of the genre elements borrowed from lament psalms is the petition.[36] There are sixty imperative verb forms in Ps 119, and all but one (v. 115) are addressed to God as petitions.[37] In addition to the imperatives, there are numerous verbs that are formally marked as jussive and others that function as jussive verbs, although they are not formally marked.[38] Most of the jussive forms are also addressed to

---

[34] On the topic of genre in general and laments in particular, see the introductory chapter. The following discussion does not address the genre of Ps 119. Similarly, the various genre elements, such as petitions or enemies, are discussed in the introductory chapter, including relevant scholarship.

[35] The presence of these elements in Ps 119 does not demonstrate that it is a lament psalm, since they are used for a different rhetorical purpose. The implications of using elements of laments is discussed in chapter 3, beginning on p. 78.

[36] Gunkel discusses the petition briefly in the chapter on communal laments (p. 83) and in more detail in the chapter on individual laments. "The most significant part of the complaint song is the *petition*. It is the heart of the genre, which is understandable since the efforts of the praying are designed to obtain something from God." Hermann Gunkel, *Introduction to the Psalms: The Genres of the Religious Lyric of Israel*, trans. James D. Nogalski (Macon, GA: Mercer University Press, 1998), 157–58.

[37] Eleven of the following verses contain two imperatives: vv. 12, 17, 18, 22, 25, 26, 27, 28, 29, 33–40, 49, 58, 64, 66, 68, 73, 86, 88, 94, 107, 108, 115–117, 122, 124, 125, 132–135, 144–146, 149, 153, 154, 156, 159, 169, 170, and 176. "The given form of the petition is the *imperative*." Gunkel, *Introduction to the Psalms*, 158.

[38] Included in the category "formally marked" are verbs that are morphologically jussive as well as those preceded by the negative אל. The verses that include a formally marked jussive are the following: 8, 10, 19, 31, 43, 76, 80, 116, 122, 133, 172, 173, and

God as petitions.[39] The author combines the petitions with a variety of motifs, and many of the examples occur in the same, or a very similar, format in lament psalms. The following table lists petitions in Ps 119 followed by other psalms that contain a similar petition.[40]

v. 8	אל תעזבני עד מאד	do not abandon me	Pss 27:9; 38:22; 71:9
v. 22	גל מעלי חרפה ובוז	remove reproach and shame	Pss 31:12; 39:9; 44:14
v. 31	אל תבישני	let me not be ashamed	Pss 25:2, 20; 31:2, 18
v. 39	העבר חרפתי אשר יגרתי	remove my reproach	Pss 44:14; 89:51; 109:25
v. 86	עזרני	help me	Pss 79:9; 109:26
v. 94	לך אני הושיעני	save me	Pss 3:8; 6:5; 7:2; 12:2
v. 116	סמכני כאמרתך	support me	Pss 37:17; 51:14; 54:6
v. 117	סעדני ואושעה	sustain me	Pss 18:4; 41:4; 80:4, 8
v. 121	בל תניחני לעשקי	do not turn me over to oppressors	Pss 72:4; 103:6; 105:14
v. 122	אל יעשקני זדים	do not let the insolent oppress me	Pss 72:4; 86:14; 103:6
v. 134	פדני מעשק אדם	redeem me	Pss 25:22; 44:27; 78:42
v. 145	ענני יהוה	answer me	Pss 4:2; 13:4; 27:7; 55:3
v. 146	הושיעני	save me	see above v. 94
v. 153	ראה עניי וחלצני	look at my affliction; deliver me	Pss 6:5; 18:20; 50:15; 81:8
v. 154	ריבה ריבי וגאלני	plead my case; redeem me	Pss 74:22; 106:10; 107:2

---

175. Some of these examples are addressed to God, although the grammatical subject is not God, e.g., v. 80 "Let my heart be blameless in your statutes" (יהי לבי).

[39] Gunkel distinguished between petitions and wishes, in part based on the form of the verb. Petitions occur with an imperative verb form, and wishes occur with a jussive verb form. But this was not the only basis for his distinction. For Gunkel the differences could be traced back into older formulaic elements, such as curses. At least some of his analysis was based on comparisons with Babylonian literature. Gunkel, *Introduction to the Psalms*, 164–68. The distinctions between wishes and petitions breaks down in Psalm 119.

[40] The translations are only partial in order to highlight the relevant phrases, and this list is only a sampling.

The cumulative case is strong that the author of Ps 119 used petitions that are patterned on traditional laments, and the repetition of this element affects the tone of the entire psalm. In the examples listed above, both the form and content correspond with laments. Other verses are formally similar to petitions, but the content would not occur in a lament psalm.

2.3.2. Enemies

One of the most common genre elements in lament psalms is a complaint about enemies.[41] Gunkel includes various examples in his description of the lament genre: "opponents surround him (Pss 17:9, 11; 22:13, 17), seek him out, lie in wait for him (59:4), gloat over his misfortune (22:18), taunt him, and laugh at him (22:7–9; 42:11; 102:9)."[42] Deissler claims, "the perilous challenge by enemies is here [Ps 119] the most frequent lament motif."[43] More than twenty verses in Ps 119 contain some element of antagonism between the speaker and the unrighteous ones who abandon God's word, such as princes who sit and slander him (נדברו v. 23), deceptive men who pursue him (רדף vv. 84, 86), and those who wait to destroy him (אבד v. 95). The speaker hopes to have an answer for those who reproach him (חרף v. 42), and he complains that the insolent mock him greatly (זדים הליצני עד מאד v. 51). The cords of the wicked surround the speaker (חבלי רשעים v. 61). Insolent men smear him with deception (שקר v. 69), dig traps for him (שיחות v. 85), and the wicked set a snare for him (נתנו רשעים פח לי v. 110).

In other examples the direct antagonism is less prominent, but words for enemies and oppression are used. The speaker declares that God's commandments make him wiser than his enemies (איבים v. 98) and "my enemies (צרי) forget your words" (v. 139). In v. 157 he laments that his persecutors and enemies (רדפי וצרי) are numerous. Some of the verses listed here overlap with the previous category of petitions. For example, vv. 121 and 122 include requests that God will deliver the speaker from the oppression of man.

---

[41] "The *enemies of the pious* are mentioned everywhere." Gunkel, *Introduction to the Psalms*, 140. See also Claus Westermann, *Praise and Lament in the Psalms*, trans. Keith Crim and Richard N. Soulen (Atlanta: John Knox, 1981), 188–89.

[42] Hermann Gunkel, *Introduction to the Psalms*, 127.

[43] "Die lebensgefährliche Anfechtung durch Feinde ist hier [Ps 119] das häufigste Klagemotiv." Deissler, 285.

2.3.3. *Claims of Innocence*

Another common element of lament psalms is the claim of innocence, which form critics explain as an attempt by the petitioner to motivate God to action.[44] Psalm 26 contains numerous examples: "I have walked blamelessly" (v. 1), "I have not entered in with the dissemblers" (v. 4), "I hate the assembly of the wicked" (v. 5), and "I have washed my hands in innocence" (v. 6). These declarations of innocence in Ps 26 provide the psalmist's reasons why God should not gather his soul with the sinners or the men who shed blood (v. 9).

Most of the claims of innocence in Ps 119 assume Torah as the standard of righteousness: "I keep your statutes" (חקיך v. 8); "I have clung to your stipulations" (עדותיך v. 31); "I have not forgotten your precepts" (פקודיך v. 93); and "I have chosen your precepts" (פקודיך v. 173). In only a few cases is the claim of innocence framed without reference to God's word: for example, "I have sought you with my whole heart" (בכל לבי v. 10), or the bold claim "I have done justice and righteousness" (משפט וצדק v. 121). The emphasis on Torah is noticeably different than other claims of innocence in the Psalter.[45] This difference is evidence that the psalmist adapted the elements of laments to his own agenda.

Some of the claims of innocence are juxtaposed with petitions or the motif of enemies, and this supports the claim that the author of Ps 119 borrowed these genre elements from lament psalms. Verse 22 provides a clear example. The first half of the verse contains a petition for God to remove his reproach, and the second half of the verse mentions the

---

[44] Gunkel discusses the "rationale of the *innocent*" as an element of individual complaint songs. Gunkel, *Introduction to the Psalms*, 176. However, he also uses the rubric "song of innocence" for Pss 5, 7, 17, and 26 (p. 186). Kwakkel expands this list to include Ps 44; see Gert Kwakkel, *According to My Righteousness: Upright Behavior as Grounds for Deliverance in Psalms 7, 17, 18, 26, and 44*, OtSt, vol. 46, ed. Johannes C. de Moor (Leiden: Brill, 2002). Kwakkel includes a detailed discussion of each of these psalms and how the claims of innocence have been interpreted in the past century. Much of that interpretation was concerned with the *Sitz im Leben*, which is not relevant for the study of Ps 119. Several interpreters of these claims of innocence, especially in the early 1900s, tended to ascribe "self righteousness" to the psalmist who made the claims. Gerhard von Rad argued against this by showing that "righteousness" in the Hebrew Bible must be interpreted in the context of a relationship rather than by an absolute standard. For the details of his argument, see the section "The Righteousness of Jahweh and of Israel" in Gerhard von Rad, *Old Testament Theology*, trans. D. M. G. Stalker, vol. 1 (New York: Harper and Row, 1962), 370–83.

[45] For this reason, Kwakkel excludes these verses in Ps 119 from his study. Kwakkel, *According to My Righteousness*, 1.

reason that God should grant the request, specifically, "for I keep your stipulations." In this instance the word כי indicates the relationship between the two stichs, while in other verses the relationship is not explicit, since the stichs are merely juxtaposed. For example, in v. 31 the two stichs are juxtaposed without any conjunction. "I cling to your stipulations; O YHWH, do not shame me." It is left to the reader to ponder the nature of the relationship between the ideas in v. 31.

There is a continuum of examples, from those which are clearly modeled on lament formulas to others which are questionable. Verse 94 is an example that is quite clear. The imperative "save me!" (הושיעני), which occurs in many lament psalms, is used in the first half of v. 94, and the second half is clearly a claim of innocence: "for I have sought your precepts" (כי פקודיך דרשתי). Verse 56 is an example that is closer to the other end of the continuum; in isolation it might not be labeled a claim of innocence. The second half of v. 56 has all of the features that occur in v. 94. It is connected to the first part of the verse with the particle כי; the speaker declares "for I keep your precepts" (כי פקודיך נצרתי). In the conception of Ps 119 keeping the precepts is the essence of innocence, but the first half of v. 56 does not include a petition or any mention of enemies. Whether or not v. 56 should be labeled a claim of innocence is open for debate, but the clear examples like v. 94 affect the interpretation of examples like v. 56.

2.3.4. *Adaptations*

Several verses in Ps 119 use genre elements of lament psalms and adapt or modify the features in some way. One repeated petition is the request "give me life" (חַיֵּנִי).[46] This imperative could have been discussed in the section on petitions, since it is formally similar to petitions in other lament psalms, such as "help me," "deliver me," "do not let my enemies succeed," and the like. All these petitions are imperatives addressed to God, and many of them include an objective suffix that refers to the supplicant. The petition "give me life" is formally the same, but the content is different. A request for "life" is not found in lament psalms, and this specific grammatical form (D imv.) occurs nowhere in the Hebrew Bible outside of Ps 119.

---

[46] The D imperative occurs in the following verses: 25, 37, 40, 88, 107, 149, 154, 156, and 159. Additionally, this word occurs in the indicative and as a jussive; see the discussion in the commentary on v. 25.

Deuteronomy emphasizes the motif of "life" (חיה); in fact, there is a direct connection between "life" and Torah observance.[47] In Deut 4:1 Moses admonishes the people, "Now, O Israel, listen to the statutes (החקים) and to the regulations (המשפטים) which I am teaching to you to do in order that you might live" (למען תחיו). The connection occurs again in Deut 6:24, "YHWH commanded us to do all these statutes (החקים)…in order to give us life" (לחיתנו D inf.). Other passages repeat this theme in Deuteronomy, and chapter 30 is especially important. Here the people are offered a choice: "See I have set before you today life and goodness, death and evil" (את החיים ואת הטוב ואת המות ואת הרע Deut 30:15). The way for the people to choose life is "to love YHWH your God, to walk in his ways, and to keep his commandments, statutes, and regulations (מצותיו וחקתיו ומשפטיו) that you might live (וחיית)…" (Deut 30:16). Thus, the content of the petition "give me life" is reminiscent of Deuteronomy, while the form is similar to other petitions found in lament psalms. The "life" that the speaker in Ps 119 is requesting is the "life" promised to those who follow God's Torah.

In my opinion, the best explanation of the above data is that the author of Ps 119 combined the content of the motif from Deuteronomy with a formal element borrowed from lament psalms. Psalm 119 and Deuteronomy share a particular way of speaking about the benefits of obedience—"life." It is not necessary to prove that the author of Ps 119 borrowed this phraseology from Deuteronomy, but the similarity does support the claim of this chapter that the author was using traditional religious language. Additionally, Ps 119 and lament psalms share a particular way of phrasing petitions. Regardless of how one explains this phenomenon, it is clear that the author of Ps 119 used traditional religious language to compose the psalm.

The motif of "forgetting" is another example that does not correspond precisely with other claims of innocence, but it can be described as an adaptation of this genre element. The speaker declares eight times that he does not, or will not, forget Torah (לא אשכח or לא שכחתי). One example occurs in v. 61, where the "forgetting" phrase is juxtaposed with a lament that the cords of the wicked surround the speaker.[48] "Forgetting Torah" is unique to Ps 119. However, forgetting God is

---

[47] See the discussion of the "life" motif in the commentary on v. 25.
[48] The other verses are 16, 83, 93, 109, 141, 153, and 176.

an important motif in Deuteronomy, and it is repeated throughout both the Former and Latter Prophets.[49] Moses exhorts the people, "Be careful that you do not forget YHWH your God, and thus fail to observe his commandments, regulations, and his statutes..." (לבלתי שמר מצותיו ומשפטיו וחקתיו Deut 8:11), but already in Judg 3:7 they were doing evil when "they forgot YHWH their God" (וישכחו את יהוה אלהיהם).[50] According to the indictments of Jeremiah, one of the reasons that the people will be punished is that they forgot YHWH their God (שכחו את יהוה אלהיהם Jer 3:21; see also Jer 13:25), and Isaiah also reproaches Israel for forgetting "the God of your salvation" (כי שכחת אלהי ישעך Isa 17:10). Psalm 44 uses the same language in a claim of innocence, "All this has come upon us, but we have not forgotten you" (ולא שכחנוך v. 18).

The author of Ps 119 appropriated the motif of "forgetting God" and adapted it for his purposes by substituting Torah in place of God. This substitution is similar to the examples of pious language discussed above. The author's use of this motif resembles a claim of innocence, since he juxtaposes the statement "I do not forget your word" with laments (vv. 16, 141) and petitions (vv. 153, 176). Thus, the form is patterned on laments psalm, while the content is reminiscent of Deuteronomy and the Former Prophets. The same could be said for other phrases, such as "wholeheartedly" (בכל לב vv. 34, 58, etc.) or "justice and righteousness" (משפט וצדק v. 121). It seems that the author of Ps 119 is portraying someone who has learned the lessons taught in the Deuteronomistic History.

2.4. The Language of Wisdom Literature

Deissler states that Ps 119 is dominated with a sapiential spirit.[51] He lists many verses that are closely connected with Proverbs and claims, "...there is no doubt that Ps 119 assumes the book of Prov and not

---

[49] The theological usage in the OT "refers...less to the human act of remembering than to practical behavior: active turning away and opposition." This is clear in passages that contrast forgetting God with keeping his commandments, or in passages that join forgetting God with abandoning him and turning to other gods. TLOT, 1325.

[50] Weinfeld explains, "Forgetting YHWH means ignoring his existence as well as his demands." Weinfeld, *Deuteronomy 1–11*, 394.

[51] Deissler, 272.

the other way around."[52] For example, Deissler lists Ps 119:59 and Prov 16:9 as an example of an intentional connection that is "most likely or completely evident."[53] Proverbs 16:9 begins, "A man's heart plans his way…" (לב אדם יחשב דרכו), and Ps 119:59 begins "I considered my ways…" (חשבתי דרכי). These are the only two verses in the Bible that use the phrase "to consider a way" (i.e., the verb חשב and the object דרך). Deissler's claim that Ps 119 is dependent on Proverbs and not the other way around is in all likelihood correct. However, proving a relationship between Ps 119 and another biblical text, including the direction of dependence between them, may be impossible given the literary form of Ps 119. In any case, my goal is not to demonstrate a specific textual relationship, but to show that Ps 119 uses phraseology and motifs of wisdom literature.

2.4.1. *Locutions Borrowed from Wisdom Literature*

Avi Hurvitz provides careful argumentation that Ps 119 uses wisdom vocabulary. First, he establishes a contrast between phraseology or vocabulary in biblical wisdom literature (Prov, Qoh, and Job) and in other biblical corpora. For example, in two verses that contain similar ideas, Proverbs uses the word הון but Leviticus uses כסף:

Lev 25:37   את כספך לא תתן לו בנשך *Do not lend him your wealth by interest*
Prov 28:8   מרבה הונו בנשך *He who amasses his wealth by interest*

These two verses show a choice between words for wealth, specifically הון and כסף. This choice, that is the possibility of using a different word, is a key element of the argument, and Hurvitz concludes that הון is a word that is characteristic of wisdom literature.[54] Since the word הון occurs in Ps 119:14, Hurvitz adduces this as evidence that Ps 119 is a wisdom psalm.

---

[52] "…kann es nicht zweifelhaft sein, daß Ps 119 das Buch der Prv voraussetzt und nicht umgekehrt." Deissler, 273.

[53] "…höchstwahrscheinlich oder gar evident." Deissler, 273.

[54] His evidence is not limited to these two verses in Lev and Prov. Avi Hurvitz, "Wisdom Vocabulary in the Hebrew Psalter: A Contribution to the Study of 'Wisdom Psalms'," *VT* 38 (1988): 42–44.

Another example that Hurvitz notes is the D participle of ל.מ.ד, which is used for "teacher" only in Proverbs and Ps 119.[55] The D participle does occur elsewhere, but in the other passages it has a different syntactic function. Thus, the usage of the participle in Prov 5:13 and Ps 119:99 is unique. These are only two examples from twelve, and Hurvitz provides similar argumentation for all of the examples. I list them here without reiterating all of the argumentation:[56]

1. הון
   (see above)
2. תורה or מצות as the object of a transitive verb
   (Prov 2:1; 3:1, 2; Ps 119:50, 99)
3. פז וזהב together with מצות, תורה, or חכמה
   (Prov 8:19; Ps 119:127)
4. שעע "take pleasure in" + object of either wisdom or Torah
   (Prov 8:30, 31; Ps 119:16, 24, 47, 70, 77, 92, 143, 174)
5. אהב "love" + object of either wisdom or Torah
   (Prov 4:6; 8:17; passim; Ps 119:47, 48, 97, 113, 119, 127)
6. צפן "store up" + object of either word or commandments
   (Prov 2:1; 7:1; Ps 119:11; see below)
7. תמימי דרך "blameless of way"
   (Prov 11:20; Ps 119:1)
8. שגה...מן "stray from…" + commandments or instruction
   (Prov 19:27; Ps 119:10, 21, 118)
9. אור // נר "lamp" and "light" used in parallel
   (see the discussion below)
10. ירא "fearing" + object of either regulations or command
    (Prov 13:13; Ps 119:120)
11. מלמד D participle used as a substantive for "teachers"
    (Prov 5:13; Ps 119:99)
12. תוגה "grief"
    (Prov 10:1; 14:13; Ps 119:28)

---

[55] Avi Hurvitz, שקיעי חכמה בספר תהלים [*Wisdom Language in Biblical Psalmody* (Hebrew)] (Jerusalem: Magnes Press, 1991), 116–17.
[56] Hurvitz, *Wisdom Language in Biblical Psalmody*, 42–44, 52–54, 58–60, 100–19.

Hurvitz focuses on wisdom locutions and makes a convincing case. In the following paragraphs I expand the discussion to include related metaphors and motifs.

2.4.2. *Metaphors and Motifs that are Characteristic of Wisdom Literature*

As noted by Hurvitz there are lexical links between Prov 2 and Ps 119, but the similarities between the two chapters extend beyond the phraseology that Hurvitz describes. Both chapters are concerned with the topic of pedagogy, and the parallels between the two chapters are striking.[57]

Prov 2:1	ומצותי תצפן אתך	*and store up my commands with you*
Ps 119:11	בלבי צפנתי אמרתך	*in my heart I stored up your word*
Prov 2:2	תטה לבך לתבונה	*incline your heart to good sense*
Ps 119:36	הט־לבי אל־עדותיך	*incline my heart to your stipulations*
Prov 2:4	אם־תבקשנה ככסף	*If you seek it like silver*
	וכמטמונים תחפשנה	*and search for it like treasures*
Ps 119:72	טוב לי תורת פיך	*the Torah of your mouth is better for me*
	מאלפי זהב וכסף	*than hoards of silver and gold*
Prov 2:7	מגן להלכי תם	*a shield for those who walk blamelessly*
Ps 119:1	אשרי תמימי דרך	*Blessed are those whose way is blameless*

These two chapters share over twenty words or phrases, a high number considering that Prov 2 has only twenty-two verses. One of the locutions identified by Hurvitz is "to store up words," specifically the verb "to store" (צפן) with the object "word" (אמרה) or "commandment" (מצוה). Psalm 119:11 specifies that the place of storing up knowledge is in the heart, "I have stored your word in my heart" (בלבי צפנתי אמרתך). The only other passage in the Hebrew Bible that uses the verb "to store" (צפן) with the location specified as the heart is Job 10:13.[58] When the author of Ps 119 formulated statements about education, he used locutions of traditional wisdom literature.

Although the phraseology discussed in the previous paragraph occurs only in wisdom literature and Ps 119, the conceptions are not

---

[57] For a discussion of the conception of pedagogy in Prov 2 see Michael V. Fox, "The Pedagogy of Proverbs 2," *JBL* 113 (1994): 233–43.

[58] See also Prov 10:14, "wise men store up knowledge" (חכמים יצפנו דעת).

limited to wisdom literature. "These words, which I am commanding you today, shall be on your heart" (על לבבך Deut 6:6). This is
repeated in Deut 11:18 with the verb שים, "You shall put these words
of mine upon your hearts and upon your souls" (ושמתם את דברי
אלה על לבבכם ועל נפשכם).[59] Both passages in Deuteronomy include
the idea of learning the commands, which is a prerequisite to obeying them.[60] Conceptually, Ps 119:11 corresponds with the passages in
Deuteronomy, but the author of Ps 119 used phraseology found in
wisdom literature to express the idea.

Another metaphor for the intellectual process in both Ps 119 and
wisdom literature is illumination. "The opening of your words gives
light" (פתח דבריך יאיר v. 130). The phrase "opening of your words" is
unique in the Hebrew Bible. There is a similar use of the word פתח in
Ps 49, which is a psalm that reflects on the problem of evil, a frequent
motif in wisdom literature. The first five verses of Ps 49 are a call to
listen to the song that follows, and they culminate in v. 5, where the
second half of the verse indicates the psalmist's intention "to open"
(פתח) or "disclose" his riddle:

Ps 49:5	אטה למשל אזני	*I will incline my ear to a parable;*
	אפתח בכנור חידתי	*with a lyre I will disclose my riddle.*

In light of this verse, the phrase "opening of your word" in Ps 119:130
can be understood as disclosure of God's word. The phrase "giving
insight to the callow" (מבין פתיים) in the second half of the verse is
reminiscent of wisdom literature, although it does not meet the strict
criteria established by Hurvitz. Yet it is clear from this phrase that the
"opening of your word" is a metaphor for an intellectual process.

Many scholars have noted the striking similarity between the following verses:

Prov 6:23	כי נר מצוה ותורה אור	*because a commandment is a lamp,* *and instruction is a light*
Ps 119:105	נר לרגלי דברך ואור לנתיבתי	*your word is a lamp for my foot* *and a light for my path*

---

[59] The concept of having words on the heart occurs in a Hittite loyalty text and
in the oath of a vassal to Esarhaddon. See D. J. Wiseman, *The Vassal Treaties of
Esarhaddon* (London: British School of Archeology, 1958).

[60] Pedagogy is clearly one emphasis of Deut 6; see Weinfeld, *Deuteronomy 1–11*,
340–42.

This is another example of the metaphor of light figuring an intellectual process, and in v. 105 it is combined with the metaphor of the path. It is noteworthy that in many verses throughout Ps 119, God's word is the path, but in v. 105 God's word is a light that illumines the path. In Prov 6:23, the first half of the verse does not include the metaphor of the path, but the second half of the verse reads, "Disciplinary reproof is the way of life" (ודרך חיים תוכחות מוסר). Regardless of whether or not Ps 119 borrows directly from this verse in Proverbs, the similarities between the two verses support the thesis that the author uses traditional language of wisdom literature.

Several of the examples provided by Deissler as evidence that Ps 119 borrowed from Proverbs include the trope of the path. One example is Ps 119:5 and Prov 4:26, which both use the verb "to establish" (כון) and the word "way" (דרך).[61] This fact alone does not prove that the author of Ps 119 borrowed from Proverbs, but regardless of the nature of the relationship between Ps 119 and Proverbs, the path is one of the most frequent metaphors in both of them. Psalm 119 begins with the metaphor of the path, concludes with it, and utilizes it in many verses in between. In the first verse, the trope is explicit; the psalmist uses the term דרך "way" and a participle of the verb הלך "walk." The speaker delights in the "way" (דרך) of God's stipulations (v. 14). He prays for insight into the "way" (דרך) of God's precepts (v. 27), and he asks that God will instruct (ירה) him in the "way" (דרך) of his statutes (v. 33). He declares that he will run in the "way" (דרך) of God's commandments (v. 33), and he asks God to make him walk in the "path" (נתיב) of his commandments (v. 35). Many other verses use the trope of the path, and it is implicit in the last verse of the psalm in the word "to go astray" (תעה v. 176).

There are many similarities between the use of the trope in Ps 119 and Proverbs. The proper path is easy to use. "The WAY OF LIFE is straight, flat, and well-lit. No one stumbles in it."[62] In Proverbs no one stumbles on the way of life; in Ps 119 the ones walking in Torah have no stumbling blocks (v. 165). Because he seeks God's precepts,

---

[61] These two verses are an illustration of the more widespread problem with Deissler's methodology. Similar locutions occur in Deut 19:3 ("prepare the way for yourself" תכין לך הדרך) and 2 Chron 27:6 ("he prepared his ways" הכין דרכיו), and their presence in these books undermines Deissler's argument.

[62] Michael V. Fox, *Proverbs 1–9. A New Translation with Introduction and Commentary*, AB, vol. 18A (New York: Doubleday, 2000), 130. The capitalization of WAY OF LIFE is a convention borrowed from George Lakoff and Mark Johnson, *Metaphors We Live By* (Chicago: University of Chicago Press, 1980).

the speaker walks in a "wide place"—that is, without impediments or dangers of ambush (v. 45). As mentioned above, the word of God illumines the path of his servant (119:105).

Both Proverbs and Ps 119 emphasize that people who are honest and faithful are on the proper path. It is better to be a poor man "who goes in his innocence than a man of crooked ways who is rich" (Prov 28:6). In Ps 119 the speaker declares that he has chosen the "way of faithfulness" (דרך אמונה v. 30) and asks God to remove the "way of deception" from him (דרך שקר v. 29). He also hates every "way of deception" (ארח שקר vv. 104 and 128) and has restrained his feet from every "evil way" (ארח רע v. 101). Although the book of Proverbs does not use the phrase "way of deception," it does contrast the fool and his deception with the wise man who considers his way (Prov 14:8).

The verses in the previous paragraph emphasize man's initiative, but both Proverbs and Ps 119 also teach that God alone is ultimately in control. Both Proverbs and Ps 119 declare that God knows the ways of man; that is, one cannot hide his actions from God. For the young man in Prov 5 who is being tempted, one of the reasons to avoid temptation is that "the ways of a man are before the eyes of YHWH" (Prov 5:21). The proper response is to avoid straying onto the path of the strange woman that leads to death. In Ps 119:168, the reason that the speaker observes God's precepts is that "all my ways are before you" (כי כל דרכי נגדך).

One of the wisdom locutions identified by Hurvitz is the phrase "to stray" from words or commandments.[63] In Proverbs the lad is warned not to "stray from words of knowledge" (לשגות מאמרי דעת Prov 19:27), and in Ps 119 one of the descriptions of the wicked is "those straying from your commandments" (השגים ממצותיך v. 21), while in v. 10 the speaker petitions, "Do not cause me to stray from your commandments" (אל תשגני ממצותיך). In Proverbs those who praise wickedness are the ones who abandon instruction (עזבי תורה 28:4). Using the same words, the author of Ps 119 describes the wicked as those who abandon God's Torah (עזבי תורתך v. 53).[64] The word "abandoning" is not necessarily an example of the metaphor of the path, but the frequency of the other verses that use the metaphor of the path affect the interpretation of these verses.

---

[63] See the listing of phraseology from Hurvitz above at p. 51.
[64] On the different translations of תורה, see Chapter 4, beginning on p. 109.

The paragraphs above emphasize the importance of the trope of the path in wisdom literature, where the metaphor plays a more central role than it does in other corpora. Yet the trope of the path does occur elsewhere. In Deuteronomy it is used exclusively to figure obedience. "Path" or "way" occurs in Deuteronomy in a literal sense, for example, in the recounting of the wanderings (1:31) or in descriptions of the pillar of fire showing the way (1:33). In every case when the word "way" (דרך) is used metaphorically in Deuteronomy, it figures obedience to God's commandments. For example, the children of Israel are exhorted to follow the path that God has commanded them to walk (5:33) and to walk in God's ways (8:6). More examples could be listed for Deuteronomy.

In the Former Prophets this trope is used as a formula to evaluate the various kings, for example, "Jehu was not careful to walk in the instruction of YHWH the God of Israel with all of his heart" (2 Kgs 10:31...ויהוא לא שמר ללכת בתורת יהוה). Using this formula links the evaluation of the kings, either positively or negatively, with exhortations in the book of Deuteronomy. One example of the formulaic language is Josh 22:5: "Only be very careful to observe the commandment and the instruction (תורה) which Moses, the servant of YHWH, commanded you—to love YHWH your God and to walk in all of his ways (ללכת בכל דרכיו) and to keep his commandments and to cling to him and serve him with all your heart and all your soul." Thus, the path is a metaphor used to figure obedience in both Deuteronomy and the Former Prophets.[65]

Again, it seems likely that the author of Ps 119 combined the conception of the path in Deuteronomy with the phraseology of wisdom literature, especially since there are numerous examples.[66] The combination is similar to the petition "give me life" (see above pp. 47–48). Regardless of the specific relationship between all of the texts, the use of traditional religious language is a constitutive literary feature of Ps 119. In the following chapter, I discuss how it contributes to the message of Ps 119.

---

[65] On the relationship between Deuteronomy and wisdom literature, see Moshe Weinfeld, *Deuteronomy and the Deuteronomic School* (Oxford: Oxford University Press, 1972), 244–319.

[66] The fact that the usage overlaps with various corpora supports the claim that Ps 119 cannot be classified into a single genre.

CHAPTER THREE

THE EXEMPLARY TORAH STUDENT

משה בירך לישראל באשריך, ודוד בירך את ישראל באשרי האיש
מדרש תהלים מזמור א

3.1. Introduction

In chapter 2 I argued that the use of traditional religious language is a constitutive literary feature of Ps 119. It is clear that the author uses locutions and motifs of wisdom literature, but as noted in the first chapter, the psalm does not praise wisdom. Elements of lament psalms are also easily identified in Ps 119, but it is not a lament psalm. Why does the author use the traditional religious language? In this chapter I argue that it contributes to the author's portrayal of the speaker as an exemplary Torah student, and that the speaker models the message. What does it mean to claim that the speaker models the message?

The author never admonishes anyone to obey Torah, rather he portrays someone who does so and thereby creates a model for the reader to follow. Part of the message being modeled is that the righteous, by definition, observe Torah. This is not merely a statement used to define the righteous, rather there is a suasive goal, namely that the readers of Ps 119 should obey Torah.[1] The portrayal of a person who obediently follows Torah communicates the message more subtly and effectively than an admonition would. The lack of admonitions or exhortations distinguishes Ps 119 from wisdom literature and provides additional evidence that Ps 119 should not be classified as a wisdom psalm.[2]

There are, of course, other facets of the message that the speaker models in addition to obedience. For example, the pious should be immersed in Torah, studying and internalizing it. But the author never

---

[1] If a particular reader is persuaded, then the goal could be described as "persuasive." Whether or not Ps 119 is persuasive varies from reader to reader, and exploring the dynamics of how readers respond to Ps 119 is beyond the purview of this study. I use the word "suasive" rather than "persuasive" to keep this distinction clear.

[2] Michael V. Fox, private communication; see chapter 1 for the discussion of genre.

admonishes anyone to be immersed in Torah, rather he constructs a
persona whose speech is permeated with traditional religious language.
By putting this language in the mouth of the speaker, the author characterizes the speaker as someone who has internalized Torah, and this
characterization contributes to the modeling of the message.

The author's characterization of the speaker is complex and
multifaceted. This complexity could not be achieved in a short poem
or in a brief, static portrait. Instead the author portrays the speaker
in a variety of situations and as a rounded character who exhibits a
variety of emotions. Instead of a portrait as an analogy, one might
think of numerous snapshots that capture the speaker in different situations and different emotional states. In this way the author is able to
construct a persona that is more rhetorically effective. Thus, the length
of the poem is not merely to fill out the acrostic; it is necessary for
the author to achieve his suasive objectives.[3] Additionally, the themes
are interrelated in a way that makes isolated descriptions difficult. For
example, the speaker's trust (בטח) can be related to believing (האמן),
hoping (יחל), loving (אהב), and so on. This complexity influences the
interpretation of any specific verse.

Many verses in Ps 119 are written with the primary goal of characterizing the speaker, and previous studies of the psalm have failed
to recognize that goal. The author emphasizes the speaker's delight
in learning Torah, his commitment even in the face of adversity, the
advantages of observing the word of God, and so on. Verse 5 illustrates
the emphasis on the speaker's attitude: "O, that my ways would be
established to keep your statutes." The reader is given no information
in v. 5 about what God's statutes are; the focus is the volition of the
speaker.

In this chapter I provide evidence to support the above claims,
including an explanation for why the author uses traditional religious
language. As a point of comparison, I first discuss other texts that
portray exemplary types of people. I then argue that the first three
verses of Ps 119 alert the reader that this psalm shares a similar rhetorical goal with these other texts. Based on this foundation, the bulk

---

[3] See the discussion in chapter 1 for citations of scholars who have lamented the
length of Ps. 119; see also the section on "Poetics" for issues related to the length,
beginning on p. 16. By overlooking the rhetorical aim that I am discussing in this
chapter, previous studies have failed to recognize one of the most important reasons
for the length of the poem.

of the chapter explores the literary techniques used to portray the exemplary Torah student, concluding with a discussion of Ps 119's suasive goals.

3.2. Exemplary Types

One of the goals of Ps 119 is to portray an exemplary Torah student, and other texts—both in the Hebrew Bible and extra-biblical Jewish religious literature—use a similar rhetorical technique. "Exemplary" indicates that something is laudable, commendable, and worthy of imitation. The examples discussed in the following paragraphs all have a similar suasive aim, specifically, persuading the reader to imitate a particular person or a type of person. Examining some of the other texts from the Hebrew Bible that share a similar rhetorical technique with Ps 119 is helpful for understanding the psalm, and the use of this technique elsewhere in the Bible supports the thesis that Ps 119 portrays an exemplary Torah student. In chapter 5, I discuss the portrayal of exemplary types in extra-biblical Jewish religious literature; the following paragraphs describe exemplary types in the Hebrew Bible, especially in Psalms and Proverbs.[4] In this section the comparisons are limited to Psalms and Proverbs, in part because the genres are more similar, but also to highlight the relationship of Ps 119 with other psalms.

3.2.1. The Righteous in Psalms

Several psalms include encomia, which are formal expressions of praise or laudatory discourse.[5] One example is Ps 1, which contains several

---

[4] Comparisons could also be made with the portrayal of characters in biblical narrative. Joseph, for example, serves as a model for the reader to emulate. Some have argued that Joseph was wise to avoid the advances of Potiphar's wife and have related this to the motif of the strange woman in Proverbs. Yet it is questionable whether this should be viewed as wisdom literature; see Michael V. Fox, "Wisdom in the Joseph Story," *VT* 51 (2001): 26–41.

[5] "Discourse" here is used in a very general sense. I am neither using the term "discourse" as a technical linguistic term, which identifies a type of direct speech, nor as a sociolinguistic term, which refers to a particular conception of reality, similar to the use of "discourse" by Foucault or Habermas. However, exploring the power of encomia to construct religious identities would be a fruitful area of discussion, and it would have conceptual overlap with my claim that Ps 119 constructs an exemplary persona.

conceptual parallels to Ps 119. Both psalms begin with a macarism, "Happy is the man…" (אשרי האיש). This formula "focuses praise on a person (or group) for his/her beneficent well-being and establishes the person as exemplary…."[6] In Ps 1 the righteous man, who is introduced in the macarism, is the notional subject of several verbs that occur without an explicit subject. That is, "the man" in v. 1 is the antecedent of the "he" implicit in the third person verbs; he is the actor. "The man" is also the antecedent of the pronominal suffix on the word חפצו "his delight." In vv. 4 and 5 the author presents the antithesis of the exemplary man, specifically the "wicked ones." Thus, the first three verses portray an exemplary righteous man whose actions should be emulated. The next two verses (vv. 4–5) describe the wicked, who are a stark contrast to the exemplary man, and the final verse of the psalm provides a fitting capstone. Since the first psalm (together with Ps 2) serves as an introduction to the Psalter and since it portrays an exemplary type of person, the author signals that portraying exemplary types is an important rhetorical aim of the book as a whole.[7] The speaker in Ps 119 resembles other descriptions of the ideal righteous man in the book of Psalms and should be understood as an instantiation of the exemplary type.

Another encomium occurs in Ps 15, a psalm that uses a question and answer format to introduce its description of the righteous man.[8] Verse 1 begins, "O YHWH, who can dwell in your tent? Who can reside in your holy mountain?" The answer is "the one who walks blamelessly (תמים), does righteousness (פעל צדק), and speaks the truth in his heart" (v. 2). The remainder of Ps 15 describes the one who walks blamelessly in more detail. Similarly, Ps 119 begins with

---

[6] TLOT, 196–97.

[7] For a discussion of Pss 1 and 2 as an introduction to the Psalter, see Erich Zenger, "Der Psalter als Wegweiser und Wegbegleiter: Ps 1–2 als Proömium des Psalmenbuchs," in *Sie wandern von Kraft zu Kraft: Aufbrüche, Wege, Begegnungen—Festgabe für Bischof Reinhard Lettman*, ed. A. Angenendt, et al. (Kevelaer: Buzon and Bercker, 1993), 29–47. In an unpublished paper, Alan Cooper argues that Ps 3 is also part of the introduction to the Psalter, specifically that it introduces the hero of the Psalter. While this is an intriguing theory, I am not convinced that it accounts for the importance of the Torah emphasis or the paradigmatic function of many psalms. See also chapter 5, where I discuss the place of Ps 119 in the Psalter.

[8] Kraus notes that "the מי question of v. 1 is answered with reference to a holistic, irreproachable type that corresponds to the covenant order of Yahweh. In a paradigmatic sense the archetypal picture of the צדיק is drawn—an exemplar." Hans-Joachim Kraus, *Psalms 1–59*, Translated by Hilton C. Oswald (Minneapolis: Augsburg Publishing, 1988), 229.

praise for "those whose way is blameless" (תמימי דרך) and "in his [God's] ways they walk" (בדרכיו הלכו). They also do not do (פעל) iniquity. It is noteworthy that there are lexical links between the two psalms, that both psalms use the metaphor of the path, and that both use participles.[9] Another feature shared between these psalms is the question and answer format found at the beginning of Ps 15 and in Ps 119:9, where the author praises the efficacy of Torah, claiming that a young man (נער) can keep his way pure by observing God's word.[10] Unlike Ps 1 or 15, Ps 119 is not formally an encomium; nevertheless, all three psalms portray exemplary pious individuals.

Like the first psalm, Ps 112 also begins with a macarism, and it also extols the virtues of a particular type of individual, specifically the one who fears YHWH (v. 1). Psalm 112 defines a righteous person in light of Ps 111 and specifically as one who fears God.[11] The ideal God-fearer in Ps 112 "delights greatly" in God's commandments (במצותיו חפץ מאד v. 1), and the exemplary righteous man in Ps 1 also delights in the Torah of YHWH (בתורת יהוה חפצו v. 2). This delight in God's commandments as a characteristic of the righteous applies to the speaker in Ps 119 as well.

Many psalms include comments on the righteous. "You will bless the righteous one (צדיק), O YHWH" (5:13). "The eyes of YHWH are upon the righteous ones (צדיקים), and his ears are [open] to their cry" (34:16). This word (צדיק) occurs more than fifty times in the Psalter.[12] In a few cases it describes an attribute of God (e.g., 119:137), but the majority of occurrences are used to describe an exemplary person

---

[9] It is not necessary—or perhaps even possible—to conclude that the author of Ps 119 borrowed directly from Ps 15. Yet the comparison does show that the rhetorical techniques are not unique to Ps 119.

[10] Kent Aaron Reynolds, "The Answer of Psalm cxix 9," *VT* 58 (2008): 265–69.

[11] The relationship between Pss 111 and 112 has been discussed in various ways. See Raymond C. van Leeuwen, "Form Criticism, Wisdom, and Psalm 111–112," in *The Changing Face of Form Criticism for the Twenty-First Century*, ed. Marvin A. Sweeney and Ehud Ben Zvi (Grand Rapids: Eerdmans, 2003), 65–84; Johannes Schildenberger, "Das Psalmenpaar 111 und 112," *Erbe und Auftrag* 56 (1980): 203–07; Erich Zenger, "Dimensionen der Tora-Weisheit in der Psalmenkomposition Ps 111–112," in *Die Weisheit—Ursprünge und Rezeption; Festschrift für Karl Löning zum 65. Geburtstag* (Münster: Aschendorff, 2003), 37–58; and Walther Zimmerli, "Zwillingspsalmen," in *Wort, Lied und Gottesspruch*, Forschung zur Bibel, vol. 2, ed. J. Schreiner (Würzburg: Echter, 1972), 105–13.

[12] It is used in lament psalms as a claim of innocence. See Gert Kwakkel, *According to My Righteousness: Upright Behavior as Grounds for Deliverance in Psalms 7, 17, 18, 26, and 44*, *OtSt*, vol. 46, ed. Johannes C. de Moor (Leiden: Brill, 2002).

or group of people. The speaker in Ps 119 is a representative of this group, and in a sense, Ps 119 defines the righteous as those who are occupied with Torah.

3.2.2. David

The encomia in the Psalter are not praising a specific person but instead a paradigmatic individual, a *type* of person. A slightly different, but related phenomenon is found in Ps 18 where David's behavior functions as a paradigm for the righteous; that is, David serves as a specific example of the more general paradigm.[13] In Ps 18:21–25 David speaks in the first person and recounts his own righteous behavior.[14] The same righteousness is the focus of vv. 26–28, which switch to the third person and exhort the readers to follow David's example.[15] In v. 21 David states that God dealt with him "according to the purity of my hands" (כבר ידי). Verse 27 promises, "with the pure you will show yourself pure" (עם נבר תתברר). Thus, David's purity in v. 21 is the same characteristic that the reader is exhorted to emulate in v. 27. David claims that he was blameless (תמים v. 24), and v. 26 states that God will deal blamelessly with a blameless man (עם גבר תמים תתמם). What David says about himself in the first person serves as a paradigm for the righteous, and the shift from David's first-person speech to the third-person statements signals the shift from the instantiation to the paradigm. The pattern is repeated in vv. 29–30 (first person) and v. 31

---

[13] For a study of the Bible's portrayal of David, see Marti J. Steussy, *David: Biblical Portraits of Power* (Columbia, SC: University of South Carolina Press, 1999). Steussy argues that the portrayal of David progresses or evolves through the Psalter. For example, "[h]is voice becomes progressively less distinct from the people's as he leads them in worship in the restored community" (p. 186). Regardless of whether or not we accept Steussy's arguments about the shape of the Psalter, it is clear that the character of David has a paradigmatic role in the book. See also the articles in *König David: biblische Schlüsselfigur und europäische Leitgestalt*, ed. Walter Dietrich and Hubert Herkommer (Stuttgart: W. Kohlhammer, 2003): Klaus Seybold, "David als Psalmsänger in der Bibel. Entstehung einer Symbolfigur," 145–63; Regine Hunziker-Rodewald, "David der Hirt. Vom «Aufstieg» eines literarischen Topos," 165–77; and Ernst-Joachim Waschke, "David redivivus. Die Hoffnungen auf einen neuen David in der Spätzeit des Alten Testaments," 179–209.

[14] This is true within the narrative world of the text; I am not making a claim either positively or negatively about the Davidic authorship of any particular psalms.

[15] Hossfeld identifies verses 26–32 as a unit and gives them the rubric "Lehre," which could be translated "teaching" or "the lesson." Frank-Lothar Hossfeld, "Der Wandel des Beters in Ps 18: Wachstumsphasen eines Dankliedes," in *Freude an der Weisung des Herrn: Beiträge zur Theologie der Psalmen*, Stuttgarter Biblische Beiträge, vol. 13 (Stuttgart: Katholisches Bibelwerk, 1986), 189.

(third person). In vv. 29–30 David proclaims his trust in YHWH; verse 31 states that YHWH is a shield for all those who trust in him.

In both sections (vv. 21–28 and vv. 29–31) the proper behavior is related in some way to God's word, which links Ps 18 with Ps 19. For example, David declares that "all of his judgments are before me and his statutes I have not removed from me" (כי כל משפטיו לנגדי וחקתיו לא אסיר מני 18:23). The focus of the second half of Ps 19 is Torah, and in his article on Ps 19, Leslie Allen argues that the second half of the chapter depicts a servant who follows God's word in light of David's model behavior in chapter 18.[16] Allen notes, "Ps 19 seems to have been placed beside Ps 18 in order that its second half might serve to develop those hints of David as a role model.... The term [servant] does not elevate him above Israel, but brings him down to the level of the individual believer committed to serving the same God."[17] This "individual believer" is not a specific individual but a *type*. Portraying a particular type of individual, specifically the righteous man, is a recurring literary technique in the book of Psalms; a specific example of the type is David. Thus, the portrayal of an exemplary Torah student in Ps 119 corresponds with an established pattern in the Psalter.

3.2.3. Exemplary Women in Proverbs

The book of Proverbs also portrays various *types* of people.[18] A few individual proverbs scattered through chapters 10–29 describe exemplary types of women, particularly exemplary wives, since the book of Proverbs is addressed to men (e.g., Prov 12:4).[19] The primary portrayal of an exemplary woman is found in the acrostic poem that concludes the book (31:10–31). "The Woman of Strength is not a particular woman, but an ideal.... She is a paragon of feminine virtues, practical

---

[16] Leslie C. Allen, "David as Exemplar of Spirituality: The Redactional Function of Psalm 19," *Bib* 67 (1986): 544–46. Allen points out many lexical parallels between the two chapters. Psalm 18 begins by labeling David as the servant of YHWH (לעבד יהוה v. 1); Ps 19 uses the term "your servant" (עבדך) twice (vv. 12 and 14). The root תמם is frequent in Ps 18 (vv. 24, 26, 31, 33), and Ps 19:8 proclaims that the Torah of YHWH is "perfect" (תמימה). Both chapters label God as "my rock" (צורי 18:3, 47; 19:15). These are only a selection of the verbal parallels.

[17] Allen, "David as Exemplar," 546.

[18] My description of the types of individuals in Proverbs is influenced by the work of Michael Fox; see the following footnotes.

[19] Michael V. Fox, *Proverbs 10–31. A New Translation with Introduction and Commentary*, The Anchor Yale Bible, vol. 18B (New Haven: Yale University Press, 2009), 548.

and ethical. She is the counterpart of the wise man portrayed throughout Proverbs and serves the same paradigmatic role."[20] In contrast,
the strange woman in chapters 1–9 is a type of woman that should be
avoided. As types, both the strange woman and the woman of strength
are not allegories, rather they are descriptions of human beings. In one
sense, the descriptions are not "actual" or "literal," since they are not
referring to a specific person, but the descriptions are realistic, since
actual instantiations of both types do exist. That is, the depictions are
not metaphors or analogies of some spiritual reality, as some interpreters suggest.[21] The portrayals contribute to Proverbs' goal of creating
personae who are worthy of imitation.

3.2.4. *The Wise in Proverbs*

No specific individual embodies all the wise behaviors discussed in
the book of Proverbs (at least not all the time), yet the many separate
descriptions of wise behavior in the individual proverbs in chapters
10–29 cohere into a portrait of a wise man. No single passage of the
book renders the paradigm, rather the book as a whole constructs it.
The result is a complex portrayal of a wise man to which the wise
reader aspires. Similarly, the various descriptions of the speaker in Ps
119 create a complex portrayal of a Torah student, who delights in
God's word, trusts God's stipulations, and is committed to both the
study and observance of Torah. The speaker in Ps 119 is one who fears
YHWH, which is the beginning of wisdom.

One of Proverbs' unique contributions to the Hebrew Bible is to
integrate the character traits of wisdom and righteousness. A cun-
ning, shrewd schemer could be called wise, but in the worldview of
Proverbs only the righteous are truly wise. Sun Myung Lyu describes
righteousness and wisdom in Proverbs as "meta-virtues" that consoli-
date other virtues, and "the relationship between the two concepts is
integrative rather than identical, in the sense that despite the real difference between them the two meta-virtues are to be co-present in
a well-developed moral character."[22] It is therefore wise to be pious,

---

[20] Fox, *Proverbs 10–31*, 912.
[21] For a discussion of various interpretations of the women in Proverbs, see the
relevant sections of Fox's commentary, especially on Prov 7 and 31.
[22] Sun Myung Lyu, "Righteousness in the Book of Proverbs" (Ph.D. diss., University
of Wisconsin—Madison, 2006), 80, italics original.

and pious people use their intellectual abilities to help them follow the path of piety.

3.2.5. *The Suasive Force of Exemplary Types*

Each of the aforementioned types serves as a paradigm for the readers to emulate. Lyu notes that the book of Proverbs invites readers to be righteous by showing them the connection between choices and their consequences.[23] Proverbs also invites readers to be wise, using the same strategy. The sages who compiled the book of Proverbs used a variety of rhetorical strategies, including exhortations, warnings, depictions of success, predictions of failure, and descriptions of what God desires and abhors. The Psalter also describes characteristics of the righteous that God loves, and it exhorts the pious to adopt certain behaviors and attitudes. Various examples of explicit admonitions could be listed, but the explicit examples are only part of the rhetorical strategy. The explicit examples and the overarching, implicit paradigms mutually reinforce one another.

The speaker in Ps 119 is an instantiation of an exemplary type of person, specifically the Torah student who is introduced in Ps 1. Psalm 119 therefore contributes to an emphasis that is found elsewhere in the Psalter, and the cumulative effect of the various passages increases the suasive force. I discuss the contribution of Ps 119 to the Psalter and the Hebrew Bible in more detail in chapter 5; the salient point here is that other biblical authors use exemplary types of people as models for the reader to emulate. Thus, the rhetorical strategy employed in Ps 119 occurs elsewhere in the Hebrew Bible; what is unique is the emphasis on Torah study, not merely Torah observance.

3.3. THE PORTRAYAL OF THE EXEMPLARY TORAH STUDENT— ITS CONSTRUCTION

Similar to the paradigmatic wise and righteous people discussed above, the speaker of Ps 119 serves as a paradigmatic Torah student. In the following pages, I describe how the author constructs the portrayal of the speaker by answering the following questions: What are the means that the author uses to portray the speaker? What textual

---

[23] Lyu, "Righteousness in the Book of Proverbs," 94.

details constitute the portrayal of the speaker? Examining these details helps explain the author's suasive goals.

The description in this section supports the thesis that the speaker models the message, and identifying this rhetorical aim provides a more complete and compelling explanation of the data found in Ps 119. For example, the repetition and variation in the psalm are a means of portraying different facets of the persona that the author seeks to create, rather than merely a result of completing the acrostic form. The elements of lament psalms, which led Will Soll to classify Ps 119 as a lament psalm, contribute to the portrayal of the speaker by depicting his emotions and responses in antagonistic situations. Similarly, the locutions borrowed from wisdom literature, which led Avi Hurvitz to classify Ps 119 as a wisdom psalm, contribute to the portrayal of character formation in the speaker.[24]

Some of the material described in the following sections necessarily overlaps with the discussion in chapter 2 of traditional religious language. In chapter 2 the argument addresses the *what* question, while here the focus is the *why* question. Dealing with these questions separately is important for sound methodology. For example, I argue in chapter 2 that the author uses the language of lament and that recognizing the usage is necessary in order to understand the meaning of individual verses and therefore the chapter as a whole. In this chapter, I argue that the author portrays the speaker using "language of distress." By depicting the speaker's responses to distress, the author is able to characterize the speaker as a faithful follower of God's instruction even during hardship. Thus, some of the verses discussed in chapter 2 under the rubric "The Language of Lament" are repeated here under the rubric "The Language of Distress." Similarly, the section in this chapter on "The Language of Character Formation" overlaps to some degree with the discussion in chapter 2 of "The Language of Wisdom Literature." For the most part, chapter 2 examines the form, and chapter 3 addresses the function.

In constructing the persona of the speaker, the author interrelates Torah observance and Torah study, and much of the following discussion can be related to both of these emphases. For example, "the

---

[24] See chapter 1 on the question of genre for the respective arguments of Soll and Hurvitz.

language of devotion" portrays the speaker's devotion both to obeying
God's instruction and to meditating on it continually. By repeating
the verbs "observe" (שמר) and "keep" (נצר), the author indicates that
Torah observance is a central commitment of the speaker. Together
the two verbs occur thirty-one times in the chapter. Their grammatical
subject is almost exclusively the speaker, and with only one exception,
the object is God's word. Similarly, the speaker repeatedly asks God
for insight and understanding of Torah. Amir notes that the sages use
the term "Torah" in two ways, and "it is not always easy to discern
between them: the system of commandments on the one hand and the
study of Torah on the other."[25] In Ps 119, it is not so much a question of the meaning of the term "Torah" as it is the mutual interde-
pendence of these activities. That is, a servant of God will, of course,
observe God's instruction, and such observance is only possible when
one knows the instruction well. True study of Torah entails observance of Torah; true Torah observance entails Torah study.

In the following pages I examine various facets of the characterization of the speaker in support of my argument that the speaker
models the message. Any facet must be considered individually for
the sake of discussion, but it is important to keep in mind that the
author constructs the persona by combining all of the various descriptions and characterizations. An apt analogy is the concept of "faith"
in the Hebrew Bible: "[it] has no specific noun for faith; it says what
we mean by faith with a multitude of expressions, in whose combined
resonance the thing becomes clear."[26] Similarly, the author of Ps 119
interrelates numerous attitudes, activities, and character traits with the
result that the speaker embodies them and should be viewed as a paradigmatic Torah student.

---

[25] "שלא תמיד קל להבחין ביניהם: מערכת מצוות מזה ותלמוד תורה מזה." Yehoshua
Amir, "מקומו של מזמור קיט בתולדות דת ישראל", in עיונים במקרא ספר זכרון ליהושע
מאיר גרינץ ["The place of Psalm 119 in the religion of Israel," in *Studies in scripture: a
volume in memory of Joshua Meir Grintz* (Hebrew)] (Tel Aviv: Hakibbutz Hamuchad
Publishing, 1982), 68. In later Judaism, rabbis debated which activity—study or observance—was more important. See, for example, BT Kiddushin 40.

[26] "Das AT hat kein Substantivum für Glaube, es sagt das was wir mit Glauben
meinen, mit mannigfaltigen Ausdrucksformen, in deren Zusammenklang die Sache
transparent wird." *RGG*, s.v. "Glaube." The same phenomenon is described in the
article on אמן in TLOT: "Where we would speak of 'believing,' the OT can also use
the verbs..." to fear, to recognize, to seek, to await, to hope. TLOT, 143.

3.3.1. *The Introductory Function of Verses 1–3*

The first three verses of Ps 119 situate the psalm in the same realm of discourse as the examples discussed above in the section "Exemplary Types." Several details in vv. 1–3 support this claim. One already mentioned (see the above discussion of Ps 1) is the macarism at the beginning of vv. 1 and 2 ("Happy are those…" [...אשרי]). The macarisms group Ps 119 together with the other texts throughout the Psalter that use this phrase.[27] Most commonly, a macarism lauds a single person rather than a group; however, a few examples extol a class of people. "Happy are the ones who dwell in your house" (Ps 84:5), and "Happy are all who fear YHWH" (Ps 128:1). These passages portray a paradigmatic class of people and encourage the readers to live in such a way that they would belong to the class of people being extolled.[28]

In addition to the macarisms, other features indicate that the first three verses of Ps 119 set the stage for the author's rhetorical goals. Plural verbs are used throughout the first three verses but are rare in the rest of the psalm. This indicates that the first three verses describe a group of people in contrast to the balance of the psalm, which portrays an individual. In v. 1 "the ones walking" (ההלכים) and in v. 2 "the ones keeping" (נצרי) are both plural participles. In addition to the participles there are three plural verbs in vv. 2 and 3 (ידרשוהו, פעלו, and הלכו). None of these verbs has an explicit subject; the notional subject for each of these plural verbs is the group of people introduced in vv. 1 and 2 by the plural participles. Plural verbs do occur throughout the remainder of the psalm, but in general they have inanimate subjects. That is, the plural verbs in the remainder of Ps 119 are not descriptions of the activity of people as they are in vv. 1–3.

---

[27] This phraseology is much more frequent in the Psalter than it is elsewhere in the Hebrew Bible. See TLOT p. 196, where M. Sæbø claims that the "formula characterizes known wisdom Psalms (Psa 1; 32; 34; 106; 112; 127; 128)." However, see chapter 1 on the question of the genre of wisdom psalms.

[28] Karin Finsterbusch makes a very similar point, although she includes v. 4 as part of the introduction. "In der ersten Strophe wird das Ideal eines torafrommen Menschen gezeichnet (v. 1–4), dem das betende Ich entsprechen will (v. 5–8)." Karin Finsterbusch, "Multiperspektivität als Programm: Das betende Ich und die Tora in Psalm 119, " in *Was ist der Mensch, dass du seiner gedenkst? (Psalm 8,5), Festschrift für Bernd Janowski zum 65. Geburtstag* (Neukirchen-Vluyn: Neukirchener, 2008), 94. Finsterbusch uses the term "perspective" differently than I do, but this terminological difference does not undermine the agreement.

Torah observance is the emphasis of the first three verses, and it is described in various ways. Verse 1 defines "those whose way is blameless" (תמימי דרך) as "the ones who walk in the Torah of YHWH," which is another way of saying "those who observe Torah." Verse 2 describes the class of people as "the ones who keep his stipulations" (נצרי עדתיו), and v. 3 declares that "they do not do iniquity; they walk in his ways." Walking in God's ways serves as a figurative description of obedience.[29] Thus, the first three verses describe a class of people who obey God's stipulations, and in these verses the author divides people into two groups—those who follow God's ways and those who do not. The contrast between the two groups of people is not explicit in the first three verses, but throughout the rest of the psalm the author uses the contrast repeatedly and explicitly. The speaker in Ps 119 belongs to the class of people who walk in God's Torah; that is, he exemplifies the characteristics introduced in vv. 1–3.

Finally, there is a change of perspective in v. 4 that indicates vv. 1–3 are introductory.[30] Beginning with v. 4 the rest of the chapter uses a first-person perspective. None of the first three verses contains a first- or second-person pronoun, but all of the following verses in the chapter do. The vast majority of the verses (153 out of 176) contain an explicit first-person singular form. The first person is realized in various ways: in the conjugation of the verb, as an independent personal pronoun, or as a pronominal suffix.[31] After accounting for the first three verses, there are twenty verses remaining that lack a first-person form; all twenty contain a second-person singular form. A second person (you) cannot occur without a person speaking the "you"; the speaker is necessarily the first person.[32] With the exception of the first three verses,

---

[29] See the discussion of the two ways above, p. 85 and the discussion of the metaphor of the path in chapter 2, pp. 54–56.

[30] Zenger considers vv. 1–4 as the introductory verses; however, he does note that the change in perspective with the second person pronoun emphasizes God's personal involvement. "V 4a: betontes Personalpronomen «Du, ja du selbst»; der Wechsel der Sprechrichtung bedeutet hier eine Hervorhebung." Frank-Lothar Hossfeld and Erich Zenger, *Psalmen 101–150*, HThKAT (Freiburg: Herder, 2008), 361 As noted above, Finsterbusch also regards vv. 1–4 as introductory; see Finsterbusch, "Multiperspektivität als Programm," 94.

[31] Lyons notes that the use of explicit first-person and second-person pronouns is not essential and gives an example from Latin in which the main verb grammaticalizes the category of person. John Lyons, *Semantics* (Cambridge: Cambridge University Press, 1977), 639.

[32] Emile Benveniste, *Problems in General Linguistics*, trans. Mary Elizabeth Meek, Miami Linguistics Series, vol. 8. (Coral Gables, FL: University of Miami Press, 1971), 218.

the entire chapter adopts a first-person perspective; that is, the words of Ps 119 are the speech of the exemplary Torah student.

Psalm 119 is primarily addressed directly to God as petitions, praises, and promises. Placing the majority of the psalm in the mouth of the speaker is a means of characterizing him, and the author portrays him as devout, reverent, and obedient—in a word, pious. Since most of the psalm is addressed directly to God, this precludes the notion that Torah is some sort of intermediary between God and man. The speaker yearns to know God's word, repeatedly asks God to teach him and give him insight, and believes that God personally instructs him (v. 102).[33] He is not obsessed with minutiae of the commandments simply to show that he knows something; God's word is not an object of academic study. The commandments are the speaker's delight, because they are an instantiation of God's favor that is graciously granted (vv. 29, 58, 132).

3.3.2. *Use of First-person Language*

The first-person perspective, which the author uses exclusively after v. 3, introduces the element of subjectivity that is essential to the author's goal of portraying the emotions and volition of an ideal student of Torah. There are many semantic overlaps in the terminology of subjectivity. The statement "The speaker is the subject in Ps 119" can be a grammatical statement. In many of the verses the grammatical subject is the "I." The statement can also be a way of noting that Ps 119 is about the persona indicated by the "I." That is, the author's subject matter is the exemplary Torah student, which the pronoun "I" references. Finally, the "I" is the thinking, feeling, desiring, and believing subject.[34]

---

[33] On the theme of YHWH as a teacher, see especially Karin Finsterbusch, *JHWH als Lehrer der Menschen: ein Beitrag zur Gottesvorstellung der Hebräischen Bibel*, vol. 90, Biblisch-theologische Studien (Neukirchen-Vluyn: Neukirchener, 2007).

[34] There is a surfeit of scholarly literature that discusses "subjectivity," the "subject," the "self," and so on. Part of the difficulty in the literature is the fact that different authors use the same terms with different definitions. I am indebted to Jonathan Schofer for parts of the following discussion, from interaction in the classroom as well as private communication. I follow him in using "self" as a general term and "subject" as a term "characterizing the self as it speaks, experiences, knows, chooses, and acts." Jonathan Wyn Schofer, *The Making of a Sage: A Study in Rabbinic Ethics* (Madison, WI: University of Wisconsin Press, 2005), 16. See also Carol Newsom, *The Self as Symbolic Space: Constructing Identity and Community at Qumran*, Studies on the Texts of the Desert of Judah, vol. 52 (Leiden: Brill, 2004).

There is more at stake than an interesting play on words between grammatical subject, subject matter, subjective, and subjectivity. "It is this property [subjectivity] that establishes the basis for individual discourse, in which each speaker takes over all the resources of language for his own behalf."[35] Benveniste is giving a linguistic description of speech, which is relevant since all but the first three verses of Ps 119 are placed in the mouth of the Torah student. Without using this property of subjectivity the author could not have constructed the persona from whose subjective perspective the reader experiences this psalm. The author could have given a description or encomium of an ideal student of Torah, but the rhetorical effect would have been very different.[36]

As mentioned above, the first-person perspective begins in v. 4 and continues through the entire psalm. The pronouns "I" and "you" occur frequently in Ps 119, and the repetition of these pronouns keeps the element of subjectivity in the foreground of the psalm. Benveniste notes, "We will perceive the nature of this 'subjectivity' even more clearly if we consider the effect on the meaning produced by…certain verbs of speaking. In saying *I promise, I guarantee*, I am actually making a promise or a guarantee."[37] An example of this occurs in Ps 119:57 where the speaker declares, "My portion is YHWH; I promise to keep your words." With this statement the speaker not only *declares* something, he also *performs* something. "Performing" with language is explored and analyzed in speech act theory, which describes verbal expressions not only as propositions but also as communicative acts.[38]

---

[35] Emile Benveniste, *Problems in General Linguistics*, 220.

[36] The relationships of linguistics, rhetorical effects, emotions, etc. are extremely complex. For a recent study of some possible pitfalls, see Joan Leach, "Rhetorical Analysis," in *Qualitative Researching with Text, Image and Sound: A Practical Handbook*, ed. Martin W. Bauer and George Gaskell, 207–26 (London: Sage Publications, 2000). See also Niko Besnier, "Language and Affect," in *Annual Review of Anthropology* 19 (1990): 419–51. This article by Besnier discusses some of the complexities, and the list of references illustrates the point. For an article of fewer than 20 full pages, Besnier gives 450 references. See also my discussion below of Ps 119's suasive force, beginning on p. 96.

[37] Emile Benveniste, *Problems in General Linguistics*, 229.

[38] On speech act theory see J. L. Austin, *How to Do Things with Words* (Cambridge, MA: Harvard University Press, 1962). John Lyons uses the term "performative" to describe what often transpires with the use of the first person but adds that sentences may qualify as performatives without using the first person. Lyons, *Semantics*, 728. See also John Searle, *Speech Acts: An Essay in the Philosophy of Language* (Cambridge: Cambridge University Press, 1970). The observations of Austin have been extended and applied in various ways, especially in the so-called "theological interpretation

I list v. 57, because it corresponds with Benveniste's example, but subjectivity is more inclusive than speech act theory. The subjectivity can be seen in verses that describe the speaker's attitude or intentions, regardless of whether or not the speaker is performing something.

3.3.3. *The Language of Devotion*

The author does not merely portray the speaker as someone who obeys and studies Torah but also as someone who is devoted to these spiritual disciplines. One nuance of the term "devoted" is commitment, and the speaker in Ps 119 is certainly committed to Torah, yet there is more than mere commitment involved. When the term "devotion" is used with reference to a relationship, it has emotional overtones. Lovers who are devoted to one another enjoy and take delight in each other's commitment. The exemplary Torah student is devoted to Torah like a young lover is devoted to a first love.

3.3.3.1. *Adverbial Phrases*

One way the author portrays the speaker's devotion is by using adverbial phrases that describe how the speaker studies and observes Torah. The adverbial phrases depict the attitudes or volition of the speaker. For example, in v. 34 the speaker declares, "I will observe it [Torah] wholeheartedly" (בכל לב), and in v. 69, "I will keep your precepts wholeheartedly" (בכל לב). The phrase "wholeheartedly" indicates the speaker's complete commitment to the task at hand. The same idea can be stated negatively—"without reservation." Deuteronomy uses this adverbial phrase to describe the way one should seek God (4:29), love God (6:5; 30:6), and serve God (10:12; 11:13). The phrase is used throughout the Former Prophets to describe how the people of Israel should repent: the repentance should be "wholehearted" (1 Sam 7:3; 1 Kgs 8:48; *passim*).[39] The speaker's declarations that he will obey God's word give the reader no new information about the nature or essence of Torah, but the adverbial phrases do give the reader information

---

of Scripture"; see for example, D. Christopher Spinks, *The Bible and the Crisis of Meaning: Debates on the Theological Interpretation of Scripture* (New York: T & T Clark, 2007).

[39] Weinfeld notes that the "phrase is predominant in Deuteronomy and the Deuteronomic literature…, though attested already in proto-Deuteronomic texts such as 1 Sam 7:3; 12:20, 24." Moshe Weinfeld, *Deuteronomy 1–11. A New Translation with Introduction and Commentary*, AB, vol. 5 (New York: Doubleday, 1991), 338.

about the speaker's volition. By using various adverbial phrases the author reveals the speaker's emotions and attitudes while he observes or meditates on Torah. His observance is willing, and his study is a delight.

The speaker's willingness is an essential element of the psalm's message. Not only does the speaker observe God's word, but he explicitly wants to observe it. The author of Ps 119 emphasizes the speaker's willingness with statements such as, "Make me walk in the path of your commandments, because in it I take delight" (v. 35) or "I restrain my feet from every wicked path, so that I might observe your word" (v. 101). By putting these statements, and many others like them, in the mouth of the speaker, the author portrays the attitudes and commitments of the speaker.

In v. 32 the speaker exclaims, "I will run in the way of your commandments, because you expand my heart."[40] Running in the path indicates an eagerness to engage in some pattern of behavior. In Prov 1:15–16 the father warns his son to avoid the gang, which proffers an enticement for companionship and wealth: "Restrain your feet from their path, because their feet run to evil and they are swift to shed blood." YHWH loathes "feet that are swift to run to evil" (Prov 6:18). Both of these passages from Proverbs characterize the wicked as eager to perform their evil deeds.[41] In Ps 119 the ideal student of Torah is eager to observe God's commandments.

3.3.3.2. *Verbs of Emotion*

In some of the examples above, the author portrays the speaker's attitudes using adverbial phrases that modify either Torah observance or Torah study. In other examples the speaker declares his emotions or volition explicitly; that is, his attitude itself is the main focus rather than being a modifier of some other activity. For example the statement "I love your commandments more than gold—even fine gold" (v. 127) says nothing about Torah study or Torah observance, and the verse provides no information about what the commandments are. Instead the emphasis is on the intensity of the speaker's love. Other

---

[40] See the commentary on v. 32 regarding the metaphor "expand my heart."

[41] "The idiom 'run to evil' appears in 1:16 and Isa 59:7, signifying eagerness and alacrity. The worthless man not only does evil, he does it with zest." Michael V. Fox, *Proverbs 1–9. A New Translation with Introduction and Commentary*, AB, vol. 18A (New York: Doubleday, 2000), 223. See also pp. 87–88.

verses in Ps 119 teach that the speaker's love of Torah leads him to obey and to study it, but in v. 127 the focus is the love itself.

The author uses the verb "to love" (אהב) ten times with the speaker as the grammatical subject and one of the eight Torah terms as the object.[42] Some of the examples juxtapose the speaker's love for God's word with either the motif of Torah observance or Torah study. In v. 97 the speaker exclaims, "How I love your Torah! All day it is my musing." The author does not explain the relationship between the speaker's love of Torah and his meditation, but the juxtaposition implies that the speaker meditates on Torah because he loves it. Verse 167 associates the outward duty—Torah observance—with the speaker's love: "My soul observes your stipulations, and I love them very much." Again, the author does not explain how the speaker's obedience and love are related, but the verse portrays the speaker as one who is eager to obey.

In verses that use the verb "to love" (אהב), the author juxtaposes the speaker's love with other emotions, such as delight and loathing. He contrasts the speaker's love for Torah with his hatred for deception and duplicity. Verse 163, which contains the verb "to love" (אהב), illustrates the problem with trying to summarize the ideas of Ps 119 under the two rubrics of Torah study and Torah observance, since the verse does not describe either Torah study or Torah observance. The speaker declares, "I hate and loathe deception; I love your Torah." The author is not describing the speaker's love of Torah for some ancillary purpose, rather he is characterizing the true servant of God as one who loves Torah. The author portrays the speaker declaring his love for God's precepts in the form of a claim of innocence, "Look—for I love your precepts—O YHWH, give me life according to your mercy" (v. 159).[43] Verse 47 is an example that links two emotions: "I will take delight in your commandments, which I love." There is no information about the nature of the commandments; the verse is exclusively about the speaker's emotions, specifically his love and delight (ש.ע.ע).

This root (ש.ע.ע) occurs eight times in Ps 119, which is more than the rest of the Bible combined.[44] In Isa 5:7 the phrase "a plant of his

---

[42] Verses 47, 48, 97, 113, 119, 127, 140, 159, 163, and 167.

[43] See the discussion in chapter 2 regarding claims of innocence and the cumulative effect of the repetition, pp. 46–48.

[44] Vv. 16, 24, 47, 70, 77, 92, 143, and 174; cf. Avi Hurvitz שעשועי תורה' במזמור", קיט, ["שעשועי תורה' מקור הביטוי ורקעו הלשוני" in Ps. 119—the Origins of the

delight" (נְטַע שַׁעֲשׁוּעָיו) is a metaphor used to describe the special place that the people of Judah had in God's attention. Elsewhere part of the semantic range of the word is "playing." For example, Isa 11:8 describes idyllic conditions when a child who is not yet weaned will be able to play (שִׁעֲשַׁע) safely near the den of a venomous snake. In Prov 8:30 it is juxtaposed with "frolic" (מְשַׂחֶקֶת). Fox argues that this describes Lady Wisdom playing before God, and her "play expresses the joy of intellect: exploring, thinking, learning."[45]

In v. 24 the word "delight" (שַׁעֲשֻׁעָי) is juxtaposed with a metaphor that describes a mental process; specifically, the speaker declares that God's stipulations are his delight and "the men of my counsel" (אַנְשֵׁי עֲצָתִי). This personification of God's stipulations as a group of counselors is unique in the Bible, and it provides a sharp contrast with the group of princes in v. 23, who sit and slander the speaker. His response to the antagonism of the princes is to meditate on God's statutes. Thus, in vv. 23 and 24 the ideal Torah student meditates on God's word in the face of adversity, and he delights in taking counsel from Torah.

In v. 16 the emphasis is on the speaker's delight in observing Torah. The speaker declares, "I will delight myself (אֶשְׁתַּעֲשָׁע) in your statutes; I will not forget your word." As noted in chapter 2, the expression "I do not forget" describes Torah observance. Using this phrase in v. 16 and juxtaposing it with the speaker's delight indicates that the speaker delights in obedience. In the second half of v. 70, the "delight" or "pleasure" (ש.ע.ע) of the speaker is contrasted with the moral and mental obtuseness of the insolent. Since "delight" is juxtaposed with a description of a mental faculty of the wicked, it seems to refer to the speaker's study of Torah. Thus, the author uses the root ש.ע.ע to describe the speaker's delight in both obedience and study. Yet trying to distinguish between the two activities of study and obedience is foreign to Ps 119; the author is portraying an exemplary person. The activities of Torah observance and Torah study can be discussed separately, but they cannot be separated in practice. The person who continually contemplates Torah will avoid straying from the path of Torah.

Phrase and Its Linguistic Background" (Hebrew)], in *Studies on Hebrew and Other Semitic Languages Presented to Chaim Rabin on the occasion of his Seventy-Fifth Birthday*, ed. M. Goshen-Gottstein et al., 105–09 (Jerusalem: Academon Press, 1990).
[45] Fox, *Proverbs 1–9*, 289.

In v. 31 the speaker declares, "I cling (דבק) to your stipulations." This verse assumes that the reader understands the metaphor of clinging to God, which occurs frequently in Deuteronomy and the Former Prophets. Clinging to God is a metaphor that connotes fearing God, serving God, and obeying God's commandments. Additionally, the metaphor has emotional overtones. Those who cling to God are devoted, and devotion is what God desires. Clinging to God's stipulations is a way to demonstrate commitment, obedience, and devotion to God.

Verse 31 is one of the examples discussed in chapter 2 under the rubric "The Language of Piety."[46] Several of the examples include verbs that are used elsewhere in the Bible with God as the object, but in Ps 119 the author substitutes Torah as the object. Verbs such as "love" (אהב), "fear" (ירא), "trust" (בטח), "believe" (אמן), and "hope" (יחל) are verbs of emotion. Because the statements are placed in the mouth of the speaker, the emotions being portrayed are his emotions. Thus, these verses contribute to the emotional portrait of the ideal Torah student, specifically his devotion to Torah.

Verse 42 includes a substitution of Torah in place of God, which it is noteworthy. In most of the Bible trust (בטח) should be placed exclusively in God, but in Ps 119 the speaker trusts (בטח) God's word. The word בטח often has a connotation of security or confidence, and this connotation fits well in Ps 119:42. In the first half of the verse the speaker declares that he will have an answer for those who reproach him (חרף); the reason that he will have an answer is his trust (בטח) in God's word.[47] Psalm 119 transforms the phrase "trust in God" into "trust in God's word," a locution that is unique in the Hebrew Bible. Another unique locution created by a similar substitution is found in v. 120: "I fear your regulations" (וממשפטיך יראתי). Throughout the Bible God is the object of fear, and in Ps 119 the speaker refers to the righteous as those who fear God (vv. 63, 74, 79). In the first half of v. 120 the speaker declares that his flesh trembles from fear of God. These statements characterize the exemplary student of Torah and elevate the status of Torah for the pious. A proper attitude towards

---

[46] The section begins on p. 34.

[47] Hakham adds that the righteous trust "in your promises that you will deliver those who cling to your Torah." (בהבטחותיך להושיע את הדבקים בתורתך) Amos Hakham, ספר תהלים בדעת מקרא [*Psalms* in *Da'at Mikra* (Hebrew)] (Jerusalem: Mossad HaRav Kook, 1990), 392.

Torah is a means by which the true servant of God demonstrates fear
and love of God.

3.3.3.3. *The Speaker's Relationship with God*

The verses discussed in the above paragraphs fuse the speaker's relationship with God and devotion to Torah. For the author of Ps 119
no one can be a servant of God without a commitment to Torah, and
no one can properly understand and observe Torah without a commitment to God. Either one—a relationship with God or a relationship with Torah—entails the other; they are inseparably intertwined.
Insight and understanding of Torah is only available for a servant of
God, and the speaker considers himself God's servant (vv. 17, 23, 49,
passim). The relationship between the speaker and God pervades Ps
119, and influences the ideas throughout the psalm.

> The triad of God-Torah-Israel is a fundamental assumption of any ancient
> Judaic world. In such worlds, God is rarely understood apart from his
> simultaneous relations with the world as its creator, with Torah as its
> revealer, and with Israel as its covenant partner or redeemer. Likewise,
> Torah rarely stands solely for a piece of wise or useful guidance. Rather
> it is something that comes from God as a message for Israel. Israel, to
> complete the triad, is rarely simply the name of an ethnic group. In
> Judaic usage, it commonly denotes a people living in covenantal relation
> to God through the guidance of Torah.[48]

The above description can be almost directly applied to Ps 119. The
conception of Torah cannot be properly understood apart from the
triad of God-Torah-Israel. The speaker, an exemplary Israelite, assumes
that God is the revealer of Torah, and he repeatedly asks God to teach
him personally. Torah is wise guidance for the speaker, and he recognizes that the guidance is a message from God for him. It is this
message and guidance that the speaker longs to understand in order
to live in a proper relationship with God.[49]

The relationship between God, Torah, and the speaker is important in Ps 119 not merely because it is "a fundamental assumption of

---

[48] Martin Jaffee, *Early Judaism: Religious Worlds of the First Judaic Millennium*,
Studies and Texts in Jewish History and Culture, ed. Bernard D. Cooperman, vol. 12
(Bethesda, MD: University Press of Maryland), 92.

[49] The focus of Ps 119 is on the individual rather than the covenant community,
which shifts the function of Torah. On the absence of the topics of nation, covenant,
etc., see the section beginning on p. 128.

any ancient Judaic world," but more to the point, because portraying
the relationship is a central rhetorical goal of Ps 119. Specifically, the
psalm describes the function of Torah in the relationship between God
and the speaker; this is a description of what Torah *does*—not what
Torah *is*. In some verses Ps 119 praises and describes Torah explicitly,
yet even the exaltation of Torah contributes to the message that Torah
should be studied and obeyed. Recognizing this rhetorical goal of the
psalm helps to explain the variation and repetition that an earlier generation of scholars disdained.[50] In order to achieve the goal of portraying the function of Torah in a relationship, the author describes the
emotion and volition of the speaker in several different ways. Although
there is repetition involved, there is also variation; thus, the author is
able to portray multiple facets of the speaker's relationship with God
and Torah.

3.3.4. *The Language of Distress*

3.3.4.1. *Repeated Petitions*

Many verses in Ps 119 portray the speaker in distress, and by using
petitions, which are formally similar to lament psalms, the author of
Ps 119 portrays the speaker as a supplicant, who continually asks for
God's help. This portrayal of the speaker characterizes him as a dependent servant of God—someone not relying on his own insight. The
author does not give any specific information about the speaker's situation; instead the focus is on his emotions and reactions in the face of
adversity. Often lament psalms emphasize an emotional state rather
than specifying a particular problem. Gunkel notes that the descriptions in many laments are too general to allow for the identification of
a specific situation or even a specific problem. Within a single context
multiple descriptions occur, and the differences cannot always be correlated with a specific setting. For example, there are three different
problems in Ps 22: sickness, wild animals, and enemies. "These observations should serve as a warning to us against taking the individual
images and concepts which occur in the complaint literally in every
case." The discontinuity of the images

---

[50] See chapter 1 for a discussion of previous scholarship.

makes it completely clear that whatever unites these images has to be sought outside the images themselves. This unity may lie in the spiritual condition of the poet. The poet does not place as much weight on a completely faithful reflection of the external circumstances as he does on communicating the internal circumstances....[51]

The *Hodayot* from Qumran are analogous. Like Ps 119 they utilize lament formulas, but they should not be classified as laments.[52] In the *Hodayot* the lament motifs throw the elements of praise into sharper relief; the contrast highlights the praise or thanksgiving similar to the way an artist uses a dark color to create contrast.

Verse 145 provides a good illustration: "I call out wholeheartedly— answer me, YHWH, so that I can keep your statutes." There is no information in the verse about the speaker's situation. The verse seems to imply that the speaker is in a situation that might cause him to go astray (perhaps similar to Prov 30:8–9), but the circumstances are not the point. The author is portraying the speaker's reliance on God.

3.3.4.2. *Enemies as a Foil*

Enemies, an important genre element of lament psalms, are a recurring motif in Ps 119. Erhard Gerstenberger states that Ps 119 includes a "portrait of the godless," but there is little, if any, characterization of the wicked in Ps 119.[53] The wicked are very flat characters. Psalm 119 does teach that the wicked are those who forsake Torah, but that does not explain the function of the enemies in the psalm. The purpose of the contrast between the speaker and enemies, throughout the entire psalm, is to characterize the speaker. They appear only as a foil for the exemplary servant of God. In almost every verse that includes the motif of enemies, their actions and attitudes are contrasted with those of the speaker, highlighting the proper behavior of the paradigmatic Torah student.

---

[51] Hermann Gunkel, *An Introduction to the Psalms: The Genres of the Religious Lyric of Israel*, trans. James D. Nogalski (Macon, GA: Mercer University Press, 1998), 134.

[52] See Eileen M. Schuller, "Petitionary Prayer and the Religion of Qumran," *Religion in the Dead Sea Scrolls*, ed. John J. Collins and Robert A. Kugler (Grand Rapids: Eerdmans, 2000), 29–45.

[53] Erhard S. Gerstenberger, *Psalms, Part 2, and Lamentations*, FOTL, vol. 15 (Grand Rapids: Eerdmans, 2001), 315.

Using the motif of enemies introduces an element of antagonism, and this allows the author to portray how the speaker reacts in antagonistic situations. The following paraphrase of v. 69 highlights the contrast: "Despite the fact that the insolent slander me, I will still keep God's precepts wholeheartedly." The author uses this depiction of the speaker being slandered in order to show that the exemplary Torah student gives unreserved commitment to God's word even in the worst circumstances.

Many examples demonstrate that the function of the enemies is to serve as a foil for the exemplary Torah student. In v. 139 the speaker's concern is not deliverance from the enemies but rather proper observance of God's word: "My zeal silences me, because my enemies forget your words" (שכחו דבריך צרי).[54] Since the speaker repeatedly declares that he does not and will not forget Torah, this description of the enemies is an explicit contrast to him. It is especially clear in v. 85 that the use of enemies in Ps 119 highlights Torah observance: the speaker declares, "The insolent dig pits for me that are not according to your Torah" (אשר לא כתורתך). One might ask, "What sort of pit *is* according to God's Torah?" Alternatively, the antecedent of the relative pronoun may be the action of digging pits rather than the pits themselves, and the action of digging pits is not something that a Torah student would undertake.[55] In any case, the author of Ps 119 is not concerned with pits; the trope is borrowed from lament psalms and redeployed to characterize the speaker.

Verses throughout the psalm state explicitly that the wicked do not observe Torah; for example, in v. 158 the treacherous ones (בגדים) are "those who do not observe your word" (אשר אמרתך לא שמרו). Yet the wicked are not being condemned; there is no exhortation to repent. The speaker always has center stage, and the relationship between the speaker and the wicked serves to highlight the speaker's piety. When he sees those who do not observe God's word, he says, "I was disgusted" (v. 158). He is a bit less caustic in v. 136, where he says that he weeps about others' failure to observe God's Torah. This

---

[54] Zenger notes that "zeal" (קנה) is often used of YHWH's demand for exclusive commitment from the people of Israel. Hossfeld and Zenger, *Psalmen 101–150*, 383.

[55] This may be the understanding of traditional Jewish interpreters (e.g., Ibn Ezra and Radaq), who connect v. 85 with the commandment in Deut 19:10 that innocent blood should not be shed ולא ישפך דם נקי.

is reminiscent of the wise man: "In Proverbs, whether *others* obey or despise wisdom causes joy or chagrin to the wise."[56]

The author uses the motif of antagonism repeatedly, and the following paraphrases highlight the contrasts between the speaker and the antagonists. "Although princes sit and gossip about me, I still meditate on your statutes" (v. 23). "Although the insolent scorn me, I do not turn aside from your Torah" (v. 51). "Although the wicked set a snare for me, I do not stray from your precepts" (v. 101). "Although the wicked wait to destroy me, I contemplate your stipulations" (v. 95). Verse 161 draws on the theme of enemies and their antagonism, and the verse contributes to the characterization of the speaker, since he responds appropriately even in the face of ill-treatment: "Princes pursued me for no reason, but my heart trembles at your word." He may fear the princes and their schemes, but that fear pales in comparison to his fear for God and his word.[57] The speaker's fear of God's word will keep him on the right path regardless of what the princes do to him. It is also a natural, contextual reading of this verse to include it as part of the contrast between the ideal Torah student and the unrighteous. The princes are not explicitly labeled unrighteous or wicked, but their antagonism against the speaker is capricious (חנם), which means that they do not fear God or his word.

In v. 150 the speaker uses a spatial metaphor to describe the wicked and contrast them with the ideal Torah student: "The ones who pursue schemes draw near, but they are far from your Torah." Elsewhere in the Hebrew Bible distance is a physical trope used to figure an attitude or spiritual condition.[58] For example, in Isa 29:13 God says that the people draw near to him with their lips but make their hearts distant.

---

[56] Michael V. Fox, private communication.

[57] "Einen existentiellen 'Schrecken' und ein 'Zittern des Herzens' (vgl. Dtn 28,66 f.) gibt es für ihn nur vor dem Gericht JHWHs." Zenger, *Psalmen 101–150*, 386. In this section of the commentary, Zenger discusses the enemies and the motifs of war that are used in the psalm, but he does not note the author's use of the enemies as a foil, which is their most important function. See my discussion of P. J. Botha's arguments in the following pages.

[58] Lakoff and Johnson note the widespread influence of spatial metaphors in language generally, and study of spatial metaphors in the Hebrew Bible has bourgeoned in the years following their work. George Lackoff and Mark Johnson, *Metaphors We Live By* (Chicago: University of Chicago Press, 1980). Eidevall notes that "nearness stands for communion" and "distance means abandonment," giving numerous citations from the Psalter (Pss 10:1; 17:8; 22:2, 12, 20; 31:23; 34:19; 38:22; 57:2; etc.). Göran Eidevall, "Spatial Metaphors in Lamentations 3,1–9," in *Metaphor in the Hebrew Bible*, ed. P. van Hecke, BEThL, vol. 187 (Dudley, MA: Peeters, 2005), 134.

Ezekiel 8:6 illustrates the spatial metaphor, since it is describing men in Jerusalem doing abominations "in order to be far off from my sanctuary."[59] Physically, the abominable men of Jerusalem cannot be distant from the temple. The spatial trope figures their spiritual condition or emotional disposition. It is a relatively common metaphor throughout the Bible, but Ps 119:150 is the only verse in Scripture that uses this spatial metaphor for an attitude towards Torah.[60]

The author continues the spatial metaphor in the following verse: "You are near, O YHWH, and all your commandments are true" (v. 151). The same spatial trope is used for salvation in v. 155, "Salvation is far from the wicked," and the second half of the verse explains that it is "because they have not sought your statutes." This implies that for those who study Torah salvation is near, which reinforces the statement in v. 151, "You are near, O YHWH." The author does not specify the nature of the moral matrix, and he never explicitly characterizes the speaker as one who is near to Torah. Yet the contrast between the schemers who are "far from Torah" and the speaker who is near to YHWH implies that Torah study brings God near.[61]

P. J. Botha, in his article "The Function of the Polarity Between the Pious and the Enemies in Psalm 119," suggests a triangle as a way to visualize the relationships in Ps 119.[62] In his visualization the three corners of the triangle are YHWH, the person praying (in my terms,

---

[59] Many translations and commentaries interpret this verse as the people doing something to drive God away from his sanctuary, but this interpretation ignores the grammar. See William Tooman, "Ezekiel's Radical Challenge to Inviolability," ZAW 121 (2009): 498–514.

[60] This metaphor should be viewed in light of how the author of Ps 119 substitutes Torah in place of God. See above "The Language of Piety," p. 34. In most cases, nearness is a figurative way of expressing God's favor, while distance figures displeasure. There exceptions in which God draws near in order to judge. One of the most common occurrences of this trope is the nearness of God in the cult, which in some instances draws its imagery from the Sinai pericope. For an overview of this metaphor see Werner E. Lemke, "The Near and Distant God: A Study of Jer 23:23–24 in Its Biblical Theological Context," JBL 100 (1981): 541–55. For comments that address its occurrence in the Psalter, see the introduction to Artur Weiser, The Psalms, in OTL. trans. H. Hartwell. (Philadelphia: Westminster, 1962).

[61] Thus these verses contribute to the author's message regarding the function of Torah; see below p. 136. Verses 150, 151 and 155 are an illustration of an associative sequence, since they all use a spatial metaphor. See the comments in the introductory chapter on "associative sequences" p. 21; the rubric is borrowed from Fox, Proverbs 10–31, 480.

[62] P. J. Botha, "The Function of the Polarity Between the Pious and the Enemies in Psalm 119," OTE 5 (1992): 252–63.

the speaker), and the enemies. In the center of this triangle is Torah as the means by which the speaker can and should relate to God and his enemies. A triangle seems to imply that the enemies are as important as the speaker, but that would give too much importance to the enemies. The focus of Ps 119 is the speaker, and the enemies are only a foil for him. Nevertheless, Botha is correct that an important facet of Ps 119 is the portrayal of relationships, since it contributes to the author's goal of characterizing the speaker.

Relationships between the speaker and other human beings in Ps 119 are either presented entirely negatively (as enemies) or are only presented in passing. The speaker calls himself a friend of those who fear God (v. 63), but the friendship is not explained or described.[63] Verses 74 and 79 include similar statements about those who fear God, but if the God-fearers were described as characters, they would certainly be flat characters. The author does not develop them, nor does he use them to develop the speaker. What is important for the author's portrayal of the speaker is the contrast between the ideal Torah student and the treacherous, insolent, wicked antagonists, who are far from Torah.

3.3.4.3. *The Speaker's Longing for Torah*
In addition to portraying the speaker in antagonistic situations, the author uses the language of distress borrowed from laments for a unique purpose, specifically to portray the speaker's intense desire for God's word. His desire is so intense that it is distressing: "My soul is ground down from longing for your judgments all the time" (v. 20). The expression "ground down" only occurs elsewhere in Lamentations, where it describes deep anguish.[64] Not only is the speaker's longing intense, it is also incessant: "My eyes fail for your word, saying 'When

---

[63] Zenger comments that those who fear YHWH form an association with the speaker of Ps 119, although it is difficult to decide if they form a "community." "Da sind aber auch solche, die, wie er selbst, die Tora als Weg zur JHWH-Furcht (vgl. Ps 111,10; 112,1) sehen und darin die Erfüllung ihres Lebens erfahren. Sie sinde seine «Genossen», mit ihnen weiß er sich nicht nur verbunden, sondern sie bilden eine Gemeinschaft (V 63); ob diese sogar festere Formen annimmet («Gemeinde»), ist schwer zu entscheiden." Hossfeld and Zenger, *Psalmen 101–150*, 371.

[64] In his commentary on Lamentations, Ulrich Berges states that the word in Ps 119:20 has a nuance of longing: "d.h. sehnt sich." Ulrich Berges, *Klagelieder*, HThKAT, ed. Erich Zenger (Freiburg: Herder, 2002), 174. However, this nuance of longing is not part of the lexical meaning of the word; if the nuance is present in Ps 119:20, it derives from the context.

will you comfort me?'" (v. 82). A similar expression occurs in the previous verse, "My soul fails for your salvation; I hope for your word"
(v. 81). A theme that is shared in these verses is the notion of waiting for God's Torah. Yet in other verses the speaker declares that he
will not forget Torah, he will observe Torah, and so on. If the speaker
promises to keep God's word, then why is he waiting for it? Thus, it is
clear from this logical gap that the author is portraying the speaker's
desire.[65]

3.3.5. *The Language of Character Formation*

Verse 104 explicitly portrays the process of character formation: "I
consider your precepts; therefore, I hate every path of deception."
Contemplating God's precepts, an intellectual process, shapes the
speaker's emotions, and the speaker himself recognizes that meditation on Torah forms his character.[66] The logical relationship between
the two stichs of v. 104 is specified by the conjunction (עַל כֵּן), which
makes the emphasis on character formation clear. In most of Ps 119
the process of character formation is less explicit, and the author
depicts the process in various ways.

Wisdom literature also addresses the topic of character formation,
and this explains, at least to some extent, why the author of Ps 119
uses the metaphors and motifs of wisdom literature. For example,
Proverbs associates learning and piety, since the "sages of Proverbs
make an essentially intellectual process—learning wisdom—proceed
both from and toward piety."[67] In Ps 119 the intellectual process of
learning Torah is a demonstration of piety, and the process makes the
Torah student more pious.

Various comparisons could be drawn between the themes or literary techniques used to portray an exemplary person in Proverbs and
Ps 119. For example, both Proverbs and Ps 119 use the metaphor of

---

[65] I discuss logical gaps beginning on p. 102.

[66] As I note above in the section on "First-person Language" pp. 70–71, the author
portrays the speaker's subjectivity in the context of Torah study and observance.
Notions of the self and subjectivity are important facets of the literature on character
formation. I am indebted especially to Jonathan Schofer for helping me think about
how Ps 119 relates to the study of character formation or virtue ethics.

[67] Michael V. Fox, "The Pedagogy of Proverbs 2," *JBL* 113 (1994): 238.

the path to emphasize the contrast between two different types of individuals.

> Corresponding to the TWO PATHS there are two classes of people. Proverbs splits the world along a moral fault line that runs between two classes, the wicked/foolish and the righteous/wise. The first class is the source of all evils and dangers; the second is innocent. The two remain apart, each type pursuing his own path.[68]

The sages of the book of Proverbs believed that the wise are on the path of life rather than the path leading to death, and similarly Ps 119 emphasizes that the righteous who follow Torah are on the right path.

Another point of comparison between the speaker in Ps 119 and the wise man in Proverbs is the depiction of self-control or repose. In Proverbs, "the ideal type is the 'silent man,' who excels not only in tactical reticence and self-control (as in earlier Wisdom) but in repose, resignation, and humility."[69] There are many examples in Ps 119 in which the speaker reacts to an antagonistic or dangerous situation by asserting that he meditates on Torah, does not forget God's statutes, or does not abandon God's precepts.

One metaphor, borrowed from wisdom literature, figures the heart as a container for the words of Torah. For the sages the faculty of wisdom is precious and should be hidden away because of its value.[70] In Ps 119 God's word is precious and should be hidden away because of its value. Torah is something to be treasured like gold or a great spoil (v. 162).[71] The goal of Torah study in Ps 119 is the internalization of Torah, which shapes the student's character.

As noted in chapter 2, internalizing God's word occurs in slightly different terminology in Deuteronomy: "These words shall be upon your heart" (על לבבך Deut 6:6). This is repeated and adapted in Deut 11:18 where the children of Israel are exhorted to put (שם) God's words "upon your heart" (על לבבכם).[72] The significance of this metaphor is

---

[68] Fox, *Proverbs 1–9*, 130.

[69] Fox, *Proverbs 1–9*, 155.

[70] Fox, *Proverbs 1–9*, 114–15.

[71] See Avi Hurvitz, שקיעי חכמה בספר תהלים [*Wisdom Language in Biblical Psalmody* (Hebrew)] (Jerusalem: Magnes Press, 1991), 52–54.

[72] See Weinfeld, *Deuteronomy 1–11*, 455, who comments that the repetition forms an inclusio.

similar to the English idiom of keeping something in mind.[73] If the children of Israel had God's word upon their heart then they would not forget God and chase other gods. According to the Deuteronomistic History they failed to internalize Torah and consequently forgot God; the prophets Ezekiel and Jeremiah declared that God would solve the problem supernaturally (Ezek 36; Jer 31).[74]

One who walks in Torah, who is by the definition of Ps 119 also a student of Torah, undergoes a spiritual and intellectual transformation by means of internalizing Torah. The process is similar to the acquisition of wisdom described by Fox in his essay "Wisdom in the Lectures."[75] The young man being addressed by his father in Proverbs does not possess all possible wisdom. In fact, as a youngster he may possess very little wisdom; he may have only the instruction (תורה) of his parents. Yet if he avoids present temptations by following instruction, then he will have opportunities to gain wisdom. Similarly, the young man in Ps 119 has a place to start: "How can the young man keep his way pure? By observing your word" (v. 9). He has some knowledge of Torah, perhaps also from his parents, and if he will walk in what he knows, then God's word will light the path ahead (v. 105). The young man in Proverbs develops a character trait, which can be called wisdom: "Wisdom is a configuration of the soul; it is *moral*

---

[73] Weinfeld notes that the practical meaning of the command to love God is loyalty and obedience, which the phrase "shall be on your heart" assumes. Weinfeld, *Deuteronomy 1–11*, 351. The trope of the heart as a tablet on which something could be written is a way of figuring the process of education; see David M. Carr, *Writing on the Tablet of the Heart* (Oxford: Oxford University Press, 2005). Others argue that "memory" is part of the range of meaning; see Georg Fischer and Norbert Lohfink, "'Diese Worte sollst du summen' Dtn 6,7 wᵉdibbartā bām—ein verlorener Schlüssel zur medatativen Kultur in Israel," in *Studien zum Deuteronomium und zur deuteronomistischen Literatur III*, Stuttgarter Biblische Aufsatzbände, vol. 20, ed. Gerhard Dautzenberg and Norbert Lohfink, 181–203 (Stuttgart: Verlag Katholisches Bibelwerk, 1995). In his comments on Prov 3:3, Fox writes that the phrase means "hold them permanently in your memory; make them an indelible part of your character." Fox, *Proverbs 1–9*, 145. His discussion in the paragraphs following this quotation defends the interpretation that more than memory is involved.

[74] Thomas M. Raitt, *A Theology of Exile: Judgment/Deliverance in Jeremiah and Ezekiel* (Philadelphia: Fortress Press, 1977). How each of these books viewed the hope for the future of Israel and whether there was any hope in the Deuteronomistic History has been discussed at length. A helpful collection of essays can be found in Gary N. Knoppers and J. Gordon McConville, eds., *Reconsidering Israel and Judah: Recent Studies on the Deuteronomistic History*, Sources for Biblical and Theological Study, vol. 8 (Winona Lake, IN: Eisenbrauns, 2000). The specifics of the debate do not affect my argument here.

[75] Fox, *Proverbs 1–9*, 347–51.

character."[76] Similarly, the student of Torah internalizes individual instructions and regulations, and this internalization develops into a character trait, specifically the fear of God.

Psalm 119 defines those who fear God as "the ones observing your precepts" (v. 63) and "the ones who know your testimonies" (v. 79). For the author of Ps 119, piety includes both the observance and knowledge of Torah. The fear of God is an important motif in the book of Proverbs, because Proverbs teaches that piety and wisdom mutually support one another. It is wise to be pious, and piety leads to wisdom. The beginning of wisdom is the fear of YHWH (Prov 1:7), and the acquisition of wisdom results in the fear of YHWH (Prov 2:5). It is a developmental process: "The simple fear of divine anger that prompted the first, juvenile steps toward wisdom matures into a reasoned, cognitive conscience."[77] The same development occurs in Ps 119 by means of the internalization of Torah.

Torah study is an ongoing and self-perpetuating process; that is, the one who gains insight of Torah develops a desire for more insight. During the process the student becomes more pious and more able "to walk in Torah." The internalization of Torah begins to protect the student from temptation, and the author repeatedly emphasizes the process is one of the heart. The speaker studies and obeys the commandments wholeheartedly. He hides God's words in his heart (v. 11). He asks God to incline his heart to the testimonies (v. 36). He requests that his heart would be continually in the statutes (v. 80). He declares that he has inclined his heart to performing the statutes (v. 112). The commands delight the speaker's heart (v. 111). As is the case elsewhere in the Bible, the heart is the center of the individual's character and desire.[78] As Fox notes, "Moral character comes down to desiring the right things, and how can we teach desire?"[79] One answer is by portraying someone whose desires are pure. This is the technique used in Ps 119, and the author borrows from wisdom literature, since it is also concerned with character formation.

---

[76] Fox, *Proverbs 1–9*, 348, italics original.

[77] Fox, *Proverbs 1–9*, 111.

[78] In rabbinic texts related to desire and instincts the heart is a common trope, and its usage is examined carefully in chapter 2 of Jonathan Wyn Schofer, *The Making of a Sage* (Madison, WI: University of Wisconsin Press, 2005).

[79] Fox, *Proverbs 1–9*, 348.

The study that Ps 119 promotes is something more than rote learning of a prescribed set of rules; it is a continual inner conversation
with Torah—for example, in the night (vv. 55, 62) and in dangerous
situations (v. 92), among others. One could add, without doing any
injustice to Ps 119, that everyone should meditate on Torah "when
you sit in your house, when you walk in the way, when you lie down,
and when you get up" (בשבתך בביתך ובלכתך בדרך ובשכבך ובקומך
Deut 6:7). Petitions for understanding imply that the study of God's
word is not a simple process and that Torah study is something more
than exegesis. The speaker declares that he meditates on God's word,
has regard for it, thinks about it in the night, and so on. All of these
activities are spiritual exercises or disciplines, not academic ones.[80]
And when the spiritual exercise is performed, the speaker depends on
God to add insight and instruction as a supernatural gift.

Torah study is not a formula that will automatically produce the
correct results. The exemplary student gains knowledge and access to
God through Torah but only when God grants him knowledge and
access. The speaker may keep all the laws, but he still needs God's intervention. Obedience has some positive effect, but it does not produce
the desired results by a mechanistic chain of cause and effect. Insight
into God's word is a benefit granted personally by God that leads to
obedience, and obedience is an activity supported and made possible
by God that yields the benefit of greater insight. This is not faulty logic
on the part of the author, since Torah observance and Torah study are
mutually reinforcing activities. The relationship between the speaker's
obedience of Torah and his understanding of Torah is an example that
demonstrates the author is portraying a process of spiritual formation.

The requests for understanding are not limited to the words "teach"
(למד) and "insight" (בין). The speaker also requests, "Open my eyes
that I may gaze on miracles from your Torah" (v. 18). He declares that
when he meditates on God's precepts, then he can see God's paths
(v. 15). He will not be ashamed "when I gaze on all of your commandments" (v. 6). He petitions God to turn his (the speaker's) eyes from

---

[80] Pierre Hadot discusses spiritual exercises in his *Philosophy as a Way of Life:
Spiritual Exercises from Socrates to Foucault*, trans. Michael Chase (New York:
Blackwell, 1995). I am not claiming that the description of Hadot applies directly to
Ps 119; studying the Hebrew Bible in light of the work of Hadot and others who have
examined early Christian literature would likely be a fruitful endeavor. My claim here
is simply that the study being described is something more than just an intellectual
process.

looking at what is vain or worthless (שָׁוְא v. 37). All of these verses figure a spiritual and intellectual process; the speaker is not talking about a literal process of reading with his eyes. True insight into God's word comes through persistent meditation combined with supernatural intervention.[81]

Psalm 119's claim that God teaches the speaker directly is striking. In Deuteronomy, a book that emphasizes teaching, God gives his revelation to Moses, who in turn teaches the people or the priests.[82] Priests and parents then repeat the instruction for later generations. In Proverbs, parents are the most important teachers. None of these teachers is significant in Psalm 119. Deissler comments, "YHWH is experienced as the great and unique teacher through learning and meditating on the divine teaching and promise, behind which all other means of instruction and advice must take second place."[83]

The emphasis on character formation in Ps 119 is not limited to locutions borrowed from wisdom literature. Many of the examples of traditional religious language discussed above contribute to this rhetorical goal as well. For example, I argue in chapter 2 that Ps 119:30 should be interpreted in light of Ps 16:8 and that v. 30 is one case in which the author substitutes Torah in place of God. If this interpretation is adopted, then the verse reads: "I set your regulations [continually before me]." Hame'iri specifies that the significance is to keep the regulations in mind: "I have set them in front of me so that I will not forget them."[84] In isolation v. 30 would not explicitly portray the process of character formation, but it dovetails with the other verses in Ps 119 that do portray character formation. The speaker repeatedly declares that he does not (or will not) forget God's word. These verses share features with other claims of innocence and with other verses in which the author substitutes Torah in the place of God. In Deuteronomy "forgetting God" results in disobedience of his commandments. The author of Ps 119 compresses the expression into a

---

[81] On the conception of God as a teacher see Finsterbusch, *JHWH als Lehrer der Menschen*.

[82] Karin Finsterbusch, *Weisung für Israel: Studien zu religiösem Lehren und Lernen im Deuteronomium und seinem Umfeld*, FAT, vol. 44, ed. Bernd Janowski et al. (Tübingen: Mohr Siebeck, 2005).

[83] Deissler, 311. "Im Lernen und Meditieren der göttlichen Weisung und Verheißung wird Jahwe als der große und einzige Lehrer erfahren, hinter dem alle andern Vermittler von Weisung und Rat zurücktreten müssen."

[84] שויתים לנגדי לבל אשכחם Ha-Keter, 165.

more concise locution—forgetting God's commandments—which implies disobedience.

3.3.6. *Inconsistencies in the Portrayal*

The portrayal of the exemplary Torah student is not always consistent. Whybray labels some of the statements paradoxes: "Such paradoxes are consistent with, and even characteristic of, a person in spiritual turmoil. They testify to the reality of the psalmist's faith, not to spiritual uncertainty and vacillation."[85] Whybray is right that there is no spiritual vacillation in Ps 119, but ascribing this sort of language to the psychological profile of the psalmist is not helpful. Any psalmist who had the time to reflect on and plan the construction of a 176-verse acrostic poem (using eight Torah terms and eight verses for each letter of the alphabet, stitching the strophes together with repeated key words, infusing the lines with traditional religious language, and more…) would be able to write without being unduly influenced by "spiritual turmoil." A better explanation of the data is to ascribe them to the psalmist's goal of constructing an effective persona.

The inconsistencies show that the author's rhetorical goals are most important. His goal is not to create perfect coherence between all the figurative language and literary techniques; it is to portray the Torah student realistically. Some of the incongruities are subtle. For example, in v. 6 the speaker declares that he will not be ashamed when he contemplates God's commandments. This confidence stems from his petition in v. 5 for God to help him observe the law. Verse 22, however, begins with a petition for God to remove his reproach. The second half of the verse provides the reason why God should do so: "I keep your stipulations." If he keeps the stipulations (v. 22), why does he petition God for help to observe them (v. 5)? In v. 101 the speaker declares, "I restrain my feet from every evil path, so that I might observe your word." But v. 9 teaches that a naïf can keep his way pure by observing God's word. Which comes first? This is the language of character formation, and it is therefore a developmental process. "Which comes first?" is the wrong question.

---

[85] Roger N. Whybray, "Psalm 119: Profile of a Psalmist," in *Wisdom, You Are My Sister*, ed. Michael L. Barré, CBQMS, vol. 29 (Washington: Catholic Biblical Association, 1997), 37.

The examples of inconsistencies listed above are subtle, but other examples are more glaring. It is impossible to reconcile v. 110 and v. 176: "From your precepts I have not erred" (תעה v. 110); "I have erred..." (תעה v. 176). In many verses the speaker declares his delight in God's word: vv. 14, 111, 162, *passim*. But in other verses he declares his longing for God's word—as if he does not possess it: "My eyes fail for your salvation and for your righteous word" (v. 123); "I hope for your salvation, O YHWH" (v. 166). In v. 82 the speaker asks, "When will you comfort (נחם) me?" Yet he has already declared that he takes comfort (נחם) when he remembers God's judgments (v. 52). If the speaker of Ps 119 never erred, never needed God's help, never experienced distressful situations, and his speech was always consistent, then he would be a character who was too idealized and therefore an unconvincing character.

Although the metaphor of the path provides unity to the chapter because of its frequency, it also is used inconsistently. Torah is itself the path (v. 1); Torah keeps the servant on the right path (v. 9); and Torah lights the way or reveals the path (v. 105). Is Torah the path, or is it the light that helps the speaker walk in the path? Many verses include the motif of danger or antagonism on the path, but in v. 45 the speaker declares that he will walk about in security and in v. 32 that he will run in the path. Running on the path and walking in security clash with the depictions of the enemies who wait in ambush or set traps for the speaker. Not all of these examples contribute directly to the rhetoric of character formation, but the inconsistencies show that the author's rhetorical aims are paramount. Additionally, the metaphor of the path, as it is used in Proverbs and Deuteronomy, emphasizes behavior: "'The way of the Lord' is the behavior God demands of humans (Deut 28:9; etc.). To 'go' in it or 'keep' it means to obey his commands."[86] Psalm 119 assumes that Torah provides guidelines for proper behavior, and what is more, Ps 119 teaches that those who internalize Torah will naturally chose the right path—that is, the right behavior. Their choices will flow from their character, which has been shaped by immersion in Torah.

Petitions and claims of innocence in the chapter also illustrate that rhetorical concerns control the portrayal of the ideal Torah student. As noted above, numerous verses juxtapose petitions with claims of

---

[86] Fox, *Proverbs 10–31*, 528.

innocence. These verses indicate that the speaker believes God will eventually vindicate those who observe Torah. The speaker repeatedly declares that he observes Torah, and he does so wholeheartedly and with delight. Yet in other verses, he petitions God to deliver him so that he can observe Torah. "Give me life (חיני) according to your mercy, and I will observe the stipulations of your mouth" (v. 88).[87] He also petitions God to instruct him so that he can observe Torah (e.g., v. 33), and in v. 5 he expresses his longing to observe God's statutes. If the speaker actually observes Torah as he claims elsewhere, then why does he petition God for help? These verses do not invalidate the speaker's claims that he observes God's commandments. The best explanation for such inconsistencies is that the author sought to portray a complex and compelling Torah student in a variety of situations.

3.3.7. The Portrayal of Settings

The author of Ps 119 depicts the speaker in various settings in order to characterize him. This is analogous to the way that an author of a narrative develops characters in different settings, although there is no narrative progression in Ps 119 and the acrostic medium does not necessarily lend itself to mimesis. Many examples occur in the chapter: "In the night I remember your name" (v. 55); "In the middle of the night I will arise to praise you" (v. 62); "All day it is my musing" (v. 97); "Princes pursue me for no reason" (v. 161); "I praise you seven times a day" (v. 164). All of these verses portray the speaker in some setting, often interacting with those who forget God's word, and all are juxtaposed with some statement about Torah. Psalm 119 might be labeled a portrait of the exemplary Torah student, but the portrayal is far from static.

Some of the scenes are almost vignettes; for example, in v. 23 the speaker declares, "Princes sit and speak against me."[88] This verse implies some sort of antagonism without giving an explanation. Due

---

[87] The logical relationship between the two halves of this verse—specifically between the verbs "give me life" and "I will observe"—is open to interpretation. The long form of the first person verb "I will observe" (ואשמרה) seems to indicate a logical consecution; however, see the comments on vv. 15 and 44. See also the section on logical gaps, beginning on p. 102.

[88] Alter uses the term "narrative vignettes" to describe some proverbs. Robert Alter, *The Art of Biblical Poetry*, (New York: Basic Books, 1985), 169. See also the comments on Prov 11:2 in Fox, *Proverbs 10–31*, 531.

to the poetic constraints the author cannot elaborate in the verse, but he gives enough information to portray a scene for the reader. By juxtaposing the comment about princes with the phrase "your servant will muse on your statutes," the author implies that the speaker responds appropriately to antagonism, specifically like a composed sage. Another interesting scene is portrayed in v. 46: "I will speak your stipulations in front of kings and not be ashamed." It is not clear whether being in front of kings includes danger for the speaker or not. Using the motif of shame seems to imply antagonism, but being in front of kings could imply that the speaker has some important function in the royal court.[89] Regardless of whether or not antagonism is involved, the author uses only a few words to create a scene in which the speaker demonstrates his commitment to God's word.

The metaphor of the path, which is so pervasive in Ps 119, is a trope that the author uses to portray different scenes.[90] The path functions as a setting in which the speaker acts or reacts to others, who are almost exclusively the wicked. For example, "Wicked men set a snare for me, but I did not stray from your precepts" (v. 101). In this example the speaker does not interact with the wicked, but he does react to danger by remaining faithful and committed to God's precepts. Just as life for the righteous is not always free from danger or antagonism, so also the path of the upright in Ps 119 is not always free from danger. Thus, there is a mimetic function to the trope that is important for the portrayal of the speaker. The trope of the path is not mimetic in the same way that a narrative is. However, the path functions as a setting in which the servant acts, or to mix similes, like a background on which different sketches of the Torah student are drawn.

The author adds depth and complexity to his portrayal of the speaker by depicting him in different situations.[91] Regarding different

---

[89] Zenger sees no antagonism here but rather the theme of passing on God's instruction to the king and the people that is found in Pss 102:20–23; 138:4–6; and Isa 2:1–5; 42:1–4. For Zenger this is the "Vision von der Weitergabe der Tora JHWHs an die Könige und die Völker." Hossfeld and Zenger, *Psalmen 101–150*, 369.

[90] See the above discussions of the trope of the path, including the comparisons with wisdom literature.

[91] Karin Finsterbusch, whose article was published after I had first written these paragraphs, describes this feature of Ps 119 as programmatic; that is, it was part of the author's agenda. She notes that the requests of the speaker come from different life perspectives. For example, in one stanza the speaker represents a young man and in another stanza an older man with life experience. Although she uses the word "perspective" in a different way than I do, the argument is essentially the same,

perspectives in narrative, Wolfgang Iser comments, "Indeed, it is this very shifting of perspectives that makes us feel that a novel is more 'true-to-life.'"[92] This is not to claim that the literary techniques in Ps 119 are the same as those used in narrative. Of course reading a novel, which is the object of Iser's concern, is different than reading Ps 119, but there is a helpful analogy. If all of the depictions of the speaker were in similar situations, the portrait would be static and flat.

3.3.8. *Repetition*

The frequent repetition and combination of the various techniques described above have a cumulative effect on interpretation. For example, in v. 161 the speaker laments, "Princes pursue me for no reason." The trope of the path is not explicit; that is, the pursuit could take place anywhere. However, since the trope of the path is so frequent throughout the chapter, it is natural to read this verse as an example of the use of the trope. Additionally, other occurrences of the trope involve some sort of danger for the speaker, such as traps or snares, which are typically placed on a path in order to be effective. Grouping v. 161 together with the other verses that use the metaphor of the path (and the motif of danger) is a natural reading of the verse, although the path is not explicit.

Some commentators have argued that various phrases in Ps 119 are simply ballast to fill out the poetic lines and to complete the expansive acrostic, but the repetition effects a more nuanced portrayal of the speaker, which is to say the repetition is not redundant.[93] Verse 44 provides a good example for discussion: "I will keep your Torah continually, forever and ever." In isolation, this verse could be interpreted as begrudging capitulation from someone who had been forced to accept the authority of Torah. Furthermore, the end of the verse "continually, forever and ever" (תמיד לעולם ועד) could be merely ballast to lengthen the poetic line. Yet in the context of so many other statements of the speaker's eagerness, the emphasis on perpetual obser-

---

and it is gratifying that we arrived at this conception independently. Finsterbusch, "Multiperspektivität als Programm," 103–04.

[92] Wolfgang Iser, *The Implied Reader: Patterns of Communication in Prose Fiction from Bunyan to Beckett* (Baltimore: The Johns Hopkins University Press, 1974), 288.

[93] See the introductory chapter for a discussion of the poetics of the psalm and examples of scholars who claim that the repetition does not have an important function in the psalm.

vance in this verse is best interpreted as a declaration of the speaker's intention, and rather than being ballast this phrase contributes to the portrayal of the exemplary Torah student. Not every verse in Ps 119 contains a reference to the speaker's attitudes or emotions, but such statements are so frequent in the chapter that they affect the tone of the entire psalm.

The cumulative effect of the various techniques is strengthened by means of being woven together. The speaker's willing obedience is interrelated with other important themes throughout the chapter. For example, a servant of God is one who is subject to God and to God's stipulations, and the speaker speaks of himself as "your servant" thirteen times.[94] In v. 125 the speaker states explicitly, "I am your servant" (עבדך אני). Although the focus of the verse seems to be knowledge and insight, the willing subject should not be ignored. The speaker asks God for insight in order to know God's stipulations. A connection between obedience and insight is not explicit in the verse, but the juxtaposition does imply that insight leads to obedience, which is willing subjection. In order to obey God's commandments, one must know them, and the speaker is convinced that God will personally teach anyone who is a committed student. With this depiction, the author portrays a view of pedagogy that reinforces his view of piety.

The portrayal of the speaker's emotions and attitudes is not a simplistic, one-dimensional portrayal. The author repeats, varies, and recombines motifs to give the portrayal texture and complexity. In difficult situations the speaker does not forget God's word; instead he is eager to follow God's commandments. He awakes in the middle of the night to praise God about his righteous judgments (v. 62), and Torah is his conversation partner all day long (v. 97). In fact, he praises God for his word "seven times a day" (v. 164). The speaker delights and rejoices in God's word, but he does not take his commitment lightly. He fears God's judgments (v. 120), and his heart trembles at God's word (v. 161). The cumulative effect demonstrates that the repetition

---

[94] Cf. vv. 17, 23, 38, 49, 65, 76, 84, 122, 124, 125, 135, 140, 176. On the theme of willing subjection see Schofer, *The Making of a Sage*. He deals with this theme throughout his work, but see the introduction on pp. 18–19, where he sets the stage for further discussion and draws some comparisons and contrasts with other theorists, such as Foucault, MacIntyre, and Ricoeur. It would be anachronistic for me to argue that the student depicted in Ps 119 looks very much like a student of a rabbi that might be depicted in the Mishnah, but there is some value in drawing this comparison. For further discussion see chapter 5, especially "The Place of Ps 119 in Judaism," p. 167.

in Ps 119 is not merely for the sake of the acrostic; it contributes to the author's rhetorical goals.

3.4. The Portrayal of the Exemplary Torah Student— Its Suasive Force

In the above paragraphs, I argue that the author constructs a persona who models the message. The author does not exhort the reader to obey and study Torah, instead he portrays someone does so.[95] To a certain extent, the reader must adopt the perspective of the speaker, and thus in the process of reading Ps 119 there is also a formation that takes place in the reader.[96] In the book of Proverbs, "the creation of

---

[95] It is "ein Wesensmerkmal von Literatur, dass sie fiktional ist (also nicht notwendigerweise Realexistierendes darstellt), gleichzeitig aber Authentizität suggeriert und die Handlung oder die Personen als möglicherweise real präsentiert; diese Grenze von Realität und Fiktion kann nur Literatur schaffen (bei anderen Texten würde man dies als Lüge bezeichnen, bei Literatur ist das ein Zeichen für das Können des Autors)." Karla Prigge, private communication.

[96] Exploring such a subjective category is a notoriously difficult enterprise, not only for the obvious reason that a reader's subjective response is unavailable for study, but also because the topic is at the intersection of so many specialized, and often isolated, disciplines. Ethnographers, for example, caution that unreflectively inserting Western ideas of the self into a field of study will have a distorting effect; see for example, Frank Johnson, "The Western Concept of Self," in *Culture and Self: Asian and Western Perspectives*, ed. A. J. Marsella et al., 91–138 (New York: Tavistock, 1985). Scholars must also grant that emotions are culturally conditioned, which complicates the study of emotional language and its effect on the readers; see Catherine Lutz, "Emotion, Thought, and Estrangement: Emotion as a Cultural Category," *Cultural Anthropology* 1 (1986): 287–309. In traditional linguistics, "affect has been consistently set aside as an essentially unexplorable aspect of linguistic behavior, a residual category to which aspects of language that cannot be handled conveniently with extant linguistic models were relegated to be forgotten." Besnier, "Language and Affect," 420. But "affect" is one of the primary emphases in Ps 119, and the effect of the affective language deserves consideration. In the study of cognition, both emotion and motivation are often bracketed out of the discussion: "Cognition and emotion and cognition and motivation are research topics for the future. I have not much to say about these topics at present, except that they are important and should no longer be neglected." Walter Kintsch, *Comprehension: A Paradigm for Cognition* (Cambridge: Cambridge University Press, 1998), 421. Yet "motivation" is precisely the point here, and the relationship between religious discourse and rhetoric complicates the question further; see Debora K. Shuger, "The Philosophical Foundations of Sacred Rhetoric," in *Rhetorical Invention and Religious Inquiry*, ed. Walter Jost and Wendy Olmstead, 47–64 (New Haven: Yale University Press, 2000). The often assumed dichotomy between rational and emotive language needs to be abandoned for a more nuanced model; see for example, Raphaël Micheli, "Emotions as Objects of Argumentative Constructions," *Argumentation* (2008): 1–17. Despite all of this complexity, we must accept that the

effective personae was instrumental in imbuing the readers not only with knowledge but also with attitudes and perspectives that will guide their behavior for the years to come."[97] The speaker fills this role in Ps 119, and in the following paragraphs I describe features of the psalm that contribute to its suasive force.

3.4.1. *Advantages and Benefits of Torah Observance*

The author describes advantages and benefits for those who observe Torah; however, the language of advantage does little to characterize the speaker. Instead it contributes to the suasive force of the chapter, and this supports the thesis that Ps 119 was written to persuade the reader to adopt the behavior, perspectives, and attitudes of the speaker. Since the advantages accrue to the speaker, the description of benefits could be considered as part of the author's portrayal of the speaker. At the same time the benefits contribute to the suasive force by depicting Torah study and observance as desirable pursuits. For example, v. 19 teaches that the giving of Torah is an instance of God granting his favor. Because the verse is phrased as a petition from the speaker, it contributes to his characterization, but there is also a message for the reader, specifically, the perceptive, pious person will take advantage of the favor that God has granted in Torah. Verses 9 and 11 both indicate that God's word is effective in preventing sin, a clear advantage for those who want to avoid sin, namely, the righteous.

The first two verses of Ps 119 laud Torah observance and teach that those who walk in Torah will be blessed. Other verses also proffer general well-being as an advantage of immersion in God's word. The teaching is explicit in v. 165: "There is great peace (שלום) for the ones who love your Torah, and there is no stumbling block for them." Elsewhere in the chapter the teaching is implicit, when the author portrays the well-being of the speaker. In v. 54 the speaker states that God's statutes are songs for him. The mention of songs implies that the statutes evoke a positive emotional response, even though other verses in Ps 119 portray the speaker in situations of distress.[98] This apparent

---

construction of meaning includes the participation of the reader, and even if we cannot specify it precisely, we cannot ignore it completely.

[97] Fox, *Proverbs 1–9*, 346.
[98] See the discussion of "*Inconsistencies in the Portrayal*" at p. 90.

discrepancy is another example that the rhetorical goal is most important. In v. 45 the speaker declares, "I walk about in a broad place, for I
seek your precepts." The verse assumes a dichotomy between openness
and constriction.[99] A constricted path is not only difficult to navigate,
but it also increases the danger of ambush. In this case, the intention
is not to characterize the speaker. Instead the author uses the spatial
metaphor to promote the benefits of Torah study, specifically a situation of security.

Another advantage of following Torah is the avoidance of shame.
This is an important motif throughout the Bible, and the secondary literature on this topic is voluminous.[100] In the prophetic books,
especially Isaiah and Jeremiah, those who trust in any god other than
YHWH will eventually be ashamed.[101] In the book of Psalms, many
laments include a petition that God would prevent the supplicant from
being ashamed. The nuances in the prophets and the Psalter are not
identical, and even an individual passage has both sociological and
psychological components. Studies of shame in the Hebrew Bible have
tended to accept and utilize anthropological theories about how an
ancient society's value system was influenced by a continuum between
honor and shame. This anthropological construct has been called into
question by some recent studies.[102] Regardless of the precise sociological framework, being shamed includes something more than merely
an emotion.

Psalm 119 includes petitions that are similar to other laments.
"Support me according to your word, and I will live. And do not let
me be ashamed of my hope" (v. 116). The juxtaposition implies that
if God will support the supplicant according to his word, then he will
not be ashamed. In v. 22 the speaker petitions, "Remove from me
reproach and contempt (חרפה ובוז), for I keep your stipulations." A
similar petition occurs in v. 39: "Make my reproach (חרפתי), which I

---

[99] Eidevall lists "the dimension of width/narrowness" as one of the commonly used
spatial tropes in the Psalter. "Width, or open space, stands for health and freedom
// narrowness, or confinement, means suffering and oppression." Göran Eidevall,
"Spatial Metaphors in Lamentations 3,1–9," 134.

[100] See the introduction in Johanna Stiebert, *The Construction of Shame in the
Hebrew Bible: The Prophetic Contribution*, JSOTSup, vol. 346 (Sheffield: Sheffield
Academic Press, 2002).

[101] The word "shame" (בוש) in various forms occurs 47 times in Isaiah and Jeremiah,
which is more than a third of the occurrences in the Bible.

[102] See, for example, W. Dennis Tucker, Jr., "Is Shame a Matter of Patronage in the
Communal Laments?" *JSOT* 31 (2007): 465–80.

fear, pass away, for your judgments are good." The verses above imply that Torah observance will prevent shame, and some verses make this explicit. "Then I will not be ashamed, when I gaze at all of your commandments" (v. 6). The conjunction "then" (אז) at the beginning of the verse makes the benefit of avoiding shame logically dependent on v. 5, which emphasizes the speaker's desire to observe God's statutes properly. Yet the second half of v. 6 makes the benefit logically dependent on "gazing at all of your commandments." This is another example of how Torah study and Torah observance are intertwined throughout the psalm.

In the examples listed above, the precise nature of the shame varies. In some cases, the shame is depicted as a strictly personal, subjective experience. In the case of "speaking in front of kings" (v. 46) or "having an answer" (v. 42), a public experience is in view. Additionally, the author uses the motif of shame in some of the contrasts between the speaker and the wicked. In v. 42 the speaker declares that he will have an answer for those who reproach him, because he trusts in God's word. "Having an answer" implies that the one who trusts in God's word will not be publicly shamed, and in contrast, the insolent who lie about the speaker will be ashamed. The nature of the shame in Ps 119 cannot be limited to a specific setting or emotion. In my opinion, the author of Ps 119 is using a traditional expression without limiting its scope. The salient point is that Ps 119 views shame from the perspective of piety, and Torah observance prevents shame, since a pious person will not experience feelings of shame nor be publicly disgraced.

Insight is another advantage for the exemplary student of Torah.[103] In v. 130 the metaphor of illumination is used to describe the benefit of insight: "The opening of your words gives light—it gives insight to the callow." The second half of this verse specifies that the metaphor figures an intellectual process. Like v. 130, the second half of v. 135 also uses the metaphor of illumination with reference to the intellect, since God's teaching illuminates the one who learns. In v. 102 the speaker declares, "I do not turn away from your judgments." What enables him to follow the path of God's judgments? The second half of the verse explains, "because you yourself have instructed me." Having God as a personal instructor is certainly an advantage, and v. 102 emphasizes the advantage of receiving God's instruction. The

---

[103] I discuss conceptions of pedagogy above in the section on character formation p. 84; see the citations of secondary literature, which I will not repeat here.

knowledge that the speaker receives leads to obedience. According to v. 7 learning God's righteous judgments results in the ability to praise God correctly, specifically "with an upright heart" (אודך בישר לבב).

In several verses the author implies that God will teach the supplicant because of God's mercy or goodness. The nature of the association between God's teaching and mercy is not specified; the author simply juxtaposes the ideas. For example, "Your mercy fills the earth, O YHWH; teach me your statutes" (v. 64), and "You are good and the one who causes good things; teach me your statutes" (v. 68). Of all the examples, v. 124 comes the closest to linking the two topics explicitly, "Deal with your servant according to your mercy, and teach me your statutes."

Several verses in Ps 119 juxtapose statements about God's mercy and grace with Torah without specifying the nature of the relationship and without including the theme of teaching. "I entreat your favor wholeheartedly; give me grace according to your word" (v. 58). Similarly in v. 76, "Let your mercy comfort me, according to your word for your servant." These verses imply that God promised to deal mercifully with those who serve him. In v. 77 the speaker petitions: "Let your compassion come to me that I might live, because your Torah is my delight." The second half of this verse implies that the speaker's delight in Torah gives him grounds for his request; that is, one of the benefits of delighting in Torah should be God's compassion. In v. 52 the speaker states that he takes comfort (אתנחם) when he remembers God's judgments.

Describing God's mercy as a benefit of Torah observance is problematic, because strictly speaking, mercy is undeserved. Yet it is clear in some verses that the psalmist believes those who observe Torah receive help from God. The speaker also claims that he would have perished in his affliction, if God's Torah had not been his delight (v. 92). Verse 93 teaches that God gives life by means of his precepts. In v. 175 the speaker states, "Your judgments help me," although he does not say how they help.

It is impossible to define the precise relationship between Torah observance and God's grace. Psalm 119, like the rest of the Hebrew Bible, does not assume a strict deed-consequence nexus.[104] The ben-

---

[104] See Gustav Boström, *The God of the Sages* (Stockholm: Almqvist & Wiksell, 1990), 90–140, who provides a corrective to the article by Klaus Koch, "Gibt es ein

efits of Torah study and observance are not doled out according to a mechanistic formula; they require God's intervention. Torah observance will result in deliverance from danger and from the wicked, but this benefit may not be immediate. Additionally, a simplistic portrayal of the motifs of comfort, giving life, and mercy would not serve the author's rhetorical goals. In some verses the speaker claims that God has granted mercy by means of Torah, but in other verses the speaker expresses his longing for God's salvation. The author's goal is not to define precisely the relationship of Torah observance and God's deliverance; his goal is a portrayal of an exemplary, pious student in different situations. The implication for the reader is that following Torah ensures God's help, even if it is delayed for some unknown reason.

3.4.2. A Secondary Function of Traditional Religious Language

The author portrays the speaker as someone whose speech is permeated with traditional religious language. As I argue in the above sections, one effect of placing this language in the mouth of the speaker is to characterize the speaker as someone who is immersed in Torah, yet this is not the only contribution of the traditional language. It has an additional rhetorical function; namely, it lends authority and legitimacy to the poem. That is, the author's intended audience are those who will recognize and embrace the traditional religious language. It is true that Ps 119 is unique, and "within Jewish piety it forms a new focus of religious relationship, which as yet had not arisen in this way."[105] At the same time, however, there is continuity with earlier tradition that is strengthened by the author's use of religious language.

Vergeltungsdogma im Alten Testament?" *ZThK* 52 (1955): 1–42, where Koch defended the concept of the *Tat-Ergehen Zusammenhang*. Although the supposed deed-consequence nexus is typically discussed in a negative sense (thus the contrast with retribution or Vergeltung), it is appropriate to discuss it in a positive sense as well. Just as there is not a strict, negative deed-consequence nexus, so also there is not a strict, positive deed-consequence nexus.

[105] בתוך הדתיות היהודית נוצר מוקד חדש להתיחסות שעד כה לא היה קיים בצורה כזאת Amir, "The place of Psalm 119 in the religion of Israel," 65. My choice of the words "religious relationship" as a translation of להתיחסות is interpretive on my part; there is nothing inherently "religious" in the word itself. But my choice is not without basis. In the preceding sentences Amir uses the verb יחס several times to discuss the way the author of Ps 119 associates Torah and God as part of a religious relationship. In the sentence quoted here, Amir is building on that discussion, and he uses the term להתיחסות, which is from the same verbal root, thus giving the discussion continuity.

This language evokes feelings and attitudes that make the reader more receptive to the message.

Evocative or emotive facets of Ps 119 must be considered, despite the inherent difficulties.[106] Relating the evocative nature of the psalm to traditional religious language adds yet another level of complexity. For example, it is tempting to describe the persona of the speaker as someone who has internalized the exhortations of Deuteronomy and is pious as defined by Deuteronomy. In chapter 2, I discussed the language of piety and cited various passages, especially from Deuteronomy and the Deuteronomistic History, where such language is found. It appears that Ps 119 is the borrowing text due to slight adaptations of the phraseology. The implication of this would be that the author of Ps 119 is drawing on networks of meanings, using allusions to Deuteronomy, in order to construct his portrayal of the ideal Torah student. This is a "tempting" description rather than a "convincing" description, because I do not believe there is sufficient evidence to defend it.[107] Even though this scenario cannot be defended, it is suggestive for heuristic purposes. Because there are verses in Ps 119 that cannot be properly understood without recognizing the traditional religious language, this implies at the very least that the language had been handed down over time. Furthermore, the religious nature of the language legitimates the psalm, since it involves unmediated, personal contact with God.

3.4.3. *The Suasive Force of Logical Gaps*

The relationship between various statements in Ps 119 is often not specified. Thus, reading Ps 119 trains the reader intellectually, since one must puzzle out the relationship between different ideas in the psalm. For many of the verses in Ps 119, the reading process is similar to reading disjointed proverbs, which omit either assumptions or conclusions.

> ...by actively supplying the missing assumptions and conclusions, the reader participates in the reasoning process, and by unpacking the argument helps teach himself. He is then more likely to interpret, amplify, and extend the message. If read carefully, then, the gapped proverbs not only transmit packets of truths, they *train* the reader in a mode of think-

---

[106] See footnotes 36 and 96 in this chapter.

[107] On the relationship between Ps 119 and other texts see the introduction to chapter 2 and chapter 5, "The Place of Psalm 119 in the Hebrew Bible," beginning on p. 160.

ing: identifying behaviors and associating them with their consequences. In other words, they train the reader to think like a sage.[108]

In some cases the author uses conjunctions that specify the nature of the relationship between the two stichs. However, for the most part the author avoids conjunctions, which forces the reader to participate and trains his patterns of thinking.

Like the sages of the book of Proverbs, the author of Ps 119 does not merely want to convey information. The author of the book of Proverbs "is aiming at a higher and harder goal: wisdom as power. The knowledge of wisdom, once achieved, resides in the learner as a potential and must be activated by God in order to become the power of wisdom, an inner light that guides its possessor through life."[109] The author of Ps 119 is also aiming at a higher goal. He is seeking to persuade the reader to internalize Torah, so that it will shape the reader's character and become an inner lamp for his feet and an inner light for his pathway.[110]

The author of Ps 119 portrays a subject who is a model for the reader in his own character formation. The subjective point-of-view is crucial for the construction of the paradigmatic student of Torah. Because of this subjectivity the author is able to portray the speaker modeling not only activities but also attitudes. The reader witnesses the speaker in the act of adopting a particular stance, experiencing an emotion, declaring his intention, or displaying an attitude. In the process of reading Ps 119, the reader begins to think like the speaker. Careful reading thus "entails the possibility that we may formulate ourselves."[111]

---

[108] Fox, *Proverbs 10–31*, 498.

[109] Fox, *Proverbs 1–9*, 347.

[110] Zenger notes that this is the promise of Jer 31, specifically that everyone will know YHWH "unmediated and through the Torah in their hearts." Hossfeld and Zenger, *Psalmen 101–150*, 391. "…unmittelbar und durch die Tora in ihrem Herzen."

[111] Iser, *The Implied Reader*, 294. One must expand "reading" here to allow for oral transmission; thus, the "hearers" should be included as well. Despite the length of Ps 119, it may have been used in a liturgical setting at Qumran. At least one fragment was found in Cave 4 that was prepared specifically for writing Ps 119. That is, the leather was cut and ruled so that the lines of Ps 119 would fit on it. Although this does not necessarily prove that Ps 119 was used liturgically, it seems to be a reasonable conclusion. See Peter W. Flint, Patrick W. Skehan, and Eugene Ulrich, "Two Manuscripts of Psalm 119 from Qumran Cave 4," *RevQ* 64 (1995): 477–86. "Traditions…can be important elements in defining selves, both because of intrinsic persuasiveness and because of the legitimacy that people claim for them." Schofer, *Making of a Sage*, 178n13.

CHAPTER FOUR

THE CONCEPT OF TORAH

‏...שלא יאמר לך אדם אין מזמורות תורה,‏
‏אלא תורה הם, ואף הנביאים תורה‏
‏מדרש תהלים מזמור עח‏

4.1. Introduction

What is the concept of Torah in Psalm 119? It promotes an expansive conception of Torah, but there is no explicit definition of Torah in the psalm. It praises and exalts Torah, but as Abraham Heschel notes, although the sages praise Torah, "praises upon praises do not fit its essence."[1] Seybold states that a definition is missing because Ps 119 is about the experience of a reality that can only be hinted at or intimated.[2] Instead of a single definition the psalmist multiplies statements, using a variety of terms. The various statements refer to different instantiations of Torah, but Torah is not limited to those instantiations. The reader must derive the overarching concept from the individual verses, many of which refer to specific instantiations of Torah. Ultimately, the conception of Torah in Ps 119 is greater than the sum of the parts.

Torah is the verbal expression of God's desires—both for humanity and for the universe. Psalm 119 does not state this explicitly, but it can be inferred from the various explicit statements in the psalm. Similarly, the following conclusions can be drawn. Since God is righteous and just, God desires that creation will be just. Since God is the powerful creator and king of the universe, God's desires have an imperative force. God's imperatives are also inherently just and demand justice. Since God is merciful and good, God desires to do good things for

---

[1] ‏תורה מן‏ Abraham Joshua Heschel, ‏תהילות ותשבחות אינן הולמות את מהותה‏ ‏השמים‏ [*Torah from Heaven in the Refraction of the Generations* (Hebrew)], vol. 2, (Jerusalem: Soncino Press, 1962ff), 3.

[2] "Eine Definition fehlt in 119, weil es gerade um die Erfahrung einer Realität geht, die begrifflich nur angedeutet werden kann." Klaus Seybold, *Die Psalmen*, HAT I/15, ed. Matthias Köckert and Rudolf Smend. (Tübingen: J. C. B. Mohr, 1996), 473.

creation, especially the creatures made in God's image. Therefore if one will follow God's instruction, it will lead to true life.

For the most part, the implications listed in the previous paragraph assume a very expansive conception of Torah. In order to construct this expansive conception, the psalmist repeats certain locutions with alterations and heaps up terms for Torah. The process of multiplying various terms is similar to the way that the book of Proverbs uses multiple words for wisdom. In reference to the prologue of the book of Proverbs (1:1–7), Gerhard von Rad first asks how the individual terms are associated with one another and then gives the following explanation:

> Apparently an expansive concept, for which there was no useful word available, is being constructed here for the reader. Several well-known terms are set in the space [of the prologue], so that through this cluster the desired expansion of the conceptual sphere would be achieved. Certainly, the individual terms that are used differ from one another but perhaps not in a sense that can be established with conceptual precision, because at the same time they obviously also overlap with each other. By amassing a number of terms, the text seems to aim for something more expansive and greater, which would be deficiently expressed with just one of the terms.[3]

Although von Rad is describing words for wisdom, his description is appropriate for the use of multiple terms for Torah in Ps 119. The author heaps up the Torah terms so that through the accumulation "the desired expansion of the conceptual sphere would be achieved." The fact that the psalmist uses multiple synonyms and the way that he uses the synonyms both point to a conception of God's word that is more inclusive than any of the individual terms.[4]

---

[3] "Wahrscheinlich soll hier ein umfassender Begriff, für den kein handliches Wort mehr zur Verfügung steht, dadurch vor dem Leser aufgebaut werden, daß gewissermaßen in seinen Raum eine Anzahl bekannter Begriffe hineingestellt werden, so daß durch diese Häufung die gewünschte Ausdehnung des Begriffsraumes erreicht wird. Sicher unterscheiden sich die einzelnen verwendeten Begriffe voneinander; aber vielleicht nicht in einem Sinne, der begrifflich präzis zu bestimmen wäre, denn offenbar überschneiden sie sich auch zugleich wieder. Der Text scheint durch die Kumulierung vieler Begriffe etwas Umfassenderes, Größeres anzuvisieren, das mit einem der verwendeten Begriffe unzureichend umschrieben wäre." Gerhard von Rad, *Weisheit in Israel* (Neukirchen-Vluyn: Neukirchener, 1970), 26–27.

[4] On the concept of "synonymous" see the discussion beginning on p. 113. In discussing the eight terms, I also use the label "lexeme." I use this label primarily for stylistic reasons. For example, it is awkward to talk about the word "word" (דבר). My arguments are not dependent on a technical definition of "lexeme." Some linguists use

The repetition of the eight Torah terms is therefore essential to the author's goal of describing and promoting an expansive conception of Torah. In addition to repeating the eight Torah terms, the author repeats various locutions, juxtaposing them in different ways and with different themes. This repetition with variation contributes to a network of interrelated ideas and enables the author to expand the conceptual sphere further. Thus, the repetition is not simply a by-product of constructing an eight-fold acrostic poem.[5]

The concept of Torah in Ps 119 extends beyond the commandments, statutes, and regulations—that is, the legal sphere. Deissler comments, "Our psalm is not a psalm of the law, but rather a psalm of the word of YHWH. What is more, word is to be taken in its most inclusive sense."[6] Within this inclusive category of word and under the idea of speech, one can include "divine creation, control of things and mankind, requirement and prohibition, promise and threat of God."[7] Deissler concludes that the psalm works at times like a magnifying glass and at times like a prism; thus one can discern "the unity and diversity of the divine speech" in Ps 119.[8]

Deissler's phrase "unity and diversity" (Einheit und Vielfalt) can be a cliché, but it is appropriate for Ps 119. "Diversity" is expressed in the variety of the instantiations and "unity" in the expansive concept. This is not to say that the expansive concept is something fundamentally different than the instantiations. Any instantiation is itself Torah and thus shares the essence of Torah. Similarly, the expansive, abstract concept of Torah does not differ in its essence from any of the instantiations. Torah includes the rules that govern the universe (vv. 89–91).

"lexeme" as a way of talking about an abstraction that is independent of specific forms; thus, "sing" and "sang" are two "words" of the same "lexeme." See Peter Matthews, *The Concise Oxford Dictionary of Linguistics* (Oxford: Oxford University Press, 1997), s.v. "lexeme" and "word." I am not using these distinctions for my argument; however, the distinction between "lexical meaning" and "contextual meaning" or "grammatical meaning" is important for my argument. On this see p. 110.

[5] Various examples of this claim occur in the scholarship on Ps 119; see the introductory chapter for scholars who denigrate the psalm. In this chapter, see the comments of Soll on "correlative uses" of the Torah terms in footnote 29.

[6] "Unser Psalm ist darum nicht ein Gesetzespsalm, sondern ein Psalm vom Worte Jahwes. Dabei ist Wort in seiner umfassendsten Bedeutung zu nehmen." Deissler, 293.

[7] "...das göttliche Erschaffen, das Lenken der Dinge und der Menschen, das Gebieten und Verbieten, das Verheißen und Drohen Gottes..." Deissler, 293.

[8] "...wirkt der Psalm wie ein Prisma, welches das Sprechen Jahwes in seinen verschiedensten Weisen farbig aufleuchten läßt. So polarisiert sich in Ps 119 Einheit und Vielfalt des göttlichen Sprechens." Deissler, 294.

It also includes the justice that God will enact upon the wicked at some future date (v. 84), and it includes any instruction, command, or rule from God for mankind (*passim*). These are all a single, unified entity, because they are all from the mouth of God.

None of the instantiations mentioned in Ps 119 are unique. For example, in both Ps 119 and in the Pentateuch, "regulations" (משפטים) is a word that refers to rules that humans should obey. The relationship between God's word and nature that is described in Ps 119:89–91 is not a frequent motif in the Hebrew Bible, but it does occur. God's control of creation by means of his word is found in the books of Psalms and Job. It also occurs in Proverbs and, of course, Genesis.[9] Since these notions are included in Ps 119, the author is promoting something more than a collection of commandments.

In the previous chapter, I argue that Ps 119 describes the function of Torah in the relationship between God and the speaker. This is a description of what Torah *does*—not what Torah *is*. Describing the conception of Torah in Ps 119 must account for this suasive goal. Some verses have a double function; specifically, they characterize the speaker while at the same time praise Torah. This is a clever literary technique, but since the two rhetorical goals are woven together, answering the question "What exactly is the conception of Torah in Ps 119?" is more complicated.

Various facets of the expansive concept of Torah can be derived from the way the author portrays the relationship between God, his servants, and Torah. For example, Torah includes stipulations about how any servant of God should act in the relationship. The stipulations, precepts, regulations, and commandments are instantiations of Torah. Additionally, Torah includes stipulations about how God should act. Because the stipulations about how God should act are self-imposed and because God is not double-minded, he will follow the stipulations (although there may be some delay). The stipulations that govern God's actions are therefore promises, which the servant of God can trust—and should trust.[10] The fact that God makes promises

---

[9] Cf. Ps 33; 78; 148; Job 26:10; 28:26; 38:10–11; Prov 8:29.

[10] In several verses Rashi describes God's word (both דבר and אמרה) as the word "which you have made me trust" (הבטחתני); see vv. 25, 38, 41, 49, 123, and 162. Note that this could be translated "you have promised me." There are related words for promise, such as "I swear to you," but the H of ב.ט.ח is the Hebrew idiom for "promise." I note the connection, since it is not always clear in translation. I discuss the aspect of promises further beginning at p. 119.

implies something about his character: God is good and desires to do good things for creation, especially humanity. For the author of Ps 119, this implication is Torah, but it is not an instantiation of Torah in the same way that a specific commandment is.

Included in the constellation of ideas about God and the relationship between God and humanity is the assumption that God desires to reveal to humanity something about the being and desires of God. How does the author know this? He knows because Torah teaches him. Since Torah teaches that God speaks to humanity and Torah is the word of God, Torah teaches about Torah. This self-referential notion is an important facet of the expansive concept of Torah, despite the fact that Ps 119 never makes it explicit.

4.2. What Psalm 119 Expresses

Although Psalm 119 does not explicitly define Torah, it does include explicit statements about Torah, and discussing these statements helps clarify the conception of Torah in the psalm. The explicit declarations demonstrate that the author's conception of Torah cannot be limited to the Pentateuch or any other specific text. One piece of evidence that supports this claim is the distinction between explicit statements that describe instantiations of Torah and statements that describe an abstract concept. This distinction provides a means of organizing some of the data in the following sections, in which I first discuss the eight Torah terms and secondly explore the explicit statements themselves.

4.2.1. *The Torah Terms*

In addition to Torah (תורה), the seven other terms in Ps 119 are "word" (אמרה), "word" (דבר), "regulation" (משפט), "commandment" (מצוה), "statutes" (חקים), "stipulations" (עדות), and "precepts" (פקודים).[11] It

---

[11] I uses these translations as consistently as possible. There are some verses in which it is not possible, and I discuss these exceptions in the course of the argument. I list the last three terms in the plural form, since they only occur in the plural in Ps 119. "Torah" occurs only in the singular; the other lexemes (מצוה, אמרה, דבר, and משפט) occur in both singular and plural forms. The Masorah Gedolah lists ten terms, adding דרך and אמונה to the eight listed here (Ha-Keter, 176). The tradition of discussing each of these words extends at least as far back as Radaq, who lists eleven terms, adding דרך, צדק, and אמונה (Ha-Keter, 160). In addition to the eight terms listed above, Deissler discusses דרך and ארח. These two terms overlap with the other synonyms due to the extensive use of the metaphor of the path. Although

should be noted from the outset that the author of Ps 119 is not using the eight terms with entirely unique meanings. If that were the case, then the psalm would be unintelligible. For example, the verb צוה ("to command") is "a specific form of speech: a superior's discourse ordering and commanding a subordinate."[12] This definition applies in Ps 119. The superior is God, and commands are a form of God's speech addressed to subordinates—a category that includes humanity as well as the heavens and earth. Similar citations from the lexica and various monographs could be given for the other seven terms; for example, a statute (חק) can be pictured as a "boundary line that the ruler draws for his subordinates."[13] This metaphor applies in Ps 119 as well, since in theological usage God takes the place of the earthly king.

Since the author is not using rare or unique meanings of the terms, studying the lexical meaning of each of the terms provides only a basic sketch of the conception of Torah.[14] Lexical meaning is the basic content that a word contributes to any context, while contextual meaning is "the enriched and complex meanings [that a word] receives by interaction with its new environment."[15] Exploring the contextual meanings of the eight Torah terms is much more helpful for establishing

---

he is cited by various commentators as arguing for ten synonyms rather than eight, Deissler emphasizes that the eight terms listed above are the eight main terms "die acht Haupttermini." Deissler, 292. This is not the only example of careless readings of Deissler. See also Deissler, 71.

[12] TLOT, 1062.

[13] TLOT, 470.

[14] There are a few noteworthy details of the terms that have no bearing on the meaning. For example, the term "precepts" (פקודים or פקדים) only occurs in the Psalter. In the Targumim, this word is used to translate "commandment" (מצוה). Hurvitz argues that its presence in the Hebrew Bible is evidence of Aramaic influence and is a characteristic of LBH. Avi Hurvitz, בין לשון ללשון: לתולדות לשון המקרא בימי בית שני [The Transition Period in Biblical Hebrew: A Study in Post-Exilic Hebrew and Its Implications for the Dating of Psalms (Hebrew)] (Jerusalem: Bialik Institute, 1972), 126–30. Another example is the feminine form חקתיך (v. 16), which occurs with no discernable difference in meaning from the masculine form of the word elsewhere in Ps 119. The masculine forms are characteristic of Deuteronomy (21 occurrences), as opposed to the feminine forms, which are characteristic of Leviticus, Numbers, and Ezekiel (Lev—26 occurrences, Ezek—24 occurrences, and Num—14 occurrences.) The distribution is statistically significant, and it confirms that Ps 119 is more closely aligned with Deuteronomy than other parts of the Hebrew Bible.

[15] Michael V. Fox, *Proverbs 1–9 A New Translation with Introduction and Commentary*, AB, vol. 18A (New York: Doubleday, 2000), 28. Linguists typically distinguish between lexical meaning and grammatical meaning. For example, the word "this" in English does not have lexical meaning; instead it has a grammatical function. See for example, Matthews, *Concise Oxford Dictionary of Linguistics*, s.v. "lexical meaning."

the conception of Torah in Ps 119, that is, the relationships between them, how they are used similarly, whether or not there are contrasts between them, and so on. In the following sections I address these issues.

4.2.1.1. *Excursus*—עֵדוֹת

One of the Torah terms "stipulations" (עֵדוֹת) must be discussed briefly, since the consonants עדות can be interpreted in different ways. Bruno Volkwein argues that the consonants עדות represent two different words, each with their own derivations and meanings.[16] One of the two words is a noun meaning "testimony," based on the noun "witness" (עֵד) or the verb "to witness" (עוּד) with the addition of the abstract ending /-ūt/. The second word is derived from the Aramaic word עֵדְיָא (pl. emphatic) or עֵדֵי (pl. construct), meaning "stipulations." According to Volkwien, when this word of Aramaic origin was adopted in Hebrew, the resulting plural form produced a homograph with the abstract noun "testimony."[17] Volkwein suggests that the plural עֵדוֹת was in some cases misunderstood by the Masoretes as עֵדוּת, which may explain many passages where "stipulations" fits the context better than "testimonies."[18]

A further complication in the MT is the occurrence of the three consonants עדת. These three consonants could theoretically represent a defective spelling of the homographs discussed in the previous paragraph or a singular construct of the word עֵדָה. Of the twenty-three occurrences in Ps 119, twenty-two are suffixed (all except v. 88). This is helpful since the *yod* preceding the suffix shows that all of the occurrences are plural, thus ruling out the possibility that the consonants are a singular construct form.[19] Since all of the other twenty-two occurrences are plural, the consonants עֵדוֹת in v. 88 should be read as a plural construct and vocalized עֵדוֹת, rather than עֵדוּת. In addition to providing a uniform explanation for all the occurrences

---

[16] Bruno Volkwein, "Masoretisches «Zeugnis» oder «Bundesbestimmungen»," *Biblische Zeitschrift* 13 (1969): 18–40.

[17] Homographs are "forms which differ phonetically but are spelled in the same way." Matthews, *Concise Oxford Dictionary of Linguistics*, 164. The important point for this discussion is that the forms were graphically identical, regardless of the pronunciation.

[18] Volkwein, "Masoretisches «Zeugnis» oder «Bundesbestimmungen»," 39.

[19] Verses 14 and 33 are two examples of plene spelling עֵדְוֹתֶיךָ, i.e., with the *waw*. Two examples of defective spelling are עֵדֹתָיו v. 2 and עֵדֹתֶיךָ v. 22.

in Ps 119, this explanation also corresponds with the use of the word in Deuteronomy. Throughout the Hebrew Bible, "stipulations" usually includes the notion of a hierarchy in which God imposes the legal conditions upon subordinates. This hierarchy is clear in Ps 119, since the stipulations all come from God.

4.2.1.2. Instantiations and an Abstract Concept

The eight terms are used in different ways to refer to two semantic levels—the abstract concept and the individual commandments. Although "semantic levels" is a spatial metaphor and is therefore not extremely precise, it provides a basis for further discussion. Initially, the eight terms can be sorted according to which terms are semantically less specific and which are more specific. The more specific terms correspond with instantiations of Torah, that is, specific commandments. The more general terms often correspond with the abstract, comprehensive concept. However, there are inconsistencies, since some of the eight terms are used for both instantiations and for the abstract conception. Despite the inconsistencies, identifying two semantic levels is valuable, and I use the distinction as a heuristic strategy. It must be emphasized that there is no bifurcation of Torah in Ps 119. Any instantiation is itself Torah and shares the essence of the expansive conception.

Several features indicate that the author uses the term "Torah" only for the abstract, expansive concept and that "Torah" is the primary term. Torah is the first of the terms to occur (v. 1). Torah occurs more frequently than the other terms, and it is the only one of the terms that does not occur in the plural. Based on this evidence, Erich Zenger suggests that the seven additional words are an explication, or to be precise, a type of commentary to what is meant by "Torah." They underline the multi-faceted meaning (multiperspektive Bedeutung) of the instruction that goes forth from YHWH.[20]

---

[20] Erich Zenger, "Torafrömmigkeit: Beobachtungen zum poetischen und theologischen Profil von Psalm 119," in *Freiheit und Recht: Festschrift für Frank Crüsemann zum 65. Geburtstag*, ed. Christof Hardmeier, Rainer Kessler, and Andreas Ruwe (Gütersloh: Verlagshaus Chr. Kaiser, 2003), 387. The word "Torah" has been the object of countless studies. The articles on "Torah" in TLOT and TDOT both include bibliographies; TDOT is much more extensive. Gerhard Liedke analyzes the distribution of the terms across different corpora in *Gestalt und Bezeichnung alttestamentlicher Rechtssätze*, WMANT vol. 39, (Neukirchen-Vluyn: Neukirchener, 1971). For more recent studies see "Tora" and "Wort Gottes" in *RGG*[4]. The following two collections of essays are not

Hyponymy is a linguistic term used to describe semantic relationships, and it is helpful for describing the eight Torah terms because it includes the notion of different levels. "Hyponymy is definable in terms of unilateral implication."[21] That is, one of the terms implies the other, but the implication does not work in both directions. John Lyons gives several examples: a cow is a kind of animal; a rose is a kind of flower; and so on. The term animal is "superordinate" to the term cow—a different "level" of meaning.[22] Similarly, any commandment, statute, or precept must be delivered to mankind in words. The statement "humanity has statutes from God" implies that "humanity has words from God," but the reverse is not necessarily the case. Words are not necessarily statutes. Thus, "statutes" (חקים) is a hyponym of "word" (דבר), and these two terms correspond with two semantic levels used throughout Ps 119.

For the two lexemes דבר and אמרה, the implication works both directions; it is bilateral.[23] Thus דבר is a kind of אמרה, and אמרה is a kind of דבר. "The definition of hyponymy in terms of unilateral implication enables us to define synonymy as bilateral, or symmetrical hyponymy: if x is a hyponym of y and y is a hyponym of x, then x and y are synonymous."[24] Using this definition the two lexemes דבר and אמרה are synonymous. The synonymity is not created in Ps 119, but it is reinforced by the author's use of the two terms. This synonymity, however, applies only to the lexical meaning of the terms. The term אמרה is used more often than דבר with the contextual meaning of "promise" (see below at p. 119). Thus, the lexical meanings may be synonymous, but there are differences between the way the author uses the two lexemes.

---

primarily focused on the meaning of the terms, but they provide explanations of how Torah grew in prominence: Eckart Otto, ed., *Tora in der Hebräischen Bibel: Studien zur Redaktionsgeschichte und synchroner Logik diachroner Transformationen*, BZAR 7, (Wiesbaden: Harrassowitz, 2007) and Gary N. Knoppers and Bernard M. Levinson, eds., *The Pentateuch as Torah: New Models for Understanding Its Promulgation and Acceptance* (Winona Lake, IL: Eisenbrauns, 2007).

[21] John Lyons, *Semantics* (Cambridge: Cambridge University Press, 1977), 292.

[22] Lyons uses the term "superordinate" and notes that the corresponding term "subordinate" is not helpful to refer to the more specific terms, since "subordinate" is a term that is already used in linguistics to describe a syntactic relationship. Lyons, *Semantics*, 291.

[23] I use "lexeme" in this section as a synonym for "term," because the discussion is about words. This is a stylistic choice, not a technical use of "lexeme."

[24] John Lyons, *Semantics*, 292.

The terms "statutes" (חקים), "stipulations" (עדות), and "precepts" (פקודים) always refer to instantiations of God's word and always occur in the plural form. In contrast, Torah always refers to the abstract concept and always occurs in the singular form. This raises the question of whether the grammatical number of the various terms corresponds with the two levels of meaning—singular for the abstract concept and plural for the instantiations. Some scholars have claimed that there is a distinction in meaning between the singular and plural of דבר in Ps 119 and that the plural form refers to specific commandments.[25] The plural form (vv. 57, 130, 139, 147k, 161k) is reminiscent of the phrase "ten words" (עשרת דברים), which is the label given to the Ten Commandments in Deut 4:13. Another example is the phrase "these words" (הדברים האלה) in the Sh°ma' (Deut 6:6). The usage of the plural "words" in Deuteronomy seems to support the contention that the plural form refers to particular instantiations of God's word, but the distinction breaks down in Ps 119, because the speaker declares that he will observe God's word (דבר singular in v. 17) as well as God's words (דברים plural in v. 57).

The use of singular and plural forms does not consistently correspond with the two different levels of meaning, but it does generally correspond. The author is not describing multiple abstract concepts, and the two terms that are always singular (תורה and אמרה) always refer to an abstract concept. The three terms that are always plural (חקים, עדות, and פקודים) always refer to instantiations. The lexeme מצוה is usually plural, and in those cases it is similar to the three terms that occur only in the plural. However, in v. 96 it occurs in the singular: "Your commandment is very expansive" (רחבה מצותך מאד). Verse 96 refers to an inclusive concept, not to commandments that can be enumerated, and this is similar to the use of the singular in v. 98: "Your commandment makes me wiser than my enemies" (מאיבי תחכמני מצותך).[26] The remaining two terms (דבר and משפט) occur in

[25] Soll's comment on the plural form דברים is representative: "The use in the plural tends to reflect the legal traditions." Will Soll, *Psalm 119: Matrix, Form, and Setting*, CBQMS, vol. 23 (Washington, D.C.: Catholic Biblical Association, 1991), 38.

[26] Although the Masoretes vocalize מצותך as a plural form, it is written without a *yod*. Elsewhere in the chapter (except vv. 96 and 115) the word is suffixed and written with a *yod*. In v. 115 the word is in construct—"commandments of my God" (מצות אלהי)—which could be either singular or plural in the consonantal text. The Masoretes vocalize it as a plural. See also the discussion of v. 175 on p. 120 and the commentary on v. 98.

both singular and plural forms and are discussed below, since they are used with various meanings.

With the exception of vv. 96 and 98 noted above, the four terms "commandments" (מצות), "statutes" (חקים), "precepts" (פקודים), and "stipulations" (עדות) denote directives that can be enumerated and should be obeyed, observed, or performed. Thus they refer to instantiations of Torah. Distinguishing between these terms is difficult, in part, because there is some semantic overlap between the terms. For example, outside of Ps 119 it might be possible to say that the term "commandments" (מצות) is a hyponym of "statutes" (חקים); that is, the lexeme "statutes" (חקים) has a broader range of meaning than "commandments" (מצות). Yet even if this is true for the lexical meaning, the distinction breaks down in Ps 119 due to the author's use of the terms. The same can be said for "precepts" (פקודים) and "stipulations" (עדות). Each of these four terms is used with the metaphor of the path, for example, "way of your statutes" (דרך חקיך v. 33), and "way of your precepts" (דרך פקודיך v. 27). The author uses the terms in similar grammatical constructions and with similar metaphors, which raises the question of whether the terms are interchangeable.

4.2.1.3. *Interchangeable Usage?*
Leidke states that when the term "statutes" (חקים) occurs in a series with other terms for commandments, "all terms are fully equalized and indicate synonymously the whole or parts of Yahweh's regulations and commandments."[27] Similarly, when the term "regulations" (משפטים) occurs with other words for commandments, the meaning "is usually completely homogenized; the words serve then, as synonymous designations for Yahweh's ordinances and commandments."[28] Is it possible that the author thoughtlessly interchanges the eight Torah terms? Does he simply follow the poetic constraints of using one of the terms in each verse? For example, the author uses "righteous" (צדק) to describe God's stipulations (עדות v. 144), and God's stipulations are not described with the word "righteous" צדק anywhere else in the Bible. Since it does not occur elsewhere, it seems possible that this description arose by coincidence. Soll refers to such uses as "correlative"

---

[27] TLOT, 471.
[28] TLOT, 1398.

and argues that the author used a Torah term in each verse in order to follow the pattern that he set for himself.[29]

One of the reasons that Soll comes to this conclusion is that he assumes God's word is found in a "book," and many of Soll's difficulties are resolved by recognizing that Torah cannot be limited to a text. Unique formulations in Ps 119, such as v. 144 where the author describes the stipulations with the description צדק, do not prove that the author was thoughtlessly using the Torah terms, because the unique formulations are generally re-affirmed elsewhere in the psalm. For example, v. 138 teaches that God actively appointed righteousness (צדק) as a characteristic of his stipulations.[30] Other verses in the psalm also describe God's commandments and regulations with the word "righteous" (צדק).[31]

The eight Torah terms all have some semantic overlap, and they are therefore interchangeable to some extent. For example, all eight of them serve as the object of the verb "observe" (שמר). Similarly, the psalmist uses the verb "to keep" (נצר) with five of the terms as the object: "stipulations" (עדות), "Torah" (תורה), "statutes" (חקים), "commandments" (מצות), and "precepts" (פקודים). The speaker declares nine times that he has not (or will not) forget (לא שכחתי) God's word, also using five of the terms: "Torah" (תורה), "statutes" (חקים), "precepts" (פקודים), "commandments" (מצות), and "word" (דברים / דבר). The verb "to love" (אהב) has five of the terms as its object: "command-

---

[29] "We will refer to such uses of the Torah words in Psalm 119 as 'correlative' uses. In these cases, the constraint of employing a Torah word in each line is accommodated by using it to refer not so much *to* the book as *through* the book to the kinds of experiences and events that are frequent subjects of biblical prayers. The presence of these correlative uses are further evidence that Torah is not, for the psalmist, an end in itself. While the author relates all of his prayer to Torah, Torah is not, strictly speaking, the subject of his psalm." Soll, *Psalm 119*, 86 (italics original). Also discussing "correlative" uses, Soll claims, "Everything that is said will be related to *tôrâ*; that is not the same thing, however as saying that everything will be *about tôrâ*. The distinction is important. To see Psalm 119 as a psalm simply or even primarily about Torah is to mistake part of its formal matrix for its subject." Ibid., 55. To my knowledge, no one else has been so bold as to claim that Ps 119 is not about Torah, and this misinterpretation is one more demonstration that his analysis of the genre as a lament psalm led him astray.

[30] Mezudat David interprets the verb צוה in v. 138 differently: "Your stipulations which you commanded, they are righteous and very faithful" (עדותיך אשר צוית המה צדק ואמונה מאד). מקראות גדולות "אורים גדולים" (Jerusalem: Even Yisrael Institute, 1992), 786. However, see my comments on v. 4 and how the author of Ps 119 uses this verb.

[31] See vv. 7, 62, 75, 106, 121, 123, 142, 160, 164, and 172.

ments" (מצות), "Torah" (תורה), "stipulations" (עדות), "word" (אמרה), and "precepts" (פקודים). The verb "meditate" (שיח) has three of the terms as its object: "precepts" (פקודים), "statutes" (חקים), and "word" (אמרה).

The fact that the terms are to some extent interchangeable does not mean that the author was haphazardly using the terms. Furthermore, the evidence discussed above fails to support Soll's conclusion that the subject of Ps 119 is not Torah. Instead, the author seeks to expand the conceptual sphere of Torah by heaping up the various terms and by building a network of interrelated ideas.

To this point, I have argued (1) that four of the terms (פקודים, חקים, מצות, and עדות) refer almost exclusively to instantiations of Torah, (2) that these four terms are not used with unique meanings in Ps 119, and (3) that distinctions between the four terms are difficult to distinguish. In contrast, the word "Torah" is used exclusively to refer to the abstract concept. Three terms (דבר, אמרה, and משפט) remain, and these three are used in various ways, which are discussed in the following paragraphs.[32] When דברים refers to words that the speaker observes (שמר), it overlaps semantically with commandments, precepts, statutes, and stipulations. A similar use of "word" is found in v. 9, which states that a young man (נער) should keep his way "according to your word" (כדברך). It is similar since it refers to a standard for behavior, but it is also different since it does not refer to directives that can be enumerated. The phrase "according to your word" deserves further consideration, because it is used differently in Ps 119 than it is anywhere else in the Hebrew Bible and because it is used in different ways within this psalm.

---

[32] Botha also isolates these three terms: "...it is evident that the words משפטים, דבר, and אמרה are markedly distinguished from the rest as a result of the relation between YHWH and the righteous." P. J. Botha, "The Measurement of Meaning: An Exercise in Field Semantics," *Journal for Semitics* 1 (1989): 16. Botha labels these three terms as the "Word Group" and the other five terms as the "Instruction Group." He also claims that the "Word Group" defines the relationship between YHWH and the righteous, while the "Instruction Group" defines the relationship between the righteous and Torah itself (p. 17). I find this description unhelpful because all of Ps 119 except vv. 1–3 is addressed directly to God; thus, distinguishing between the speaker's relationship to God and his relationship to Torah is impossible. Additionally, Botha claims that the "Word Group" displays a juridical inclination, but if anything, I would argue the opposite. That is, the so-called "Instruction Group" displays a juridical inclination. Perhaps this objection is due to the imprecision of the phrase "juridical inclination."

4.2.1.4. *"According to Your Word"*—כדברך
Outside Ps 119 the phrase "according to your word(s)" or "according to these words" refers to specific words found in the immediate context. For example, in Genesis 47 Jacob calls Joseph to his deathbed and asks his son not to leave him buried in Egypt. Joseph replies that he would do "according to your word" (כדברך Gen 47:30). The referent of "word" is also clear when the phrase includes a proper name, for example, "according to the word of Moses" (Exod 8:9). It is especially common in Kings with the divine name, "according to the word of YHWH." In these cases, the "words" are explicit in the context.

There is a slight change in the use of the phrase in 2 Chron 35:6, which is the account of Josiah reinstating the Passover celebration. Josiah commands the people to sanctify themselves "in order to act according to the word of YHWH by the hand of Moses." In this context, the "word of YHWH" is the book of the covenant that was found in the temple. In all of these examples the content or referent of the "word(s)" is specified in the immediate context, but that is not the case in Ps 119, where the referent of the "word" is never specified.

The psalmist uses the phrase "according to your word" six times (vv. 9, 25, 28, 65, 107, and 169). Verses 25 and 107 both contain the imperative "give me life" (חיני) followed by the phrase "according to your word." These two verses could also be linked with verse 28, which contains a similar request, "establish me (קימני) according to your word." In these three verses (vv. 25, 28, and 107) the author assumes that God's word constrains even God and that a reminder of this word will motivate God to act. God should keep God's own word. Verse 65 can also fit in this category, "You have done what is good for your servant, O YHWH, according to your word." That is, God's actions have been in keeping with God's word. All of these examples have semantic overlap with the word "promise." This is not to say that the lexical meaning of דבר is "promise," but it is used in locutions that communicate this concept.

Uses of the phrase "according to your word" support the thesis that the conception of Torah in Ps 119 is expansive. On the one hand, the psalmist argues in v. 9 that a young man can purify his behavior by keeping it "according to your word." On the other hand, he assumes that God should also act according to God's word. Surely God does not need any sort of guidelines or regulations to keep the way of God pure. Furthermore, the notion that Torah includes comforting promises for God's servant is not limited to the specific phrase "according to

your word." In v. 49 the speaker petitions, "Remember the word (זכר
דבר) for your servant, upon which you made me hope." The author
repeats the combination of hoping on God's word several times in the
remainder of the psalm. Four different verses (74, 81, 114, and 147)
end with the phrase "I hope for your word" (לדברך יחלתי).

There is an additional dimension to the statements discussed in the
previous paragraph, due to the fact that God is obligated to keep God's
word. It is not merely a possibility that God will act in a certain way,
but rather, more importantly, a certainty. By giving God's word, God
obligates God; the petitions of the speaker are therefore not simply
that God will act in a certain way but that God will do it now. "It is
not about a promise for *this* person in particular, but about one for
any given person in any given time. For that reason the speaker now
requests that he would be exactly that person."[33] Thus, these verses
have a double function. Namely, they indicate that Torah includes
promises for God's servant, and at the same time they characterize
God's servant as one who trusts on the promises of Torah.

4.2.1.5. "Word"—אמרה

Throughout my translation of Ps 119, I use "word" to translate אמרה
and I include the Hebrew in order to distinguish it from דבר. This is
the lexical meaning of the term, but it does not necessarily reflect the
contextual meaning. The author of Ps 119 uses the lexeme אמרה for
both "promise" as well as for teaching that should be obeyed. Most
of the occurrences of אמרה in Ps 119 refer to promises, and several
English translations consistently use "promise" as a translation.[34] One
example is found in v. 38, "Establish for your servant your promise
(אמרה), which belongs to those who fear you." David uses similar language in 2 Sam 7:25, "Now, YHWH God, the word which you spoke
concerning your servant and concerning his dynasty, establish (הקם)
[it] forever, and do just as you said." What the speaker requests in Ps
119:38 is the establishment or fulfillment of the word that was already
given. In vv. 67, 133, and 158, however, the term אמרה refers to teaching about how humans should act. In v. 67 the speaker declares that
he observes God's word (אמרתך שמרתי); it does not make sense to

---

[33] "Es geht dann nicht um ein Versprechen für *diesen* Menschen im speziellen,
sondern um eines für irgendeinen Menschen zu irgendeiner Zeit; der Sprecher bittet
nun darum, dass genau er derjenige sei." Karla Prigge, private communication.
[34] For example, RSV, NAB, NEB.

argue that the speaker observes God's promises. In v. 133 the speaker petitions God to establish his steps in God's word (אמרה), and v. 158 defines the treacherous as those who do not observe God's word (אמרה). The translation "promise" distorts the meaning of all three of these verses.

4.2.1.6. *"Regulations"*—משפטים

The term משפט is used in various ways throughout Ps 119. The "righteous regulations" (משפטי צדק) are rules that the servant of God should follow. This use of the term corresponds with its use throughout the Pentateuch, where the plural (משפטים) refers to regulations that the people should observe and teach to their children. It is especially common in Deuteronomy, where the twenty occurrences in the plural all refer to the commandments.[35] Several of the explicit statements discussed above, such as "your regulations are good," can also be grouped in this category. The occurrences of the plural overlap with the four terms discussed above (פקודים, עדות, מצות, חקים) and thus reference instantiations of Torah.

In different manuscripts there is variation between singular and plural forms of the word משפט in four verses (vv. 43, 149, 160, and 175). This variation is not particularly noteworthy, since both singular and plural forms of the word occur within a single manuscript. However, verse 175 is noteworthy, since in some manuscripts the form occurs without a *yod* (indicating a singular) yet is vocalized with a *seghol* (indicating a plural). Furthermore, the verb form is not decisive, since it is written defectively (מִשְׁפָּטֶךָ יַעְזְרֻנִי).[36]

In several verses the singular form (משפט) clearly does not refer to rules that should be obeyed. For example, "How long until you execute judgment on the ones who oppress me?" (מתי תעשה ברדפי משפט v. 84). In this case משפט refers to some action that God will undertake in the future. Verse 84 assumes that justice has been delayed for some reason, but the speaker is confident that God will eventually set things straight. In v. 121 the speaker declares, "I have done justice (משפט) and righteousness." Verse 132 reads, "Give me grace according to the right (משפט) of those who love your name."

---

[35] Deuteronomy 33:21 is a possible exception.
[36] See the commentary on v. 98 and the discussion of the variations in number in the ancient witnesses beginning on p. 185. There is enough variation the manuscript traditions that it is difficult to draw any firm conclusions.

In v. 20 the speaker declares his incessant longing for God's
מִשְׁפָּטִים. Deissler states, "The sense of mišpaṭîm appears to be ambiguous here. The preceding context speaks for the meaning 'regulations',
but the following [speaks] more for 'justice'."[37] If this verse is considered in light of my arguments in chapter 3, then the primary goal of
the verse is to portray the speaker's longing. It is similar to v. 19, where
the speaker petitions God not to hide the commandments. Of course,
he knows the commandments; they are not literally hidden from him.
These examples illustrate that the rhetorical goal must be taken into
account when drawing conclusions about the conception of Torah in
Ps 119.

There is a cumulative effect of amassing the eight Torah terms,
an affect which expands the conceptual sphere of Torah. That is, the
overlapping meanings of the terms influences the interpretation of the
other verses even when a particular term does not occur explicitly. For
example, I noted that the author uses both דבר and אמרה in locutions
to indicate that Torah includes promises for those who obey. A similar
concept occurs in other verses without using either of these two terms.
"Remove reproach and shame from me, because I have kept your precepts" (v. 22). "Save me because I have sought your precepts" (v. 94).
"Let your hand help me, because I have chosen your precepts" (v. 173).
"Look at my affliction and deliver me, because I have not forgotten
your Torah" (v. 153). None of these verses explicitly mention promises
or use the terms דבר or אמרה, but they assume that someone who follows God's precepts will receive God's help, an assumption that is in
harmony with the verses that refer to promises. By interrelating ideas
and motifs in this manner, the author is able to promote an expansive
concept of Torah.

4.2.2. Attributes of Torah

Several classifying verbless clauses provide information about the
nature of Torah or the attributes of Torah.[38] "Your regulations are
good" (טוב v. 39b). "All of your commandments are righteous" (צדק

---

[37] "Der Sinn von mišpaṭîm scheint hier zweideutig. Der vorausgehende Kontext
spricht für die Bedeutung 'Bestimmungen', der nachfolgende eher für 'Gericht'."
Deissler, 113.
[38] IBHS, 132–35. These types of clauses are called "descriptive nominal clauses" in
JM, 566.

v. 172b). "Your commandments are upright" (ישר v. 137b). "Your Torah is true" (אמת v. 142b). "All of your commandments are faithful" (אמונה v. 86a). Elsewhere in the Hebrew Bible these are attributes of God. Since Torah comes from the mouth of God (vv. 13, 72, 88), Torah could not be anything other than good, righteous, upright, and true.

In addition to using verbless clauses, the author also specifies that Torah is righteous by using the construct phrase משפטי צדקך (vv. 7, 62, 106, 160, 164).[39] In this phrase צדק functions as an adjective; thus it can be translated "your righteous regulations."[40] A similar construction occurs in v. 123, "your righteous word" (אמרת צדקך). By using these concise construct phrases the author is able to state that God's word is righteous, while at the same time making another statement. For example, in v. 7 the speaker declares that he will praise God with an upright heart when he learns God's righteous regulations. This is one example of a verse with a double function. The construct phrase states explicitly that God's regulations are righteous. The verse also implies that learning Torah is a prerequisite for proper praise.[41]

Verse 129 contains an explicit statement that is grammatically straightforward, but it is difficult to establish the precise nuance of the phrase: "Your testimonies are miraculous" (פלאות עדותיך). Twice in Ps 119 the author uses a word from the same root (נפלאות vv. 18 and 27)—a word traditionally translated as "wonders."[42] Elsewhere in the Bible the root is used in reference to God's supernatural intervention on behalf of Israel, especially bringing them out of Egypt. The psalmist repeatedly declares his praise for God's miracles or expresses his intention to recount God's miracles to others, using some word based on this root.[43] In Ps 119, both vv. 18 and 27 include a request for insight

---

[39] The *yod* (plural construct) is missing in the MT of v. 160b ולעולם כל משפט צדקך. This omission may be a scribal error; multiple Hebrew MSS, LXX, Syriac, and Targumim have a plural form. Alternatively, the author could be emphasizing that every single judgment of God will last forever, in which case the other ancient witnesses are flattening the distinction and assimilating v. 160 to the other four occurrences in the chapter. See the discussion of משפט above at p. 120, the commentary on v. 98, and the discussion of the ancient witnesses beginning on p. 185.

[40] GKC, § 128p: *IBHS*, 149.

[41] Using this technique enables the author to compress complex arguments into very few words; I discuss this technique below beginning on p. 144.

[42] See Fritz Stolz, "Zeichen und Wunder: die prophetische Legitimation und ihre Geschichte," *ZThK* 69 (1972): 125–44.

[43] TLOT, 982.

or revelation, so that the speaker can see or meditate on the miracles in
God's word. These examples could indicate that God's word contains
a record of God's miraculous intervention, namely, the text describes
miraculous events. If that is the case in vv. 18 and 27, then the event is
the miracle. However, v. 129 states that God's stipulations are miraculous (פלאות עדותיך), which indicates that Torah is something more
than a record of God's actions. The word of God is itself miraculous.

The explicit statements discussed in the above paragraphs are what
might be expected. If God is righteous, then it goes without saying that
the word of God is righteous. God would not say anything unrighteous. The same is true for other attributes as well, such as true, faithful,
refined (i.e., free of contaminants), and so on. However, explicit statements using the term עולם show that the conception of God's word in
Ps 119 includes more than the Pentateuch or written Torah.

Out of the eleven occurrences of the word עולם in Ps 119, ten of
them are prefixed with the preposition ל, indicating a duration of
time stretching into the future.[44] In v. 142 the speaker states, "Your
righteousness is righteous forever (לעולם), and your Torah is true."
Verse 142 does not explicitly state that Torah will last forever but that
God's righteousness will last forever. Yet the juxtaposition of the two
halves of the verse implies that Torah will last forever. Similarly, v.
160 implies that God's regulations are eternal by declaring that they
will be righteous forever (לעולם). Other verses with the prepositional
phrase לעולם use it to describe the speaker's observance of Torah.
For example, in v. 44 the speaker declares that he will observe (שמר)
God's Torah continually, forever and ever (תמיד לעולם ועד).[45] A similar statement of intent occurs in v. 112, "I have inclined my heart to
do your statutes forever."

Verse 52 is the only example of the eleven verses with the word עולם
that points backward in time rather than forward, by using the phrase
"from of old" (מעולם). This phrase can indicate the eternal past.[46]
However, v. 52 does not indicate explicitly that God's word existed
into the *eternal* past. The speaker's declaration, "I remembered your

---

[44] TLOT, 856.

[45] Radaq lists an alternate interpretation of this verse, in which "forever and ever" is
a characteristic of Torah itself. או פירוש: תורתך, שהיא עומדת לעולם ועד—אשמרה
אותה תמיד Ha-Keter, 167.

[46] "There are two great aeons: past and future. They are both called ʿolam and
extend indefinitely in both directions." Fox, *Proverbs 1–9*, 281.

regulations from of old," (v. 52) implies that they were given long ago but not necessarily that they existed from eternity past.

The author of Ps 119 also points backward in time by using the motif of creation. In v. 152 the speaker declares that God has founded his testimonies forever (לעולם יסדתם). This verse explicitly states that God's stipulations will last forever, yet the use of the verb "founded" (יסד) intimates that the stipulations were in place long before the writing of Ps 119. The grammatical form יסדתם "you founded them" occurs only one other time in the Bible, specifically in Ps 89:12 where the topic is creation and the suffix "them" refers to the "heavens and earth."[47] Many passages about creation in the book of Psalms include some indication that God's creative activity took place in "ancient days" (e.g., Ps 44:2 בימי קדם), and v. 152 begins with the word קדם. The lexical meaning of קדם can be simply "beforehand," yet in the book of Psalms it has the connotation of long ago, especially due to its use in contexts about creation.[48] Verse 152 does not specify exactly when God's stipulations came into being. Nonetheless, the use of both קדם and יסד evokes the motif of creation and an association with ancient times.

Like v. 152, vv. 89–91 include both the creation motif and a statement that God's word will last forever. The explicit statements in these verses provide some grammatical challenges and demonstrate that the conception of Torah in Ps 119 cannot be limited to the Pentateuch.

| Ps 119:89 | לעולם יהוה | Forever, O YHWH, |
| | דברך נצב בשמים | your word is established in the heavens. |

Verse 89 states that God's word will last forever (לעולם) and that it is stationed in the heavens. Deissler argues that the psalmist, with the use of this verb "stationed" (נצב), intends "evidently a personification of the divine word."[49] Booij disagrees with Deissler and claims that this verb "represents a special usage"; he translates, "Your word is in command in heaven."[50] Both interpretations are reading too much into a single word, but v. 89 does indicate that the author's conception of

---

[47] See also Ps 78:69 and 102:26. The suffix in Ps 119:152 ("them") refers to God's stipulations (עדות).

[48] HALOT, 1070.

[49] "…offenbar eine Personifikation des göttlichen Worts." Deissler, 190.

[50] Thijs Booij, "Psalm 119:89–91," *Bib* 79 (1998): 539.

Torah was expansive. Torah is in some way transcendent; it is independent of the physical manifestations or instantiations of it.

Ps 119:90   לדר ודר אמונתך   *Your faithfulness [endures] for generations.*

כוננת ארץ ותעמד   *You founded the earth, and it stood.*

The first half of v. 90 reiterates the motif of endurance with the phrase "for generations" or "from generation to generation." Supplying the verb "endures" in the translation is an attempt to render a verbless clause into idiomatic English. Another option would be to interpret the verse as an example of what Watson calls the "pivot pattern."[51] The second half of the verse begins with the verb "you founded" (כון), and it could function as the verb in the first half of the verse as well. If this is the case, then the verse would read, "You founded your faithfulness for generations." Reading the first half of the verse as a verbless clause is a more simple solution, and there is very little difference in meaning.

Ps 119:91   למשפטיך עמדו היום   *According to your regulations they stand today,*

כי הכל עבדיך   *because all are your servants.*

In v. 91 there is no explicit subject for the verb "they stand" (עמדו). The subject of the plural verb must be the heavens (v. 89) and the earth (v. 90), indicating a merism for the universe. In other words, *everything* stands today according to your regulations. This interpretation is supported by "all" (הכל) in the second half of the verse. Ibn Ezra reads "heavens and earth" as the subject; he states that the heavens and earth are standing like servants to do your regulations.[52] His interpretation emphasizes that all of creation is ready to do God's bidding, but the emphasis of vv. 89–91 is not that creation performs something or is prepared to act. Instead it is that God's word controls and sustains the universe. It is tempting to interpret these verses in light of the later rabbinic notion that God used Torah as a blueprint for creation.[53] Although that trope can be correlated with these verses, there is no

---

[51] Wilfred Watson, *Classical Hebrew Poetry: A Guide to its Techniques*, JSOTSup. vol. 26, (Sheffield: Sheffield Academic Press. 1995), 214–21.

[52] Ha-Keter, 173. הזכיר השמים והארץ והם עומדים כעבדים לעשות משפטיך

[53] Like an artisan uses a plan, "so the Holy One, blessed be He, looked in Torah and created the world." Gen. Rabba 1:4. כך היה הקב"ה מביט בתורה, ובורא את העולם. ברשית רבה פ"א ד

evidence anywhere in Ps 119 that Torah existed before the created order.

The use of the creation motif and words for "former times" show that the psalmist's conception of God's word includes something that extends back before Sinai. The universe did not wait until the events of Sinai to begin following God's rules. All of creation has been obedient since God first spoke the world into existence, and part of the psalmist's conception of Torah is that it gives order to the universe. This evidence is a strong argument against limiting Torah to something written. Certainly, whatever authoritative texts the psalmist had would have been included in his conception of God's word, but it cannot be limited to those written instantiations.

Explicit statements in Ps 119 declare that Torah is true, faithful, righteous, miraculous, good, upright, and without impurities. Such statements apply attributes of God to Torah. It may seem self-evident that Torah would have these characteristics, since the source of Torah is God. However, the author uses the same vocabulary of both God and Torah in order to make the connection explicit. For example, v. 39 declares that God's regulations are good. Verse 68 declares that God is good and one who does good things, and v. 65 also declares that God has done good. Another attribute of both God and God's word is righteousness (צדק); Ps 119 ascribes it to Torah (vv. 7, 62, 75, *passim*) as well as to God (v. 142).

Ascribing the same attributes to both God and Torah is one example of phenomena found throughout the psalm that expand the conceptual sphere of Torah. Through the repetition of terms and locutions and the juxtaposition of those locutions in different ways, a network of relationships emerges. The resulting web of interrelated ideas is greater than the sum of the individual verses. This undermines the notion that the repetition is merely for the sake of completing the acrostic.

4.2.3. *Torah Study*

Psalm 119 contains a new vision of pedagogy; the new vision includes the contemplation of Torah as a facet of ethical and religious instruction. The speaker repeatedly petitions God to teach him (למד vv. 12, 26, 64, 66, 68, 108, 124, 135, 171), to instruct him (הורני v. 33), and to give him insight (בין vv. 27, 34, 73, 125, 144, 169). Instruction directly from God keeps the speaker from turning aside from the path of Torah: "I do not turn aside from your regulations, because you yourself have instructed me" (כי אתה הורתני v. 102). The content of the instruction is frequently God's statutes (חקים).[54] In chapter 3, I describe Torah study as a spiritual discipline that contributes to the speaker's character formation; Torah study is discussed again here, since it is interrelated with the psalm's conception of Torah.

Jon Levenson and Yehoshua Amir come to very different conclusions about the nature of Torah study in Ps 119, and at the root of their differences are their respective assumptions about what Torah is in Ps 119. Levenson states:

> On the one hand, he knows the Torah and has spent his life learning it. On the other, he prays to have it disclosed to him as if it is new. The likelihood is that the psalmist's Torah lacks a constant identity. It is like the *tôrâh* of a prophet, which comes sporadically. Between oracles, the prophet can only cherish the old ones and prepare himself spiritually for a new one.[55]

Levenson also suggests that "the psalm was written to serve as an inducement for the kind of revelation and illumination for which it petitions."[56] Levenson's claim that Torah "lacks a constant identity" is at least partially based on the repeated requests for insight. He argues that the length of the poem with the repetition of the terms for Torah function together "like a mantra."[57] He concludes that there were three sources of Torah for the author of Ps 119: (1) received tradition, (2) cosmic or natural law, and (3) unmediated divine teaching.[58] The relationship between Torah study and the identity of Torah is at the center of Levenson's argument.

Amir's view of Torah is quite different. "The Torah is surely laid out before him [the psalmist], and he certainly reads in it.... Nevertheless he requires divine assistance in order to understand it."[59] According

---

[54] Seven verses have "statutes" (חקים) as the object of the verb "teach" (למד), specifically vv. 12, 26, 68, 71, 124, 135, and 171.

[55] Jon D. Levenson, "The Sources of Torah: Psalm 119 and the Modes of Revelation in Second Temple Judaism," in *Ancient Israelite Religion: Essays in Honor of Frank Moore Cross*, ed. Patrick D. Miller, Paul D. Hanson, and S. D. McBride, (Philadelphia: Fortress, 1987), 565.

[56] Levenson, "The Sources of Torah," 566.

[57] Levenson, "The Sources of Torah," 566.

[58] Levenson, "The Sources of Torah," 570.

[59] התורה אמנם מונחת לפניו, ויש רגליים להנחה שהוא קורא בה....ואף על פי כן "מקומו של מזמור קיט" ,Yehoshua Amir הוא צריך לסייעתא דשמייא כדי להבין אותה עיונים במקרא ספר זכרון ליהושע מאיר גריץ, in ,"בתולדות דת ישראל" ["The Place of Psalm 119 in the religion of Israel," in *Studies in Scripture: a volume in memory of Joshua Meir Grintz* (Hebrew)] (Tel Aviv: Hakibbutz Hamuchad Publishing, 1982), 76.

to Amir the psalmist stares with admiration at "the unlimited expanse that is open to him when he begins to study Torah."[60] It is possible, Amir suggests, that the psalmist believes God's word is hidden within this unlimited expanse (cf. v. 19 "Do not hide your commandments from me"). The reader must seek (דרש) for the hidden word within the written word in a type of process that gradually developed into the halakhic process. Amir admits that there is no way to prove this, yet it is noteworthy that he lists some of the same verses that Levenson cites in support of the idea that the psalmist is seeking unmediated revelation.

Their different conclusions stem, at least in part, from their different assumptions about what Torah is. Amir assumes that Torah is a written text, and Levenson argues that Torah "lacks a constant identity." Amir recognizes that the full interpretive tools and strategies found in later rabbinic writings were not operative for the author of Ps 119; nevertheless, his claim that there is a wide open expanse within the limits of a written text imposes a later rabbinic notion of Torah back onto Ps 119. Similarly, there is no indication that the speaker receives unmediated revelation as Levenson suggests. Whatever insight the speaker receives is available for any committed student of Torah. Both Levenson and Amir fail to account for the author's goal of characterizing an exemplary student of Torah and portraying the process of the student's character formation. This oversight leads them to unnecessary conclusions about the conception of Torah.

4.3. What Psalm 119 Does Not Express

The relationship of juxtaposed ideas in Ps 119 is often open to interpretation due to the literary shape of Ps 119, specifically the lack of conjunctions and the terseness of the poetic lines. The lack of specificity contributes to the author's rhetoric, since the reader is forced to contemplate the nature of Torah itself. Although the indeterminacy serves a suasive goal, it also raises the possibility of reading ideas into Ps 119 that are not present in the psalm itself.[61] Noting what the

---

[60] מרחב אין סופי הנפתח לפניו עם צאתו לעסוק בתורה...Amir, "The place of Psalm 119 in the religion of Israel" (Hebrew), 77.

[61] I discuss the notion of indeterminacy further in § 4.4. p. 136.

psalmist does not say is therefore important for describing his conception of Torah.

4.3.1. *Concepts that are Avoided*

Several expressions and themes that the author of Ps 119 avoids are glaring in their absence, for example, the cult, Moses, words for writing, and covenant. These omissions cannot be attributed to mere coincidence or to an oversight on the part of the author, but how does their omission help one understand the concept of Torah in Ps 119? The absence of words for writing, scribes, or books (ספר, סופרים, כתב, כתובים) is striking, since the author of Ps 119 was certainly concerned with texts and writing.[62] Moshe Greenberg notes, "The absence of reference to a book agrees quite well with the speeches of Moses in the first part of Deuteronomy, where the very specific commandments of God are to be taught not from a book but by hearing them from parents."[63] Since Ps 119 has so many affinities with Deuteronomy, this is a good observation, but it cannot be the full explanation.

Correlating these omissions with the author's rhetoric provides a more complete explanation. If the term "covenant" were used in Ps 119, it would almost certainly be understood as a reference to the covenant between God and Israel at Sinai.[64] Of course there are other covenants in the Hebrew Bible, but in the context of commandments, statutes, precepts, and stipulations (מצות, חקים, פקודים, and עדות), the natural point of reference would be Sinai. Therefore the referent of Torah would be implicitly limited, and this would undermine the author's promotion of Torah without limits (v. 96).

---

[62] The author does use the word ספר as a verb: "With my lips I recount…" (v. 13) and "I recount my ways…" (v. 26). However, a noun from this root never occurs in Ps 119.

[63] Moshe Greenberg, "Three Conceptions of the Torah in Hebrew Scriptures," in *Studies in the Bible and Jewish Thought* (Philadelphia: Jewish Publication Society, 1995), 24.

[64] Zenger notes that the word "covenant" (ברית) does not occur in Ps 119, but he argues that the connection to covenant theology of Deuteronomy is unmistakable. Although I agree that the connections to Deuteronomy are striking, the question of why the author avoided the term "covenant" is still an important one when trying to specify the conception of Torah in the psalm. "Zwar fehlt im ganzen Psalm der Begriff «Bund», aber der Bezug auf die deuteronomische Bundestheologie is unüberhörbar…" Frank-Lothar Hossfeld and Erich Zenger, *Psalmen 101–150*, HThKAT (Freiburg: Herder, 2008), 361.

Deissler argues that the psalmist does not use the term "covenant" because Ps 119 is a psalm of the individual.[65] As I argue in the introductory chapter, the designation "psalm of the individual" has unwarranted implications, since it is derived from the form critical method of Gunkel.[66] However, Deissler is correct that the term "covenant" would evoke the relationship between God and a community of people rather than an individual. This would undermine the author's portrayal of an exemplary Torah student. Thus, the term "covenant" would be counterproductive for both of the author's suasive goals, specifically promoting an expansive concept of Torah and portraying an exemplary Torah student.

Another topic that is never mentioned in Ps 119 is the cult: "No cultic wind wafts through this Psalm."[67] There are no references to the temple, priests, or ritual purity. Verse 108 does use a word for offerings (נדבות), but it is used metaphorically of prayer or praise: "Let the offerings of my mouth be pleasing, O YHWH." Since the stipulations regarding the proper performance of the cult were revealed at Sinai, any discussion of the cult would likely bring the events of Sinai to mind. In Leviticus specifications for the cult are called "torah," and any mention of the cult would evoke the textual details in the Pentateuch and limit the referent of Torah to specific texts, namely priestly regulations.[68]

---

[65] "Der naheliegende Begriff $b^e r\hat{\imath}t$ (Bund) wird vom Verfasser augenscheinlich wegen seiner kollektiven Bedeutung vermieden." Deissler, 282; see also Deissler, 303. Other explanations for why Ps 119 does not use the term "covenant" (ברית) are less than satisfactory. In earlier critical scholarship there was a claim that covenant and law were separated in post-exilic Judaism. Kraus effectively rebuts this claim. There were at least two problems with the discussion: (1) it assumed that post-exilic thought was monolithic and (2) it was influenced by Wellhausen's caricature of post-exilic "Jewish nomistic piety." See Hans-Joachim Kraus, "Freude an Gottes Gesetz: Ein Beitrag zur Auslegung der Psalmen 1; 19B und 119." *EvTh* 10 (1950): 337–51. Greenberg states that the "absence of allusion to the covenant anticipates the situation in talmudic Judaism where the terminology of laws and commandments virtually excludes the term ברית." Greenberg, "Three Conceptions of the Torah," 24. However, stating that Ps 119 "anticipates" a later situation explains nothing. It is merely an observation not an explanation.

[66] See the section on Genre (§ 1.3, p. 21).

[67] "Durch diesen Psalm weht keine kultische Luft." Deissler, 282.

[68] I want to emphasize that my claim here is not a claim about the composition of the Pentateuch or the relationship of Ps 119 to a P source. Some might want to argue that due to the omission of cultic references, the author of Ps 119 subscribed to an anti-priestly ideology. In my opinion, there is simply too little evidence in Ps 119 itself to support this type of argument. See chapter 5 for a discussion of the relationship of Ps 119 to other parts of the Hebrew Bible.

Any mention of the cult would also introduce an element that runs counter to the psalms' rhetoric, specifically a hierarchy of authority. A hierarchy by its very nature excludes people, and many verses in the Bible explicitly associate Torah with the priesthood.[69] For the author of Ps 119, Torah is not a possession of cultic officials, and Torah could not "belong" to anyone in particular. The young man (נער v. 9) who wants to keep his way pure has access to God's word and can even surpass his teachers by meditating on Torah. The speaker inherits God's testimonies (v. 111), which implies that the readers can inherit them as well. Part of the message of Ps 119 is that everyone should study Torah. References to the cult, Sinai, or the Torah of Moses would have limited the author's ability to emphasize that God will teach anyone who meditates on Torah.

4.3.2. The Relationship Between Torah and Wisdom

As noted in the introduction, several scholars classify Ps 119 as a wisdom psalm, and Hurvitz presents convincing evidence that Ps 119 uses wisdom locutions. I argue that the author of Ps 119 appropriates locutions of wisdom literature and uses them to portray the process of character formation. Since wisdom and Torah are linked in some way in Judaism (see the following paragraph), this raises the question of whether Ps 119 equates wisdom and Torah, replaces wisdom with Torah, or prioritizes Torah above wisdom.

Psalm 119 borrows the praises of wisdom in order to praise the benefits of Torah, but in doing so the author of Ps 119 avoids using words for wisdom. "Among all the synonyms for teaching and knowledge used in Ps 119, a notable set of words is missing, the wisdom-words: חכמה and חכם; בנה, תבונה, and נבון; שכל and משכיל."[70] It is well-discussed that the apocryphal books Ben Sira, Baruch, and Wisdom of Solomon all link wisdom and Torah.[71] In Ben Sira wisdom

---

[69] Passages that associate Torah with priests are numerous and span various corpora: Lev 10:11; Deut 17:11; 24:8; 2 Kgs 12:3; 17:28; Jer 18:18; and Ezek 7:26.

[70] Michael V. Fox, *Proverbs 10–31 A New Translation with Introduction and Commentary*, The Anchor Yale Bible, vol. 18B (New Haven: Yale University Press, 2009), 955.

[71] Erich Zenger, "Die späte Weisheit und das Gesetz," in *Literatur und Religion des Frühjudentums*, ed. Johann Maier und Josef Schreiner (Würzburg: Echter Verlag, 1973), 43–56. Eckhard J. Schnabel, *Law and Wisdom from Ben Sira to Paul*, Wissenschaftliche Untersuchungen zum Neuen Testament, vol. 16 (Tübingen: J. C. B. Mohr, 1985). Bauckmann states that in Ben Sira "ist das alte Ziel der Weisheitslehre

is specifically the "book of the covenant of the Most High" (24:23). If the author of Ps 119 wanted to equate Torah with wisdom, he would not have avoided the terms for wisdom.

Because the author of Ps 119 does not use characteristic wisdom terminology, there is not sufficient evidence to establish precisely his conception of wisdom and its relationship to Torah. As Fox notes, texts in the Hebrew Bible tend to "assign wisdom a lesser status relative to revealed Torah."[72] If there was any tension, Ben Sira resolves it by explicitly equating wisdom and Torah, but Ps 119 does not take that step. The use of locutions and motifs of wisdom literature is best explained in light of the rhetorical goals described in chapter 3. Psalm 119 shares a rhetorical goal with wisdom literature, specifically the portrayal of the process of character formation, and due to this common objective the locutions of wisdom literature were an attractive and useful resource for the author of Ps 119.

Of all the verses in Ps 119 on the topic of Torah study and pedagogy, vv. 99 and 100 are the best evidence that the author prioritizes Torah above wisdom. In v. 99 the speaker makes the bold claim that he has more understanding than his teachers. Such arrogance would be condemned by the sages who transmitted wisdom literature, and the speaker adds to his brashness in v. 100 by claiming that he has more insight than elders. Why can the speaker make this bold claim? The reason given in v. 99 is that God's stipulations are his meditation or conversation (שיחה לי), and if one can receive instruction directly from God (vv. 102 and 171), then other teachers pale by comparison. Deissler states, "His wish is that one might first and foremost sit at

---

das neue Ziel des Gesetzes geworden." E. G. Bauckmann, "Die Proverbien und die Sprüche des Jesus Sirach," ZAW 72 (1960): 55. Sheppard argues that in order to support this innovation Ben Sira and Baruch were forced to "construct an elaborate proof to demonstrate a close connection between them [Wisdom and Torah]." Gerald T. Sheppard, *Wisdom as a Hermeneutical Construct: A Study in the Sapientializing of the Old Testament*, BZAW, vol. 151 (Berlin: de Gruyter, 1980), 15. However, the identification of Torah as part of God's wisdom for mankind is already implied in Deut 4:6 when Moses tells the people that their obedience to all of God's statutes (חקים) and regulations (משפטים) will be their wisdom (חכמה) and insight (בינה) in the eyes of all the other nations. Fox notes that the implication is also found in the book of Proverbs and that "there is thus no radical innovation in Ben Sira's claim that wisdom found its home in Israel (24:1–22), where it took the form of Torah" (19:20). Fox, *Proverbs 1–9*, 358.

[72] Fox, *Proverbs 10–31*, 951.

the feet of YHWH as the one and only teacher of wisdom."[73] Since Ps 119 does not use words for wisdom, the word "wisdom" should be replaced with "Torah"; that is, the speaker desires to sit at the feet of God as the one and only teacher of Torah.

4.3.3. *Torah as a Hypostasis?*

Because the author exalts Torah throughout the Ps 119, Torah seems to take on a life of its own. It is clear in some texts that God's word was hypostasized, but is Torah in Ps 119 a hypostasis? Can the conception of Torah in Ps 119 be correlated with the *Logos* of Greek philosophy or the *Memra* in Aramaic translations and commentaries on Scripture? Various scholars have described the *Memra* as an attempt to preserve the transcendence of God without positing a separate entity, but Boyarin argues that this position is self-contradictory, since there must either be a separate entity or God's transcendence is not preserved.[74] Boyarin's thesis is that the prologue of John, in which Jesus is described as the Word of God in flesh, is not a radical departure from Jewish ideas but instead draws on common and thoroughly Jewish conceptions. According to Boyarin, the prologue of John represents "old common Judaic patterns of religious thought, a way from which later rabbinism has parted."[75] One need not agree with all of Boyarin's arguments to accept the minimal claim that at least some strands of early Judaism hypostasized God's word.

On the other end of the chronological spectrum Jack Lawson states, "in all its essential aspects Logos, as expounded by the Stoics, has precursors within the literature and thought of ancient Mesopotamia."[76] Lawson is not concerned with how the connections between Greek philosophy and ancient Mesopotamia took place; in fact, for him the question of how these connections took place is immaterial. "What is of importance is that for at least two millennia prior to the rise of the Stoic school of philosophy, neighboring civilizations in the East

---

[73] "Sein Wunsch ist es, daß man zuerst und zuletzt Jahwe als dem einen und einzigen Lehrer der Weisheit zu Füßen säße." Deissler, 200.

[74] Daniel Boyarin, "The Gospel of the Memra: Jewish Binitarianism and the Prologue to John," *HTR* 94 (2001): 255.

[75] Boyarin, "The Gospel of the Memra," 283.

[76] Jack Lawson, "Mesopotamian Precursors to the Stoic Concept of Logos," in *Proceedings of the Second Annual Symposium of the Assyrian and Babylonian Intellectual Heritage Project*, ed. R. M. Whiting, The Neo-Assyrian Text Corpus Project (Stuttgart: Franz Steiner, 2001), 91.

had produced literature which expounded ideas of a cosmic, creative principle, ideas which were organized around the divine speech or 'word.'[77] Lawson provides evidence that the ideas found in texts that hypostasize God's word also existed in much earlier texts, specifically in the conceptions of divine speech.

Of course, the answer to whether God's word is hypostasized in Ps 119 depends on how hypostasis is defined. In some texts the term is used simply for "being that has attained reality."[78] This is a statement about ontological status, and of course, in the conception of Ps 119, the word of God has "attained reality." But this seems trivial. It does not help to explain the conception of Torah in Ps 119 to note that it has "attained reality."

The *Logos* concept, however, includes the notion of an "independent and separate personification" of a divine being or universal principle.[79] Modern uses of the term "hypostasis" typically include this aspect of independence or separation from the deity.[80] One might say that a hypostasis assumes its own identity and acts independently from the deity, although the hypostasis is not a separate deity. The element of independence is missing in Ps 119. Separation between God and his word cannot be developed in Ps 119, since almost every verse is addressed directly to God.[81]

The development of Torah into a distinct, separate entity is a logical conclusion of some of the assumptions in Ps 119. It is self-evident that whatever God says is distinct from God's being. Combined with the belief that God's word will never pass away—a belief that Ps 119

---

[77] Lawson, "Mesopotamian Precursors to the Stoic Concept of Logos," 91.

[78] Note that the quotation is not "a being" but "being." *The Encyclopedia of Religion*, s.v. hypostasis.

[79] *Encyclopedia of Religion*, s.v. "logos."

[80] For the sake of this discussion, I am bracketing out the use of the term "hypostasis" in the New Testament and subsequent Christian theological reflection on the Trinity. One reason is that this is chronologically later than Ps 119, and a second reason is that it develops into a technical term in the study of patristics and dogmatics.

[81] Whether any hypostases exist in the Hebrew Bible is a matter of scholarly debate. See for example Azzan Yadin, "*Qol* as Hypostasis in the Hebrew Bible," *JBL* 122 (2003): 601–26. There are verses that seem to indicate God's word has a separate existence. For example, "My word, which goes forth from my mouth, will not return to me emptily." (Isa 55:11; see also Ps 147:15). Yet these verses only "teach the power of the Holy One (blessed be he) in this world; there is no indication of an independent existence of the word of God in the supernal world." "ללמד את גבורותיו של הקדוש ברוך הוא בעולם הזה, אבל אין רמז למציאות עצמאית של דבר ה' בעולם העליון." Heschel, תורה מן השמים [*Torah from Heaven* (Hebrew)], vol. 2, p. 21.

affirms—it is easy to imagine how Torah came to be hypostasized. But this step is not taken in Ps 119. In any case, a hypostasis of God's word would run counter to the rhetorical goals of Ps 119. One of those goals is to define piety in terms of fealty to Torah, but this does not remove God from the equation. Psalm 119 is written about the relationship between God and the speaker. Nothing in Ps 119 can be taken outside of the context of this relationship, and a hypostasis would blur this focus.[82]

If the term "hypostasis" is not helpful, can Torah be labeled a universal? Fox labels wisdom "the perfect and transcendent universal, of which the infinite instances of human wisdom are imperfect images or realizations."[83] The following descriptions are adapted from his descriptions of wisdom as a universal in the essay "Wisdom in the Interludes."[84] Torah exists independently of human minds and is unbounded by space, since it is established in the heavens. Torah is somehow active in the realm of nature, since the heavens and earth stand by it. The many requests for insight confirm that Torah must be accessed, understood, and then obeyed. Torah will last forever, and it is apprehended by intellect not sensory perception. Torah exists objectively; it is not a mental construct.

At first glance, the above descriptions and the definition of "universal" from the *Encyclopedia of Philosophy* seem to describe well the expansive conception of Torah in Ps 119. A universal is a "single substance or Form, existing timelessly and independently of any of its particular manifestations and apprehended not by sense but by intellect."[85] On closer examination, however, there are fundamental differences between a universal and the conception of Torah in Ps 119. Nowhere does Ps 119 claim that Torah exists timelessly—that is, into the eternal past.[86] Another difference becomes clear by considering an analogy used in the essay by Fox. "To use an analogy from modern linguistics, we can say that the limitless teachings and wise ideas that

---

[82] It would be an interesting hypothesis to claim that Ps 119 was written as a polemical response to Greek philosophy, i.e., Judaism had its equivalent for the *Logos* in Torah. But there is no evidence to support such a hypothesis.

[83] Fox, *Proverbs 1–9*, 356.

[84] Fox, *Proverbs 1–9*, 352–59.

[85] A. D. Woozley, "Universals," in *The Encyclopedia of Philosophy*.

[86] Michael Fox comments that starting from creation is enough to consider Torah timeless, (private communication). Later sages, i.e., of the Mishnah and *midrashim*, explore the question of the origins of Torah, but Ps 119 does not.

humans can shape, learn, and transmit are *generated* from the transcendent wisdom in the same way as an infinity of possible utterances are 'generated' from the deep structure of language."[87] Thus, wise human beings can formulate new wisdom based on the universal Wisdom; however, the idea that human beings could generate new Torah would be completely foreign to Ps 119. God is the source of Torah; it comes directly from God's mouth. Humans can discover various implications of Torah, but discovering the implications of Torah is fundamentally different than generating new Torah.

4.4. A Concept that is Greater than the Sum of the Parts

The expansive, abstract concept of Torah in Ps 119 is greater than the sum of the parts. Despite the fact that this phrase is a cliché, it describes something essential about the conception of Torah. The "parts" are the instantiations of Torah, that is, the individual commandments, stipulations, and promises. Torah comprises all of the commandments and stipulations, but there is more. Whatever collection the author of Ps 119 had, his conception of Torah was more inclusive than the collection of texts.[88]

4.4.1. *Definition*

In some cases it is necessary to describe something's function in order to define or describe it adequately. For example, an electric motor can be described by listing its components and their configuration in relationship to one another. The description may even include a materials list and detailed schematics that would allow someone with the proper tools and training to assemble the motor, but all of that would not suffice as a definition. Any sufficient definition of an electric motor must include some mention of what it *does*. A dominant rhetorical goal of Ps 119 is to portray the function of Torah in the life of the pious. This emphasis on the function of Torah is one way that the concept of Torah in Ps 119 extends beyond the sum of the parts.

---

[87] Michael V. Fox, *Proverbs 1–9*, 356.

[88] In my opinion, the author of Ps 119 knew most, if not all, of the texts that constitute the Hebrew Bible, but the argument here is not dependent on identifying which texts he knew.

Torah functions to bring the supernal and natural worlds together. As I have already noted, Torah does not serve as a mediator in Ps 119, but Torah exists in the heavens, which is the realm of God. Torah finds expression in human language, but at the same time Torah is God's word. Psalm 119 does not explore the implications of these statements, nor does it address any of the philosophical questions that the various statements raise. The author repeatedly focuses on the efficacy of Torah observance and Torah study.

A quilt or a tapestry can serve as an analogy for describing the psalmist's conception of Torah. All of the various commandments, precepts, regulations, and promises are woven together like the threads of a tapestry into Torah, which transcends a random collection of commandments both in form and function. Any particular commandment is like a thread of the tapestry. Without being woven together by the artist, the individual threads are just that—threads. When the threads are woven together, the threads do not change in essence, but the tapestry itself transcends a mere collection of threads. Similarly, when a quilt is finished, the component squares of fabric do not change in essence, but they take on added dimensions of beauty and functionality, such as providing warmth. Individual commandments can be compared to the squares of fabric, and the concept of Torah can be compared to the quilt. Yet any individual commandment is Torah, since it comes from God.

4.4.2. Evidence that the Concept is Greater than the Sum of the Parts

There are meaningful patterns of repetition and a network of interrelated ideas in Ps 119. The nature of these relationships is not necessarily specified by the author, and the network of ideas is constituted in various ways. Repeating the eight Torah terms is an essential component of the framework, but the relationships are not created only by means of the Torah terms. By repeating and varying motifs and locutions, the author communicates a conception of Torah that is greater than the sum of the parts.

The repetitions are not merely ballast; they constitute an argument. One example that illustrates a meaningful pattern of repetition is the phrase "teach me your statutes" (למדני חקיך vv. 12, 26, 64, 68, 124, and 135). This petition is repeatedly juxtaposed with statements about God's goodness. Verse 68 is explicit, "You are good and the one who causes good things; teach me your statutes." Verses 64 and 124 juxtapose the request with statements about God's mercy, and v. 12 begins, "Blessed are you, O YHWH." These juxtapositions and the fact that they are repeated several times reveal part of the message of Ps 119: Because God is good, God will personally teach the pious. Elsewhere in the psalm, the speaker declares that Torah is good, and the reason Torah is good is that it comes from God, who is good.

The network of interrelated ideas within the chapter can be explored by tracing a particular motif or repeated word. One example is the petition "give me life" (חַיֵּנִי) that occurs nine times in Ps 119 and nowhere else in the Bible. The petition is followed by various prepositional phrases: "according to your word" (דבר vv. 25, 107), "according to your justice" (משפט vv 149, 156), and "according to your promise" (אמרה v. 154). The speaker also uses this imperative with phrases that do not include any of the Torah terms, for example, "according to your mercy" (חסד vv. 88, 159), "in your way" (דרך v. 37), "by your righteousness" (צדק v. 40).

The interrelationship of ideas can be seen in the following:

1. a) Give me life (חיה) according to your way (דרך v. 37).
   b) Give me life (חיה) according to your word (דבר vv. 25, 107).
   c) Your word is the way to walk (v. 1, *passim*).
2. a) Give me life (חיה) according to your righteousness (v. 40).
   b) Give me life (חיה) according to your word (vv. 25, 107).
   c) Your word is righteous (v. 7, *passim*).
3. a) Give me life (חיה) according to your mercy (vv. 88, 159).
   b) Give me life (חיה) according to your word (vv. 25, 107).
   c) Your word says that you will be merciful (v. 76).

The above groups are not syllogisms. None of the above statements in c) follows logically from the statements in a) and b). Furthermore, the relationships in c) "X is Y" are different in all of the above examples. Listing the above verses side by side simply illustrates how different concepts are woven together in the psalm into a network that ultimately expands the conception of Torah.

In addition to the imperative forms of the verb חיה, other occurrences of the word provide further illustration of the interconnection of ideas. In v. 50 the speaker states that God's word (אמרה) gives him life. In v. 93 the speaker declares that God gives him life by means of the precepts (פקודים). The author juxtaposes several other petitions with the word חיה: "Deal [well] with your servant so that I may live"

(v. 17); "Let your compassions come to me that I might live" (v. 77); and "Support me according to your word, and I will live" (v. 116). These examples link "life" with God's goodness and compassion.

Verse 37 includes a text critical question that illustrates how closely interrelated the various terms are.

Ps 119:37 העבר עיני מראות שוא   *Turn my eyes away from seeing worthlessness;*

בדרכך חיני   *give me life in your way.*[89]

Many commentators find the lack of one of the eight Torah terms in v. 37 unacceptable and read "give me life in your words" (בדבריך instead of בדרכך). This reading does have support from the Targum, which translates בדביריך. Perhaps the translator was exploiting the graphic similarity between the two words דרכך and דבריך.[90] The difference between these two readings for v. 37 (either דרך or דבר) is graphically minor, and it is easy to imagine a scribal error as the source of the variant readings. Furthermore, God's word (דבר) and God's way (דרך) are linked throughout the psalm, and the psalmist does not specify the nature of the relationship. It is not a question of semantics; the psalmist is not providing a definition of either term. He is arguing "God's word is God's way," by means of the network of related ideas. It is left to the reader to decide specifically how God's word and God's way relate.

The author's use of the verb "to look at" (נבט) also creates a relationship between God's way and God's word. In v. 6 the speaker declares that he will not be ashamed "when I look at all your commandments" (כל מצותיך), and in v. 18 he expresses his desire to gaze on "miracles from your Torah" (נפלאות מתורתך). In v. 15 he states, "I will look at your paths" (ארחותיך). "Paths" are not typically an object of contemplation—words are. Elsewhere, the focus of the speaker's mental processes is God's word. What does the author mean with the phrase "look at your paths"?

---

[89] Many MSS have a plural form ("ways" בדרכיך), but that does not affect the argument here.

[90] Interpretation based on graphic similarity was common place, and therefore the Targum is not good evidence for a different *Vorlage*. One classic article that provides examples of this type of interpretation is I. L. Seeligmann, "Voraussetzungen der Midraschexegese," VTSup, vol. 1 (1953), 150–81. For a more recent study see Alexander Samely, *Rabbinic Interpretation of Scripture in the Mishnah* (New York: Oxford University Press, 2002).

A phrase similar to "I will look at your paths" (Ps 119:15) does not occur anywhere else in the Bible. If the path is a metaphor for behavior in v. 15 as it is elsewhere, then the speaker is declaring that he will look at the way God acts.[91] This is a possible interpretation, which would mean that the speaker contemplates God's actions, actions presumably recorded or preserved in traditional narratives. Perhaps this is over-interpretation—pressing the metaphor too far. In any case, v. 15 makes sense in the context of Ps 119 without any textual change, because the author juxtaposes the metaphor of the path with other terms for Torah throughout the chapter. There is only one correct path—namely Torah. It is no accident that some commentators include "way" (דרך) as one of the terms for God's word.[92]

Tracing the theme of love through Ps 119 highlights the network of interrelated ideas and how the relationships affect interpretation. The author juxtaposes statements about love with various ideas. The speaker repeatedly declares that he loves Torah; these verses could be grouped together with the verses discussed above that substitute Torah in place of God. One theme that is juxtaposed with the speaker's love is the purity of Torah. In v. 140 the speaker states that he loves God's word, which is free of impurities. He also loves God's stipulations because God puts an end to the dross (v. 119). In v. 127 the speaker exclaims, "I love your commandments more than gold—even fine gold." These examples share an underlying metallurgy metaphor. The point of the metaphor is that God's word is refined (צרופה). By using these juxtapositions, the author is promoting Torah as something that is worthy of love, because it is pure and true.

In other verses the author makes a similar argument by contrasting the speaker's love for Torah with his hate for deception and duplicity. For example, v. 113 reads, "I hate divided things, but I love your Torah" (סעפים שנאתי ותורתך אהבתי). The verse implies that God's word is unified. That is, Torah speaks with one voice; it contains no contradictions. Since the source is God, it cannot contain contradictions. Verse 163 also contrasts what the speaker loves and hates: "I

---

[91] I discuss the metaphor of the path in chapters 2 and 3. The metaphor of the path figures behavior, both in Ps 119 as well as the rest of the Bible. Even in Isa 2:3 (// Mic 4:2), which juxtaposes a mental process with the metaphor of the path, the emphasis is proper behavior. "He will teach us his ways, and we will walk in his paths" (וירנו מדרכיו ונלכו בארחתיו). Walking in God's path is a way of figuring obedience.

[92] One example is Levenson, "The Sources of Torah."

hate and loathe deception; I love your Torah." (שקר שנאתי ואתעבה תורתך אהבתי). Neither of these examples explicitly states that Torah is free of deception, but in light of the network of ideas both v. 113 and v. 163 imply that Torah is true.

Verse 159 is an example that juxtaposes love with several different motifs: "Look, for I love your precepts; O YHWH, give me life (חיה) according to your mercy." The verb "give me life" provides a lexical link between this verse and v. 156: "Your compassions are numerous, O YHWH; give me life (חיה) according to your regulations." The repetition of the word "numerous" (רבים) links vv. 156 and 157: God's compassions are numerous (v. 156), and the speaker's foes are numerous (v. 157). The second half of v. 157 contains a claim of innocence, and v. 158 provides a contrast between the speaker and his antagonists who ignore God's commands. Thus, there is an associative sequence that extends from v. 156 to v. 159.[93]

The associative sequence in these four verses is an example of the network of interrelated ideas that the author builds throughout Ps 119, and the relationship of ideas affects the interpretation of individual verses. In v. 159 the speaker's love for Torah is used as a claim of innocence. This conclusion would be unwarranted if there were no other claims of innocence in Ps 119. Furthermore, the motif of antagonism occurs in the preceding verses, which sets the stage for the claim of innocence in v. 159. Another example is the petition that God would give the speaker "life" according to the mercy of God. On the basis of this verse alone, one should not conclude that God's regulations are an expression of mercy. However, the author makes that argument elsewhere in the chapter, and the repetition of the verb "life" (חיה) associates v. 159 with other verses that use the word.

Substituting Torah for God, as discussed in chapters 2 and 3, is another example of meaningful repetition. Collectively, the verses that include this substitution promote Torah to a new level of importance for the pious, even if that is not the case for the verses individually. If the substitutions occurred in only one or two verses, it might not be significant, but there are multiple examples. The pattern of substitutions contributes to the network of ideas that expand the conception of Torah. In chapter 3, I discuss how the substitutions contribute to

---

[93] On "associative sequence" see p. 21. There is also a lexical link between v. 157 and v. 161, and this could be described as part of the same sequence.

the author's portrayal of the speaker's emotions, yet these verses also contribute to the conception of Torah in Ps 119. Thus, these verses are additional examples that have a double function.[94]

One of the substitutions occurs in v. 66, and it results in a unique locution within the Hebrew Bible: "I believe in your commandments" (במצותיך האמנתי). Nowhere else is the word "commandments" the object of verb "to believe"; instead God is the expected object of this verb.[95] There are two possibilities for interpreting the verse; one is that the verse emphasizes God's promises. The term "commandment" (מצות) is not typically juxtaposed with the idea of a promise, but one of the Ten Commandments does include an explicit promise, "Honor your father and mother *in order that your days may be long upon the land*, which the Lord your God is giving you" (Exod 20:12; cf. Deut 5:16 and Eph 6:2). Since the idea that Torah includes promises occurs elsewhere in Ps 119, Deissler adopts this as the best explanation of v. 66.[96]

Another possible interpretation is that v. 66 contains a statement of belief in an abstract concept, similar to the statement "I believe in justice." This statement could mean several different things: (1) I believe justice exists (even though it does not seem like it); (2) I believe that justice will ultimately prevail; (3) I believe it is worth the effort to fight for justice. An abstract statement, such as "I believe in your commandments," fits well with the tone of Ps 119. The precise significance of the verse would then be open to various interpretations, similar to the three examples listed above. Radaq explains, "I believe in them, because you commanded them, and because they are righteous regulations."[97]

The first interpretation of v. 66 is corroborated by verses that imply Torah includes promises, even if this argument is not explicit. One example is v. 49 where the speaker requests, "Remember the word for your servant, upon which you have made me hope" (יחל). The expectation that God will "remember" indicates that the word has already been given; the psalmist is not hoping for some new information. This verse also indicates that God's word in Ps 119 is not limited to com-

---

[94] For further discussion of the phenomenon, see p. 144.
[95] See also the discussion and notes on p. 41.
[96] Deissler, p. 168.
[97] האמנתי בהם, שאתה צוית אותם, ושהם משפטי צדק Ha-Keter, 171.

mandments or instructions for mankind. The expression "hoping on God's word" is one example with the implication that Torah includes promises.

However, this corroborating evidence for the first interpretation does not necessarily exclude the second interpretation. The two options are not mutually exclusive, and due to the rhetorical goal of portraying the speaker's emotions and volition, it may not be possible or necessary to decide between these two interpretations of v. 66. This is not to say that the author was sloppy or that the meaning of Ps 119 is indeterminate. On the contrary, it "is actually effective mimesis of a determinate but complex reality"; that complex reality is the expansive concept of Torah.[98]

Some verses depict Torah as performing functions that are elsewhere attributed to God or requested from God; thus, these verses are similar to the substitutions listed above. Technically, these examples amount to personifications of Torah, but they remain only incipient. That is, they are used in passing and are not developed; nonetheless, they contribute to an expansive conception of Torah. For example, many prayers throughout the Hebrew Bible, including in the book of Psalms and Ps 119, request God's help. In v. 173 the speaker says, "Let your hand be my help," and in v. 86 he simply petitions, "Help me!" God's justice is the grammatical subject of the verb in v. 175, "Your justice helps me" (ומשפטך יעזרני).[99] As noted above, the speaker petitions God to give him life, and in v. 50 the speaker declares, "Your word has given me life" (אמרתך חיתני), which provides yet another example of Torah being substituted for God.[100] God's word is the life-giving agent.

Another example of an incipient personification occurs in v. 24, where the speaker calls God's stipulations "men of my counsel" (אנשי עצתי). Although this precise phrase does not occur elsewhere in the Bible, the idea of seeking counsel from others is praised in many proverbs (Prov 11:14; 12:20; 13:10; 15:22; 20:18; 24:6). The idea is also similar to "counsel of the wicked" in Ps 1:1. The author of Ps 119 finds

---

[98] In its original context this phrase does not refer to Torah, but it is an appropriate phrase, since I am discussing indeterminacy. The phrase is from Michael V. Fox, "The Uses of Indeterminacy," *Semeia* 71 (1995): 173–92.

[99] Alternatively, "Your regulations help me." In the MT the subject appears to be singular, but the verb is vocalized as a plural; see the discussion of משפט on p. 120 and the commentary on v. 98.

[100] See the comments on v. 50 regarding the verb "give life" (חיה).

his counsel not from mere human advisors but in God's stipulations. Furthermore, in v. 98 the speaker attributes the act of teaching to the commandments: "Your commandments make me wiser than my enemies" (v. 98). There are multiple requests in the chapter for God to teach the speaker, but in v. 98 the author substitutes commandments for God.

Many of the examples discussed in the above paragraphs have a double function.[101] They contribute both to the author's portrayal of the exemplary Torah student and to the promotion of Torah. Verses with the motif of love, for example, reveal something about the speaker's attitudes and emotions. At the same time, they argue that Torah is free of deception and division and thus contribute to the conception of Torah. This double function occurs in many verses of Ps 119 because the author frames the poem in the first person. With the exception of the first three verses, the entire psalm contributes to the characterization of the speaker. Separating the two topics—that is, the exemplary student and the conception of Torah—is necessary for the sake of discussion, but the portrayal of the Torah student and the promotion of Torah are woven together in Ps 119.

Two of the verses discussed above (vv. 113 and 163) end with the phrase "I love your Torah," and both verses use the topic of deception in the first stich. By means of the juxtaposition these verses imply that Torah is free of deception, and since other verses in Ps 119 state explicitly that God's word is true, this implication corresponds with the message that occurs elsewhere in the psalm. At the same time, it is clear from these verses that the paradigmatic Torah student does not lie; such activity is abhorrent to him. Again, these verses have the double function of promoting Torah and portraying a student of Torah.

Another example of this double function occurs in v. 140, which begins, "Your word is completely refined," namely, free of impurities. The second half of the verse states, "And your servant loves it." The verse is explicitly describing both the nature of Torah and the character of the speaker, but the logical relationship between the two halves of the verse is not explicit. The conjunction between the two stichs is a *waw* (ו). In v. 119, which also uses the motif of refining metal, the author joins the stichs with a causal conjunction: "You put an end to

---

[101] There are numerous examples of this phenomenon; see the discussion of v. 7 on p. 122.

all the wicked of the land—the dross; therefore, I love your stipula-tions." Based in part on v. 119, a causal relationship between the two stichs of v. 140 is a likely interpretation, and the verses implies that the speaker loves God's word because it is pure.

There are logical gaps in the verses, but it is not difficult to fill those gaps, since the phenomenon occurs frequently and the ideas required to fill the gaps occur elsewhere in the psalm. In v. 144 the speaker petitions God for insight so that he might live (הבינני ואחיה). This is quite different than the other requests for insight in Ps 119. Elsewhere the speaker asks for insight in order to learn God's word and observe it properly. Additionally, the requests for "life" are juxtaposed with claims of innocence, which indicates that Torah observance leads to "life." Verse 144 omits several steps of the process: insight leads to learning, which leads to obedience, which is rewarded with "life." Verse 144 jumps from insight directly to "life" and expects the reader to fill in the other steps. This conclusion would be unwarranted if v. 144 were the only example that required the reader to supply the logi-cal connections; however, there are multiple examples throughout the chapter. Verses that include logical gaps are similar to "disjointed prov-erbs," and some, for example v. 144, can be classified as enthymemes.[102] The author rarely explains the nature of the relationships between the stichs, and the logical gaps force the reader to think about them.[103]

To a certain extent, one can demarcate the conception of Torah in Ps 119 by contrasting it with other conceptions of Torah. Several contrasts have already been drawn. Psalm 119 does not equate Torah with wis-dom as do Ben Sira, Wisdom of Solomon, and Genesis Rabba. Torah is not a universal, an ideal, or a hypostasis. Contrary to Levenson, there is no evidence that Torah is new unmediated revelation that comes to the supplicant in some altered state of consciousness. Although Amir may be correct that Ps 119 contains precursors to *halakah*, his argu-ment that the author saw a wide open expanse hidden within the text

---

[102] Michael V. Fox, "The Rhetoric of Disjointed Proverbs." *JSOT* 29 (2004): 165–77.

[103] Fox's description of the parallelism found in individual proverbs is a fitting description of verses in Ps 119 as well: "The parallelism has the effect of framing an idea in the first line so that it may be modified and commented on in the second. Unlike the monostich, the couplet allows for a little compressed dialectic. It embodies an intellectual process appropriately called wisdom, for it involves thinking about an idea as well as simply stating it." Fox, *Proverbs 10–31*, 493.

of the written Torah cannot be defended from Ps 119. Finally, Torah is not the *Logos* or *Memra*.

The above notions may be in Ps 119 in inchoate form, but there is a danger of imposing later ideas onto Ps 119. This danger is particularly acute for Ps 119 due to the literary form, the juxtapositions that are not explained, the use of traditional religious language, and the rhetorical goal of portraying an exemplary Torah student. In different ways, all of these features encourage the reader to contemplate the expansive conception of Torah. That is, the lack of an explicit definition contributes to the suasive goals.

The conception of Torah in Ps 119 is a composite of ideas about God's word that can be found in various passages throughout the Hebrew Bible, passages that portray YHWH as a God who communicates with humanity. Psalm 119 promotes the benefits that God's communication, in any and all of its modes, provides. Systematically working out the various implications of the belief that God verbally expresses desires in Torah would likely lead to the claim that Torah is eternal, unchanging, and the blueprint of the universe. But Ps 119 does not work out the implications in a systematic fashion as later rabbis did. Although it is on the way, Torah in Ps 119 is not yet *the* Torah of Rabbinic Judaism.

CHAPTER FIVE

PSALM 119 IN CONTEXT

משה נתן חמשה חומשי תורה לישראל,
ודוד נתן חמשה ספרים שבתהלים לישראל
מדרש תהלים מזמור א

5.1. INTRODUCTION

Because Deissler gives such a positive evaluation of Ps 119, it seems that
he has moved beyond the disdain of Duhm.[1] However, in his conclusion it becomes clear that Deissler merely shifts his disdain to another
timeframe. According to Deissler, Ps 119 was written before 200 B.C.E.
and Judaism was not yet characterized by the "narrow-minded legalism" (*engstirniger Nomismus*) that many authors ascribe to the early
Hellenistic period. "The opinion of R. Kittel that the time of the Mac-
cabees first brought the backward slide into the 'strict anxiety of the
priestly statute' and the 'petty casuistry of the priestly ritual doctrine' is
freshly supported through our study."[2] Deissler recognizes that Ps 119
does not contain a narrow-minded legalism, which is an improvement
over Duhm, but his comments raise other questions, especially in light
of the developments in the study of the Psalter and Second Temple
Judaism since the time of Deissler. How does Ps 119 fit into the composition of the Psalter and the completion of the Hebrew Bible? What
is the contribution of Ps 119 to the development of Judaism?

In this chapter I argue that Ps 119 contributes to the centrality
of Torah study in Judaism and to the conception of Torah that is
found in the Hebrew Bible. When individual psalms, or, more likely,
previous collections of psalms, were compiled into the Psalter, the
compiler emphasized a complex theological conception of Torah. The

---

[1] See the introduction.
[2] "Die Ansicht von R. Kittel, daß erst die Zeit der Makkabäer den Rückschlag in die
'enge Ängstlichkeit der priesterlichen Satzung' und die 'kleine Kasuistik der priesterlichen Rituallehre' brachte, wird durch unsere Studie neu gestützt." Deissler, 317–18.
The quote of Kittel is from the second edition of Kittel's history of Israel, published
in 1929.

same concept influenced the compilation of the Hebrew Bible as a whole. Both the compilation of the Psalter and the Hebrew Bible were undertaken by individuals who were dedicated to the study of Scripture, especially Torah study and observance. Occupation with Torah, which includes both Torah study and Torah observance, is an axiom of Rabbinic Judaism. By emphasizing the value and benefits of Torah study, Ps 119 contributed to the centrality of Torah study, and this emphasis is unique in the Hebrew Bible.

To this point, I have described the conceptions and rhetoric in Ps 119 with very little reference to its literary and historical contexts. Discussing "context" as the conclusion rather than the introduction is atypical in biblical studies, but in the case of Ps 119, it is warranted due to the literary features of the psalm and the lack of historical references. As I argued in the introduction, form criticism is ill-suited for the study of Ps 119 since the psalm had no pre-literary stage. My methodology is therefore to sketch a trajectory of developing Judaism and then examine how my study of Ps 119 corresponds with that trajectory. The following sections address progressively broader contexts, beginning with the place of Ps 119 in the Psalter, followed by its place in the Hebrew Bible, and concluding with its place in developing Judaism.

5.2. THE PLACE OF PSALM 119 IN THE PSALTER

5.2.1. *The Problem of Integrating Psalm 119 into the Structure of the Psalter*

Prior to the groundbreaking work of Gerald Wilson, the question of Ps 119's place in the Psalter received little attention; instead research focused on individual psalms and their respective *Sitz im Leben*.[3]

---

[3] With the word "Psalter" I am referring to the 150 psalms preserved in the Masoretic tradition. I do not accept the theory of Sanders, Wilson, and Flint that there were multiple "Psalters." One problem with this theory is its disproportionate dependence on 11QPs[a]. For example, Flint gives tables of evidence and claims that the differences between 1–89 are considerably fewer than in 90–150. This is an argument based on statistics, but the statistics are skewed since much of the evidence derives from a single manuscript. As Talmon notes, this is an argument from silence, since 11QPs[a] does not contain any of the first 100 Psalms. See Talmon's review of Flint in *JBL* 118 (1999): 545–47. Additionally, even if the data at Qumran indicates a relatively late date for the compilation of the Psalter, this does not mean that different Psalters were in existence. Using the same term in this way clouds the issues. Flint provides a sketch

However, study of the Psalter has undergone a dramatic change in the past twenty-five years; numerous articles and monographs have appeared that discuss the arrangement of the Psalter and how the arrangement affects interpretation.[4] Psalm 119 occurs in the final section of the five-part Psalter (Pss 107–150), yet its contribution to Book V and to the Psalter is still a matter of debate.[5] Koch states that Ps 119 "does not reveal anything of the redactional outline by its membership."[6] Zenger notes that various proposals regarding the editing of the fifth book all "have difficulty ordering the long Psalm 119 into the structure."[7]

One of the most recent studies of Book V is by Martin Leuenberger, who subordinates the theme of Torah to the kingship of God. He considers Ps 119 an older individual psalm that was inserted into

---

of the argument in his introduction to *The Dead Sea Psalms Scrolls and the Book of Psalms*, Studies on the Texts of the Desert of Judah, vol. XVII, ed. F. García Martínez and A. S. van der Woude. vol. XVII (Leiden: Brill, 1997), see especially pp. 7–9; he provides his conclusions in chapter 9, which is entitled "True Psalter or Secondary Collection?" pp. 202–27.

[4] Gerald Wilson, *The Editing of the Hebrew Psalter*, SBL Dissertation Series, vol. 76 (Chico, CA: Scholars Press, 1985). Wellhausen claims that Ps 119 is not a psalm and therefore does not belong in the Psalter. Julius Wellhausen, *The Book of Psalms* (New York: Dodd, Mead, and Co., 1898). Despite this claim of Wellhausen, there are important works before Wilson that address the redaction of the Psalter. In the introduction to his commentary on the Psalter, Delitzsch discusses the five-part division of the Psalter and cites earlier works that at least mention the meaningful organization of the individual psalms, including *midrashim*, the Talmud, and several church fathers. Franz Delitzsch, *Biblical Commentary on the Psalms*, 3 vols., 2d ed. (Edinburgh: T & T Clark, 1885). From the same period, see W. Riedel, "Zur Redaktion des Psalters," *ZAW* 19 (1899): 169–72. Some of the comments in Smend's work foreshadow the conclusions of Wilson. Rudolph Smend, *Die Entstehung des Alten Testaments*, Theologische Wissenschaft: Sammelwerk für Studium und Beruf, vol. 1 (Stuttgart: W. Kohlhammer, 1978). See also, H. Gese, "Die Entstehung der Büchereinteilung des Psalters," in *Vom Sinai zum Zion*, Beiträge zur Evangelischen Theologie, vol. 64 (München: Kaiser, 1974), 147–58 and Matthias Millard, *Die Komposition des Psalters*, FAT, vol. 9, ed. Bernd Janowski and Hermann Spieckermann (Tübingen: J. C. B. Mohr, 1994). Many more recent works are cited in the following pages, and it is clear that Wilson deserves a great deal of the credit for revivifying the discussion of the final shaping of the Psalter.

[5] See the discussion below on the five-part division.

[6] "... läßt von einer Zugehörigkeit zum redaktionellen Aufriß nichts erkennen." Klaus Koch, "Der Psalter und seine Redaktionsgeschichte," in *Neue Wege der Psalmenforschung*, ed. Klaus Seybold and Erich Zenger, HBS, vol. 1 (Freiburg: Herder, 1995), 254.

[7] Erich Zenger, "The Composition and Theology of the Fifth Book of Psalms," *JSOT* 80 (1998): 87. This is a revised, English translation of Erich Zenger, "Komposition und Theologie des 5. Psalmenbuchs 107–145," *Biblische Notizen* 82 (1996): 97–116.

the fifth division of the Psalter without any editorial changes.[8] It was included as an instructional poem, which teaches about the relationship between Torah observance and a successful life. The obedience described in Ps 119 is the proper response of anyone who has experienced the deliverance of God, which is the emphasis of Ps 118, and this relationship between Pss 118 and 119 is the reason that Ps 119 was included.[9] Leuenberger underestimates the importance of Ps 119 in the Psalter, and he dismisses Zenger's proposal for the concentric arrangement of Book V too quickly, claiming that the connections between Pss 107 and 145 cannot carry the weight of the claims made by Wilson.[10] Furthermore, he does not give sufficient consideration to the work of Reinhard Kratz, in which Kratz shows that the conception of Torah has a "programmatic function" in the Psalter.[11]

5.2.2. The Frequency and Placement of the Theme of Torah in the Psalter

Before discussing how the study of Kratz contributes to a solution, it is first necessary to consider the frequency and placement of the theme of Torah in the Psalter. James Mays identifies seventeen psalms that are part of the latest stratum of the Psalter and each of them includes

---

[8] Ps 119 was inserted "unverändert." Martin Leuenberger, *Konzeptionen des Königtums Gottes im Psalter*, Abhandlungen zur Theologie des Alten und Neuen Testaments, ed. Erhard Blum et al., vol. 83 (Zürich: Theologischer Verlag Zürich, 2004), 372. He discusses Ps 119 at several places (see 275, 299, 300, 370–72), but he minimizes the importance of Ps 119 in the final composition of the Psalter.

[9] Leuenberger, *Konzeptionen des Königtums Gottes im Psalter*, 370–72.

[10] "Schließlich wird die (im Gefolge Wilsons) behauptete Rahmung 107/145 erheblich relativiert durch eine Gegenprobe der von Zenger angeführten Leitwörter und Themen, die zeigt, daß diese auch sonst in V wichtig (und bes. in der Entsprechung 136/145 signifikanter) sind; sie ist lediglich als vergleichsweise schwache drittrangige Großklammer plausibel, als welche sie keinesfalls einen inklusorischen Aufbau von V überhaupt tragend mitbegründen kann." Leuenberger, *Konzeptionen des Königtums Gottes im Psalter*, 275. He claims that the works of Wilson, Millard, Koch, Kratz, and Zenger emphasize different thematic trajectories or "catch-word-connections," and the different emphases result in different arrangements (p. 276). The same thing can be said for Leuenberger's work itself. His emphasis is the kingdom of God, and through this prioritization, Leuenberger subordinates other concerns.

[11] Reinhard Kratz explores the theme of Torah and argues that the Psalter promotes an extremely complex theological Torah-concept in his article, "Die Tora Davids. Psalm I und die doxologische Fünfteilung des Psalters," *Zeitschrift für Theologie und Kirche* 93 (1996): 1–34. I explore his arguments more fully in the following section.

verses with the theme of Torah.[12] The introduction, conclusion, and redactional seams of the Psalter all include an emphasis on Torah, and Mays' observations have been confirmed by various scholars. In the following paragraphs I highlight some of the relevant data as a basis for further discussion.

Doxologies divide the Psalter into five sections, which are typically referred to as books (Book I, chaps. 1–41; II, chaps. 42–72; III, chaps. 73–89; IV, chaps. 90–106; and V, chaps. 107–150). At least since the first centuries of the Common Era, the five parts have been viewed as following the pattern of the five-part division of the Pentateuch.[13] Within this macrostructure scholars have identified various groupings of psalms. Some of the groupings correspond with the superscriptions, such as the so-called "ascent psalms" (Pss 120–134).[14] Other groupings are established by thematic and lexical links, such as the concentric arrangement of Pss 15–24 or the collection of Pss 93–100.[15] The salient point for my study is that both the five-part macrostructure and other groupings within the macrostructure can be established—or at least outlined—without reference to the theme of Torah. For example, one of the structuring devices in the Psalter is the placement of the royal psalms, and Howard concludes "that the organizing principle of the Psalter ultimately has to do with the reign of God as King."[16] This is methodologically significant, since it mitigates against the problem of circular reasoning.[17] There are several psalms, whose placement is structurally significant, that are linked with Ps 119 in some way.

---

[12] James L. Mays, "The Place of the Torah-Psalms in the Psalter," *JBL* 106 (1987): 8.

[13] See footnote 4 in this chapter.

[14] Klaus Seybold, *Die Wallfahrtspsalmen: Studien zur Entstehungsgeschichte von Psalm 120–134*, Biblisch-Theologische Studien, ed. Ferdinand Hahn et al., vol. 35 (Neukirchen-Vluyn: Neukirchener, 1978).

[15] On Psalms 15–24 see Patrick D. Miller, "Kingship, Torah Obedience, and Prayer," in *Neue Wege der Psalmenforschung*, ed. K. Seybold and E. Zenger, HBS, vol. 1 (Freiburg: Herder, 1995), 127–42. On Psalms 93–100 see David M. Howard, *The Structure of Psalms 93–100*, BJS, vol. 5 (Winona Lake, IN: Eisenbrauns, 1997). For a survey of the research up to 1993 see David M. Howard, "Editorial Activity in the Psalter: A State-of-the-Field Survey," in *The Shape and Shaping of the Psalter*, ed. J. Clinton McCann, JSOTSup, vol. 159 (Sheffield: JSOT Press, 1993), 52–70. Leuenberger incorporates more recent articles and monographs in his work on the composition of Books IV and V; Leuenberger, *Konzeptionen des Königtums Gottes im Psalter*.

[16] Howard, *The Structure of Psalms 93–100*, 207.

[17] If the structure was established by the Torah theme alone, then explaining the complex Torah concept on the basis of the structure could degenerate into a viciously circular argument.

Both the introduction (Pss 1, 2) and conclusion (Pss 146–150) have multiple lexical connections with Ps 119. The first verse of both Pss 1 and 119 begins with אשרי, and the last verse of both psalms uses the root א.ב.ד. In Ps 1 the last word of the last verse begins with ת, and since the first word begins with א, Ps 1 runs from א to ת like the acrostic in Ps 119. Both Ps 1 and Ps 119 use the phrase "Torah of YHWH" (תורת יהוה), which only occurs in one other psalm, namely Ps 19. Both Ps 1 and Ps 119 portray a person whose "delight" (חפץ) is in Torah and who contemplates God's word day and night. The contrast between the righteous and the wicked is an important motif in both Pss 1 and 119, and both use the metaphor of the path to figure behavior. All of these details cannot be mere coincidence, and various scholars have noted the connections.[18]

In the conclusion to the Psalter (Pss 146–150) the word "Torah" does not occur, but various synonyms for Torah, which are used in Ps 119, do occur. Psalm 146:7 identifies God as the one who brings justice (משפט) for the oppressed, and Ps 149:9 describes God's punishment of the wicked as his fulfillment of a "written judgment" (משפט כתוב). Psalm 148 emphasizes God's control of nature by means of his command (צוה v. 5) and his word (דבר v. 8). Psalm 147 also describes the power of God's word: "He sends his word (אמרה) to the earth; his word (דבר) runs very swiftly" (Ps 147:15).[19] This same word of God can melt ice and snow (Ps 147:18), and it was a special gift to Israel:

Ps 147:19	מגיד דברו ליעקב	He announced his word to Jacob,
	חקיו ומשפטיו לישראל	his statutes and his judgments to Israel.
Ps 147:20	לא עשה כן לכל גוי	He did not do so for all the nations,
	ומשפטים בל ידעום הללו יה	and they do not know the regulations. Hallelujah!

---

[18] Reinhard Kratz is a recent example, who cites numerous other authors. "Nur hier [Ps 119:1] begegnet wie in 1,2 der Ausdruck *twrt yhwh*; 19,15 hat zum Abschluß die Wurzel *hgh* wie 1,2 (*whgywn lby lpnyk*), 119,1 ist eingeleitet mit *'šry* wie 1,1, eröffnet auch hier einen akrostischen Durchgang von Alef bis Taw (mit der Wurzel *'bd* im letzten Vers 119,176 wie 1,6) und verbindet wie 1,1f Tora und Wegmetapher (*tmymy drk, hhlkym btwrt yhwh*)." Kratz, "Die Tora Davids," 8.

[19] "Ps 147,15.18 vollzieht zum einen durch die in beiden Versen gleiche Formulierung *šlḥ* + *dbr* die im Horizont von Sir 24 und Bar 3,9–44 zu interpretierende Identifikation von *dbr* = Schöpfungsordnung und *dbr* = Offenbarungs-Tora – beide als Konsequenz/ Ausdruck von JHWHs Königsherrschaft. Zugleich wird dieser *dbr* konkretisiert als *hqjm wmšptjm*, d. h. als die konkrete Tora Israels (vgl. Dtn 4,8)." Erich Zenger, "Daß alles Fleisch den Namen seiner Heiligung segne," *Biblische Zeitschrift* 41 (1997): 19.

In addition to the introduction and conclusion, the theme of Torah also figures prominently in psalms that are part of the structuring arrangement of the Psalter, such as 19, 73, 89, 94, 111, and 112. Psalm 19 is the centerpiece of a group of psalms (15–24) that are concentrically arranged, and this group of psalms has multiple lexical and thematic links with Pss 1, 2, and 119.[20] Psalms 73 and 89, which both include verses that emphasize Torah observance, are the first and last psalms of the third division of the Psalter and therefore frame the third book.[21] David Howard argues that Ps 94 "serves as an appropriate hinge between the early part of book 4—which raises many questions about life's purpose and God's relationship with his people—and the middle part of the book, in which unfettered praise of Yhwh the king breaks forth."[22] Psalm 94 contains one of the few verses outside of Ps 119 that depicts YHWH (in this verse יה) as the one who teaches Torah to his followers:

| Ps 94:12 | אשרי הגבר אשר תיסרנו יה | *Blessed is the man whom you admonish, O YH,* |
| | ומתורתך תלמדנו | *and from your Torah you teach him.* |

The similarities between this verse and many verses in Ps 119 are striking, including the macarism. The following two verses provide another striking example:

Ps 94:17	לולי יהוה עזרתה לי	*If YHWH had not been my help,*
	כמעט שכנה דומה נפשי	*my soul would have quickly lain down in silence.*
Ps 119:92	לולי תורתך שעשעי	*If your Torah had not been my delight,*
	אז אבדתי בעניי	*then I would have perished in my affliction.*

Like many other verses in Ps 119 that substitute Torah in place of God, v. 92 substitutes Torah in place of YHWH's help.[23] It is also

---

[20] For a discussion of this group of psalms and its relationship to Torah see Miller, "Kingship, Torah Obedience, and Prayer."

[21] For a discussion of Ps 73 and its relationship to Torah see Walter Brueggemann and Patrick D. Miller, "Psalm 73 as a Canonical Marker," *JSOT* 72 (1996): 45–55. On Ps 89 see Mays, "The Place of the Torah-Psalms in the Psalter."

[22] David M. Howard, "Psalm 94 among the Kingship-of-Yhwh Psalms," *CBQ* 61 (1999): 668.

[23] This statement must be understood in light of the discussion of similar substitutions in chapters 2 and 4. In isolation, this surface feature of the text (the substitution) would not be sufficient evidence to argue that the author of Ps 119 was elevating the

noteworthy—and likely not a coincidence—that the author of Ps 94 uses the root ש.ע.ע, which is one of the favorite terms of the author of Ps 119. "Your compassions delight my soul" (Ps 94:19 תנחומיך ישעשעו נפשי). The links between Pss 94 and 119 support the claim that Ps 119 is one of the latest layers of the composition of the Psalter, because, as Howard has shown, Ps 94 is one of the latest layers within Book IV.

Psalms 111 and 112, both acrostics, deserve further consideration, since they contribute to the concentric structure of Book V, which has Ps 119 at the center. Psalm 111 is a hymn of praise for YHWH's mighty acts (גדלים מעשי יהוה v. 2), his grace and mercy (חנון ורחום יהוה v. 4), and the establishment of his eternal covenant (צוה לעולם בריתו v. 9). Verse 10 concludes the psalm:

| Ps 111:10 | ראשית חכמה יראת יהוה | *The beginning of wisdom is the fear of YHWH.* |
| | שכל טוב לכל עשיהם | *There is good insight for all who do them.* |

The plural suffix "them" in the second stich poses a problem and is interpreted in various ways. The LXX has a feminine singular pronoun, which refers to "wisdom," and many commentators follow the Greek on this point. The nearest plural antecedent in the MT is "his precepts" (פקודיו v. 7), and in my opinion, reading "precepts" as the antecedent is the proper interpretation, which indicates that the author of Ps 111 is arguing that it is wise to obey God's precepts. Psalm 112:1 supports this interpretation, since the motif of the fear of YHWH stitches the two psalms together and also characterizes the God-fearer as one who delights in the commandments:

| Ps 112:1 | אשרי איש ירא את יהוה | *Blessed is the man who fears YHWH,* |
| | במצותיו חפץ מאד | *who delights greatly in his commandments.* |

Psalms 111 and 112 are paired as "twin psalms."[24] Psalm 112 repeats the attributes of God that are praised in Ps 111 and praises the righteous who display the same character traits. For example, just as

---

status of Torah; however, due to the repetition of this phenomenon, it cannot be dismissed as coincidence.

[24] Walther Zimmerli, "Zwillingspsalmen," in *Wort, Leid und Gottesspruch*, Forschung zur Bibel, vol. 2, ed. J. Schreiner 105–13 (Würzburg: Echter, 1972).

YHWH is gracious (Ps 111:4), so also the righteous should be gracious (Ps 112:4). The description in Ps 112 uses the same vocabulary as Ps 111 and follows the same order. Based on the pattern in Ps 111, the author of Ps 112 composes an encomium about the one who delights in God's commandments. There are numerous thematic and lexical links between Ps 112 and Pss 1, 19, and 119.[25] For example, Pss 1, 112, and 119 all begin with אשרי and the root א.ב.ד occurs in the last verse of all three psalms.

5.2.3. Zenger's Proposal

It is clear that the theme of Torah is important in the composition of the Psalter as a book. There is broad scholarly consensus on this point, but there is less consensus on how the data should be interpreted. Because Book V is part of the final editing of the Psalter, it is one of the keys to understanding the message of the book as a whole. Zenger describes the structure of Book V as a concentric arrangement, in which Ps 119 is framed by three layers that he summarizes in the following table:[26]

R A		A		R A
107, 108–10, 111 and 112	113–118	119	120–136, 137	138–144, 145
David (eschatological/ messianic)	Exodus (Pesach)	Torah (Shabuoth)	Zion (Sukkoth)	David (eschatological/ messianic)

(R = royal psalm; A = acrostic psalm)

---

[25] Various scholars have noted the connections between Pss 1, 19b, and 119. "Nur in Ps 112,1 begegnet noch das 'šry (h)'yš von 1,1; es ist hier entsprechend Ps 111 im Akrostichon von Alef ('šry) bis Taw (t'wt rš'ym t'bd) durchgeführt, das Ps 1 mit dem ersten und lezten Wort nur andeutet; vgl. auch… [the list continues]." Kratz, "Die Tora Davids," 10. There are many other examples; see the bibliography for Cole, Mays, Pinto, and Zenger.

[26] Martin Leuenberger grants that Ps 119 is difficult to integrate into the structure of the fifth book but claims that Zenger makes the problem into a virtue without solving the difficulty. "Wenn nun Zenger allerdings die Not zur Tugend macht, indem er 119 schlicht ins Zentrum stellt, löst das noch keine sachlichen oder kompsitionellen Probleme…." Leuenberger, *Konzeptionen des Königtums Gottes im Psalter*, 275.

The following table highlights the concentric arrangement:

A	107			
B		108–110 + 111–112		
C			113–118	Exodus
			119	Torah
C'			120–136 + 137	Zion
B'		138–144 + 145		
A'	145			

Zenger argues for this arrangement by noting "structural signals" in Book V and draws several conclusions.[27] Psalms 111 and 112 "are the response to the oracles of Psalm 110.... The composition directs the reader to see in the *'îš* of Psalm 112 the king whom YHWH has called to his side in Psalm 110."[28] In the center of Book V, "Psalm 119 is a prayer for a life according to the Torah which is the precondition for the advent of the universal reign of the God of the Exodus and of Zion celebrated in the fifth book of psalms (God of the Exodus: Pss 113–118; God of Zion: Pss. 120–136, 137)."[29] Psalm 119 "is a prayer for the grace to keep and love the Torah as the fundamental law of the announced and praised kingdom of God, so that the kingdom may come. In terms of the literary form it is an individual who is speaking here. But in terms of the compositional context, those praying are from Israel *and* the nations."[30] The psalms of Book V are "meant to be recited/meditated upon as a 'spiritual pilgrimage' to Zion which is the seat of the universal king YHWH and of the God of Sinai who teaches his Torah from Zion."[31] And the sequence at the center of Book V "is meant to be a meditative actualization of the canonical history of the origin of Israel (Pss 113–118: the Exodus; Ps 119: Sinai; Pss 120–135: entry into the Promised Land with Zion/Jerusalem as the heart of the land)."[32] Thus, according to Zenger those who meditate on the sequence at the center of Book V as a "spiritual pilgrimage" appropriate the psalms for their own lives. Zenger's hermeneutic is a "spiritualization" of the Psalter, and he argues that the singing of YHWH's praise functions as

---

[27] Zenger, "The Composition and Theology of the Fifth Book of Psalms," 88.
[28] Zenger, "The Composition and Theology of the Fifth Book of Psalms," 91.
[29] Zenger, "The Composition and Theology of the Fifth Book of Psalms," 98.
[30] Zenger, "The Composition and Theology of the Fifth Book of Psalms," 99.
[31] Zenger, "The Composition and Theology of the Fifth Book of Psalms," 100.
[32] Zenger, "The Composition and Theology of the Fifth Book of Psalms," 101.

the deliverance for the one singing, similar to the function of song of the three youngsters in the fire in Dan 3 (LXX).

> This is also the hermeneutic, which the final "hallel" creates for the entire book of Psalms: the Psalms are... the book of the praises of the God of the Torah and of the provident, good king of the world. They are the prayers, in which the poor and oppressed find the strength to rely on YHWH – and thus to become a community of the pious, where the kingdom of God can break in and dawn...[33]

On the one hand, Zenger's spiritualization or appropriation of the Psalter is unfalsifiable; that is, any reader may appropriate the Psalter however they wish. On the other hand, Zenger is making a historical claim, namely that psalms were appropriated by the pious living in the last centuries of the pre-Christian era.[34] There is evidence within the Psalter that it was meant to be appropriated; for example, that the prayer and praise in the Psalter were meant to serve either as a supplement or a substitute for the cult:

Ps 141:2   תכון תפלתי קטרת לפניך   *May my prayer be arranged as an incense offering before you,*

משאת כפי מנחת ערב   *the lifting up of my hands as the evening obligation.*[35]

Millard notes that the theology of Jochanan ben Zakkai, which depicts prayer and good works as substitutes for the cult after its cessation in 70 C.E., already occurs here in the Psalter.[36] For Zenger, the appropriation or meditation on the psalms by a group of people shapes the group into a community of believers that "actualizes" God's kingdom,

---

[33] "Das ist auch die Hermeneutik, die das Schlußhallel für das ganze Psalmenbuch entwirft: Die Psalmen sind... das Buch der Preisungen des Gottes der Tora und des fürsorglichen guten Weltkönigs. Sie sind die Gebete, in denen Arme und Bedrängte die Kraft finden, auf JHWH zu setzen – und so zu einer Gemeinschaft der Frommen (*qhl ḥsjdjm*) zu werden, wo das Gottesreich ein- und anbrechen kann..." Zenger, "Daß alles Fleisch den Namen seiner Heiligung segne," 20.

[34] Zenger does not always distinguish between the two types of discussion—that is, between his historical claims and the current relevance of the Psalter.

[35] On the "lifting up of the hands" see the comments on Ps 119:48 at p. 41.

[36] "Die Theologie im Umfeld von Jochanan ben Zakkai, die Wohltaten und Gebet als möglichen Ersatz für Opfer ansieht und damit die Überlebensgrundlage des Judentums als religiöser Gemeinschaft nach der Zweiten Tempelzerstörung 70 n. Chr bildet, ist also im Judentum vorher bereits angelegt. Als eine dieser Ersatzfunktionen für den wirklichen Gottesdienstbesuch im Tempel können wir das Lesen des Psalters annehmen, da, so die Theologie etwa von Ps 141, Gebete Opfer ersetzen." Millard, *Die Komposition des Psalters*, 229.

and according to Ps 119, Torah observance is a precondition for this kingdom.

Like any attempt to interpret the Psalter as a book, Zenger faces the difficulty of synthesizing a considerable amount of data. Zenger's attempt to correlate the theme of God's kingdom with the emphasis on Torah illustrates the difficulty. Part of the message of the Psalter is that God will someday judge the wicked, thereby establishing his kingdom and instituting the justice for which the psalmists pray. Yet if Torah observance "is the precondition for the advent of the universal reign of the God" as Zenger argues, then one conclusion of his interpretation is that the obedience of the righteous is a precondition for the judgment of the wicked.[37] Clearly, this is not part of the message of the Psalter. If the Psalter does not teach that Torah observance is a precondition of God's reign, how should these themes be related? This question is important, not only for establishing the message of the Psalter but also for establishing the place of Ps 119 within the book.

5.2.4. *Psalm 119's Contribution to the Theology of the Psalter*

The juxtaposition of Pss 1 and 2, which together serve as an introduction to the Psalter, demonstrates that these two themes are central concerns. In a recent article Robert Cole lists the many lexical connections between the first two psalms, and concludes that they both describe the same person. "It becomes increasingly clear that Psalms 1 and 2 at the head of the Psalter do not present two different themes of wisdom and/or Torah and kingship respectively, but rather *both* depict the ideal kingly warrior who enjoys complete domination of his enemies."[38] Similarly, Mitchell, who emphasizes the messianic message of the Psalter, equates the two. Mitchell claims that the figure in Ps 1, "who does not associate with evildoers, who meditates in YHWH's Torah, who is like a fruitful tree, who succeeds in all he does, is really the same figure as the hero of Ps ii; that is YHWH's *mashiah*."[39] These

---

[37] Zenger does not claim that this is part of the message, yet it seems to be an unavoidable conclusion of his various arguments. Although I do not know, I assume that Zenger recognizes the tension, but I do not see where he specifically addresses the tension.

[38] Robert L. Cole, "An Integrated Reading of Psalms 1 and 2," *JSOT* 98 (2002): 80.

[39] David C. Mitchell, "Lord, Remember David: G. H. Wilson and the Message of the Psalter," *VT* 56 (2006): 542–43.

arguments are similar to Zenger's claims about "the man" of Ps 112; that is, Zenger identifies the man of Ps 112 with the king of Ps 110.

Lexical links, repetitions of motifs, and juxtapositions do indicate that there is a relationship between the motifs, but they do not support the conclusions described in the previous paragraph. Juxtaposition does not necessarily imply equation, and one of the themes is not necessarily prioritized by the juxtaposition. Jesper Høgenhaven also interprets Pss 1 and 2 as a unity, but he describes it as a "double theological introduction"—the ethical (Ps 1) and the eschatological (Ps 2).[40] "Psalm 1 sees the righteous in opposition to the wicked, those whose delight is not in the *tora* of Yahweh, and looks forward to the final divine judgment. In Psalm 2 our view is broadened to encompass the great drama of the Messianic age to come."[41] A "double introduction" is more consistent with the message of the Psalter than the conclusion that one of the two themes is more important than the other.

Cole, Mitchell, and Zenger all fail to account for the paradigmatic function of Pss 1 and 112, which is also part of the rhetoric of Ps 119, and this oversight weakens their respective arguments. One might argue that the "hero" of Ps 2 fits the paradigm of "the man" in Ps 1—or that hero is the successful, righteous man *par excellence*. But that would be a different claim than suggesting he is "really the same figure" as Mitchell does. There is a suasive goal in the first psalm, specifically that the reader should choose the path of the righteous; Mitchell's claim that the figure in Ps 1 is the Messiah of Ps 2 obscures this rhetorical goal, which is not only important for Ps 1 but for the Psalter as a whole, including Pss 19, 112, and 119.[42]

Accounting for the paradigmatic function of various psalms, which I have argued is paramount in Ps 119, allows one to relate the themes of the Psalter as follows: The exemplary student of Torah, portrayed throughout the Psalter, internalizes Torah, which teaches that God desires justice; thus he believes that God will ultimately judge the wicked by divine decree and establish the kingdom of God, righting

---

[40] Jesper Høgenhaven, "The Opening of the Psalter: A Study in Jewish Theology," *Scandinavian Journal of the Old Testament* 15 (2001): 179.

[41] Høgenhaven, "The Opening of the Psalter: A Study in Jewish Theology," 178.

[42] Patrick Miller notes that "the man" of Ps 1 is anyone. Patrick D. Miller, "The Psalter as a Book of Theology," in *Psalms in Community*, ed. Harold W. Attridge and Margot E. Fassler, Society of Biblical Literature Symposium Series, vol. 25 (Leiden: Brill, 2004), 91. This suasive goal is least explicit in Ps 19, but when Ps 19 is read together with Ps 18, the rhetoric is then clear.

the wrongs of the present world. This does not exclude the possibility that God will judge individuals in the present or that individuals who follow Torah can actualize God's kingdom in their own lives, but these serve only as precursors to the messianic kingdom. The ideal Torah student serves God in fear (Ps 2:11) and hopes for God's coming kingdom.[43] Meditating on Torah thus leads the righteous to praise God despite the current delay of justice, because justice will prevail for all who trust in him (כל חוסי בו Ps 2:12). All of the prayers and praises of the Psalter can be incorporated into this framework, and because the latest redactional layers, especially Ps 119, portray an exemplary Torah student, the collection of prayers and praises in the book of Psalms is intended to function paradigmatically for the righteous. The conception of Torah in Ps 119 is consistent with the conception of Torah throughout the entire Psalter—not only consistent but mutually reinforcing.

5.3. The Place of Psalm 119 in the Hebrew Bible

The arguments of Reinhard Kratz support the conclusion that Ps 119 is part of the final editing of the Psalter, and his interpretation raises the issue of the relationship of the Psalter with the rest of the Hebrew Bible. Because he addresses the Psalter as a whole, much of his discussion overlaps with the previous section of this study. I include his contribution in this section, since he argues that the introduction (especially Ps 1) as well as the five-part division both relate the Psalter to a literary entity outside of itself, specifically the Torah of YHWH, and this raises the issue of the relationship between the Psalter and the rest of the Hebrew Bible. His description of the Torah of YHWH as a complex, expansive concept involves several steps, which I summarize in the following paragraphs.

According to Kratz, the formulation of Ps 1:2, 3 is supplied from Josh 1:7, 8 and Jer 17:5–8.[44] Joshua 1 describes the Torah of Moses, which is primarily Deuteronomy and secondarily the entire Pentateuch;

---

[43] Kratz notes that in the latter part of the Psalter David loses his historical role and functions as a model of righteousness Kratz. "Die Tora Davids," 22–23.

[44] "Bekanntlich ist die Formulierung von V. 2b und V. 3b aus Jos 1,7–9 (V. 8), in V. 3a (mit dem Gegenbild in V. 4) aus Jer 17,5–8 (V. 8) gespeist." Kratz, "Die Tora Davids," 6.

however, Ps 1 uses the label "Torah of YHWH" rather than "Torah of Moses." This more inclusive label, which is suited for the purpose of the Psalter, is used in Chronicles and may be borrowed by the psalmist from 1 Chron 22:12: "Surely YHWH will give you understanding and insight, and he will give you command over Israel, that you should keep the Torah of YHWH your God."[45] This verse from 1 Chronicles assumes its parallel verse in 1 Kgs 2:3, which in turn sounds like the passage in Josh 1:7–9, and all of these details point to a late layer in the composition of the Psalter.

> In addition, the expression "Torah of Jhwh" in Ps 1... may have experienced an expansion of meaning, which in Chronicles was not yet intended, that in certain cases is oriented to the sources of the work of Chronicles and therefore, aside from the Pentateuch, included the preexisting, authoritative writings of the later part of the canon, the prophets (Nebiim), which were collected in the "Book of the Kings of Israel and Judah" (cf. 2 Chron 35:26f.), i.e., what is in Josh – 2 Kgs and the latter prophets.
>
> Through the double citation from Josh 1:7f. and Jer 17:5–8 in any case, they [that is, Joshua and Jeremiah] are viewed as a unity, and in addition the citation of Josh 1:8 in Ps 1:2 brings the citation of Josh 1:7 at the end of the prophets in Mal 3:22 clearly to mind. Psalm 1 intentionally uses the term "Torah of YHWH," which has a somewhat broader scope [broader than "Torah of Moses"] and increases its authority, and thereby points to an entity outside of the Psalter, surely the Pentateuch and in all likelihood also already the collection of the Former and Latter Prophets....[46]

---

[45] אַךְ יִתֶּן לְךָ יהוה שֵׂכֶל וּבִינָה וִיצַוְּךָ עַל יִשְׂרָאֵל וְלִשְׁמוֹר אֶת תּוֹרַת יהוה אֱלֹהֶיךָ Several details of this verse are open to interpretation, including the semantics of the words "understanding" (שכל, which may also be translated "success") and "command" (צוה, for the meaning "to give command" see BDB, 845), as well as the syntactic relationships between the clauses. Deciding between these possibilities is not essential for this study, but I mention it here since the interpretation affects how one views the possible relationship between Ps 1 and 1 Chron 22.

[46] "Daneben könnte der Ausdruck »Tora Jhwhs« in Ps 1...eine in der Chronik selbst so wohl noch nicht intendierte Bedeutungserweiterung erfahren haben, die sich gegebenenfalls am Quellenbestand des chronistischen Werkes orientiert und also neben dem Pentateuch die im »Buch der Könige von Israel und Juda« gesammelten (vgl. 2 Chr. 35,26f) d.h. die in Jos—2 Kön und den hinteren Propheten vorliegenden autoritativen Schriften des späteren Kanonteils »Propheten« (Nebiim) mit umfaßt. Im Doppelzitat aus Jos 1,7f und Jer 17,5–8 jedenfalls werden sie als Einheit betrachtet, und im übrigen erinnert das Zitat von Jos 1,8 in Ps 1,2 sehr an das Zitat von Jos 1,7 am Schluß von Nebiim in Mal 3,22. Ps 1 verwendet bewußt den etwas weiter gefaßten, die Autorität steigernden Begriff »Torah Jhwhs« und weist damit auf eine Größe außerhalb des Psalters, sicher den Pentateuch und womöglich auch schon auf die Sammlung der vorderen und hinteren Propheten...." Kratz, "Die Tora Davids," 7.

Zenger contends that Kratz has brought the ideas of the Psalter—or at least the fifth division of the Psalter—into "too close a relationship to the theology of Chronicles or to the theology of the historical work of the Chronicler."[47] Yet even if direct textual dependence between Ps 1 and 1 Chron 22 cannot be proven, the broader claims of Kratz are still defensible. Furthermore, Kratz is arguing that the Psalter extends the meaning of "Torah of YHWH" beyond what is meant by this phrase in Chronicles, since in Chronicles it is essentially coreferential with the "Torah of Moses," that is, the Pentateuch. "In fact, the result allows one to conclude that the 'Torah of Moses' from Josh 1:7f. has developed in Ps 1 to the 'Torah of YHWH,' not only in the sense of Chronicles but also in consideration of the following Torah passages in the Psalter, and the conception of Torah in this way also fulfills a programmatic function within the Psalter."[48] This function is in part to establish the behavior of the righteous; that is, the literary entity that the successful righteous man has in his heart and mouth—the Torah of YHWH—directs his behavior.[49] The literary entity "includes primarily the Pentateuch and in addition the later part of the canon, the 'Prophets,' which is based on the Torah."[50] The various and diverse

---

[47] Zenger, "The Composition and Theology of the Fifth Book of Psalms," 88.

[48] "Vielmehr läßt der Befund darauf schließen, daß die »Torah des Mose« aus Jos 1,7f in Ps 1 nicht nur im chronistischen Sinne, sondern eben auch in Rücksicht auf die folgenden Tora-Stellen im Psalter zur »Tora Jhwhs« geworden ist und der Torabegriff so auch innerhalb des Psalters eine programmatische Funktion erfüllt." Kratz, "Die Tora Davids," 8.

[49] "Nach allem umfaßt die »Tora Jhwhs« in Ps 1 mehr als nur »Gesetz« und »Gesetzesgehorsam«, mehr als bloße Gesetzlichkeit und Vergeltungslehre. Tora Jhwhs, das ist für Ps 1 und in seinem Sinne für den ganzen Psalter eine literarische, in Herz und Mund zu bewegende Größe, die den individuellen Lebensvollzug des glücklich gepriesenen Gerechten in verschiedener Hinsicht grundlegend bestimmt, persönlich in seiner das ganze Leben umgreifenden Relation zur Tora (Ps 19; 119), kosmologisch in der Artikulation der Himmelskunde von der Herrlichkeit Gottes (Ps 19), sozial im Konflikt zwischen Gerechten und Frevlern (Ps 37 und 94), kultisch im Sprechen des Lobpreises (Ps 40) und geschichtlich im Konnex mit der Erwählung des Volkes Israel und des davidischen Königs (Ps 78; 89; 105). Im Lesen und Meditieren der literarischen Größe »Tora Jhwhs« eröffnen sich dem schriftgelehrten Gerechten von Ps 1 alle diese Lebensbezüge, und eben davon, von den Wirkungen und Prägungen der Tora im Leben des Grechten, handelt in der Sicht von Ps 1 der Psalter. So sind Tora Jhwhs und Psalter zwar nich dasselbe Buch, aber in der Sache kongruent, wenn nicht identisch. Nach Ps 1 mach der Psalter explizit, was Pentateuch (und Propheten) als Torah Jhwhs für das Leben eines Grechten implizieren." Kratz, "Die Tora Davids," 11.

[50] "Das Proömium wie die doxologische Fünfteilung gehören somit zu einer der letzten Bearbeitungen des Psalters. Beide beziehen den Psalter auf eine literarische Größe außerhalb seiner selbst, die »Tora Jhwhs«, die in der Hauptsache den Pentateuch und zusätzlich den seinerseits auf die Tora bezogenen späteren Kanonteil

themes of the Psalter are joined in "a unified, albeit extremely complex, theological Torah concept."[51]

As Seeligmann notes, "it is an important innovation when the entire complex of instructions, together with the historical frame in which it is placed, appears with the claim to be Torah."[52] This "entire complex" is assumed by the author of Ps 119 and by the compiler of the Psalter. Since the codex had not yet been invented, the various texts that constituted the literary entity could not be collected in a single, physical "book." Nevertheless, there was an awareness of a literary entity, constituted by a group of sacred, authoritative texts, whose authors self-consciously related their own writings to other texts in the group. This is not to say that every component of the literary entity was finalized. Sara Japhet observes that an authoritative collection of texts can exist without the precise form of the texts being established: "In a paradoxical way what may be called 'a religion of the book' was not in fact 'a religion of the letter.'"[53]

The paragraphs above include various words that I have largely avoided, such as *text, literary entity, Pentateuch, canon,* and so on. As noted in chapter 4, the author of Ps 119 also avoided words for writing and scrolls, and I argue there that such words would have limited the scope of Torah to a literary entity. That limitation would have undermined the author's suasive goals. At first, there may seem to be a contradiction between the claims of Kratz that the Psalter relates to a literary entity, including both the Pentateuch and the Prophets, but

---

»Propheten« umfaßt." Kratz, "Die Tora Davids. Psalm I und die doxologische Fünfteilung des Psalters," 32.

[51] "So verschieden und vielfältig all diese Themen sind, mit Ps 1 und den Doxologien, gelesen im und für den Kontext des Psalters, verbinden sie sich zu einem einheitlichen, wenn auch höchst komplexen theologischen Tora-Konzept." Kratz, "Die Tora Davids," 32.

[52] "Eine wichtige Neuerung bedeutet es, wenn der ganze Komplex von Vorschriften samt dem historischen Rahmen, in den er hineingestellt ist, mit dem Anspruch auftritt, Torah zu sein." I. L. Seeligmann, "Voraussetzungen der Midraschexegese," VTSup, vol. 1 (1953), 177–78. This is similar to the comments by Lindars on the use of the word "Torah" in Deuteronomy: "The choice of *twrh* to designate the whole corpus is thus dictated by the fact that the code is regarded as a single and complete entity, given by God through the mediation of Moses for men to ponder and lay to heart." Barnabas Lindars, "Torah in Deuteronomy," in *Words and Meanings: Essays Presented to David Winton Thomas*, ed. P. R. Ackroyd and B. Lindars (Cambridge: Cambridge University Press, 1968), 130.

[53] Sara Japhet, "Law and 'The Law' in Ezra-Nehemiah," in *Proceedings of the Ninth World Congress of Jewish Studies* (Jerusalem: Magnes Press, 1988), 115.

there is not necessarily a contradiction. The conception of Torah in Ps 119 certainly includes texts; however, it cannot be limited to texts. Psalm 119 refers both to a collection of stipulations and to promises about how those stipulations will affect someone's well-being. The laws function as instruction about the relationship between human beings and God, yet Torah is established in the heavens (v. 89) and has no limits (v. 96). Thus, my conclusions fit well with the "programmatic, complex Torah-concept" that Kratz describes.

In addition to the rhetorical reasons for avoiding any reference to specific texts, the poetic features of Ps 119 make it difficult to demonstrate any textual relationships. Nevertheless there are a few examples that indicate the author of Ps 119 was using passages from elsewhere in the Hebrew Bible; these deserve consideration. Chapter 2 begins with a discussion of Ps 119:19; however, in chapter 2, I did not address the change in word order.

Ps 119:19b	אל תסתר ממני מצוותיך	*Do not hide **from me** your commandments*
Ps 27:9a	אל תסתר פניך ממני	*Do not hide your face **from me***
Ps 69:18a	ואל תסתר פניך מעבדך	*Do not hide your face **from your servant***
Ps 102:3a	אל תסתר פניך ממני	*Do not hide your face **from me***
Ps 143:7b	אל תסתר פניך ממני	*Do not hide your face **from me***

In each of the examples outside of Ps 119 the word order is verb, object, prepositional phrase (VOP); in v. 19b the order is VPO. Beentjes shows that this sort of inversion is a technique used when authors are alluding to another text.[54] One example is found in Ezekiel's use of the Holiness Code. Ezekiel 34:27a states, "and the land will give its produce" (והארץ תתן יבולה; word order SVO); this verse draws on Leviticus 26:4b, which states, "and the land gave its produce" (ונתנה הארץ יבולה; word order VSO).[55] Beentjes gives numerous examples in a variety of ancient sources, and he states "By this *deviating* model he [the author] attains a moment of extra attention in the listener (or

[54] Pancratius Beentjes, "Discovering a New Path of Intertextuality: Inverted Quotations and Their Dynamics," in *Literary Structure and Rhetorical Strategies in the Hebrew Bible*, ed. J. de Waard, L. J. de Regt, and J. P. Fokkelman (Winona Lake, Ind.: Eisenbrauns, 1996), 31–49. See also Moshe Seidel, "Parallels Between Isaiah and Psalms," [Hebrew] *Sinai* 38 (1955–56): 149–72, 229–40, 272–80, 335–55.

[55] See Michael A. Lyons, *From Law to Prophecy: Ezekiel's Use of the Holiness Code*, Library of Hebrew Bible / Old Testament Studies, vol. 507 (New York: T & T Clark, 2009), 71.

the reader), because the latter hears something else than the traditional words."[56] It seems likely that this phenomenon would have been
used by authors who were interacting with other written texts; but this
could be a purely oral phenomenon.

The use of the Priestly Blessing in Ps 119 provides more plausible
evidence that the author was using written texts.[57] There are details
in Ps 119:132 that are based on a visual similarity between the words,
which cannot be explained by the recitation of the Priestly Blessing.[58]
Verse 132 begins, "Turn to me, and be gracious to me." This sequence
of letters is almost identical to a sequence of letters in the Priestly
Blessing (both underlined in the following table), but the syntax and
meaning are different.

Num 6:25	פָּנָיו אֵלֶיךָ וִיחֻנֶּךָּ	יָאֵר יהוה
Ps 119:132	כְּמִשְׁפָּט	פְּנֵה אֵלַי וְחָנֵּנִי

In Numbers 6, "his face" (פָּנָיו) is the object of the verb "cause to shine"
(יָאֵר). In Ps 119 the corresponding letters are a verb, and together with
the preposition could be translated "face me." The following translation highlights the similarities between the verses:

Num 6:25   *May YHWH cause his face to shine upon you, and be gra-*
               cious to you.
Ps 119:132   *Face me, and be gracious to me.*

Using this sequence of letters with a different syntactic relationship
supports the argument that the author of Ps 119 was using a text, but
the text could have been limited to the Priestly Blessing itself—that is,
without any necessary connection to the book of Numbers. The silver
amulet discovered at Ketef Hinnom shows that the Priestly Blessing
was used without a literary context.[59]

However, additional evidence indicates that the author of Ps 119
was using the text of the Priestly Blessing as well as its context in

---

[56] Pancratius Beentjes, "Discovering a New Path of Intertextuality: Inverted Quotations and Their Dynamics," 49, italics original.

[57] Fishbane notes that Ps 119 uses the Priestly Blessing; see Michael Fishbane, *The
Garments of Torah: Essays in Biblical Hermeneutics*, Indiana Studies in Biblical Literature (Bloomington, IN: Indiana University Press, 1989), 66.

[58] On the "performance" of texts in the ancient world, see the discussion of David
M. Carr, *Writing on the Tablet of the Heart* (Oxford: Oxford University Press, 2005).

[59] Gabriel Barkay et al., "The Challenges of Ketef Hinnom: Using Advanced Technologies to Reclaim the Earliest Biblical Texts and Their Context," *Near Eastern
Archaeology* 66 (2003): 162–71.

Num 6, specifically the word "name" at the end of Ps 119:132. Verse 132 ends with the following phrase: "according to what is due to those who love your name" (כמשפט לאהבי שמך). Thus, there is a lexical connection between Num 6:27 and Ps 119:132; the underlining in the following table highlights the words that are used in Ps 119:60.

Num 6:25	יאר יהוה פניו אליך	May YHWH cause his face to shine upon you
Num 6:26	ישא יהוה פניו אליך	May YHWH lift up his face to you
Num 6:27	ושמו את שמי על בני ישראל	So will they put my name on the children of Israel.[60]

Num 6:27 explains the function of the Priestly Blessing and together with verses 22 and 23 provides a framework that integrates it into the book of Numbers. Since the Priestly Blessing ends at Num 6:26, the use of Num 6:27 shows that the author of Ps 119 was most likely using the blessing from its context of Numbers 6.

The use of the Priestly Blessing is the best evidence that the author of Ps 119 borrowed a passage from a written text. This observation corresponds well with the conclusion of Kratz that the Psalter relates to a literary entity outside of itself; furthermore, this literary entity is the object of study for the paradigmatic student who is portrayed in Ps 119. In my opinion, all of the evidence supports the conclusion that Ps 119 is part of one of the latest redactions of the Psalter and the Hebrew Bible altogether; at least we can say that none of the evidence contradicts this conclusion.

Alexander Rofé argues that an emphasis on Torah study is a relatively late development, saying it "does not reflect the ideal of leadership of the Dtr school in any phase of its existence."[61] According to Rofé, leaders are evaluated in the Deuteronomistic History on the basis of their obedience to Torah, not their study of Torah.[62] The praise of Joshua (Josh 1:8) as one who studies Torah day and night demonstrates the

---

[60] Having the name of God "put upon them" is a figurative expression indicating a special relationship. The concept occurs in various configurations throughout the Hebrew Bible; one example is 2 Chron 7:14, "If my people, who have my name called upon them..."

[61] Alexander Rofé, "The Piety of the Torah-Disciples at the Winding-Up of the Hebrew Bible," in *Bibel in jüdischer und christlicher Tradition: Festschrift für Johann Maier zum 60. Geburtstag*, ed. Helmut Merklein (Frankfurt: Anton Hain, 1993), 80.

[62] Rofé, "The Piety of the Torah-Disciples at the Winding-Up of the Hebrew Bible," 79.

incorporation of a "later Jewish ideal" that is also present in Ps 1.[63]
By "later" Rofé means it is later than the composition of the Deuter-
onomistic History, and it corresponds with the "winding-up of the
Hebrew Bible" when the function of prophecy—"the Lord's address to
Israel"—was transferred to Torah and its students.[64]

It is impossible to be more precise, given the literary shape of Ps 119
and the lack of any historical references. Claiming that Ps 119 comes
at or near the end of the composition of the Hebrew Bible raises the
question of the place of Ps 119 in developing Judaism. This is the focus
of the following section, and it reinforces the above arguments.

5.4. THE PLACE OF PSALM 119 IN DEVELOPING JUDAISM

How does Ps 119 fit into the trajectory of developing Judaism? By
raising this question, I do not mean to explore the history of Ps 119's
interpretation and appropriation in Judaism.[65] That discussion is
interesting as a distinct study, but the question I am raising is about
the composition of Ps 119 not its transmission history. Michael Fishbane argues that the "onset of classical Judaism" is marked by an
"axial transformation," which was a "movement from a culture based
on direct divine revelation to one based on their [texts] study and
reinterpretation."[66] In ancient Israel "sage-scribes" wrote the divine
revelation and thereby preserved it for future generations, but in classical Judaism "sage-scholars" extended the divine revelation through
interpretation.[67] Joseph Blenkinsopp makes a similar claim when he
states that what was once direct revelation to the prophet from God
himself became "inspired interpretation of Biblical texts. In other
words the exegete and theologian is now the prophet."[68] It should be
noted that scholars are not describing a sudden transformation. For

---

[63] Rofé, "The Piety of the Torah-Disciples at the Winding-Up of the Hebrew Bible,"
80.

[64] Rofé, "The Piety of the Torah-Disciples at the Winding-Up of the Hebrew Bible,"
84.

[65] As the earliest extant textual witnesses show, the interpretation of Ps 119 began
before the turn of the eras. See the discussion of the textual witnesses beginning on
p. 185.

[66] Michael Fishbane, *The Garments of Torah: Essays in Biblical Hermeneutics*, 65.

[67] Michael Fishbane, *The Garments of Torah: Essays in Biblical Hermeneutics*, 65.

[68] Joseph Blenkinsopp, *Prophecy and Canon* (Notre Dame: Notre Dame Press,
1977), 129.

example, when Fishbane uses terms such as "axial transformation," he may be trying to emphasize the importance of the transformation, but he is quite clear that there is considerable continuity between classical Judaism and the biblical period. In fact one of the central tenants of Fishbane's book *Biblical Interpretation in Ancient Israel* is that the methods of interpreting the Hebrew Bible that are in use in the post-biblical literature can be traced back into the biblical literature itself.[69]

Both scholars mentioned above point to the increased emphasis on the interpretation of texts in the Second Temple period as a foundation for later Rabbinic Judaism, and Fishbane finds evidence of this transition in Ps 119. He claims that the phrase "open my eyes" (גל עיני) in Ps 119:18 is a reuse of mantic terminology to form "a petition for divine aid in the interpretation of Scripture."[70] Regardless of whether or not this is a reuse of mantic terminology, it is a petition for understanding of God's word, and it implies an awareness that God's word is a source of authority. Of interest for this study is how Ps 119 fits into the trajectory that begins in biblical literature and culminates—via the Tannaim and Amoraim—in the two Talmudic corpora of Palestine and Babylon.

Eventually the sages who complied the Talmudic literature achieved a level of authority equal—or even above—Torah itself.

> The words of the sages are serious, because the one who transgresses their words is like the one who transgresses the words of the Torah. Indeed, the words of the sages are more serious than the words of the Torah, because in the words of Torah there are insignificant and serious [words], whereas the words of the sages are all serious.[71]

How did they achieve such authority? Initially their authority was based upon their interpretation of Scripture, and their methods of interpretation were developed from careful reading of Scripture itself. Seeligmann argues that "the oldest midrashic exegesis developed organically out of the uniqueness of the biblical literature."[72] Deissler

---

[69] Michael Fishbane, *Biblical Interpretation in Ancient Israel*, (Oxford: Clarendon Press, 1985).

[70] Michael Fishbane, *The Garments of Torah: Essays in Biblical Hermeneutics*, 66.

[71] חמורים דברי חכמים שכל העובר על דבריהם כעובר על דברי תורה ועוד חמורים דברי חכמים מדברי תורה שדברי תורה יש בהן קלות וחמורות ודברי חכמים כולן חמורות. (מדרש תנאים לדברים פרק יז פסוק יא) Midrash Tanaim on Deut 17:11.

[72] "… dass sich die älteste Midraschexegese organisch aus der Eigenart der biblischen Literatur entwickelt hat." I. L. Seeligmann, "Voraussetzungen der Midraschexegese," 151.

makes the same point. He notes that even if the term *"midrash"* in Chronicles describes a different phenomenon than later *"midrashim,"* the beginnings of the phenomenon must be sought in the history of the transmission of the Bible, and the literary character of the book of Chronicles testifies to that.[73] Additionally, at the beginning of the second century B.C.E. Ben Sira "testifies that at that time the Holy Scriptures were the quintessence of wisdom for the believing Israelite, who lived, thought, and spoke in and from them [the Scriptures]. The beginnings of such a posture must reach further back into the postexilic time."[74] Deissler lists the book of Chronicles and Ben Sira as examples of an "anthological style" that has its roots in the latest biblical books and is exemplified in the interpretative texts of the Dead Sea Scrolls.

Scholarship of the past century has described the trajectory to which I am referring in very different ways. For example, in 1907, Cornill contended that the Psalter provides a bridge between the Old Testament and the New Testament, because the piety of the Psalter shows that the rise of legalism did not entirely kill the "religious genius of Israel."[75] Alan Cooper rightly critiques this claim as nonsense, but then he continues: "the Book of Psalms *is* a 'building link'—not primarily between the Old and New Testaments, however, but between Israelite religions and *Judaism.*"[76]

Eric Meyers argues that indications of a transformation can be discerned in the period before the building of the second temple; locating the shift in the exilic or post-exilic period is much earlier than more recent scholarship. Meyers describes the era as "an epoch of continuity-with-change in the post-exilic period when prophecy

---

[73] "Selbst wenn der schon in II Chron (13,22; 24,27) auftretende Terminus 'Midrasch' nicht zur Kategorie der späteren 'Midraschim' zu zählen wäre, muß die Grundtendenz dieses Genus, im biblischen Überlieferungsstrom seinen Ansatz zu suchen, ihre längere Vorgeschichte haben, wie der literarische Charakter der Chronikbücher im ganzen ja auch bezeugt." Deissler, 25.

[74] "Jes Sir bezeugt also für den Anfang des 2. Jahrhunderts, daß damals die Heilige Schrift für den gläubigen Israeliten der Inbegriff all Weisheit war, er darum in und aus ihr lebte, dachte und redete. Die Anfänge einer solchen Haltung müssen weiter in die nachexilische Zeit hinaufreichen." Deissler, 26.

[75] C. H. Cornill, *Introduction to the Canonical Books of the Old Testament,* (London: Williams and Norgate, 1907), 399.

[76] Alan Cooper, "Biblical Studies and Jewish Studies," in *The Oxford Handbook of Jewish Studies,* ed. Martin Goodman, et al. (Oxford: Oxford University Press, 2002), 23, italics original.

declines."[77] He notes that in Hag 2:11 the prophet, using typical prophetic language (כה אמר יהוה צבאות), exhorts the people, "Ask the
priests for torah" (שאל נא את הכהנים תורה). A similar idiom occurs
in Mal 2:7, which states men will seek "torah" from the priests (ותורה
יבקשו מפיהו). Meyers claims that these verses indicate a shift in the
nuance of the word Torah, which "has moved from designating the
word of God, as in much of the prophetic literature, to designating the
regulations for specific cultic or ritual practices, as in the pentateuchal
literature."[78] Additionally, Meyers considers these phrases in Haggai
and Malachi to be predecessors of pěsaq dîn, which is a later rabbinic
phrase used to describe a halakhic ruling or adjudication, and even
labels the idioms "proto-rabbinic."[79] Meyers assumes that the priests
depicted in Haggai are interpreting texts, and because the prophet
sends people to the priests, Meyers argues that these passages show
a link between priests and prophets. For Meyers this is a preliminary
step towards later developments in which "the sages saw themselves
as heirs to the prophets."[80]

More recent critical scholarship, especially on the Pentateuch,
includes several different theories about the development of texts in
the Second Temple period. Jean-Louis Ska theorizes that the development of various texts was likely associated with a library of the second
temple.[81] David Carr argues that the Pentateuch arose as a central text
in the collection of texts that was used in the cultural education of the
elite, literate class of the Second Temple period.[82] Eckart Otto describes

---

[77] Eric Meyers, "The Use of Tôrâ in Haggai 2:11 and the Role of the Prophet in the
Restoration Community," in The Word of the Lord Shall go Forth: Essays in Honor of
David Noel Freedman in Celebration of his Sixtieth Birthday, ed. Carol L. Meyers and
M. O'Connor (Winona Lake, Ind.: Eisenbrauns, 1983), 70.

[78] Meyers, "The Use of Tôrâ in Haggai 2:11 and the Role of the Prophet in the
Restoration Community," 74.

[79] Meyers, "The Use of Tôrâ in Haggai 2:11 and the Role of the Prophet in the
Restoration Community," 71.

[80] Meyers, "The Use of Tôrâ in Haggai 2:11 and the Role of the Prophet in the
Restoration Community," 70.

[81] For an overview of his position see his article "From History Writing to Library
Building: The End of History and the Birth of the Book," in The Pentateuch as Torah:
New Models for Understanding its Promulgation and Acceptance, ed. Gary N. Knop-
pers and Bernard M. Levinson, 143–70. (Winona Lake: Eisenbrauns, 2007). See also
Jean-Louis Ska, Introduction to Reading the Pentateuch (Winona Lake: Eisenbrauns,
2006).

[82] David M. Carr, Writing on the Tablet of the Heart, (Oxford: Oxford University
Press, 2005).

the relationship between prophets and priest as an antagonistic one; he claims that the texts of the Hebrew Bible grow out of the various ways that this conflict was negotiated and resolved.[83]

Although various scholars frame the issues differently, the common thread in the above comments is an emphasis on texts. Thus, a relevant question for situating Ps 119 in relationship to the development of Judaism is how the author of Ps 119 related to texts. Deissler argues that the author uses Scripture to create Scripture. He interprets various locutions in Ps 119 by arguing that the author was borrowing from elsewhere in the Hebrew Bible and that the verse in Ps 119 must be understood in light of the ideas present in the original context.[84] The example of the Priestly Blessing discussed above supports Deissler's claim that the author was using Scripture to create Scripture, but in most cases a specific textual dependence cannot be demonstrated. Thus, Deissler's interpretation of individual verses in Ps 119 based on similar locutions elsewhere in the Bible is too far reaching. The function of what Deissler calls an "anthological style" is not primarily to import ideas from elsewhere in Scripture but to create a pious tone in the characterization of the speaker.

Studies on how and why biblical authors used antecedent texts have blossomed, especially since the work of Michael Fishbane, but many of the details of those studies are not helpful for analyzing how the author of Ps 119 used texts.[85] One reason that they are not helpful is that the various studies are often explaining how biblical authors exegete or

---

[83] Otto develops this argument in various works; for one of his most recent articles, see "Jeremia und die Tora. Ein nachexilischer Diskurs," in *Tora in der Hebräischen Bibel: Studien zur Redaktionsgeschichte und synchronen Logik diachroner Transformationen*. BZAR 7, 134–82. (Wiesbaden: Harrassowitz, 2007).

[84] Deissler is not the only scholar who makes this claim. For example, Hurvitz claims Ps 119 borrows the word "delights" (שעשעים) from Prov 8; however, his arguments are unconvincing. See my discussion of this in chapter 2, beginning on p. 50. The word occurs elsewhere in the Bible, including Ps 94, and there is no necessary literary dependence between Prov 8 and Ps 119.

[85] Michael Fishbane, *Biblical Interpretation in Ancient Israel* (Oxford: Clarendon Press, 1985). Some other examples are Bernard M. Levinson, *Deuteronomy and the Hermeneutics of Legal Innovation* (New York: Oxford University Press, 1998); Benjamin Sommer, *A Prophet Reads Scripture: Allusion in Isaiah 40–66* (Stanford: Stanford University Press, 1998); Michael A. Lyons, *From Law to Prophecy: Ezekiel's Use of the Holiness Code*, in the Library of Hebrew Bible / Old Testament Studies, vol. 507 (New York: T & T Clark, 2009). These are just a sampling, and of course earlier scholars recognized this phenomenon as well. Yet Fishbane's work sparked a new interest and emphasis on inner-biblical exegesis. See also my discussion at the beginning of chapter 2 and the relevant footnotes.

interpret earlier passages, but the author of Ps 119 is not interpreting anything. Different variations of this could be mentioned; for example, some legal material is updated and applied to new situations, or narratives are reworked with different theological or ideological emphases.[86] These are very different concerns than one finds in Ps 119.

There is another important reason why these studies are not particularly germane to Ps 119; specifically the processes of reworking a biblical narrative or innovatively applying a legal text are processes that take place as a text is being transmitted. This is not to say that there is a discreet line between composition and transmission; there is certainly not. Yet because Ps 119 did not have a long history of transmission, there was little time for tradents to alter the text.[87] Despite the fact that these recent studies are not particularly helpful, I have mentioned them because they provide a sense of text-handling procedures during the period when the Hebrew Bible was achieving its final form. And if Ps 119 was composed during this period, why is there no evidence that the author of Ps 119 was familiar with such procedures?

There are two occurrences of the word עֵקֶב in Ps 119 (at the end of vv. 33 and 112) that may indicate the author was familiar with such procedures. Both Ps 119:33 and 112 are complete and grammatically correct without the word עֵקֶב, and the addition of the word at the end of both verses creates a syntactic problem. Thus, the author is using the word עֵקֶב in an unusual way—that is, in a way that would catch the attention of a careful reader. The word is "extraneous to the understanding of its home verse" and thus freed for the sake of referencing other Scriptural verses (מופנה להקיש).[88] Yadin argues that according to the interpretational strategies of the Mekhilta, the occurrence of a word in two verses was not sufficient for drawing an analogy between the two verses. Instead an analogy may be drawn only when Scripture itself indicates that one of the occurrences does not have an essential function in its "home" verse. In this case the home verses are Ps 119:33

---

[86] See the previous footnote; see also the various works on Chronicles, such as Sara Japhet, *The Ideology of Chronicles and Its Place in Biblical Thought* (Winona Lake, IN: Eisenbrauns, 2009); Thomas Willi, *Die Chronik als Auslegung*, FRLANT, vol. 106 (Göttingen: Vandenhoeck & Ruprecht, 1972); or studies of Ezra-Nehemiah, such as Jacob Wright, *Rebuilding Identity: The Nehemiah-Memoir and Its Earliest Readers*, BZAW, vol. 348 (Berlin: de Gruyter, 2004).

[87] I discuss this further in the section on the earliest textual witnesses; see p. 185.

[88] This quote is taken from Azzan Yadin, *Scripture as Logos: Rabbi Ishmael and the Origins of Midrash* (Philadelphia: University of Pennsylvania Press, 2004), 60.

and 112, where not only does the word עקב not have an essential function, but it is used in a way that is syntactically and semantically unique within the Hebrew Bible.[89]

BDB lists Ps 119:33 and 112 as evidence that the word עקב means "until the end of time."[90] HALOT lists these verses with the translation "right to the end."[91] But neither lexicon gives other examples of this meaning, and the impetus for this supposed definition seems to be the juxtaposition with "forever" (לעולם) in v. 112, where the speaker declares, "I have inclined my heart to do your statutes forever עקב." Almost without exception, English translations render the word with "to the end" or some slight variation—"even to the end," "to the very end."[92] Another possible explanation for the translation "to the end" may be an etymology, since the consonants עקב can mean "heel," which is in some sense the end of the body. The choice "at every step" in the JPS translation (1917) seems to be related to this etymology, and it likely draws on Rashi's interpretation: "I will keep it in all of its courses and the footprints of its paths."[93] Neither "at every step" nor "to the end" is an attested use of this word elsewhere in the Hebrew Bible.

The New Jerusalem Bible opts for another possibility in v. 112: "Their recompense is eternal."[94] Other verses in the Hebrew Bible use עקב with the meaning "consequence" or by extension "reward," and in these verses the word functions as an adverbial accusative. For example, Isa 5:23 pronounces a woe upon "those who justify the wicked as a consequence of a bribe" (מצדיקי רשע עקב שחד), and Prov 22:4 teaches that "the reward of humility is the fear of the Lord" (עקב ענוה יראת יהוה). Psalm 19:12 teaches that "in keeping them [i.e., YHWH's regulations] there is great reward" (בשמרם עקב רב).

---

[89] Only one of these occurrences is preserved in the various fragments of the DSS, specifically v. 112 in 11QPs[a], and in the photo plate in the DJD volume there is nothing unusual about the writing of the word. See James Sanders, ed., *Qumran Cave 11*, DJD IV (Oxford: Clarendon Press, 1965). There are very small fragments of v. 33 preserved in 1QPs[a], but the end of the verse, where the word עקב occurs, is missing. See Dominique Barthélemy and J. T. Milik, eds., *Qumran Cave I*, DJD I (Oxford: Clarendon Press, 1955).

[90] BDB, 784.

[91] HALOT, 873.

[92] ASV, BBE, DBY, ESV, GNV, KJV, NAS, NET, NIV, NKJ, NLT, RSV, YLT.

[93] אשמרנה בכל מעגלותיה ועקבי נתיבותיה Ha-Keter, 166.

[94] The New Jerusalem Bible's translation of v. 33 is "Teach me, Yahweh, the way of your will and I will observe it." This ignores the word עקב completely.

Because there are so many thematic and lexical links between Pss 19 and 119, it is plausible to conclude that the author of Ps 119 expects the reader to interpret the word עקב in light of Ps 19:12.[95] However, the syntax of both verses in Ps 119 is different than any of the other verses in the Hebrew Bible that use the word עקב with the meaning "consequence" or "reward." Whenever the word is used with the meaning "reward," it is a substantive. An adverbial use of a substantive is possible in Hebrew, but if this is adopted in Ps 119:112, the result is syntactically awkward: "… to do your statutes forever rewardwise." This could be smoothed into better English by supplying several words "… to do your statutes forever [for the sake of the] reward." But this use would also be unattested elsewhere in the Hebrew Bible.

I remain unconvinced by any of the explanations of the syntax of these verses; nor am I convinced with the explanations of עקב given in the various lexica. What other explanation can be found? I propose that the word עקב in Ps 119:33 and 112 is a cross-reference to Deut 7:12, 8:20, and perhaps Gen 26:5. In addition to the word עקב, the verses in Genesis and Deuteronomy include lists of Torah words—commandments, statutes, and regulations—all of which occur in Ps 119. The verses are provided in the following table along with some of the context, since this suggestion is dependent on a contextual reading of these passages. That is, if the author of Ps 119 is cross-referencing these passages by using the word עקב, then he is referencing the ideas of the context, not merely the verse where the word עקב occurs.

Gen 26:4	והרביתי את־זרעך ככוכבי השמים	And I will multiply your seed like the stars of the heavens,
	ונתתי לזרעך את כל־הארצת האל	and I will give all of these lands to your seed,
	והתברכו בזרעך כל גויי הארץ	and in your seed all nations of the earth will be blessed
Gen 26:5	עֵקֶב אשר־שמע אברהם בקלי	as a consequence of the fact that Abraham obeyed my voice
	וישמר משמרתי מצותי חקותי ותורתי	and observed my injunction, my commandments, my statutes, and my Torah.
Deut 7:11	ושמרת את־המצוה	And you shall observe the commandment,

---

[95] This is Deissler's view (p. 211), and various commentators adopt his interpretation.

ואת־החקים ואת־המשפטים	*and the statutes, and the regulations,*
אשר אנכי מצוך היום לעשותם	*which I am commanding you today to observe.*
Deut 7:12 והיה עקב תשמעון את המשפטים האלה	*Then it will happen – as a consequence of your obeying these regulations,*
ושמרתם ועשיתם אתם	*and observing and doing them –*
ושמר יהוה אלהיך לך את־הברית	*that YHWH your God will keep the covenant*
ואת־החסד אשר נשבע לאבתיך	*and the faithfulness which he swore to your fathers.*
Deut 8:19 והיה אם־שכח תשכח את־יהוה אלהיך	*And it will happen that if you utterly forget YHWH your God,*
והלכת אחרי אלהים אחרים	*and walk after other gods,*
ועבדתם והשתחוית להם	*and serve them, and bow down to them –*
העדתי בכם היום כי אבד תאבדון	*I testify against you today that you will utterly perish*
Deut 8:20 כגוים אשר יהוה מאביד מפניכם	*like the nations which YHWH destroyed*[96] *from before you,*
כן תאבדון	*thus you will perish,*
עקב לא תשמעון בקול יהוה אלהיכם	*as a consequence of your not obeying the voice of YHWH your God.*

Genesis 26:5 has generated much discussion, since Abraham, who lived long before the giving of Torah at Sinai, is described as one who obeys the stipulations of Torah. Rashi explains the "commandments" as those which are in Torah, and he explains "Torah," which Abraham obeyed, as the oral Torah that came to Moses at Sinai.[97] Some rabbis cite this passage as proof that Torah existed before its official revelation at Sinai.[98] Some critical scholars explain this as part of the Deuteronomic redaction of Genesis.[99]

In any case, Gen 26:5 contributes to the emphasis on obedience of God's revelation, an emphasis that is repeated in Deut 7:12–8:20. This

---

[96] The word "destroyed" is from the same root as "perish" (א.ב.ד).

[97] מצותי הן מצות שבתורה...ותורתי להביא תורה שבעל פה הלכה למשה מסיני Ha-Keter, Genesis vol. 2, pp. 8, 10. See also Talmud Babli, Yoma 28:2.

[98] עד שלא נברא העולם צפן הקב"ה את התורה עד שיעמוד אברהם ויטול אותה, שנאמר עקב אשר שמע... (אגדת בראשית פרק יג ד"ה [א])

[99] For one example of many see Erhard Blum, *Studien zur Komposition des Pentateuch*, BZAW, vol. 189 (Berlin: de Gruyter, 1990), 103–04.

section of Deuteronomy is a unit that is demarcated by the repetition of the words עקב and תשמעון in Deut 7:12 and 8:20.[100] Furthermore, this section is a fitting précis of the entire book of Deuteronomy. It contains a brief review of Israel's history and exhortations to obey God's commandments. The exhortations are accompanied by a description of the benefits of obedience and the dangers of disobedience, that is, a foreshadowing of the blessings and cursings found later in the book of Deuteronomy. Much more could be said about the contributions of these passages to the theology of the Pentateuch, yet by any interpretation they are freighted with the same theology that permeates Ps 119.

The benefit of this suggestion for the exegesis of Ps 119:33 and 112 is not only that it helps to explain the difficult syntax, but it also activates the theology of Deuteronomy. That is to say, the message of the section in Deuteronomy (7:12–8:20) is that one's attitude to Torah has consequences. On the one hand, the pious can expect that God will keep his promises to those who obey. On the other hand, disobedience will lead to punishment. If the author was using the textual strategy that I have described above, then Ps 119 provides further evidence to support Seeligmann's claim that "midrashic exegesis" grew organically out of the biblical literature itself. The use of this textual strategy is also consistent with the thesis that Ps 119 is part of the latest redaction of the Psalter and the Hebrew Bible altogether.

My central thesis does not stand or fall with the above suggestion about the word עקב, nor does the claim that Ps 119 fits well with the trajectory from the Hebrew Bible into developing Judaism. In the dis-

---

[100] זה סיום כל הפרשה, שפתח והיה עקב תשמעון ...אהרן מירסקי, ספר דברים בדעת מקרא, עמ קמב Deuteronomy 7:12 is the beginning of the עקב section of Torah readings. Charles Perrot discusses the evidence for the reading portions and claims that there was likely a tradition of reading specific portions prior to 70 C.E.; however, there is almost no evidence for whether or not the Torah was divided into particular reading portions that early. Charles Perrot, "The Reading of the Bible in the Ancient Synagogue," in *Mikra: Text, Translation, Reading and Interpretation of the Hebrew Bible in Ancient Judaism and Early Christianity.* ed. Martin Jan Mulder et al. 137–59. Compendia Rerum Iudaicarum ad Novum Testamentum. (Assen/Maastricht: Van Gorcum, 1990). This verse also is the beginning of one of the *Sedarim* that is marked in the Leningrad Codex with ס (see Aron Dotan's introduction to BHL, p. xviii). Unfortunately neither Deut 7:12 nor 8:20 is extant in the DSS, so we cannot determine if the division existed at that time. On the scribal practice of including divisions cf. Emanuel Tov, *Scribal Practices and Approaches Reflected in the Texts Found in the Judean Desert,* Studies on the Texts of the Desert of Judah, ed. Florentino García Martínez, vol. 54 (Leiden: Brill, 2004).

cussion of the portrayal of the speaker in chapter 3, I include various examples of paradigmatic types from texts that are earlier than Ps 119.[101] A comparison with other examples from the literature of developing Judaism helps to situate Ps 119 in its historical context. Some of the types are explored in the book *Ideal Figures in Ancient Judaism: Profiles and Paradigms*.[102] The introduction states that a "number of the figures lend themselves readily enough as examples to be imitated; they are paradigmatic."[103] The essays deal with three types of figures: (1) figures from the ancient past, (2) messianic figures, and (3) ideal conceptions generated by roles, such as a visionary, martyr, or charismatic. "Other types, such as zealot or righteous man could be added."[104]

In his essay on Noah, James VanderKam explores some of the different literary functions of Noah's righteousness. In Ben Sira and the Wisdom of Solomon, Noah is portrayed as both righteous and wise—characteristics that the reader should imitate. In Jubilees and I Enoch, Noah's righteousness is the reason that he was delivered at the time of judgment, and the discerning readers will recognize that righteousness will deliver them in the final judgment.[105] Thus, the rhetorical goals determine the way that the figure is used or portrayed. For example, VanderKam does not discuss the Genesis Apocryphon, because Noah's righteousness does not function paradigmatically. That is, his righteousness is not portrayed as something to emulate, instead it is the reason that he receives a vision and has access to information that others do not possess.[106]

Although Noah's vision in the Genesis Apocryphon is not paradigmatic, there are other examples in which the role of a visionary is developed as a paradigm for emulation. In the article entitled "The Visionary," Susan Niditch discusses various examples of individuals

---

[101] See the section beginning on p. 59.

[102] John J. Collins and George W. E. Nickelsburg, eds., *Ideal Figures in Ancient Judaism: Profiles and Paradigms*, Society of Biblical Literature Septuagint and Cognate Studies, ed. George W. E. Nickelsburg and Harry M. Orlinsky, vol. 12 (Chico, CA: Scholars Press, 1980).

[103] Collins, *Ideal Figures in Ancient Judaism*, 5.

[104] Collins, *Ideal Figures in Ancient Judaism*, 5.

[105] James C. VanderKam, "The Righteousness of Noah," in *Ideal Figures in Ancient Judaism: Profiles and Paradigms*, ed. John J. Collins and George W. E. Nickelsburg (Chico, CA: Scholars Press, 1980), 23–25.

[106] Dan Machiela, private communication.

who actively seek to achieve an altered state of consciousness.[107] Michael Fishbane discusses the rabbinic prototypes of Rabbi Akiva and Johanan ben Zakkai who transcend a normal state of consciousness through the study of Torah.[108]

Clear differences emerge between Ps 119 and the above examples. There is no evidence that Ps 119 encourages one to seek an altered state of consciousness, and Ps 119 does not use a specific individual from the ancient past, such as Noah. A better example for comparison with Ps 119 is the portrayal of the sage in Ben Sira. The speaker in Ps 119 repeatedly asks for insight, and his search for insight into Torah can be compared to the sage in Ben Sira, who is portrayed as one searching for wisdom. The sage in Ben Sira "did not acquire wisdom by the allegorizing exegetical techniques and the Hellenistic philosophical jargon of the book of Wisdom [or] the visionary experiences of the heavenly realm described in the book of Enoch."[109] Similarly, the speaker in Ps 119 does not become wise through visions or philosophical speculation. In Ben Sira, "wisdom is both a gift from God and something to be acquired by personal effort. It is nourished by prayer, study, reflection, and good conduct."[110] These descriptions can be applied to Ps 119 by replacing "wisdom" with "understanding of Torah."

It is noteworthy that ideal figures in Judaism after the time of Ps 119 could all be described as Torah students. Of course, there are distinctions in the portrayals. The Teacher of Righteousness, who is portrayed in the DSS, interprets God's word correctly due to supernatural revelation, and this sort of revelation is not a characteristic of other ideal figures. Martin Jaffee describes a sage as one who embodies Torah. In rabbinic literature this embodiment involves the sage's transmission of Torah teaching to his disciples, but it also includes the sage's actions that conform to the commandments and to the traditional interpretation of the commandments.[111]

---

[107] Susan Niditch, "The Visionary," in *Ideal Figures in Ancient Judaism: Profiles and Paradigms*, ed. John J. Collins and George W. E. Nickelsburg (Chico, CA: Scholars Press, 1980), 153–79.

[108] Michael Fishbane, *The Kiss of God: Spiritual and Mystical Death in Judaism* (Seattle: University of Washington Press, 1994).

[109] Daniel J. Harrington, "The Wisdom of the Scribe According to Ben Sira," in *Ideal Figures in Ancient Judaism: Profiles and Paradigms*, ed. John J. Collins and George W. E. Nickelsburg (Chico, CA: Scholars Press, 1980), 184.

[110] Harrington, "The Wisdom of the Scribe According to Ben Sira," 184.

[111] Martin S. Jaffee, *Early Judaism: Religious Worlds of the First Judaic Millennium*, Studies and Texts in Jewish History and Culture, ed. Bernard D. Cooperman,

What is assumed in a wide variety of texts after 200 B.C.E. is that the righteous are immersed in the study and observance of Torah. Psalm 119 is not the only reason, of course. Deuteronomy already teaches that the commandments must be learned, and Ezra was a scribe "skilled in the Torah of Moses" (Ezra 7:6). Had Ps 119 never been written, personal Torah study would likely have still developed as a central virtue in Judaism. Yet both the intensity of devotion in Ps 119 and the emphasis on the transformative power of Torah in the life of individuals are unmatched within the Hebrew Bible. Thus, Ps 119 certainly contributed to the centrality of Torah study, which became axiomatic in Judaism.

---

vol. 13 (Bethesda, MD: University Press of Maryland, 2006). The notion of embodying Torah is used throughout his book; for specific comments see pp. 74–86; 114–55; and 230–40.

CONCLUSION

I have argued that Ps 119 uses traditional religious language to construct an acrostic poem with a striking message. The message, which the speaker models throughout the psalm, is that the righteous should internalize Torah to the point that it forms one's character. By placing the majority of the psalm in the mouth of the speaker, the author portrays the speaker in the process of spiritual formation, and as a result the reader experiences the psalm from the subjective perspective of the speaker. By using meaningful patterns of repetition the author expands the conception of Torah. Since the Psalter relates itself to the Pentateuch and since Ps 119 is in one of the latest layers of the Psalter, the conception of Torah includes the Pentateuch. However, the conception of Torah cannot be limited to any specific text, and this expansive conception of Torah adumbrates later Rabbinic Judaism, including the development of the oral Torah.

Psalm 119's praise of the benefits of Torah and portrayal of the exemplary student's immersion in Torah promotes Torah to the center of religious practice. Later Judaism is characterized by the centrality of Torah: "Torah is the life forming basic principle of the Jewish faith—of Jewish existence altogether. It is the center of Jewish piety and praxis."[1] As Amir notes, this centrality of Torah is already present in Ps 119, which "epitomizes the world of Judaism, of which the central life value is the occupation with Torah."[2] If the caricature of Judaism as nothing but "narrow-minded legalism" had been avoided by scholars like Duhm, they could have recognized that Ps 119 contributes to the message of the Psalter, the Hebrew Bible, and developing Judaism. Specifically, Ps 119 contributes to the belief that Torah is God's life-giving word and that the wise servant of God is devoted to its study and observance.

---

[1] "Tora ist das lebensformende Grundprinzip des jüdischen Glaubens, der jüdischen Existenz insgesamt. Sie ist die Mitte jüdischer Frömmigkeit und Lebenspraxis." Shemaryahu Talmon, "TORA—NOMOS—GESETZ: Die Bedeutung des Judentums für die Christliche Theologie," in *Lernen in Jerusalem, Lernen mit Israel; Anstöße zur Erneuerung in Theologie und Kirche* (Berlin: Institut Kirche und Judentum, 1993), 132.

[2] Amir, הוא מביע את עולמו של היהודי שהערך המרכזי שבחייו הוא העיסוק בתורה "The place of Psalm 119 in the religion of Israel [Hebrew]," 57.

The Hebrew Bible emphasizes Torah *observance* not Torah *study*. In fact, there is almost no emphasis on Torah study in the Hebrew Bible except Ps 119, which highlights Torah study as a private spiritual exercise. Beginning with extra-biblical texts discovered in the Judean Desert and continuing into texts that eventually define Rabbinic Judaism the emphasis shifts to Torah study. In the last two centuries before the destruction of the second temple, the obligation to observe Torah is already assumed, and the obligation to study Torah is being advocated. Of course, Torah observance continues to be discussed, and as I have noted above rabbis debate which activity is more important. The salient point is that there is a dramatic shift in emphasis from Torah observance to Torah study, and one of the earliest, attested texts that provides evidence of the shift is Ps 119.

The author's strategy for promoting Torah study is to portray an ideal Torah student, and the author constructs the student's persona using the first-person perspective. That is, throughout the majority of Ps 119, the speaker repeatedly uses first- and second-person pronouns. Using these pronouns enables the author to introduce subjectivity, volitional assertions, emotions, and affective language—all of which contribute to a complex characterization of a Torah student. Building up such a multi-layered portrayal of the speaker requires a poem of great length, and this rhetorical goal demonstrates that the length of Ps 119 has a function. The psalm is not long merely to fill out the acrostic format or to demonstrate the poet's facility with the language as some have claimed. Rather the length, repetition, and variation contribute to Ps 119's portrayal of an exemplary Torah student.

In addition to the affective language, the author formulates the words of the speaker using traditional religious language. The speaker uses locutions and motifs of wisdom literature, but he does not praise wisdom. He uses elements of lament psalms, but he is not lamenting. The author uses this religious language to characterize the speaker as someone who has internalized Torah so completely that it shapes his speech. Because the words are traditional, they resonate with the beliefs of the pious, and this resonance increases the rhetorical effectiveness of the psalm.

Just as the author of Ps 119 builds a complex portrayal of an exemplary student of Torah, so also he builds a complex conception of Torah that is greater than the sum of the parts. The author does this using various means. Perhaps most importantly, Ps 119 emphasizes the function of Torah in the life of the righteous. In a subtle way this emphasis on what Torah *does* contributes to an expansive conception of Torah that cannot be limited to the five books of Moses. If the author had specified exactly what Torah *is*, that specification would have worked against the rhetorical goals of portraying a Torah student and encouraging the reader to emulate the student. Along with stipulations and statutes, Torah also includes promises, and any instantiation of Torah may include various implications. I describe Ps 119's conception of Torah in chapter 4, which concludes with the observation that although Ps 119 is moving towards a Rabbinic conception of Torah, it has not yet arrived.

Despite the lack of overt historical information in Ps 119, the descriptions in the previous paragraphs are all consistent with a composition that took place at or near the end of the compilation of the Psalter and the Hebrew Bible as a whole (TNK). If one contrasts the emphasis on Torah study in later Judaism with the lack of such emphasis in most of the Hebrew Bible, the shift is indeed dramatic. However, the emphasis on Torah study in Ps 119 indicates that Rabbinic conceptions of Torah and Torah study were not radical innovations. Rather, rabbis transmitted tradition that they received from previous generations, and over the course of time their transmission of tradition became the tradition itself.

COMMENTARY

Many psalms likely had a history of oral transmission, and the notion of an *Urtext* for such psalms is unhelpful, even for heuristic purposes. In contrast, Ps 119 is a literary composition with a single author and without an oral prehistory. This study therefore assumes that an *Urtext* did exist for Ps 119 and that of the extant witnesses, the MT preserves a text that is closest to the *Urtext*. The basis for this claim is not simply a preference for the MT but rather an evaluation of the relationship between the witnesses. Almost all of the differences between the MT and the other witnesses can be explained as a development from a pre-Masoretic text (sometimes labeled "proto-MT") to the other textual traditions.[1] Thus, in my opinion, the textual witnesses that differ from the MT—primarily the DSS and Greek translations—provide the earliest evidence for the history of interpretation of Ps 119 rather than evidence for a different *Urtext* or true variants. In the following paragraphs, I provide examples in support of this claim and a brief characterization of textual witnesses.

One series of examples is represented in the MT, LXX, DSS, Syriac, and Targumim, specifically the grammatical number for the Torah terms is inconsistent. What was "originally" singular is transmitted or vocalized as plural; for example, "your word" becomes "your words."[2] There are numerous examples—too many to dismiss as scribal errors, especially since the words affected are only the Torah terms and not merely a random sampling. None of the witnesses consistently replaces all the singular forms with plurals forms. In my judgment, it is more probable that a tradent would replace "commandment" with "commandments" rather than vice versa, since any copyist or translator would be well aware that there are numerous commandments.[3]

---

* This commentary is intended as a supplement to the argument presented in the body of the book and is therefore selective rather than exhaustive.

[1] It is anachronistic to use the label "the MT" for the pre-Christian period, which is when the Psalter was translated into Greek. Furthermore, there is a group of manuscripts rather than a single Masoretic text. Similarly, "the LXX" is a problematic label, since there was no single Greek translation. Nevertheless, these labels are used for the sake of convenience.

[2] I use quotation marks here for "originally" since this is an evaluative statement.

[3] My discussion of instantiations and an abstract concept in chapter 4 is relevant here; see p. 112.

Another example of a group of differences is the addition of a vocative "O Lord" (κύριε) in six verses of the LXX.[4] There are many verses
in the MT that include the divine name as a vocative (e.g., 31, 52,
89, *passim*), so additional vocatives are not out of place in the psalm
and do not significantly alter its meaning. However, these additions
are likely evidence of a different Hebrew *Vorlage*, because the LXX
Psalter generally provides a word-for-word translation of the Hebrew.[5]
This is not to say that the LXX preserves a tradition that is closer to
the *Urtext*; on the contrary, it is more likely that a tradent would add
a vocative rather than omit it. What this evidence shows is that the
process of interpretation began in the transmission of the Hebrew text
and that differences between Greek and Hebrew exemplars should not
necessarily be attributed to the translator.

The claim that the LXX of Ps 119 generally provides evidence for
the history of interpretation rather than a different *Urtext* is partially
based on the study of Frank Austermann.[6] The first half of his study is
a characterization of the LXX Psalter and a description of its translation technique without reference to Ps 119. In the second half of the
book he tests and confirms his conclusions by comparing them with
the evidence in Ps 119. Thus, the following descriptions are valid specifically for Ps 119 as well as the Psalter in general.[7]

1. The translation of the Torah terms follows the translation of the
same terms in the Pentateuch with very few exceptions; this indicates that the translator knew and consulted a Greek translation of

---

[4] Vv. 7, 68, 85, 93, 97, and 168.

[5] "Beim Septuaginta-Psalter handelt es [sic] hinsichtlich von Aspekten der quan-
titativen Entsprechung bezüglich der Segmentierung im großen und ganzen um eine
Wort-für-Wort-Übersetzung, jedenfalls was das Ergebnis der Wiedergabetätigkeit
betrifft. [...] Insgesamt läßt sich feststellen, daß der Übersetzer das Ziel verfolgt, seine
Vorlage quantitativ und qualitativ bewahrend wiederzugeben, was ihm oft und in gro-
ßem Ausmaß gelingt." Frank Austermann, *Von der Tora zum Nomos: Untersuchungen zur Übersetzungsweise und Interpretation im Septuaginta-Psalter*, Mitteilungen des
Septuaginta-Unternehmens, vol. XXVII (Göttingen: Vandenhoeck & Ruprecht, 2003),
102, 104. Austermann applies the same characterization specifically to Ps 119 (p. 169),
with some exceptions that I summarize in the following paragraphs.

[6] See the previous footnote. In Greek, this is Ps 118. Discussions of both Hebrew
and Greek often indicate this difference as "Ps 119 (118)." I find the repetition of both
numbers to be unnecessary and therefore avoid it.

[7] The following enumerated characteristics are summarized from Austermann's
work as a whole, so it is not possible to cite a particular page number.

the Pentateuch for his translation of the Psalter.[8] The word "precepts" (פקדים) only occurs in the Psalter, and is therefore not relevant. The translation of "regulations" (משפטים) is an exception, since it is translated with several terms. The differences are due to the fact that the term is used with different meanings; that is, the translator was aware of the context and the different uses of the term.[9]

2. Sin, wickedness, unrighteousness, and even scheming are represented with words that indicate a transgression specifically against Torah. Austermann's evidence for this claim is extensive, involving many Hebrew words, e.g., רשע, חמס, פשע, עוה. These Hebrew words are consistently translated with some variation of "lawlessness" (ἄνομος). The translator could have used other words, such as unrighteousness, wickedness, sinfulness, and the like. His consistent use of "lawlessness" indicates that he defined sinfulness as a violation of the law, that is, Torah.[10]

3. The translator was especially concerned with Torah study and meditation and emphasizes these activities more than the Hebrew text does. He repeatedly translates נצר ("to keep") with some form of ἐξερευνάω ("to search or investigate"); this translation only occurs in the Psalter. He also translates שיח, שעה, and שעע with some form of μελετάω ("to meditate").

In summary the translator "by his rendering, characterizes explicitly and emphatically *misconduct as lawlessness, an evildoer as a law breaker,* and *God as law giver and interpreter.* In addition he accents the handling of the central impartation of the will of God to Israel in the form of searching study and intensive meditation."[11]

---

[8] The evidence that the translator consulted a Greek Pentateuch is much more extensive than only the Torah terms. Austermann argues for this position throughout his book.

[9] See the discussion of the term משפטים beginning on p. 120.

[10] For the specific words and translation equivalents see Austermann, 176–206.

[11] The translator "charakterisiert bei seiner Wiedergabe ausdrücklich und nachdrücklich *Fehlverhalten als Gesetzwidrigkeit, Übeltäter als Gesetzesgegner* und *Gott als Gesetzgeber* und *Gesetzesausleger.* Zudem betont er den Umgang mit der zentralen Willensmitteilung Gottes an Israel in Form forschenden Studierens und intensivieren [sic] Meditierens." Austermann, 208, italics original. My translation of the second sentence is literal, since this is my practice throughout this study; however, the literal translation is not particularly helpful in this case. It is more transparent in German that the words "the central impartation of the will of God" refer to a single entity, that is, God's revelation. Austermann's point is that the translator emphasizes *study* and *meditation* as the means by which one interacts with Torah.

With only one exception the Dead Sea Psalms Scroll replaces the imperative "give me life" (חיני) with "give me grace" or "be gracious to me" (חונני).[12] This statement is true, of course, only for the verses that are extant, and the claim that it "replaces" the word חיה is my evaluation.[13] However, there are other fragments of DSS that preserve "give me life."[14] It is improbable that only one witness would preserve the reading of the *Urtext*, and the reading in 11QPsᵃ can be explained as early evidence of the notion that Torah can be referenced with the word חן.[15]

There are additional, isolated textual differences that are treated in the following comments. They are isolated in the sense that they do not involve multiple verses, as do the examples listed above. Most of Ps 119 is straightforward; that is, the individual phrases and clauses are not difficult to understand. There are a few rare words, and occasionally a stich is open to several interpretations. Ambiguities are generally due to the concision of the verses, but ambiguity is the exception rather than the rule. Thus, the purpose of the following discussion of individual verses is not to provide a comprehensive commentary; I do not comment on every verse of the psalm. These comments provide my interpretation when it differs from other commentaries and illustrate how the thesis of this work influences interpretation.

What is more often open to interpretation than the individual words or clauses is the relationship between the two halves of a verse, since they are typically juxtaposed without a particle that specifies the relationship. As is well known, a *waw* conjunction has a wide range of possible interpretations; it shows that the stichs are related—but little more than that. There are very few verses that specify the relationship by the use of a conjunction; one example is v. 11 in which the two stichs are joined by למען ("so that"). The word כי is sometimes used as a conjunction, but it is not always clear how it should be interpreted.

---

[12] This scroll (11QPsᵃ) is often called "The Dead Sea Psalms Scroll," due in part to its publication by James Sanders in *The Dead Sea Psalms Scroll* (Ithaca, NY: Cornell University Press, 1967).

[13] The extant verses in 11QPsᵃ are vv. 37, 40, 88, 107, 156, and 159. The exception is v. 154.

[14] For example, 4QPsᵍ is extant for both vv. 37 and 40, and in both cases it reads "give me life."

[15] See Seeligmann, I. L. "Voraussetzungen der Midraschexegese," In *Congress Volume: Copenhagen, 1953*, ed. G. W. Anderson, 150–81. VTSup, vol. 1. (Leiden: Brill, 1953), 179.

Verse 1: On the אשרי formula see p. 60. The relationship between the two stichs is apposition.[16] That is, the two halves of the verse are coreferential. Those who walk in the Torah of YHWH are the same people whose way is blameless or who will be reckoned blameless. I use this definition of apposition throughout the commentary, and there are numerous verses that use apposition both to define the righteous and to define the wicked.

Verse 2: The suffixes "his" and "him" refer to YHWH in v. 1.

Verse 3: The first word of the verse (אף) indicates a continuation. That is, v. 3 continues to describe the same type of people who are the topic of vv. 1 and 2. Rashi's comments support this interpretation: "Happy are they if all this is in them."[17] The antecedent of "this" (זה) is the behavior in the first two verses.

On the second half of the verse Rashi comments that walking in God's ways means doing good. Thus the righteous not only avoid evil but they also do good.[18]

Verse 4: The precise meaning and syntax of this verse are not readily apparent; English translations of the verse vary widely.

> Thou hast commanded us to keep thy precepts diligently. (KJV)
> Thou has ordained Thy precepts, That we should keep them diligently. (NASB)
> Thou hast commanded thy precepts to be kept diligently. (RSV)
> You have commanded your precepts to be kept diligently. (NRSV)
> You have laid down precepts that are to be fully obeyed. (NIV)
> You have given us your laws to obey. (Living)
> You have charged us to keep your commandments carefully. (NLT)

---

[16] The majority of the verses in Ps 119 are divided with an 'atnach. I use the term "stich" to refer to one of these divisions—either the first half of the verse or the second half of the verse, although "half" is a generalization. I represent each stich on a different line of the translation.

[17] אשריהם אם כל זה בהם Ha-Keter, 160. For medieval commentaries I rely on the Ha-Keter edition of Miqra'ot Gedolot. Mayer Gruber criticizes this edition for producing an eclectic text, and in his work on Rashi he publishes the text of a single Hebrew manuscript, specifically Cod. Hebr. 220 from the Austrian National Library. Mayer Gruber, Rashi's Commentary on Psalms, Brill Reference Library of Judaism, vol. 18. (Leiden: Brill, 2004), 801–61. This manuscript often contains additional words (perhaps explanatory glosses); in this case the reading is אשריהם הצדיקים אם כל זה בהם, which strengthens the argument that v. 3 is describing the same people as the first two verses.

[18] אין הכל שלם אלא אם כן תעשה טוב Ha-Keter, 160.

Commentaries also translate the verse in various ways and generally do not comment on the difficulties.

> You yourself have commanded that your charges be carefully complied with.[19]
> It was you who commanded your precepts to be diligently observed.[20]
> You yourself have announced your ordinances to have them kept diligently.[21]
> You have commanded your orders to be carried out diligently.[22]
> Thou hast thyself given thy precepts, that they may be kept diligently.[23]

There are two grammatical questions that must be answered: (1) What is the object of the verb "command / appoint" (צוה)? and (2) What is the function of the infinitive "to keep" (לשמר)?

I interpret "precepts" as the direct object of the verb צוה. Outside the book of Psalms, this verb generally has a person or group of people as its direct object; however, within the book of Psalms, the opposite is true. Of the fifteen occurrences of the verb in the Psalter, only two have a person as the object of the verb. In Ps 68:29 the object is strength. In Ps 133:3 the object is blessing. One might argue that these are examples of personifications, in which the "strength" and "blessing" obey God's commands like obedient servants. In any case, the usage of this verb (צוה) within the Psalter supports the interpretation that "precepts" is the direct object of the verb.[24] A similar case occurs in Ps 119:138 where the object of the verb צוה is either "righteousness" or "stipulations."

Given this interpretation for the first part of the verse the last two words of the verse (לשמר מאד) present another difficulty. Several

---

[19] Leslie Allen, *Psalms 101–150*, Word Biblical Commentary, vol. 21 (Waco, TX: Word, 1983).

[20] Mitchell J. Dahood, *The Psalms*, The Anchor Bible, vol. 17A (Garden City, NY: Doubleday, 1970).

[21] Hans-Joachim Kraus, *Psalms 60–150*, trans. Hilton C. Oswald (Minneapolis: Augsburg/Fortress, 1989).

[22] Will Soll, *Psalm 119: Matrix, Form, and Setting.* CBQMS, vol. 23. Washington, D.C.: Catholic Biblical Association, 1991.

[23] A. Weiser, *The Psalms*, trans. H. Hartwell, OTL, (Philadelphia: Westminster, 1962).

[24] BDB lists further references in support of the meaning "appoint" on p. 846. The LXX translates the word for "precepts" in the accusative case, indicating that the translator understood "precepts" as the object of the verb. Ehrlich states, "פקדיך ist Objekt zu צויתה, und der folg. Infinitiv ist erklärend." Ehrlich, 301.

translations convert the infinitive to a passive ("...to be kept dili-
gently"), but a passive is impossible for the G stem of this verb. It is
always active.[25] If both the subject and object are not explicit, they are
always implied. For example, the infinitive לשמר occurs in casuistic
law without repetition of the object. "If a man gives money or stuff to
his friend to keep (לשמר) and it is stolen...." (Exod 22:6) It is clear
from the context that the friend is the notional subject of the infinitive
"to keep," and the money (or "stuff") is the notional object.

I have supplied "everyone" in my translation of Ps 119:4. In a
discussion of infinitival syntax, Noonan notes that there may be no
argument in the matrix clause that is identical with the agent of the
infinitive. In such cases, it is either clear from the context who the
subject is, or "subjects may not be overt when they have a general
or non-specific reference."[26] A "general or non-specific" subject works
well in Ps 119:4, i.e., "everyone."

Verse 6: The verb נבט is commonly translated "to look at" or "to
gaze at," but it has connotations that are not captured by this translation. For example, God commands Samuel not to look at (נבט) Saul's
physical appearance (1 Sam 16:7), but surely we are not to assume that
Samuel averted his eyes. Samuel was to avoid having regard, respect,
or esteem for Saul based on his appearance. In Ps 119:15 the speaker
states he will "look at" (נבט) God's paths (ארחות)—clearly not a literal
gaze. The parallel half of verse 15 indicates that a mental activity is
involved; "I will muse (שיח) on your precepts" (פקודים).[27] The action
in v. 6 must also be an intellectual process.

There is a connection between vv. 5 and 6, which is indicated by
the word "then" (אז) at the beginning of v. 6. This implies that if the

---

[25] Contrary to JM § 124s and *IBHS* § 36.2.e the infinitive is not "voiceless." Of the
more than 200 examples of G infinitives construct that occur in Genesis (excluding
לאמר) none are passive. Both grammars also fail to explain why infinitives occur in
the passive stems. If the infinitive is "voiceless" as they would have us believe, why
would it be necessary to form any infinitives in the N stem? The examples listed in
both grammars to support this claim are not convincing. A better explanation is to
identify correctly the agent of the action. See my forthcoming study of the voice of
infinitives in *ZAH*.
[26] Michael Noonan, "Complementation," in *Language Typology and Syntactic
Description*, ed. Timothy Shopen, vol. II, *Complex Constructions* (Cambridge: University Press, 1985), 68.
[27] See also Num 23:21 and BDB, 613.

speaker behaves properly (v. 5), then he will not be ashamed as he
meditates on God's commandments (v. 6).

Verse 7: In the construct phrase מִשְׁפְּטֵי צִדְקֶךָ, the noun צדק functions as an adjective describing an attribute or quality of the construct
noun מִשְׁפָּט.[28] This construction also occurs in vv. 62, 106, 160, and 164.

Verse 9: See my short note "The Answer of Psalm cxix 9" in which
I argue that the second half of this verse provides the answer to the
question posed in the first half of the verse.[29]

Verse 10: Note that the phrase "with all my heart" (בכל לבי) is conceptually the same as "wholeheartedly" (בכל לב), e.g., v. 2. The English
translation masks the similarity in Hebrew.

Verse 11: Hiding God's word in the heart indicates the speaker's
intention to remember it. Rashi comments "I did not allow it to be
forgotten by me."[30]

Verse 14: The suggestion in BHS (based on the Syriac) to read מעל
instead of כעל is not necessary, and it is more likely that the reading
in the MT would give rise to the reading in Syriac than vice versa.
The translation given here assumes that the verb "delight" is elided
from the second half of the verse. When this is the case, the subject of
the verb can change; consequently, I have translated the second half,
"like [one delights] in all wealth."[31] The verb "rejoice" (שיש) can be
followed with either ב or על to mark its object. (For ב see Ps 35:9 and
Isa 61:10; for על see Deut 28:63; 30:9; and Jer 32:41.)

Verse 15: Cf. v. 6. Both verbs in this verse are long forms of the
first person imperfect, i.e., cohortatives ("I will muse" אשיחה and "I
will gaze" ואביטה). Cohortatives generally include some sort of logical
consecution (GKC § 108; but see also IBHS § 34.5.3 where examples
are listed with no readily apparent logically consecutive function). The
occurrence of two cohortatives together in this verse is strong evidence
against mapping the form to some logical relationship. One might be
able to explain the second cohortative as being somehow dependent on
the first half of the verse, but the same rational could not be applied to
the first half of the verse. It has no apparent connection to the previous
verse and thus no logical consecution. See also the comments on v. 44.

---

[28] See GKC § 128p.
[29] Kent Aaron Reynolds, "The Answer of Psalm cxix 9," VT 58 (2008): 265–69.
[30] לא נתתיה להשתכח ממני Ha-Keter, 162.
[31] Cynthia Miller, "Patterns of Verbal Ellipsis in Ugaritic Poetry," UF 31 (2000):
333–72.

Cohortatives occur in the following verses: 15 [2x], 17, 18, 27, 34, 44, 45, 46, 48, 73, 88, 115, 117, 125, 134, 145, and 146.

Verse 16: Rashi juxtaposes the word "take delight" (אשתעשע) with "busy myself" (אתעסק), which is often used as a technical term for the study of Torah (cf. Jastrow, 1098). The interpretative tradition of associating these ideas—that is, delight and study—is also found in the LXX; cf. the comments on the text beginning at p. 185. Ehrlich comments that the phrase means busy oneself, but he gives no support for the claim.[32]

Verse 17: The verb גמל "is not exactly 'recompense,' but a response to a prior deed."[33] I have supplied "well," since the following verb "live" (חיה) implies that the speaker expects God to act in his favor. The verb "live" denotes more than mere existence (cf. v. 25). Rashi links this with God's kindness (חסד).[34]

Verse 18: Cf. v. 6; "gazing at miracles from your Torah" is one example of a cluster of "seeing" metaphors in Ps 119 used to figure the intellectual process. Rashi states that these miracles are hidden in Torah but are not explained.[35]

Verse 19: Contrary to Soll, who posits that גר is a literal reference to the author's location, i.e., exile, the phrase should be understood as a reference to the speaker's mortality; so Rashi "my days are few."[36] Ehrlich claims that the combination of the word גר with the petition in this verse shows that the poet was a foreigner and a proselyte, since any Jewish person would know the commandments.[37] His claim

---

[32] "השתעשע ב heißt sich mit etwas gern beschäftigen, nicht sich daran ergötzen." Ehrlich, 303. This quote is his entire comment on v. 16; he provides no evidence in support of this claim. Perhaps he is explaining the phrase based on the Greek.

[33] Michael V. Fox, *Proverbs 10–31 A New Translation with Introduction and Commentary*, The Anchor Yale Bible, vol. 18B (New Haven: Yale University Press, 2009), 893.

[34] The full text of Rashi's comment includes an ambiguity that is not preserved in English translations. "Grant your servant a word that I may live by it; grant your kindness." גמל על עבדך דבר שאחיה בו—גמול חסדך Ha-Keter, 164. The ambiguity lies in the object that Rashi supplies for the verb, specifically "word" (דבר), since it can also mean "something." In the context of Ps 119, it seems unlikely that Rashi is using the term דבר with such a non-specific meaning. Instead, the "word" must be Torah, and Rashi is arguing that the granting of Torah is evidence of God's goodness. Cf. the discussion of v. 19 at the beginning of chapter 2, p. 31.

[35] דברים המכוסים בה שאינן מפורשים בה Ha-Keter, 164.

[36] ימי מועטים Ha-Keter, 164. Soll associates "sojourning" with the exile in various places throughout his book; for one example, see p. 152.

[37] Ehrlich, 303.

lacks sufficient evidence, but it does indicate that the petition must be understood in light of the traditional religious language being used (cf. chapter 2).

Verse 20: The only other occurrence of the word "grinds" (גרס) in the Hebrew Bible is Lam 3:16, where it occurs in the H stem: "He ground my teeth with gravel; he covered me with ashes." In Lamentations it is a figurative description of the author's deep anguish.

The word for "longing" (תאבה) occurs only in Ps 119—in this verse as a noun and in vv. 40 and 174 as a verb. BDB (p. 1060) suggests (with a question mark) this might be a ת preformative noun from the root א.ב.ה, but "to be willing" does not seem to fit the context. Jastrow provides ample evidence (p. 1641) that the word was understood to mean "longing" in later Jewish texts.

Verse 21: The second stich is appositional to the first. The ones going astray are the insolent ones. The construction is similar to v. 1.

Verse 23: The "also" (גם) seems to connect this verse with the concept of shame in the previous verse. Although shame is not explicit in v. 23, the princes are slandering the speaker (on "speak against me" cf. Ezek 33:30 and Mal 3:13). This is an example of an "associative sequence" (see p. 21).

Rashi explains "muse on your statutes" as Torah study; cf. the comments on v. 16.[38]

Verse 24: The second half of v. 23 and the first half of v. 24 could easily stand as a couplet, i.e., "Your servant meditates on your statutes; also your stipulations are my delight." Additionally, there is a contrast between vv. 23a and 24b, specifically between the men in v. 23a who are antagonistic towards the speaker and the personified stipulations, which (or "who") give the speaker counsel. Thus, there is a chiasm linking the two verses, while each of the verses can stand alone as a meaningful couplet. The associations between vv. 22, 23, and 24 are important for understanding the individual verses. The same is true of other associative sequences throughout the chapter.

Verse 25: It is difficult to find a suitable English equivalent for the verb חיה, which occurs as an imperative in vv. 25, 37, 40, 88, 107, 149, 154, 156, and 159; as an indicative in vv. 17, 50, 77, 93, 116, and 144; and as a jussive in v. 175. The old English word "quicken" may be the closest approximation in meaning but is obsolete. The word חיה

---

[38] שאני עוסק בתורה Ha-Keter, 164.

is used in contexts of war when the victor keeps some of the people alive (e.g., Deut 20:16 and Josh 9:15). It is also used to declare that ultimately God is the one who holds the power of life, "I am the one who kills and preserves alive" (חיה Deut 32:39). I have translated the nine occurrences of the D imv. as "give me life," although this may mask some of the intended urgency. Gerleman argues that the contrasting idea "'to be dead, to die' is always involved somehow, even if it is not explicitly expressed."[39]

Norbert Lohfink argues that the D infinitive of this word in Deut 6:24 should be understood as "to maintain us." He paraphrases the verse as follows: "(Obedience to the laws would imply), to our favor, without time limit, that he will maintain us, as is now the case."[40] Part of his evidence is that usage of this root (ח.י.ה) in Deuteronomy is typically not in the D, so the phrase in 6:24 may include a different nuance. Lohfink then appeals to Jer 49:11, where a soldier tells his dying partner that he will "maintain" (D אחיה) his orphans.[41]

Verse 26: Rashi expands "I have recounted my ways" to "my needs and my sins."[42] This can be understood as petitions and confessions, but confession of sin is not mentioned elsewhere in the psalm.

Verse 27: The word נפלאות is generally translated "wonders." The translation "miracles" emphasizes the supernatural facet of the word; cf. v. 18.

Verse 30: See p. 41.

Verse 31: See pp. 47 and 76.

Verse 32: The phrase "because you expand my heart" (כי תרחיב לבי) is rare. The construct phrase "broadness of heart" is a figure of speech for arrogance in Ps 101:5 (רחב לבב) and in Prov 21:4 (רחב לב). Certainly the speaker in Ps 119 is not declaring that God makes him arrogant. One other passage also contains the construct phrase "broadness of heart," specifically 1 Kgs 5:9 [Eng. 4:29]. This verse refers to the

---

[39] TLOT, 413.

[40] Norbert Lohfink, "Deuteronomy 6:24: לחיתנו 'to Maintain Us'," in *Sha'arei Talmon: Studies in the Bible, Qumran, and the Ancient Near East Presented to Shemaryahu Talmon*, ed. Michael Fishbane and Emmanuel Tov (Winona Lake, IN: Eisenbrauns, 1992), 111.

[41] Lohfink states that the D of חיה is "overrepresented in the Psalter (twenty instances out of fifty-six)." Norbert Lohfink, "Deuteronomy 6:24: לחיתנו 'to Maintain Us'," 115. However these statistics are skewed by the fact that the D occurs sixteen times in Ps 119.

[42] את צרכי ואת חטאתי Ha-Keter, 164.

great wisdom that God gave to Solomon. "Then God gave Solomon wisdom and great understanding and broadness of heart (רחב לב) like the sand on the seashore." By means of its juxtaposition with wisdom and understanding, the construct phrase seems to denote an intellectual ability, and it is possible to read it as related to the trope of storing knowledge in the heart (cf. Prov 2:1).

Another bit of evidence supports the interpretation that "expanding the heart" refers to wisdom, specifically the lecture in Prov 4:10–19 about how to find the right path. The message of the lecture is "Choose the right path and avoid the evil one."[43] The father admonishes his son to accept his teaching, to hold on to instruction, and to keep it (נצר). If the son will do that, then he will not trip when he needs to run (ואם תרוץ לא תכשל Prov 4:12). The entire lecture contrasts the way of wisdom with the way of evil. Although there is nothing in Ps 119:32 about tripping, in the first part of the verse the speaker declares, "I will run in the way of your commandments" (דרך מצותיך ארוץ). The second half of the verse provides the reason the speaker is able to run. Like the lecture in Prov 4, the reason is that he possesses wisdom.

Verse 33: See the discussion beginning on p. 172. Ehrlich translates "Show me, YHWH, the way of your statutes, since I want to observe them assiduously." He then comments, "The articulation of עקב is not clear, but its sense can only be expressed by the above translation."[44] Ehrlich's translation of the cohortative form is interesting ("so will ich"). It could be translated into English with several different nuances, but that is not the point here. I cite him as an example of the uncertainty among commentators on how to interpret the word עקב.

Verse 36: "To 'incline the heart' (or for the heart to incline) means to desire and choose something, not only to pay attention."[45]

Verse 37: The sense of the request is for God to keep the speaker from looking at worthless or vain things. "Turn my eyes away from seeing…" (העבר עיני מראות) is a unique idiom in the Hebrew Bible. Isaiah 33:15 commends the one who "shuts his eyes from seeing evil" (עצם עיניו מראות ברע), and Ps 69:24 [Eng. v. 25] reads, "Let their eyes be darkened from seeing" (תחשכנה עיניהם מראות).

---

[43] Michael V. Fox, *Proverbs 1–9*, 183.

[44] "Zeige mir, JHVH, den Weg deiner Satzungen, so will ich ihn fleissig einhalten." He then comments, "Die Aussprache von עקב ist unsicher, sein Sinn aber kann nur der in obiger Uebersetzung ausgedrückte sien." Ehrlich, 305.

[45] Michael V. Fox, *Proverbs 1–9*, 109.

Verse 38: The antecedent of the relative pronoun (אשר) is either the servant (עבד) or God's word (אמרה). I interpret the antecedent to be God's word; the addition of "leads" is only an attempt to render the Hebrew into idiomatic English. A literal translation of the clause would be, "...your word, which is to your fear." The KJV is one example that interprets the antecedent to be the servant, "...who is devoted to thy fear." But including the concept of devotion is unwarranted.

Verse 39: The verb "to make pass away" (H ע.ב.ר) is the same form that occurs in v. 37, and is translated there as "turn away." Rashi's interpretation implies that this is a request for forgiveness, and the reproach is a result of iniquity.[46] But the speaker does not admit to iniquity elsewhere; cf. v. 26.

Verse 40: Cf. v. 20.

Verse 41: The idiom "come to me" is a way of describing an event that happens to someone. For examples, see Ps 44:18 [Eng. v. 19] and Isa 28:15. The verb is elided from the second stich; that is, "Let your mercy come...Let your salvation come...." Rashi makes this explicit, "Your salvation comes to me."[47]

Verse 42: see v. 43.

Verse 43: Deissler interprets the first half of v. 43 as a continuation of the idea in v. 42 of responding to a reproach.[48] Idiomatic English masks the repetition of דבר, which occurs in both stichs of v. 42 and in the first stich of v. 43. A stilted English rendering of the beginning of both verses highlights the connection: v. 42 "I will answer a word..."; v. 43 "Do not withhold a true word...." Combining the ideas in the first stichs of vv. 42 and 43 gives the full sense: "Do not hinder me from having a true response."[49]

Instead of the verb "remove" (נצל), I read "withhold" (אצל), which is a plausible aural error (cf. Num 11:25). However, the difference in

---

[46] מחול לי על אותו עון ושוב לא יוכלו אויבי לחרפני בו Ha-Keter, 166.

[47] תשועתך תבא לי Ha-Keter, 166.

[48] Deissler, 142–43. Other scholars note the connection as well, such as Ehrlich, 306 and Amos Hakham, ספר תהלים בדעת מקרא [Psalms in Da'at Mikra (Hebrew)] (Jerusalem: Mossad HaRav Kook, 1990), 392.

[49] There are various ideas about the nature of the response. Rabbis have suggested that it is the words of Torah itself, or that the poet who is immersed in Torah will know what to answer his reproachers from the words of Torah. Another interpretation is that the words "I trust on your word" is the answer. That is, the poet will respond that there is no reproach in trusting God's word, but rather it is his great joy to trust in the word of God. Amos Hakham lists various interpretations; Hakham, ספר תהלים, 392.

meaning is minimal, since "removal" (נצל) of a word would result
in the inability to answer and "withholding" (אצל) a word would
also. Hakham explains, "Do not distance from my mouth the word
of truth," yet he also cites Gen 31:9 where Jacob declares that God
"removed" Laban's property and gave it to him.[50]

Hakham notes that it is possible that what the psalmist is hoping
for is the judgment (משפט) that God will enact upon the wicked.
Included in these wicked would be those who reproach the psalmist
in v. 42, and this provides yet another link between the two verses.[51]

Verse 44: This verse as well as vv. 45 and 46 all begin with a cohortative; see the comments on v. 15. There is no necessary connection
between any of these three verses and the preceding verses, which provides further evidence that the form is used for its poetic effect (presumably its aural effect) rather than its semantic content.

Verse 45: On the metaphor "broad place," see p. 98. Rashi includes
a word play on the word "walk" (*hlk*) and *halakhah*.[52] Ehrlich suggests that "broad" should be understood in connection with "Torah"
in the previous verse and cites v. 96 as support.[53] This is an interesting
midrash, but there is no reason to interpret the verse in this way.

Verse 48: See p. 42.

Verse 49: Compare the last word of this verse "you have made me
hope" (יחלתני) with other occurrences of this word in Ps 119 (vv. 43,
74, 81, 114, and 147). All of the forms are D, and there is no apparent
reason why this occurrence includes the causative sense. *HALOT* lists
this verse as the only time when the D has a causative sense (p. 407),
but it also suggests that perhaps the suffix is a textual error. Hakham
simply states that the sense is causative without providing an explanation.[54]

Verse 50: There are no feminine nouns in the preceding verses
that can serve as the antecedent of the demonstrative pronoun "this"
(זאת). Conceptually, the antecedent is the hope of the speaker that is
expressed in v. 49, despite the fact that the "hope" in v. 49 is a verb.

---

[50] אל תרחק מפי את דבר האמת Hakham, ספר תהלים, 392.
[51] ואפשר ש׳למשפטך׳ רומז לדין שיעשה ה׳ ברשעים, והמשורר מצפה, שיעשה ה׳
משפט בחורפו הנזכר בפסוק שלמעלה מכאן. Hakham, ספר תהלים, 392.
[52] ואתהלכה ברחבה—בהלכה הרווחת ופושטת בישראל Ha-Keter, 167.
[53] Ehrlich, 307.
[54] Hakham, ספר תהלים, 394.

Cf. Gen 31:41, where the word זה functions similarly; see also v. 56. Another interpretation: the pronoun (זאת) could be prospective, and its conceptual reference is the clause in the second half of the verse: "your word gives me life." As previously noted, the semantic range of the verb חיה is not adequately expressed by the English "give life." In this verse it might be translated "sustained me" or "kept me alive." Cf. the comments on v. 25.

Verse 53: "The ones who abandon your Torah" is appositional to the "wicked" (רשעים). The apposition defines wickedness as abandoning Torah.

Verse 56: Like v. 50, the antecedent of "this" (זאת) cannot be linked to a specific noun; see the comment on v. 50.[55] The conceptual antecedent must be in the previous verses, specifically comfort (v. 52), songs (v. 54), and the memory of the name of YHWH (v. 55). There are benefits for the speaker, because he keeps God's precepts. This is an example of an associative sequence influencing my interpretation. The lexical repetition of היה לי in vv. 54 and 56 supports this conclusion, although the repetition alone would not be convincing evidence.

Verse 57: Conceptually, the line breaks after the first two words: "My portion is YHWH." The Masoretic division falls on the third word of the verse, and this is one of the cases where the accent does not correspond with the syntax. Perhaps it is significant that the accent is a rᵉbia' rather than the stronger disjunctive 'atnach. In Ps 16:5, where the psalmist declares that YHWH is his portion, the divine name is first; however, the acrostic format is sufficient reason to alter the word order. Furthermore, the word order is not fixed, since in Ps 73:26 the word "portion" precedes "God" (וחלקי אלהים לעולם).

Verse 59: The phrase "turn my feet to your stipulations" assumes the metaphor of the path and figures obedience.

Verse 63: "The ones who observe your precepts" is appositional with "all who fear you." This verse defines fearing God as observing his precepts; this definition corresponds with the theme of Torah observance that occurs throughout the Psalter.

Verse 66: The first word of the MT (טוב) is likely a dittography from the first word of the previous line. On the phrase "believe your commandments" see p. 142.

---

[55] The Babylonian Talmud recognizes the exegetical problem and provides a midrashic solution; cf. 'Abodah Zara 44a.

Verse 67: On the use of טרם with an impf. see *IBHS* § 31.1.1d, which states that such forms should be understood as preterites. The MT points the word אענה as a G, but the translation here assumes an N or Dp (vv. 71 and 75); the LXX translates with a passive—ταπεινωθῆναι. Rashi interrelates an active ("to answer") and a passive ("be afflicted") in his interpretation: "Before I answered you with the commandments—before I meditated [or recited] on them in the houses of study, I went astray by them [i.e., regarding them] and sinned. But now I have been humbled by them, and I observe your Torah, because the study teaches me to turn from transgression."[56]

Verse 69: See v. 70.

Verse 70: The verb טפש is a *hapax legomenon*. The word is an Aramaism meaning "to be dull."[57] The same metaphor occurs in Isa 6:10.

Verse 70 is dependent on the ideas in verse 69 (as Ehrlich notes, p. 310), and together these two verses provide several examples of motifs that are important for the author's portrayal of the speaker elsewhere in the chapter. A smooth translation of v. 69 conceals literary features of the verse that emphasize the contrast between the righteous and the wicked. The verse is constructed as a chiasm. "Insolent" (זדים) is the last word of the first half of the verse, and the independent personal pronoun "I" (אני) is the beginning of the second half of the verse. Thus, the insolent and the speaker are juxtaposed at the center of the verse. A stilted translation represents the contrast: "They smear upon me deception—the insolent ones, but I—wholeheartedly I keep your precepts." Juxtaposing "them" and "I" in the center of the verse and emphasizes the contrast between the wicked and the speaker. There are additional lexical links between the two verses. The third person plural suffix of "their heart" (לבם v. 70) refers back to the insolent in v. 69. The word "heart" (לב) occurs in both verses, although the connotations are different. In v. 69 "heart" is part of the phrase "wholeheartedly," which describes the speaker's commitment. In v. 70 the heart of the wicked introduces a different motif, specifically the intellect. By calling the wicked "dull," which is the sense of the first half of v. 70, the author equates those who are morally obtuse and those who are

---

[56] טרם אענה אותך במצותיך—טרם הגיתי בהם בבתי מדרשות , אני שוגג בהם וחוטא: ועתה משעניתי בהם, תורתך שמרתי, שהמדרש מלמדני לסור מן העבירה Ha-Keter, 170.

[57] Jastrow, 549.

mentally obtuse. In the book of Proverbs too, intellectual and moral failings are related, although finer distinctions can be discerned.

The use of various motifs in vv. 69 and 70 supports the thesis that a central goal of Ps 119 is to characterize the speaker, and the motifs in vv. 69 and 70 are repeated throughout the psalm—deception, keeping God's precepts, antagonism between the speaker and his enemies, the speaker's complete commitment, the speaker's delight in Torah, and the relationship of piety and pedagogy. All of these contribute primarily to the portrait of the speaker. The speaker declares in v. 69 that he keeps God's precepts, but the important point is that he keeps them "wholeheartedly." The insolent are labeled "dull" in v. 70, and this is used as a contrast to the intellectual curiosity of the speaker.

Verse 74: This is one of the few verses that mentions other righteous people. As Ehrlich notes, there is a wordplay between the first two words of the verse—יְרֵאֶיךָ יִרְאוּנִי.[58]

Verse 77: Cf. v. 41.

Verse 80: Cf. v. 1.

Verse 81: The translation "fails for" is not good English; it is an attempt to represent a construction in Hebrew that is somewhat elliptical. Both BDB (p. 477) and *HALOT* (p. 477) suggest that the concept of longing is implied, which could be paraphrased "my soul is exhausted from longing for your salvation," but this connotation is from the second half of the verse rather than from the meaning of the verb כלה.[59] See also the following verse.

Verse 82: The idiom "eyes failing" (using the verb כלה) can be a way of describing disease and death (1 Sam 2:33; Jer 14:6; Job 11:20), but the idiom is also used in contexts where imminent death is not the focus. It seems to be similar to the English hyperbolic idiom "I am dying to...." (Possible examples are Ps 69:4; Lam 4:17).

Verse 85: See p. 80.

---

[58] Ehrlich, 311.

[59] It seems that the lexica have confused the notions of lexical and contextual meaning by including "desire" as part of the range of meaning for the word כלה. In Ps 84:3 this word is juxtaposed with a word that does have "desire" as part of its denotation, but it is illegitimate simply to transfer "desire" to other contexts where the word כלה occurs. Intense longing is a motif that contributes to the characterization of the speaker and fits the context of Ps 119, but the motif is not based on this lexical item.

Verse 86: Instead of "with deception," Rashi interprets this phrase with the Hebrew word שוא, meaning "nothing," i.e., "They persecuted me for no reason."[60]

Verses 89–91: See pp. 124–126.

Verse 90: Literally, "Your faithfulness is for generations." I supply "endures" for the sake of English idiom. This is another example of an associative sequence, since the phrase "from generation to generation" overlaps conceptually with "forever" (לעולם) in v. 89.

Verse 91: The translation "the whole are your servants" pairs a singular subject with a plural verb. In Hebrew the clause is verbless, yet it juxtaposes a singular substantive with a plural substantive. All of creation can be referred to as a single entity, and all of the beings that constitute creation are God's servants. The lack of concord reflects this reality. (In Josh 23:14 "the whole" [הכל] is paired with a plural verb, but this is rare.)

Verse 92: See p. 153 and Ps 94:17.

Verse 96: The word תכלה is a *hapax legomenon* that BDB translates as "completeness, perfection" (p. 479). In Job 11:7 a related word (תכלית) means "extremity" or "boundary." If the word תכלה indicates a boundary, then the word קץ seems redundant, and Delitzsch describes it as a gloss inserted to explain the meaning of the difficult word תכלה.[61] Deissler interprets the verse in light of Job 11:7 and 28:3, both of which contain the idea that there is a boundary (תכלית) to mankind's ability for discovery. Because Deissler sees connections between Ps 119 and other biblical passages whenever possible, he imports this idea into v. 96, but his arguments are not convincing. Even if it is not possible to explain תכלה precisely, there is a distinct contrast between God's expansive commandment and other entities. Rashi's interpretation makes this contrast clear: "For the completion of everything there is an end and a boundary, but of your commandment

---

[60] לשוא רדפוני אויבי Ha-Keter, 172. Gruber (p. 393) suggests that this is based on the use of the two words in Exod 20:16 and Deut 5:17. (The versification is Deut 5:20 in BHS.) These two verses are the commandment, "You shall not bear false witness." The phrase "false witness" occurs in Exodus as עד שקר, and in Deuteronomy as עד שוא, which allows Rashi to make this connection.

[61] Friedrich Delitzsch, *Die Lese- und Schreibfehler im Alten Testament* (Berlin: de Gruyter, 1920), 136.

there is no boundary for its completion."[62] Ehrlich suggests that this verse is a reference to Oral Torah, since the written Torah certainly has a boundary.[63]

Verse 98: In the word "commandment" (מצותך) there is not a *yod* (י) preceding the suffix as there most commonly is with plural nouns. The pronoun "it" (היא) in the second stich, referring back to "commandment" (מצותך) is feminine singular. Additionally, the verb in the first half of the verse is singular. Despite all of this, the Masoretes vocalized the word with the vowels that are most commonly the vocalization of a plural noun, specifically with a *seghol* before the suffix. See also the discussion of v. 96 on p. 114 and of the early textual witnesses beginning on p. 185.

Verse 99: In theory the first half of this verse could be translated, "I have discretion from all my teachers."[64] This translation reflects Rashi's understanding of the verse: "I learned a little from this one and a little from that one."[65] At issue is the function of the preposition (מן) at the beginning of the verse. Two factors support interpreting the preposition as a comparative מן ("more than my teachers") instead of a מן of source ("from all my teachers"). One is the function of the preposition in v. 98, which is undoubtedly a מן of comparison. Since the comparative interpretation of the preposition is required in v. 98 and since vv. 98 and 99 are syntactically similar [מן...כי] is the pattern for both verses], it is also a natural reading of v. 99. The second factor is the relationship between the two halves of v. 99. If the first stich is read "from all my teachers," then the second half of the verse is a non-sequitur. Levenson interprets the preposition as source ("from").[66] His argument is not convincing, and it is rebutted effectively by Greenberg.[67]

---

[62] לכל סיום דבר קץ וגבול, אבל מצותך—אין גבול לתכליתה Ha-Keter, 172.

[63] Ehrlich, 314.

[64] On the words "discretion" and "insight" see Michael V. Fox, *Proverbs 1–9*, 30, 36, 37. There is not sufficient context in Ps 119 to draw fine distinctions between the various words for intellectual activities.

[65] מזי למדתי קצת ומזה קצת Ha-Keter, 174.

[66] Jon D. Levenson, "The Sources of Torah: Psalm 119 and the Modes of Revelation in Second Temple Judaism," in *Ancient Israelite Religion: Essays in Honor of Frank Moore Cross*, ed. Paul D. Hanson, S. D. McBride, and Patrick D. Miller (Philadelphia: Fortress, 1987), 566.

[67] Moshe Greenberg, "Three Conceptions of the Torah in Hebrew Scriptures," in *Studies in the Bible and Jewish Thought* (Philadelphia: Jewish Publication Society, 1995), 11–23.

Verse 100: This verse is constructed with the same template as vv. 98 and 99 [מ...כי], and the same arguments regarding the function of the initial preposition (מן) apply here as well.

Verse 102: The pronoun אתה, which I indicate in the translation with "yourself," is not necessary to complete the syntax, and thus seems to emphasize the fact that God is the teacher.

Verse 103: Rashi glosses the *hapax logomenon* נמלצו with נמקו "to be sweet."[68] The translation "smooth" is suggested by BDB (p. 576), but it is not certain.

Verse 106: Various interpretations of this verse are possible. KJV interprets the second verb (ואקימה) as parenthetical, and this interpretation is adopted in the translation. Without including the parenthetical verb, the syntax of the remainder of the verse is straightforward. The infinitive clause functions as the complement of the verb "to swear" (נשבעתי), which is a verb that commonly has an infinitive as a complement. The parenthetical verb is then emphatic—"I really will do it."

Another possibility is that the first two verbs are coordinate, i.e., on the same syntactic level, and thus form a compound verb. Both NKJ ("I have sworn and confirmed that I will keep Your righteous judgments") and TNK ("I have firmly sworn to keep Your just rules") apparently interpret the verbs as a compound phrase. A third option involves two levels of subordination. In the third option, the verb נשבעתי is the matrix verb or at the "highest" level. The verb ואקימה is then subordinate to the verb נשבעתי, and the infinitive לשמר is subordinate to the verb ואקימה. These other options do not significantly change the meaning of the verse, and I find the first option to be the simplest solution.

Verse 108: This is the only verse in Ps 119 that alludes to sacrifice, and the offering here is prayer and praise rather than literal sacrifice. Psalm 141:2 explicitly asks God to accept prayer as a supplement to the cult—or perhaps as a substitute for the cult.

Verse 109: "My life is in my hand" describes a situation of danger elsewhere in the Hebrew Bible (cf. Judg 12:3 and 1 Sam 19:5). Ehrlich translates "ständig in Gefahr."[69] This verse is one example of many in

---

[68] Ha-Keter, 174.
[69] Ehrlich, 317.

which the relationship between the two stichs is not specified. Rashi specifies the relationship with "nevertheless" (אע"פ).[70]

Verse 112: See v. 33 and the discussion beginning on p. 172.

Verse 113: The word "divided" (סעפים) is listed in BDB as people who are divided "in a religious sense" (p. 704). Rashi also explains the word as a reference to people.[71] If the word refers to people then BDB may be correct; however, there is no reason that it cannot denote concepts or ideas. It is an adjective functioning as a substantive. This spelling does not appear elsewhere in the Hebrew Bible; the closest parallel occurs in 1 Kgs 18:21. In that context the word denotes different sides of a debate. Instead of understanding the word as referring to people (BDB), it is best to understand the term as a contrast between the second half of the verse. The verse as a whole is then a positive statement about the unity of Torah.

Verse 116: Elsewhere in the psalm the speaker states that his hope is in God's word, and it is an assumption throughout the psalm that God's word will not fail.

Verse 118: "Tossed aside" is a suggestion from BDB based in part on Akkadian evidence. Another possibility is the Aramaic word סלא "to reject." The only other occurrence of the word is in Lam 1:15, where some translations derive the meaning from the parallelism and gloss the word with "trample." Rashi cites this verse in support of the meaning "to trample."[72] The precise meaning of the word is difficult to ascertain, not only because it is rare but also because it is being used as a figure of speech.

In the second half of the verse, the MT has two different words for deception (תרמיתם and שקר) that seem to result in a tautology: "...their deceitfulness is deception." The ancient versions may be reading "thoughts" (תדעיתם) instead of "deceitfulness," but this is poor evidence for a different *Vorlage*. It is more likely that the versions are attempting to explain a difficult Hebrew text. The verse must be emphasizing the injurious nature of their deceit, since the word שקר has an element of harm as part of its semantic range. See also v. 163. In any case, those who stray from God's statutes should not be trusted.

---

[70] Ha-Keter, 174.
[71] Ha-Keter, 174.
[72] Ha-Keter, 176.

Verse 119: The first stich of this verse has conceptual parallels with the first stich of v. 118. This is another example of an associative sequence. The second stich indicates that the stipulations of a just God—i.e., one who brings an end to the wicked—deserve to be loved.[73]

Verse 120: See v. 161. Rashi explains the fear as fear of divine punishment.[74] The motivation for obedience in v. 119 is love; the motivation in this verse is fear. There is no contradiction between the two, and both fear and love are motivations used in Proverbs to encourage the addressee to find and follow a wise path. Hakham notes that the second half of the verse continues the idea of fear, which is found in the first half of the verse.[75]

Verse 121: Ehrlich interprets the relationship between the stichs as follows: the speaker does what is just so that God will ensure what is just for him.[76] This interpretation illustrates how the relationship between the verses is open to interpretation. Ehrlich's suggestion is not required by the Hebrew, but it is possible.

Verse 122: *HALOT* (p. 876) notes that this is a metaphorical use of the word ערב and interprets it "to lend support for someone's cause." See also Isa 38:14.

Verse 123: On the idiom "my eyes fail" see v. 82. "My eyes fail" is followed by two coordinate prepositional phrases that indicate the object of the speaker's longing. The juxtaposition of "salvation" and "your righteous word" implies some relationship between them, but the verse does not specify the nature of the relationship. Rashi specifies the relationship by interpreting the second half of the verse as a reference to a promise. Ehrlich notes that in parallel with ישועה, the word צדק often means salvation ("Heil").[77]

Verse 126: Rashi connects this verse with the previous verse: "[This] continues the verse of scripture which is above—'Give me insight to know your stipulations' in order to understand 'the time to act' for your name."[78] Rashi's interpretation raises the question of who is

---

[73] So Ehrlich, 318.
[74] ממשפטיך יראתי—מפורענות גזרותיך Ha-Keter, 176.
[75] Hakham, ספר תהלים, 417.
[76] "Der Sänger übt Recht und Gerechtigkeit, damit JHVH dafür sorge, dass auch ihm Recht geschieht." Ehrlich, 318.
[77] Ehrlich, 319.
[78] וגו" מוסב אל מקרא שלפניו הביני ואדעה עדותיך להבין עת לעשות לשמך Ha-Keter, 176.

acting—people for the sake of God or God for the sake of people. If the actors are people, then the second half of the verse seems out of place, and Rashi's solution is that the "action" is to seek for forgiveness. Ehrlich also argues, based on the word order, that God cannot be the actor, but word order is not sufficient evidence in this case. The repeated theme of enemies and the contrast in this verse support the translation given here; that is, God is the actor, and the action is judgment against those who have broken God's rules. One problematic detail is the ל preposition prefixed to the divine name. Deissler simply states that the preposition is a mistake and deletes it.[79]

Nowhere else in the Hebrew Bible is Torah the object of the verb "to break" (פרר), which is the typical verb for breaking a covenant.

Verse 127: The beginning of this verse ("therefore" על כן) is problematic, since there is no apparent connection with the previous verse or verses. Some commentators substitute "above all" (על כל) for the MT "therefore" (על כן); this is a conjectural, albeit minor, emendation. Rashi argues that there are numerous examples of על כן that should be understood as על אשר, which is to say, "because," and he lists Gen 33:10, Num 10:31, and Isa 15:7 as examples.[80] Allen comments that "therefore" can be understood in relationship to v. 126, which contains a petition for God to act. The speaker anticipates that God will intervene in response to his petition, and based on this anticipation he "therefore" declares his love of God's commandments.[81]

The speaker frequently expresses his love for God's commandments, e.g., vv. 47 and 72; see the discussion of the speaker's emotions in chapter 3.

Verse 128: The "therefore" (על כן) at the beginning of the verse associates the speaker's love of God's commandments, which is expressed in v. 127, with his complete obedience, which is expressed in this verse in the phrase "walk straight." This understanding of the verse is based on the verb ישר in combination with the trope of the path. When the verb occurs in D it is often related to the metaphor of a path, for example, to make a path straight (Isa 40:3) or to walk straight (Prov

---

[79] "Dem Kontext entsprechend ist mit einer hebräischen Handschrift und hier das *le* vor Jahwe im MT zu streichen. Es muß beim Abschreiben durch Ideenassoziation mit ähnlichen Wendungen (cf. Jer 51, 6) eingedrungen sein." Deissler, 223.

[80] יש על כן הרבה שפתרונם כמו על אשר Ha-Keter, 178.

[81] Allen, *Psalms 101–150*, 138.

15:21). This idiom is used by TNK: "...by all Your precepts I walk straight." Because the second half of the verse includes the metaphor of the path, this possibility is plausible.

Rashi gives an alternate explanation (adopted by KJV) that is based on the idiom "it was upright in his eyes" (ישר followed by עינים). "They are upright in my eyes, and I said about them, 'They are upright.'"[82] Supplying this idiom without any contextual support seems less likely than the interpretation given above, and the idiom requires G rather than D. Regardless of which interpretation is adopted, the speaker's actions are presumably the same. That is, if the speaker esteems the precepts correct, then he will walk in them.

Following this clause Rashi adds an interesting comment: "On account of this I am deserving of your forgiveness and your favor on me."[83] Nothing in this verse indicates that the speaker deserves God's favor, but as I argue in chapters 3 and 4, some relationship between obedience and God's favor is part of the psalmist's conception of Torah observance and his relationship with God. It is not clear why Rashi includes the idea in his comments on this verse, but he seems to be influenced by ideas that are present elsewhere in Ps 119.

The construction כל X כל (i.e., the repetition of כל with an intervening word) is rare in the Hebrew Bible, and the versions struggle to translate it. Many commentators make some change to the consonantal text; one of the simplest solutions is to delete the ל of the second כל and read the remaining כ as the second person pronominal suffix, namely, instead of כל פקודי כל read כל פקודיך. This solution is plausible, since almost every occurrence of the Torah terms in Ps 119 are suffixed with the second person pronoun. Despite the fact that the construction with a repetition of כל is rare, it does occur in Ezek 44:30, where it indicates that there are no exceptions: "all the first fruits of everything" (כל בכורי כל). The phrase in the MT indicates that the speaker behaves righteously with regard to "every single last one" of God's precepts.

Verse 129: Rashi explains that the stipulations are wonderful because they are so simple and yet their reward is so great. As an example, he

---

[82] ישרתי—ישרו בעיני, ואמרתי עליהם ישרו Ha-Keter, 178.

[83] על זה כדי אני שתמחל ותרצה לי Ha-Keter, 178. Note the words "forgiveness" and "favor" are verbs in Hebrew; I translate them with nominalizations here for the sake of English style.

cites the commandment against taking both a bird and her eggs at the same time (Deut 22:6, 7).[84] The reward for obeying this simple commandment is long life.

Verse 130: See the discussion beginning on p. 53. Rashi interprets "opening" as the beginning.[85] He continues by stating God granted understanding to the simple when he said, "I am the LORD your God…" (Exod 20:2). This interpretation assumes the notion, common in rabbinic writings, that the beginning of the Ten Commandments is in some sense the beginning of Torah. Rashi also adds that another interpretation is that the "light" in this verse is an allusion to the creation, which is also the beginning of Torah (Gen 1). Ehrlich notes that revelation, which the word פתח implies, is conceptually related to the "hidden" wonders in v. 129.[86] This interpretation assumes a connection between vv. 18 and 129, since the word פלאות occurs in both verses.

Verse 131: On "longing" see v. 20.

Verse 132: "The justice of those who love your name" is the right or privilege belonging to those who love your name (BDB, 1049). The verse implies that those who love God's name can expect to receive God's grace, but this raises the question of the definition of "grace" (חנן). If the speaker is requesting something that is his "right," then in what sense is it undeserved, i.e., "grace"? The author of Ps 119 does not try to work out the logical relationship between the notion that those who love God's name have some claim on God and his requests for mercy.

Verse 135: See p. 99.

Verse 136: See p. 80. Ehrlich argues that the word על indicates what the speaker is crying about and therefore interprets the phrase as a substantive—"those who do not observe…."[87] He is correct about the function of the word על, but the substantive is not the people themselves. Instead, it is the *fact* that they do not observe. The word "because" renders "regarding the fact" more elegantly in English.

Verse 138: See v. 4.

Verse 139: See v. 136 and p. 80.

---

[84] יש מצות קלות שהרביתה במתן שכרן, כגון שילוח הקן Ha-Keter, 178.
[85] Ha-Keter, 178.
[86] Ehrlich, 320.
[87] Ehrlich, 321.

Verse 145: The translation "so that," in this verse and the following verse, is based on the use of the cohortative form. However, it is not clear how the form should be mapped to function in Ps 119. On this problem see v. 15.

Verse 146: See v. 145.

Verse 147: The timeframe is not entirely clear; the word "twilight" (נשׁף) can be either the evening or the morning (cf. Job 7:4). Both Ibn Ezra and Radaq interpret the verse as referring to early in the morning.[88] Several English translations (ESV, JPS, NAS, NKJV, RSV) adopt a similar rendering. If this is the case, then vv. 147 and 148 can be understood to mean that the speaker contemplates God's word before he falls asleep and immediately when he awakes. The translation "I arose" is based on the assumption that this verse refers to the early morning, although the verb "to arise" is not in the Hebrew. Ibn Ezra explains the verb קדמתי as "before people arise."[89] This is not to say that the verb means "to arise," but rather that the context implies the action of rising.

Verse 148: See v. 147. The translation "my eyes anticipated" might be paraphrased, "I looked forward to...." Wagner argues that this nuance of the word is an example of Aramaic influence.[90]

Verse 149: On "justice" see chapter 4. See also v. 156.

Verse 150: On the use of near and far, see the discussion beginning on p. 81 and cf. v. 155.

Verse 152: The first word of the verse "beforehand" (קדם) is a substantive that is often used adverbially to indicate an earlier time, and in this verse it modifies the verb "I know" (ידעתי). Combining these English equivalents would give the translation, "I knew beforehand...," but this raises the question: before what? Joüon states "קדם Ps 119.152 is used with the meaning of מקדם *from of old.*"[91] But his interpretation is impossible, since the speaker did not exist "from of old."

The point of the verse is not prior knowledge but rather the beginning of knowledge. The statement could be paraphrased as follows: The first stage of my knowledge was from your stipulations. A similar

---

[88] Ha-Keter, 181.

[89] קדמתי—קודם שיקומו בני אדם Ha-Keter, 181.

[90] Max Wagner, *Die lexikalischen und grammatikalischen Aramaismen im alttestamentlichen Hebräisch*, BZAW, vol. 96 (Berlin: Töpelmann, 1966).

[91] JM § 126.i.

use of the word קדם occurs in Prov 8:22. Radaq explains, "The beginning of what I know and what I understand is from your precepts."[92]

Verse 155: Cf. v. 150.

Verse 158: The antecedent of אשר is "the treacherous ones" (בגדים),
and thus the verse defines the treacherous as those who disobey God's
word. On the speaker's attitude toward the wicked see v. 136.

Verse 160: The word translated "beginning" (ראש) is used in various ways throughout the Hebrew Bible, such as "beginning," "chief," or
"best." Any interpretation of this verse based on the meanings "chief,"
"best," or "top" would be open to the inference that some lesser part of
God's word is not true. Radaq implicitly contrasts the two halves of the
verse and emphasizes that God's word was and is always true, "From
the beginning of the world unto forever..." (מראש העולם ולעולם).[93]
Other medieval commentators (Ibn Ezra, Rashi, Metsudat Zion,
Hame'iri) associate this verse with the beginning of the ten commandments by citing, "I am YHWH your God" (Exod 20:2); cf. v. 130.

Verse 161: See v. 120, and cf. Isa 66:2, 5 and Ezra 9:4; 10:3. The
speaker does not specify that he is not afraid of princes, but the juxtaposition implies that. Ibn Ezra says, "I am not afraid of them only
your word."[94]

Verse 162: Ibn Ezra associates the ideas in this verse with the previous verse. There is a contrast between the speaker's joy (שש) and fear
(פחד), and the mention of princes seems to bring the idea of spoil to
mind. "I am not afraid of princes and I do not worry. I only delight in
your word, as if I defeated the princes and took their spoil."[95]

Verse 163: Deception is a common motif; see, e.g., v. 118. Ibn Ezra
states that "deception" (שקר) is "not doing" the commandments, and
loving Torah is "doing" the commandments.[96] Radaq explains that
Torah is the opposite of "deception" (שקר) and he loves the truth.[97]

Verse 168: Rashi specifies that the phrase "my ways are before you"
means that God knows the speaker's ways.[98]

---

[92] קדם—תחלה מה שידעתי ומה שהבינותי מעדותיך Ha-Keter, 183.

[93] Ha-Keter, 183.

[94] ולא פחדתי מהם רק מדברך Ha-Keter, 183.

[95] דבק פדוק העליון: לא פחדתי מהשרים ולא דאגתי רק ששתי באמרתך כאילו נצחתי
השרים ולקחתי שללם Ha-Keter, 183.

[96] שקר—מצות לא תעשה תורתך אהבתי מצות עשה Ha-Keter, 183.

[97] כי הוא בהפך השקר ואהבתי האמת Ha-Keter, 183.

[98] אתה יודע כל דרכי Ha-Keter, 184. So also Ehrlich, 324.

Verse 171: Cf. v. 7.

Verse 174: Cf. v. 20.

Verse 176: The statement "I have gone astray" is somewhat surprising, since throughout most of the psalm the speaker declares his fealty to the commandments and even declares that he does not stray from them. On such inconsistencies see the discussion beginning on p. 90.

BIBLIOGRAPHY

Achenbach, Reinhard. "Der Pentateuch, seine theokratischen Bearbeitungen und Josua–2 Könige." In Les dernières rédactions du Pentateuque, de l'Hexateuque et de l'Ennéteuque, ed. Thomas Römer and Konrad Schmid, 225–53. BEThL 203. Leuven: Leuven University Press, 2007.

———. *Die Vollendung der Tora: Studien zur Redaktionsgeschichte des Numeribuches im Kontext von Hexateuch und Pentateuch.* BZAR 3. Wiesbaden: Harrassowitz, 2007.

———. "Pentateuch, Hexateuch und Enneateuch. Eine Verhältnisbestimmung." *ZAR* 11 (2005): 122–54.

———. "The Pentateuch, the Prophets, and the Torah in the Fifth and Fourth Centuries B.C.E." In *Judah and the Judeans in the Fourth Century B.C.E.*, ed. Oded Lipschits et al., 247–80. Winona Lake, IN: Eisenbrauns, 2007.

Albertz, Rainer. *Persönliche Frömmigkeit und offizielle Religion: religionsinterner Pluralismus in Israel und Babylon.* Calwer theologische Monographien, vol. 8. Stuttgart: Calwer Verlag, 1978.

———. *Religionsgeschichte Israels in alttestamentlicher Zeit.* Vol. 2, *Das Alte Testament Deutsch, Ergänzungsreihe.* Göttingen: Vandenhoeck & Ruprecht, 1992.

Albright, William Foxwell. "The Names 'Israel' and 'Judah' with an Excursion on the Etymology of Todah and Torah." *JBL* 46 (1927): 151–85.

———. "The Supposed Babylonian Derivation of the Logos." *JBL* 39 (1920): 143–51.

Allen, Leslie C. "David as Exemplar of Spirituality: The Redactional Function of Psalm 19." *Bib* 67 (1986): 544–46.

———. *Psalms 101–150.* Word Biblical Commentary. Waco, TX: Word, 1983.

Alter, Robert. *The Art of Biblical Poetry.* New York: Basic Books, 1985.

Amir, Yehoshua. "Die 'Mitte der Schrift' aus der Sicht des hellenistischen Judentums." In *Mitte der Schrift? Ein jüdisch-christliches Gespräch*, ed. Martin Klopfenstein et al., 217–36. Judaica et Christiana, vol. 11. Bern: Peter Lang, 1987.

———. "מקומו של מזמור קיט בתולדות דת ישראל" in עיונים במקרא ספר זכרון ליהושע מאיר גריץ ["The place of Psalm 119 in the religion of Israel." in *Studies in scripture: a volume in memory of Joshua Meir Grintz* (Hebrew)]. Tel Aviv: Hakibbutz Hamuchad Publishing, 1982.

Andersen, Francis I. and David Noel Freedman. *Amos: A New Translation with Introduction and Commentary.* The Anchor Bible, vol. 24A. New York: Doubleday, 1989.

Anderson, A. A. *The Book of Psalms.* 2 vols. London: Oliphants, 1972.

Anton, J. P. "Aristotle on the Nature of Logos." *The Philosophy of Logos* 1 (1996): 11–21.

Arneth, Martin. "Psalm 19: Tora oder Messias?" *ZAR* 6 (2000): 82–112.

Ashburn, Daniel G. "Creation and Torah in Psalm 19." *JBQ* 22 (1994): 241–48.

Auffret, Pierre. *Mais tu élargiras mon cœr: Nouvelle etude structurelle du psaume 119.* BZAW, vol. 359. Berlin: Walter de Gruyter, 2006.

Austermann, Frank. *Von der Tora zum Nomos: Untersuchungen zur Übersetzungweise und Interpretation im Septuaginta-Psalter.* Mitteilungen des Septuaginta-Unternehmens, vol. 27. Göttingen: Vandenhoeck & Ruprecht, 2003.

Austin, J. L. *How to do Things with Words.* Cambridge, MA: Harvard University Press, 1962.

Balentine, Samuel E. *The Hidden God: The Hiding of the Face of God in the Old Testament.* Oxford Theological Monographs, ed. James Barr et al. Oxford: Oxford University Press, 1983.

Ballhorn, Egbert. *Zum Telos des Psalters: der Textzusammenhang des Vierten und Fünften Psalmenbuches*. Bonner biblische Beiträge, vol. 138. Berlin: Philo, 2004.

Barkay, Gabriel, Marilyn J. Lundberg, Andrew G. Vaughn, Bruce Zuckerman, and Kenneth Zuckerman. "The Challenges of Ketef Hinnom: Using Advanced Technologies to Reclaim the Earliest Biblical Texts and Their Context." *Near Eastern Archaeology* 66 (2003): 162–71.

Barth, C. *Introduction to the Psalms*. Oxford: Basil Blackwell, 1966.

Barthélemy, Dominique and J. T. Milik, eds. *Qumran Cave I*. DJD I. Oxford: Clarendon Press, 1955.

Barthes, Roland. "Theory of the Text." In *Untying the Text: A Post-Structuralist Reader*, ed. R. Young, 31–47. Boston: Routledge and Kegan Paul, 1981.

Bauckmann, E. G. "Die Proverbien und die Sprüche des Jesus Sirach." *ZAW* 72 (1960): 33–63.

Baumgarten, A. I. "The Pharisaic *Paradosis*." *HTR* 80 (1987): 63–77.

———. "The Torah as a Public Document." *Studies in Religion* 14 (1985): 17–24.

Bautch, Richard J. *Developments in Genre between Post-Exilic Penitential Prayers and the Psalms of Communal Lament*. Academia Biblica, vol. 7. Atlanta, GA: Society of Biblical Literature, 2003.

Beck, Brenda E. F. "The Metaphor as a Mediator Between Semantic and Analogic Modes of Thought." *Current Anthropology* 19 (1978): 83–97.

Beck, David R. "The Narrative Function of Anonymity in Fourth Gospel Characterization." *Semeia* 63 (1993): 143–58.

Beckwith, Roger T. "The Early History of the Psalter." *Tyndale Bulletin* 46 (1995): 1–27.

Beentjes, Pancratius. "Discovering a New Path of Intertextuality: Inverted Quotations and their Dynamics." In *Literary Structure and Rhetorical Strategies in the Hebrew Bible*, ed. J. de Waard, L. J. de Regt, and J. P. Fokkelman, 31–49. Winona Lake, IN: Eisenbrauns, 1996.

———. "Inverted Quotations." *Bib* 63 (1982): 506–23.

Begrich, Joachim. "Die priesterliche Tora." In *Werden und Wesen des Alten Testaments*, ed. P. Volz et al., 63–88. BZAW, vol. 66. Berlin: Töpelmann, 1936.

Ben-Porat, Ziva. "The Poetics of Literary Allusion." *PTL: A Journal for Descriptive Poetics and Theory of Literature* 1 (1976): 105–28.

Benveniste, Emile. *Problems in General Linguistics*. Translated by Mary Elizabeth Meek. Miami Linguistics Series, vol. 8. Coral Gables, FL: University of Miami Press, 1971.

Berges, Ulrich. "Die Knechte im Psalter. Ein Beitrag zu seiner Kompositionsgeschichte." *Bib* 81 (2000): 153–78.

———. *Klagelieder*. HThKAT. Freiburg: Herder, 2002.

Bernstein, Moshe J. "Torah and Its Study in the Targum of Psalms." In *Hazon Nahum: Studies in Jewish Law, Thought, and History Presented to Dr. Norman Lamm on the Occasion of his Seventieth Birthday*, ed. Yaakov Elman and Jeffrey S. Gurock, 39–67. New York: Yeshiva University Press, 1997.

Besnier, Niko. "Language and Affect." *Annual Review of Anthropology* 19 (1990): 419–51.

Birkeland, H. *The Evildoers in the Book of Psalms*. Oslo: J. Dybwad, 1955.

Blank, Sheldon. "The LXX Renderings of Old Testament Terms for Law." *HUCA* 7 (1930): 259–83.

Blenkinsopp, Joseph. *Ezra-Nehemiah*. OTL. Philadelphia: Westminster, 1989.

———. *A History of Prophecy in Israel: From the Settlement in the Land to the Hellenistic Period*. Philadelphia: Westminster, 1984.

———. *Prophecy and Canon*. Notre Dame, IN: Notre Dame Press, 1977.

———. *Sage, Priest, Prophet: Religious and Intellectual Leadership in Ancient Israel*. Louisville, KY: Westminster John Knox, 1995.

——. *Wisdom and Law in the Old Testament: The Ordering of Life in Israel and Early Judaism*. Oxford: Oxford University Press, 1995.

Bloom, Harold. *The Anxiety of Influence: A Theory of Poetry*. New York: Oxford University Press, 1973.

Blum, Erhard. *Studien zur Komposition des Pentateuch*. BZAW, vol. 189. Berlin: Walter de Gruyter, 1990.

Boccaccini, Gabriele. "The Preexistence of the Torah." *Henoch* 17 (1995): 329–50.

——. *Roots of Rabbinic Judaism*. Grand Rapids, MI: Eerdmans, 2002.

Boda, Mark J. *Praying the Tradition: The Origin and Use of Tradition in Nehemiah 9*. BZAW, vol. 277. Berlin: Walter de Gruyter, 1999.

Bonkamp, Bernhard. *Die Psalmen nach dem hebräischen Grundtext*. Freiburg: Willhelm Visarius, 1949.

Booij, Thijs. "Psalm 119:89–91." *Bib* 79 (1998): 539–41.

Booth, Wayne C. "Distance and Point-of-View: An Essay in Classification." *Essays in Criticism* 11 (1961): 60–79.

Boström, Gustav. *The God of the Sages*. Stockholm: Almqvist & Wiksell, 1990.

Botha, P. J. "The Function of the Polarity Between the Pious and the Enemies in Psalm 119." *OTE* 5 (1992): 252–63.

——. "Intertextuality and the Interpretation of Psalm 1." *OTE* 18 (2005): 503–20.

——. "The Measurement of Meaning: An Exercise in Field Semantics." *Journal for Semitics* 1 (1989): 3–22.

——. "Shame and the Social Setting of Psalm 119." *OTE* 12 (1999): 389–400.

Boyarin, Daniel. "The Gospel of the Memra: Jewish Binitarianism and the Prologue to John." *HTR* 94 (2001): 243–84.

Braude, William G. *The Midrash on Psalms*. Yale Judaica Series, vol. 13. ed. Leon Nemoy. New Haven, CT: Yale University Press, 1959.

Braulik, Georg. "Die Ausdrücke für *Gesetz* im Buch Deuteronomium." *Bib* 51 (1970): 39–66.

——. "Gesetz als Evangelium." *ZThK* 79 (1982): 127–60.

——. "The Sequence of the Laws in Deuteronomy 12–26 and in the Decalogue." In *The Song of Power and the Power of Song: Essays on the Book of Deuteronomy*, ed. D. L. Christensen, 313–35. SBTS, vol. 3. Winona Lake, IN: Eisenbrauns, 1993.

Brekelmans, Christian. "Wisdom Influence in Deuteronomy." In *La sagesse de l'Ancien Testament*, ed. Maurice Gilbert, 28–38. Gembloux: J. Duculot, 1979.

Bridges, Charles. *Exposition of Psalm CXIX*. London: Seeley, Jackson, and Halliday, 1857.

Briggs, Charles A. and Emilie G. *The Psalms*. 2 vols. ICC. Edinburgh: T & T Clark, 1906.

Bright, Pamela. "Singing the Psalms; Augustine and Athanasius on the Integration of the Self." In *The Whole and Divided Self: The Bible and Theological Anthropology*, ed. David E. Aune and John McCarthy, 115–29. New York: Crossroad Publishing Company, 1997.

Brock, Brian. "Bonhoeffer and the Bible in Christian Ethics: Psalm 119, The Mandates, and Ethics as a 'Way'." *Studies in Christian Ethics* 18 (2005): 7–29.

Brownlee, W. "Psalms 1–2 as a Coronation Liturgy." *Bib* 52 (1971): 321–36.

Broyles, Craig C. *The Conflict of Faith and Experience in the Psalms: a Form-Critical and Theological Study*. JSOTSup, vol. 52. Sheffield: Sheffield Academic Press, 1989.

Brueggemann, Walter. *The Creative Word*. Philadelphia: Fortress, 1982.

Brueggemann, Walter and Patrick D. Miller. "Psalm 73 as a Canonical Marker." *JSOT* 72 (1996): 45–55.

Burger, Johan A. "Psalm 1 and Wisdom." *OTE* 8 (1995): 327–39.

Burkes, Shannon. "Wisdom and Law: Choosing Life in Ben Sira and Baruch." *Journal for the Study of Judaism* 30 (1999): 254–76.

Burkett, Ken. "Psalm 119: A Thematic and Literary Analysis." Ph.D. diss., Bob Jones University, 1994.

Buttenwieser, M. *The Psalms*. 1938. New York: Ktav, 1969.

Carr, David M. *Writing on the Tablet of the Heart*. Oxford: Oxford University Press, 2005.

Carroll, R. P. "Inscribing the Covenant: Writing and the Written in Jeremiah." In *Understanding Poets and Prophets: Essays in Honour of George Wishart Anderson*, ed. A. G. Auld, 61–76, JSOTSup, vol. 152. Sheffield: JSOT Press, 1993.

——. "Manuscripts Don't Burn—Inscribing the Prophetic Tradition: Reflections on Jeremiah 36." In *Dort ziehen Schiffe dahin*, ed. M. Augustin et al., 31–42. International Organization for the Study of the Old Testament Congress. Frankfurt am Main: Peter Lang, 1996.

Ceresko, Anthony R. "The ABCs of Wisdom in Psalm XXXIV." *VT* 35 (1985): 99–104.

——. "The Sage in the Psalms." In *The Sage in Israel and the Ancient Near East*, ed. J. G. Gammie and L. G. Perdue, 217–30. Winona Lake, IN: Eisenbrauns, 1990.

Chandler, James K. "Romantic Allusiveness." *Critical Inquiry* 8 (1982): 461–87.

Chapman, Stephen B. "'The Law and the Words' as a Canonical Formula within the Old Testament." In *The Interpretation of Scripture in Judaism and Early Christianity*, ed. Craig Evans, 26–74. Sheffield: Sheffield, 2000.

Charlesworth, James. "Isaiah 40:3 and the Serek Ha-Yaúad." In *The Quest for Context and Meaning: Studies in Biblical Intertextuality in Honor of James A. Sanders*, ed. Craig Evans and Shemaryahu Talmon, 197–224. Biblical Interpretation Series, vol. 28. Leiden: Brill, 1997.

Charlesworth, James, ed. *The Old Testament Pseudepigrapha*. 2 vols. Garden City, NY: Doubleday, 1983.

Cheyne, T. K. *The Book of Psalms*. New York: Thomas Whittaker, 1888.

——. *The Origin and Religious Contents of the Psalter*. New York: Thomas Whittaker, 1892.

Childs, Brevard S. "The Canon in Recent Biblical Studies: Reflections on an Era." *Pro Ecclesia* 14 (2005): 26–45.

——. "Psalm Titles and Midrashic Exegesis." *JSS* 16 (1971): 137–50.

Christensen, Duane L. "The Book of Psalms within the Canonical Process in Ancient Israel." *JETS* 39 (1996): 421–32.

Cohen, Menachem, ed. ב חלק תהלים ספר הכתר גדולות מקראות [Mikra'ot Gedolot 'Ha-keter.' The Book of Psalms, vol. 2] Ramat-Gan, Israel: Bar Ilan University, 2003.

Cole, Robert L. "An Integrated Reading of Psalms 1 and 2." *JSOT* 98 (2002): 75–88.

——. *The Shape and Message of Book III (Psalms 73–89)*. JSOTSup, vol. 307. Sheffield: Sheffield Academic Press, 2000.

Collins, John J. "Amazing Grace: The Transformation of the Thanksgiving Hymn at Qumran." In *Psalms in Community*, ed. Harold W. Attridge and Margot E. Fassler, 75–85. Society of Biblical Literature Symposium Series, vol. 25. Leiden: Brill, 2004.

——. "Before the Canon: Scriptures in Second Temple Judaism." In *Old Testament Interpretation: Past, Present and Future, Essays in Honour of Gene M. Tucker*, 225–41. Edinburgh: T & T Clark, 1995.

——. *Jewish Wisdom in the Hellenistic Age*. OTL. Philadelphia: Westminster, 1997.

——. *Seer, Sybils, & Sages*. JSJSup, vol. 54. Leiden: Brill, 1997.

——. "Wisdom and The Law." In *Jewish Wisdom in the Hellenistic Age*, ed. John J. Collins. OTL. Louisville, KY: Westminster John Knox Press, 1997.

Collins, John J. and George W. E. Nickelsburg. *Ideal Figures in Ancient Judaism: Profiles and Paradigms*, ed. George W. E. Nickelsburg and Harry M. Orlinsky. Society of Biblical Literature Septuagint and Cognate Studies, vol. 12. Chico, CA: Scholars Press, 1980.

Coogan, M. D. "Alphabets and Elements." *BASOR* 216 (1974): 61–63.

Cooper, Alan. "Biblical Studies and Jewish Studies." In *The Oxford Handbook of Jewish Studies*, ed. Martin Goodman, et al., 14–35. Oxford: Oxford University Press, 2002.

——. "Creation, Philosophy and Spirituality: Aspects of Jewish Interpretation of Psalm 19." In *Pursuing the Text: Studies in Honor of Ben Zion Wacholder on the Occasion of His Seventieth Birthday*, ed. John C. Reeves and John Kampen, 15–33. JSOTSup, vol. 184. Sheffield: Sheffield Academic Press, 1994.

Copeland, E. Luther. "*Nomos* as a Medium of Revelation—Paralleling *Logos*—in Ante-Nicene Christianity." *Studia Theologica* 27 (1973): 51–61.

Corley, Jeremy. "An Intertextual Study of Proverbs and Ben Sira." In *Intertextual Studies in Ben Sira and Tobit: Essays in Honor of Alexander di Lella*, ed. Jeremy Corley and Vincent Skemp, 155–82. CBQMS, vol. 38. Washington, D.C.: Catholic Biblical Association, 2005.

Cornill, C. H. *Introduction to the Canonical Books of the Old Testament*. London: Williams and Norgate, 1907.

Craigie, Peter C. *Psalms 1–50*. Word Biblical Commentary. Waco, TX: Word, 1983.

Creach, Jerome. "Like a Tree Planted by the Temple Stream: The Portrait of the Righteous in Psalm 1:3." *CBQ* 61 (1999): 34–46.

——. *Yahweh as Refuge and the Editing of the Hebrew Psalter*. JSOTSup, vol. 217. Sheffield: Sheffield Academic Press, 1996.

Crenshaw, James L. "Method in Determining Wisdom Influence on 'Historical' Literature." In *Studies in Ancient Israelite Wisdom*, ed. James L. Crenshaw. New York: Ktav, 1976.

——. *Old Testament Wisdom: An Introduction*. Atlanta, GA: John Knox, 1981.

——. "The Primacy of Listening in Ben Sira's Pedagogy." In *Wisdom, You are my Sister*, ed. Michael L. Barre, 172–87. CBQMS, vol. 29. Washington: Catholic Biblical Association, 1997.

——. "Prolegomenon." In *Studies in Ancient Israelite Wisdom*, ed. James L. Crenshaw. New York: Ktav, 1976.

Crim, Keith R. *The Royal Psalms*. Richmond: John Knox, 1962.

Croft, S. *The Identity of the Individual in the Psalms*. JSOTSup, vol. 44. Sheffield: Sheffield Academic Press, 1987.

Cross, Frank Moore, Peter Flint, Patrick Skehan, Emmanuel Tov, J. Trebolle Barrera, and Eugene Ulrich. *Qumran Cave 4.XI: Psalms to Chronicles*. DJD 16. Oxford: Clarendon Press, 2000.

Crutchfield, John C. "The Redactional Agenda of the Book of Psalms." *HUCA* 74 (2003): 21–47.

Crüsemann, Frank. *The Torah: Theology and Social History of Old Testament Law*. Translated by Allan W. Mahnke. Minneapolis, MN: Fortress, 1996.

Dahood, Mitchell J. *The Psalms: Psalms 100–150*. The Anchor Bible, vol. 17A. Garden City, NY: Doubleday, 1970.

Daube, David. "Rabbinic Methods of Interpretation and Hellenistic Rhetoric." *HUCA* 22 (1949): 239–64.

Davison, Lisa Wilson. "'Your Word is a Lamp unto My Feet': A Study of the Vocabulary, Grammar, and Semantics of Psalm 119." Ph.D. diss., Vanderbilt, 1999.

de Beor, P.A. "The Counsellor." In *Wisdom in Israel and in the Ancient Near East*. ed. M. Noth and D. W. Thomas, 42–71. VTSup, vol. 3. Leiden: Brill, 1955.

Deissler, Alfons. *Psalm 119 und seine Theologie. Ein Beitrag zur Erforschung der anthologischen Stilgattung im Alten Testament*. Münchener Theologische Studien, vol. I/11. Munich: Karl Zink, 1955.

Delitzsch, Franz. *Biblical Commentary on the Psalms*. 2nd ed. 3 vols. Edinburgh: T & T Clark, 1885.

——. "Psalms." Translated by Francis Bolton. In *Commentary on the Old Testament*, vol. 5. Peabody, MA: Hendrickson, 2001.

Delitzsch, Friedrich. *Die Lese- und Schreibfehler im Alten Testament*. Berlin: de Gruyter, 1920.

Dell, Katharine J. "'I will solve my riddle to the music of the lyre' (Psalm XLIX 4 [5]): A Cultic Setting for Wisdom Psalms?" *VT* 54 (2004): 445–58.

Dempster, Stephen. "An 'Extraordinary Fact': *Torah and Temple* and the Contours of the Hebrew Canon: Part 2." *Tyndale Bulletin* 48 (1997): 191–218.

Derrida, Jacques. "Living On: Border Lines." In *Deconstruction and Criticism*, ed. Harold Bloom et al. Translated by James Hulbert, 75–176. New York: Seabury Press, 1979.

Di Lella, Alexander. "The Meaning of Wisdom in Ben Sira." In *In Search of Wisdom: Essays in Memory of John G. Gammie*, ed. Leo G. Perdue, 139–48. Louisville, KY: Westminster/John Knox Press, 1993.

Dick, Michael. "Prophetic Poiesis and the Verbal Icon." *CBQ* 46 (1984): 226–46.

Diedrich, Friedrich. "Lehre mich, Jahwe! Überlegungen zu einer Gebetsbitte in den Psalmen." In *Die Alttestamentliche Botschaft als Wegweisung; Festschrift für Heinz Reinelt*, 59–74. Stuttgart: Katholisches Bibelwerk, 1990.

Dijkstra, Meindert. "The Law of Moses: the Memory of Mosaic Religion in and after the Exile." In *Yahwism After the Exile: Perspectives on Israelite Religion in the Persian Period*, ed. Rainer Albertz and Bob Becking, 70–98. Studies in Theology and Religion, vol. 5. Assen, The Netherlands: Royal van Gorcum, 2003.

Docherty, Thomas. *Reading (Absent) Character: Towards A Theory of Characterization in Fiction*. Oxford: Clarendon Press, 1983.

Drijvers, P. *The Psalms: Their Structure and Meaning*. New York: Herder and Herder, 1965.

Duhm, Bernhard. *Die Psalmen*. 2nd ed. Kurzer Hand-Kommentar zum Alten Testament, ed. D. Karl Marti, vol. 14. Tübingen: J. C. B. Mohr, 1922.

Eaton, J. H. *Kingship and the Psalms*. 2nd ed. Sheffield: Sheffield Academic Press, 1986.

——. "Proposals in Psalms XCIX and CXIX." *VT* 18 (1968): 555–58.

——. *The Psalms of the Way and the Kingdom*. JSOTSup, vol. 199. Sheffield: Sheffield Academic Press, 1995.

——. *The Psalms*. Torch Bible Commentaries. London: SCM, 1967.

Eerdmans, B. D. *The Hebrew Book of Psalms*. Leiden: Brill, 1947.

Ehrlich, Arnold B. *Die Psalmen. Neu Uebersetzt und Erklaert*. Berlin: Poppelauer, 1905.

Eidevall, Göran. "Spatial Metaphors in Lamentations 3,1–9." In *Metaphor in the Hebrew Bible*, ed. P. van Hecke, 133–37. BEThL, vol. 187. Dudley, MA: Peeters, 2005.

Elman, Yaakov. "The Book of Deuteronomy as Revelation: Nahmanides and Abarbanel." In *Hazon Nahum: Studies in Jewish Law, Thought, and History Presented to Dr. Norman Lamm on the Occasion of his Seventieth Birthday*, ed. Yaakov Elman and Jeffrey S. Gurock, 229–50. New York: Yeshiva University Press, 1997.

Eshel, Hanan and John Strugnell. "Alphabetic Acrostics in Pre-Tannaitic Hebrew." *CBQ* 62 (2000): 441–58.

Eskenazi, Tamara Cohn. "Torah as Narrative and Narrative as Torah." In *Old Testament Interpretation: Past, Present and Future, Essays in Honour of Gene M. Tucker*, ed. James Luther Mays, David L. Petersen, and Kent Harold Richards, 13–30. Edinburgh: T & T Clark, 1995.

Even-Shoshan, Abraham. מילון אבן־שושן המרוכז. [Milon Even-Shoshan. A New Dictionary of Hebrew, revised 1 vol. edition.] Jerusalem: Magnes Press, 2004.

Falk, Daniel K. "Psalms and Prayers." In *Justification and Variegated Nomism: The Complexities of Second Temple Judaism*, ed. D. A. Carson et al., 1–56. Grand Rapids, MI: Baker Academic, 2001.

——. "Qumran Prayer Texts and the Temple." In *Sapiential, Liturgical and Poetical Texts from Qumran*, ed. Florentino García Martínez, Daniel K. Falk, and Eileen M. Schuler, 106–26. Leiden: Brill, 2000.

Fernandez, James W. *Persuasions and Performances: The Play of Tropes in Culture*. Bloomington, IN: Indiana University Press, 1986.

Finsterbusch, Karin. *JHWH als Lehrer der Menschen: ein Beitrag zur Gottesvorstellung der Hebräischen Bibel*. Biblisch-theologische Studien, vol. 90. Neukirchen-Vluyn: Neukirchener, 2007.

——. "Multiperspektivität als Programm: Das betende Ich und die Tora in Psalm 119." In *Was ist der Mensch, dass du seiner gedenkst? (Psalm 8,5): Festschrift für Bernd Janowski zum 65. Geburtstag*, 93–104. Neukirchen-Vluyn: Neukirchener, 2008.

——. *Weisung für Israel: Studien zu religiösem Lehren und Lernen im Deuteronomium und seinem Umfeld*, ed. Bernd Janowski et al. FAT (Diss.), vol. 44, Tübingen: Mohr Siebeck, 2005.

Fischer, Georg and Norbert Lohfink. "'Diese Worte sollst du summen' Dtn 6,7 *wᵉdibbartā bām*—ein verlorener Schlüssel zur meditativen Kultur in Israel." In *Studien zum Deuteronomium und zur deuteronomistischen Literatur III*, ed. Gerhard Dautzenberg and Norbert Lohfink, 181–203. Stuttgarter Biblische Aufsatzbände, vol. 20. Stuttgart: Verlag Katholisches Bibelwerk, 1995.

Fishbane, Michael. *Biblical Interpretation in Ancient Israel*. Oxford: Clarendon Press, 1985.

——. *The Garments of Torah: Essays in Biblical Hermeneutics*. Indiana Studies in Biblical Literature. Bloomington, IN: Indiana University Press, 1989.

——. "The Hebrew Bible and Exegetical Tradition." In *Intertextuality in Ugarit and the Bible*, ed. Johannes Cornelis de Moor, 15–30. OtSt, vol. 40. Leiden: Brill, 1998.

——. *The Kiss of God: Spiritual and Mystical Death in Judaism*. Seattle: University of Washington Press, 1994.

——. "Revelation and Tradition: Aspects of Inner-Biblical Exegesis." *JBL* 99 (1980): 343–61.

——. *Text and Texture: Close Readings of Selected Biblical Texts*. New York: Schocken Books, 1979.

——. "Types of Biblical Intertextuality." In *Congress Volume: Oslo 1998*, ed. A. Lemaire et al., 39–44. VTSup, vol. 80. Leiden: Brill, 2000.

Flint, Peter W. *The Dead Sea Psalms Scrolls and the Book of Psalms*. Studies on the Texts of the Desert of Judah, ed. F. García Martínez and A. S. van der Woude, vol. 17. Leiden: Brill, 1997.

——. "Variant Readings of the Dead Sea Psalms Scrolls against the Massoretic Text and the Septuagint Psalter." In *Der Septuaginta-Psalter und seine Tochterübersetzungen*, ed. Anneli Aejmelaeus and Udo Quast, 337–65. Mitteilungen des Septuaginta-Unternehmens, vol. 24, Göttingen: Vandenhoeck & Ruprecht, 2000.

Flint, Peter W., Patrick W. Skehan, and Eugene Ulrich. "Two Manuscripts of Psalm 119 from Qumran Cave 4." *RevQ* 64 (1995): 477–86.

Fokkema, Aleid. *Postmodern Characters: A Study of Characterization in British and American Postmodern Fiction*. Postmodern Studies, vol. 4. Amsterdam: Rodopi, 1991.

Fowler, Alastair. "The Life and Death of Literary Forms." *New Literary History* 2 (1971): 199–216.

Fox, Michael V. "Aspects of the Religion of the Book of Proverbs." *HUCA* 39 (1968): 55–69.

——. "Ideas of Wisdom in Proverbs 1–9." *JBL* 116 (1997): 613–33.

——. "Job 38 and God's Rhetoric." *Semeia* 19 (1981): 53–61.

——. "LXX Proverbs 3:28 and Ancient Egyptian Wisdom." *HAR* 8 (1985): 63–69.

——. "LXX-Proverbs as a Text-Critical Resource." *Textus* 22 (2005): 95–128.

——. "The Pedagogy of Proverbs 2." *JBL* 113 (1994): 233–43.

——. *Proverbs 1–9: A New Translation with Introduction and Commentary*. The Anchor Bible, vol. 18A. New York: Doubleday, 2000.

——. *Proverbs 10–31: A New Translation with Introduction and Commentary*. The Anchor Yale Bible, vol. 18B. New Haven, CT: Yale University Press, 2009.

——. "The Rhetoric of Disjointed Proverbs." *JSOT* 29 (2004): 165–77.

——. "The Rhetoric of Ezekiel's Vision of the Valley of the Bones." *HUCA* 51 (1980): 1–15.

——. "The Social Location of the Book of Proverbs." In *Texts, Temples, and Traditions: A Tribute to Menahem Haran*, ed. Michael V. Fox et al., 227–39. Winona Lake, IN: Eisenbrauns, 1996.

——. "The Strange Woman in Septuagint Proverbs." *JNSL* 22 (1996): 31–34.

——. *A Time to Tear Down and A Time to Build Up*. Grand Rapids, MI: Eerdmans, 1999.

——. "The Uses of Indeterminacy." *Semeia* 71 (1995): 173–92.

——. "What the Book of Proverbs is About." In *Congress Volume: Cambridge 1995*, ed. J. E. Emerton, 153–67. VTSup, vol. 48, 1997.

——. "Wisdom in the Joseph Story." *VT* 51 (2001): 26–41.

Fraade, Steven. *From Tradition to Commentary: Torah and Its Interpretation in the Midrash Sifre to Deuteronomy*. Albany: State University of New York Press, 1991.

——. "Interpretive Authority in the Studying Community at Qumran." *JJS* 44 (1993): 46–69.

Fraenkel, Jonah. "Die 'Mitte des Tanach' aus der Sicht des Rabbinischen Judentums." In *Mitte der Schrift? Ein jüdisch-christliches Gespräch*, ed. Martin Klopfenstein et al., 97–118. Judaica et Christiana, vol. 11. Bern: Peter Lang, 1987.

Freedman, David Noel. "Acrostic Poems in the Hebrew Bible: Alphabetic and Otherwise." *CBQ* 48 (1986): 408–31.

——. "Acrostics and Metrics in Hebrew Poetry." *HTR* 65 (1972): 367–92.

——. *Psalm 119 the Exaltation of Torah*. Winona Lake, IN: Eisenbrauns, 1999.

——. "The Structure of Psalm 119, part 2." *HAR* 14 (1994): 55–87.

——. "The Structure of Psalm 119." In *Pomegranates and Golden Bells*, 725–56. Winona Lake, IN: Eisenbrauns, 1995.

Friedman, R. E. "The Biblical Expression *mastir panim*." *HAR* 1 (1977): 139–47.

——. *The Hidden Face of God*. New York: Harper Collins, 1997.

——. "The Hiding of the Face: An Essay on the Literary Unity of Biblical Narrative." In *Judaic Perspectives on Ancient Israel*, ed. Jacob Neusner et al., 207–22. Philadelphia: Fortress Press, 1987.

Gaster, Theodor H. "A Qumran Reading of Deuteronomy xxxiii 10." *VT* 8 (1958): 217–19.

Gerleman, Gillis. "Der 'Einzelne' der Klage- und Dankpsalmen." *VT* 32 (1982): 33–49.

Gerstenberger, Erhard S. *Der bittende Mensch: Bittritual und Klagelied des Einzelnen im Alten Testament*. WMANT, vol. 51. Neukirchen-Vluyn: Neukirchener, 1980.

——. "Psalms." In *Old Testament Form Criticism*, ed. John Hayes. Trinity University Monograph Series in Religion, vol. 2. San Antonio: Trinity University, 1974.

——. *Psalms, Part 1, with an Introduction to Cultic Poetry*. FOTL, vol. 14. Grand Rapids, MI: Eerdmans, 1988.

——. *Psalms, Part 2, and Lamentations*. FOTL, vol. 15. Grand Rapids, MI: Eerdmans, 2001.

——. "Der Psalter als Buch und als Sammlung." In *Neue Wege der Psalmenforschung*, ed. Klaus Seybold and Erich Zenger, 2–13. HBS, vol. 1. Freiburg: Herder, 1995.

Gertner, M. "Midrashim in the New Testament." *JSS* 7 (1962): 267–92.

Gese, H. "Die Entstehung der Büchereinteilung des Psalters." In *Vom Sinai zum Zion*, 147–58. Beiträge zur evangelischen Theologie, vol. 64. Munich: Kaiser, 1974.

Gesenius, W., E. Kautzsch, and A. E. Cowley. *Gensenius' Hebrew Grammar*. Oxford: Clarendon Press, 1910.

Ghosh, Ranjan. "The Concept of the Poet in the Psalms." *Darshana International* 39 (1999): 68–77.

Gillingham, Sue. "From Liturgy to Prophecy: The Use of Psalmody in Second Temple Judaism." *CBQ* 64 (2002): 470–89.

Gitay, Yehoshua. "Psalm 1 and the Rhetoric of Religious Argumentation." In *Literary Structure and Rhetorical Strategies in the Hebrew Bible*, ed. J. de Waard, L. J. de Regt, and J. P. Fokkelman, 232–40. Winona Lake, IN: Eisenbrauns, 1996.

Glass, Jonathan T. "Some Observations on Psalm 19." In *The Listening Heart: Essays in Wisdom and the Psalms in Honor of Roland E. Murphy*, ed. K. G. Hogland et al., 147–59. JSOTSup, vol. 58. Sheffield: Sheffield Academic Press, 1987.

Goldberg, Arnold. "The Rabbinic View of Scripture." In *A Tribute to Geza Vermes: Essays on Jewish and Christian Literature and History*, ed. Philip Davies and Richard White, 153–66. JSOTSup, vol. 100. Sheffield: Sheffield Academic Press, 1990.

Goldberg, Hillel. "The Emergence of Man: a Musar Approach to Mizmor 19." *Jewish Thought* 2 (1991): 125–34.

Gordis, Robert. "The Social Background of Wisdom Literature." *HUCA* 18 (1943): 77–118.

Goshen-Gottstein, M. H. "The Psalms Scroll (11QPs^a): A Problem of Canon and Text." *Textus* 5 (1966): 22–33.

Goulder, M. D. *The Psalms of the Return (Book V, Psalms 107–150): Studies in the Psalter, IV*. JSOTSup, vol. 258. Sheffield: Sheffield Academic Press, 1998.

Grabbe, Lester L. *Wisdom of Solomon*. Guides to Apocrypha and Pseudepigrapha. Sheffield: Sheffield Academic Press, 1997.

Gray, G. B. *The Forms of Hebrew Poetry*. 1915. Reprint, New York: Ktav, 1972.

Greenberg, Moshe. "Three Conceptions of the Torah in Hebrew Scriptures." In *Studies in the Bible and Jewish Thought*, 11–23. Philadelphia: Jewish Publication Society, 1995.

Groenewald, Alphonso. "'And Please, do not Hide Your Face from Your Servant' (Ps 69:18a): The Image of the 'Hidden God'." In *vom Ausdruck zum Inhalt, vom Inhalt zum Ausdruck, Festschrift der Schülerinnen und Schüler für Theodor Seidl*, ed. Maria Häusl and David Volgger, 121–38. Arbeiten zu Text und Sprache im Alten Testament, vol. 75. St. Ottilien: Eos Verlag, 2005.

Gruber, Mayer. *Rashi's Commentary on Psalms*. Brill Reference Library of Judaism, vol. 18. Leiden: Brill, 2004.

Grund, Alexandra. *Die Himmel erzählen die Herrlichkeit Gottes: Psalm 19 im Kontext der nachexilischen Toraweisheit*. WMANT, vol. 103. Neukirchen-Vluyn: Neukirchener, 2004.

——. "Die Torah JHWHs is vollkommen: Psalm 19 als Dokument jüdischen Glaubens." *Leqach* 3 (2002): 7–32.

Gunkel, Hermann. *An Introduction to the Psalms: The Genres of the Religious Lyric of Israel*. Translated by James D. Nogalski. Macon, GA: Mercer University Press, 1998.

——. *Die Psalmen*. HKAT. Göttingen: Vandenhoeck & Ruprecht, 1926.

——. *The Psalms: A Form-Critical Introduction*. Translated by Thomas M. Horner. Philadelphia: Fortress, 1967.

Hadot, Pierre. *Philosophy as a Way of Life: Spiritual Exercises from Socrates to Foucault*. Translated by Michael Chase. New York: Blackwell, 1995.

Hakham, Amos. ספר תהלים בדעת מקרא [*Psalms in Da'at Mikra* (Hebrew)]. Jerusalem: Mossad HaRav Kook, 1990.

Hall, Stuart. "Introduction: Who Needs Identity?" In *Questions of Cultural Identity*, ed. Stuart Hall and Paul du Gay, 1–17. London: Sage, 1996.

Hamp, Vinzenz. *Der Begriff "Wort" in den aramäischen Bibelübersetzungen*. Munich: Neuer Filser, 1938.

Hanson, K. C. "Alphabetic Acrostics: A Form Critical Study." Ph.D. diss., Claremont Graduate School, 1984.

Hardison, O. B. Jr. and Ernst H. Behler. "Topos." In *The New Princeton Encyclopedia of Poetry and Poetics*, ed. Alex Preminger and T. V. F. Brogan, 1294. Princeton, New Jersey: Princeton University Press, 1993.

Harrington, Daniel J. "The Wisdom of the Scribe According to Ben Sira." In *Ideal Figures in Ancient Judaism: Profiles and Paradigms*, ed. John J. Collins and George W. E. Nickelsburg, 181–88. Chico, CA: Scholars Press, 1980.

Harris, Scott. "Proverbs 1:18–19, 20–33 as Introduction." *RB* 107 (2000): 205–31.

Hayes, John, ed. *Old Testament Form Criticism*. Trinity University Monograph Series in Religion, vol. 2. San Antonio, TX: Trinity University Press, 1974.

Hayward, Robert. "The Priestly Blessing in *Targum Pseudo-Jonathan*." *Journal for the Study of the Pseudepigrapha* 19 (1999): 81–101.

Heinemann, Joseph. התפילה בתקופת התנאים והאמוראים: טיבה ורפוסיה [*Prayer in the period of the Tanna'im and the Amora'im: Its nature and its patterns* (Hebrew)]. Jerusalem: Magnes Press, 1966.

——. *Prayer in the Talmud: Forms and Patterns*. Studia Judaica, vol. 9. Berlin: de Gruyter, 1977.

Hentschke, Richard. *Satzung und Setzender: ein Beitrag zur israelitischen Rechtsterminologie*. Beiträge zur Wissenschaft vom Alten und Neuen Testament, vol. 5. Stuttgart: W. Kohlhammer, 1963.

Hermisson, Hans-Jürgen. "Der verborgene Gott im Buch Jesaja." In *Studien zu Prophetie und Weisheit*, ed. Bernd Janowski and Hermann Spieckermann. 105–16. FAT, vol. 23. Tübingen: Mohr Siebeck, 1998.

——. "Zeitbezug des prophetischen Wortes." *Kerygma und Dogma* 27 (1981): 96–110.

Heschel, Abraham Joshua. תורה מן השמים באספקלריה של הדורות [*Torah from Heaven in the refraction of the generations* (Hebrew)]. Jerusalem: Soncino Press, 1962.

Hiebert, Robert J. V. "The Place of the Syriac Versions in the Textual History of the Psalter." In *The Book of Psalms: Composition and Reception*, ed. Peter W. Flint and Patrick D. Miller, Jr., 505–36. VTSup, vol. 99. Formation and Interpretation of Old Testament Literature Series, vol. 4. Leiden: Brill, 2005.

——. "Syriac Biblical Textual History and the Greek Psalter." *The Old Greek Psalter: Studies in Honour of Albert Pietersma*, ed. Robert J. V. Hiebert, et al., 178–204. JSOTSup, vol. 332. Sheffield: Sheffield Academic Press, 2001.

——. *The "Syrohexaplaric" Psalter*. SBL Septuagint and Cognate Studies Series, vol. 27. Atlanta, GA: Scholars Press, 1989.

Hirshman, Marc. "Rabbinic Universalism in the Second and Third Centuries." *HTR* 93 (2000): 101–15.

Ho, Shirley S. "Wisdom, Life, and Restoration of Zion: A Compositional Study of Psalm 119 and the Song of Ascents." Ph.D. diss., Trinity International University, 2005.

Holm-Nielsen, Svend. *Hodayot: Psalms from Qumran*. Denmark: Aarhuus Stiftsbogtrykkerie, 1960.

——. "The Importance of Late Jewish Psalmody for the Understanding of Old Testament Psalmodic Tradition." *ST* 14 (1960): 1–53.

——. "'Ich' in den Hodajoth und die Qumrangemeinde." In *Qumran-Probleme: Vorträge des Leipziger Symposions über Qumran-Probleme vom 9. bis 14. Oktober 1961*, ed. Ursula Treu, 217–29. Schriften der Sektion für Altertumswissenschaft, vol. 42. Berlin: Akademie Verlag, 1963.

Hossfeld, Frank-Lothar. "Bund und Torah in den Psalmen." In *Bibel in jüdischer und christlicher Tradition: Festschrift für Johann Maier zum 60. Geburtstag*, 66–77. Athenäums Monografien, vol. 88. Frankfurt am Main: Anton Hain, 1993.

——. "Der Wandel des Beters in Ps 18: Wachstumsphasen eines Dankliedes." In *Freude an der Weisung des Herrn: Beiträge zur Theologie der Psalmen*, 171–90. Stuttgarter Biblische Beiträge, vol. 13. Stuttgart: Katholisches Bibelwerk, 1986.

Hossfeld, Frank-Lothar and Erich Zenger. *Die Psalmen I*. NEB. Würzburg: Echter, 1993.

——. *Psalmen 101–150.* HThKAT. Freiburg: Herder, 2008.

——. "Neue und alte Wege der Psalmen-Exegese. Antworten auf die Fragen von M. Millard und R. Rendtorff." *Biblical Interpretation* 4 (1996): 332–43.

Howard, David M. "Editorial Activity in the Psalter: A State-of-the-Field Survey." In *The Shape and Shaping of the Psalter*, ed. J. Clinton McCann, 52–70. JSOTSup, vol. 159. Sheffield: JSOT Press, 1993.

——. "Psalm 94 among the Kingship-of-Yhwh Psalms." *CBQ* 61 (1999): 667–85.

——. *The Structure of Psalms 93–100.* BJS, vol. 5. Winona Lake, IN: Eisenbrauns, 1997.

Høgenhaven, Jesper. "The Opening of the Psalter: A Study in Jewish Theology." *Scandinavian Journal of the Old Testament* 15 (2001): 169–80.

Hunziker-Rodewald, Regine. "David der Hirt. Vom «Aufstieg» eines literarischen Topos." In *König David: biblische Schlüsselfigur und europäische Leitgestalt*, ed. Walter Dietrich and Hubert Herkommer, 165–77. Stuttgart: W. Kohlhammer, 2003.

Hurvitz, Avi. "Further Comments on the Linguistic Profile of Ben Sira: Syntactic Affinities with Late Biblical Hebrew." In *Sirach, Scrolls, and Sages*, ed. T. Muraoka and J. F. Elwolde, 132–45. Studies on the Texts of the Desert of Judah, vol. 33. Leiden: Brill, 1999.

——. בין לשון ללשון: לתולדות לשון המקרא בימי בית שני [*The transition period in biblical Hebrew: a study in post-exilic Hebrew and its implications for the dating of psalms* (Hebrew)]. Jerusalem: Bialik Institute, 1972.

——. "Was QH a 'Spoken' Language? on Some Recent Views and Positions: Comments." In *Diggers at the Well*, ed. T. Muraoka and J. F. Elwolde, 110–14. Studies on the Texts of the Desert of Judah, vol. 36. Leiden: Brill, 2000.

——. 'שעשועי תורה'" ["שעשועי תורה במזמור קיט—מקור הביטוי ורקעו הלשוני"] in Ps. 119—the origins of the phrase and its linguistic background" (Hebrew)]. In *Studies on Hebrew and Other Semitic Languages presented to Chaim Rabin on the occasion of his Seventy-Fifth Birthday*, ed. M. Goshen-Gottstein et al., 105–9. Jerusalem: Academon Press, 1990.

——. שקיעי חכמה בספר תהלים [*Wisdom language in biblical psalmody* (Hebrew)]. Jerusalem: Magnes Press, 1991.

——. "Wisdom Vocabulary in the Hebrew Psalter: A Contribution to the Study of 'Wisdom Psalms'." *VT* 38 (1988): 41–51.

Instone-Brewer, David. *Techniques and Assumptions in Jewish Exegesis before 70 C.E.* Texte und Studien zum antiken Judentum, vol. 30. Tübingen: J. C. B. Mohr, 1992.

Iser, Wolfgang. *The Implied Reader: Patterns of Communication in Prose Fiction from Bunyan to Beckett.* Baltimore, MD: The Johns Hopkins University Press, 1974.

Jacobson, Rolf A. *Many are Saying: The Function of Direct Discourse in the Hebrew Psalter.* JSOTSup, vol. 397. New York: T & T Clark, 2004.

Jaffee, Martin S. *Early Judaism: Religious Worlds of the First Judaic Millennium.* Studies and Texts in Jewish History and Culture, vol. 13. Bethesda, MD: University Press of Maryland, 2006.

——. *Torah in the Mouth: Writing and Oral Tradition in Palestinian Judaism, 200 B.C.E.–400 C.E.* Oxford: Oxford University Press, 2001.

Japhet, Sara. *The Ideology of Chronicles and Its Place in Biblical Thought.* Winona Lake, IN: Eisenbrauns, 2009.

——. "'Law' and 'The Law' in Ezra-Nehemiah." In *Proceedings of the Ninth World Congress of Jewish Studies*, 99–115. Jerusalem: Magnes Press, 1988.

Jastrow, Marcus. *A Dictionary of the Targumim.* New York: Judaica Press, 1971.

Jenni, Ernst and Claus Westermann. *Theological Lexicon of the Old Testament.* Translated by Mark E. Biddle. Peabody, MA: Hendrickson, 1997.

Jensen, Joseph. *The Use of Tôrâ by Isaiah: His Debate with the Wisdom Tradition.* CBQMS, vol. 3. Washington, D.C.: Catholic Biblical Association of America, 1973.

Jeremias, Jörg. "Die Anfänge der Schriftprophetie." *ZThK* 93 (1996): 481–99.

——. *The Book of Amos*. Translated by Douglas W. Stott. OTL. Louisville, KY: Westminster John Knox, 1998.

Johnson, Frank. "The Western Concept of Self." In *Culture and Self: Asian and Western Perspectives*, ed. A. J. Marsella et al., 91–138. New York: Tavistock, 1985.

Joosten, Jan. "The Knowledge and Use of Hebrew in the Hellenistic Period, Qumran, and the Septuagint." In *Diggers at the Well*, ed. T. Muraoka and J. F. Elwolde, 115–30. Studies on the Texts of the Desert of Judah, vol. 36. Leiden: Brill, 2000.

——. *People and Land in the Holiness Code*. VTSup, vol. 67. Leiden: Brill, 1996.

——. "Pseudo-Classicisms in Late Biblical Hebrew, in Ben Sira, and Qumran Hebrew." In *Sirach, Scrolls, and Sages*, ed. T. Muraoka and J. F. Elwolde, 146–59. Studies on the Texts of the Desert of Judah, vol. 33. Leiden: Brill, 1999.

Joüon, Paul and Takamitsu Muraoka. *A Grammar of Biblical Hebrew*. Rome: Pontifical Biblical Institute, 1996.

Kaiser, Otto. "Erwägungen zu Psalm 8." In *Neue Wege der Psalmenforschung*, ed. Klaus Seybold and Erich Zenger, 208–21. HBS, vol. 1. Freiburg: Herder, 1995.

——. "The Law as Center of the Hebrew Bible." In *"Sha'arei Talmon" Studies in the Bible, Qumran, and the Ancient Near East Presented to Shemaryahu Talmon*, ed. Michael Fishbane and Emmanuel Tov, 93–103. Winona Lake, IN: Eisenbrauns, 1992.

Keenan, Edward L. "Passive in the World's Languages." In *Clause Structure*. Vol. I, *Language Typology and Syntactic Description*, ed. Timothy Shopen, 243–81. Cambridge: Cambridge University Press, 1985.

Kellermann, Ulrich. "Anmerkungen zum Verständnis der Tora in den chronistischen Schriften." *Biblische Notizen* 42 (1988): 49–92.

Kintsch, Walter. *Comprehension: A Paradigm for Cognition*. Cambridge: Cambridge University Press, 1998.

Kleinig, John. "The Attentive Heart: Meditation in the Old Testament." *The Reformed Theological Review* 51 (1992): 50–63.

Knierim, Rolf. "Old Testament Form Criticism Reconsidered." *Int* 27 (1963): 435–68.

Knoppers, Gary N. and J. Gordon McConville, eds. *Reconsidering Israel and Judah: Recent Studies on the Deuteronomistic History*. Sources for Biblical and Theological Study, vol. 8. Winona Lake, IN: Eisenbrauns, 2000.

Knoppers, Gary N. and Bernard M. Levinson, eds. *The Pentateuch as Torah: New Models for Understanding its Promulgation and Acceptance*. Winona Lake, IN: Eisenbrauns, 2007.

Koch, Klaus. "Der Psalter und seine Redaktionsgeschichte." In *Neue Wege der Psalmenforschung*, ed. Klaus Seybold and Erich Zenger, 243–77. HBS, vol. 1. Freiburg: Herder, 1995.

——. "Gibt es ein Vergeltungsdogma im Alten Testament?" *ZThK* 52 (1955): 1–42.

——. "Review of Alfons Deissler Psalm 119 (118) und seine Theologie." *Theologische Literaturzeitung* 83 (1958): 186–87.

Kolbet, Paul R. "Athanasius, the Psalms, and the Reformation of the Self." *HTR* 99 (2006): 85–101.

Koehler, Ludwig, Walter Baumgartner, and Johann Jakob Stamm. *Hebrew and Aramaic Lexicon of the Old Testament*. Translated by M. E. J. Richardson. Leiden: Brill, 1994–2001.

Konradt, Matthias. "Die vollkommene Erfüllung der Tora und der Konflikt mit den Pharisäern im Matthäusevangelium." In *Das Gesetz im frühen Judentum und im Neuen Testament*, ed. Dieter Sänger and Matthias Konradt, 129–52. Göttingen: Vandenhoeck & Ruprecht, 2006.

Koole, J. L. "Die Bibel des Ben-Sira." *OtSt* 14 (1965): 374–96.

Kooy, Vernon H. "The Fear and Love of God in Deuteronomy." In *Grace upon Grace*. ed. James I. Cook, 106–16. Grand Rapids, MI: Eerdmans, 1975.

Kratz, Reinhard Gregor. "Die Tora Davids. Psalm I und die doxologische Fünfteilung des Psalters." *Zeitschrift für Theologie und Kirche* 93 (1996): 1–34.

——. *Translatio imperii. Untersuchungen zu den aramäischen Danielerzählungen und ihrem theologiegeschichtlichen Umfeld.* WMANT, vol. 63. Neukirchen-Vluyn: Neukirchener, 1991.

Kraus, Hans-Joachim. "Freude an Gottes Gesetz: Ein Beitrag zur Auslegung der Psalmen 1; 19B und 119." *EvTh* 10 (1950): 337–51.

——. *Psalms 1–59.* Translated by Hilton C. Oswald. Minneapolis, MN: Augsburg Publishing, 1988. [German edition: *Psalmen 1–59.* BKAT, vol. 15/1. Neukirchen-Vluyn: Neukirchener, 1961.]

——. *Psalms 60–150.* Translated by Hilton C. Oswald. Minneapolis, MN: Augsburg Publishing, 1989. [German edition: *Psalmen 60–150.* BKAT, vol. 15/2. Neukirchen-Vluyn: Neukirchener, 1978.]

——. *Theology of the Psalms.* Translated by Keith Crim. Minneapolis, MN: Augsburg Publishing, 1986. [German edition: *Theologie der Psalmen.* BKAT, vol. 15/3. Neukirchen-Vluyn: Neukirchener, 1979.]

Kristeva, Julia. *Revolution in Poetic Language.* Translated by Margaret Waller. New York: Columbia University Press, 1984.

——. "Word, Dialogue, and Novel." In *Desire in Language: A Semiotic Approach to Literature and Art*, translated by Thomas Gora, Leon S. Roudiez, and Alice Jardine, 64–91. New York: Columbia University Press, 1980.

Kugel, James L. "The Scripturalization of Prayer." In *Prayers that Cite Scripture*, ed. James L. Kugel, 1–5. Cambridge, MA: Harvard University Press, 2006.

Kuntz, J. Kenneth. "The Canonical Wisdom Psalms of Ancient Israel: Their Rhetorical, Thematic, and Formal Dimensions." In *Rhetorical Criticism*, ed. J. J. Jackson and M. Kessler, 186–222. Pittsburgh, PA: Pickwick, 1974.

——. "Psalm 18: A Rhetorical-critical Analysis." *JSOT* 26 (1983): 3–31.

——. "Reclaiming Biblical Wisdom Psalms: A Response to Crenshaw." *CBR* 1 (2003): 145–54.

——. "Wisdom Psalms and the Shaping of the Hebrew Psalter." In *For a Later Generation*, 144–60. Harrisburg, PA: Trinity Press International, 2000.

Küchler, Max. *Frühjüdische Weisheitstradition.* OBO, vol. 26. Göttingen: Vandenhoeck & Ruprecht, 1979.

Kwakkel, Gert. *According to My Righteousness: Upright Behavior as Grounds for Deliverance in Psalms 7, 17, 18, 26, and 44.* OtSt, vol. 46. Leiden: Brill, 2002.

Lakoff, George and Mark Johnson. *Metaphors we Live by.* Chicago: University of Chicago Press, 1980.

Lauterbach, Jacob Z. "The Belief in the Power of the Word." *HUCA* 14 (1939): 287–302.

Lawson, Jack. "Mesopotamian Precursors to the Stoic Concept of Logos." In *Mythology and Mythologies: Methodological Approaches to Intercultural Influences*, ed. R. M. Whiting, 68–91. The Neo-Assyrian Text Corpus Project. Stuttgart: Franz Steiner, 2001.

Leach, Joan. "Rhetorical Analysis." In *Qualitative Researching with Text, Image and Sound: A Practical Handbook*, ed. Martin W. Bauer and George Gaskell, 207–26. London: Sage Publications, 2000.

Lehrman, S. M. "Psalm 119." *Jewish Bible Quarterly* 23 (1995): 55–56.

Lemke, Werner E. "The Near and Distant God: A Study of Jer 23:23–24 in Its Biblical Theological Context." *JBL* 100 (1981): 541–55.

Leonhard, Clemens. *Ishodad of Merw's Exegesis of the Psalms 119 and 139–147.* Corpus Scriptorum Christianorum Orientalium, vol. 585. Leuven: Peeters, 2001.

Lesslie, E. A. *The Psalms.* New York: Abingdon-Cokesbury, 1949.

Leuenberger, Martin. *Konzeptionen des Königtums Gottes im Psalter.* Abhandlungen zur Theologie des Alten und Neuen Testaments, vol. 83. Zürich: Theologischer Verlag Zürich, 2004.

Levenson, Jon D. "The Sources of Torah: Psalm 119 and the Modes of Revelation in Second Temple Judaism." In *Ancient Israelite Religion: Essays in Honor of Frank Moore Cross*, ed. Paul D. Hanson, S. D. McBride, and Patrick D. Miller, 559–74. Philadelphia: Fortress, 1987.

———. "The Theologies of Commandment in Biblical Israel." *HTR* 73 (1980): 17–33.

Levin, Christoph. "Die Entstehung der Büchereinteilung des Psalters." *VT* 54 (2004): 83–90.

Levinson, Bernard M. *Deuteronomy and the Hermeneutics of Legal Innovation*. New York: Oxford University Press, 1998.

Liebreich, Leon. "The Songs of Ascents and the Priestly Blessing." *JBL* 74 (1955): 33–36.

Liedke, Gerhard. *Gestalt und Bezeichnung alttestamentlicher Rechtsätze*. WMANT, vol. 39. Neukirchen-Vluyn: Neukirchener, 1971.

Lindars, Barnabas. *Law and Religion: Essays on the Place of the Law in Israel and Early Christianity*. Cambridge: J. Clark, 1988.

———. "Torah in Deuteronomy." In *Words and Meanings: Essays Presented to David Winton Thomas*, ed. P. R. Ackroyd and Barnabas Lindars, 117–36. Cambridge: Cambridge University Press, 1968.

Lindstrom, Fredrik. *Suffering and Sin: Interpretations of Illness in the Individual Complaint Psalms*. Coniectanea Biblica, Old Testament Series, vol. 37. Stockholm: Almquist & Wiksell International, 1994.

Lipinski, E. "Macarismes et Psaumes de Congratulation." *RB* 75 (1968): 321–67.

Lohfink, Norbert. "Der Begriff 'Bund' in der biblischen Theologie." *ThPh* 66 (1991): 161–76.

———. "Das Deuteronomium: Jahwegesetz oder Mosegesetz? Die Subjektzuordnung bei Wörtern für 'Gesetz' im Dtn und in der dtr Literatur." *ThPh* 65 (1990): 387–91.

———. "Deuteronomy 6:24: לחיתנו 'to Maintain Us'." In *Sha'arei Talmon: Studies in the Bible, Qumran, and the Ancient Near East Presented to Shemaryahu Talmon*. ed. Michael Fishbane and Emmanuel Tov, 111–19. Winona Lake, IN: Eisenbrauns, 1992.

———. *Das Hauptgebot: Eine Untersuchung literarischer Einleitungsfragen zu Dtn 5–11*. Analecta Biblica, vol. 20. Rome: Pontifical Biblical Institute, 1963.

———. "Die Sicherung der Wirksamkeit des Gotteswortes durch das Prinzip der Schriftlichkeit der Tora und durch das Prinzip der Gewaltenteilung nach den Ämtergesetzen des Buches Deuteronomium (DT 16,18–18,22)." In *Testimonium Veritati: philosophische und theologische Studien zu kirchlichen Fragen der Gegenwart*, ed. Hans Wolter, 143–55. Frankfurter Theologische Studien, vol. 7. Frankfurt am Main: Josef Knecht, 1971.

Lutz, Catherine. "Emotion Thought, and Estrangement: Emotion as a Cultural Category." *Cultural Anthropology* 1 (1986): 287–309.

Luyten, J. "Psalm 73 and Wisdom." In *La Sagasse de l'Ancien Testament*, ed. M. Gilbert, 59–81. Paris: Gembloux, 1979.

Lyons, John. *Semantics*. Cambridge: Cambridge University Press, 1977.

Lyons, Michael A. *From Law to Prophecy: Ezekiel's use of the Holiness Code*. Library of Hebrew Bible / Old Testament Studies, vol. 507. New York: T & T Clark, 2009.

Lyu, Sun Myung. "Righteousness in the Book of Proverbs." Ph.D. diss., University of Wisconsin—Madison, 2006.

Maier, Christl. *Jeremia als Lehrer der Tora: soziale Gebote des Deuteronomiums in Fortschreibungen des Jeremiabuches*. FRLANT, vol. 196. Göttingen: Vandenhoeck & Ruprecht, 2001.

Maier, J. "Torah und Pentateuch, Gesetz und Moral. Beobachtungen zum jüdischen und christlich-theologischen Befund." In *Biblische und judaistische Studien: Festschrift für Paolo Sacchi*, 1–54. Frankfurt am Main: Peter Lang, 1990.

Marcus, R. "Alphabetic Acrostics in the Hellenistic and Roman Periods." *JNES* 6 (1947): 109–15.

Mathys, Hans-Peter. *Dichter und Beter: Theologen aus spätalttestamentlicher Zeit.* Orbis Biblicus et Orientalis, vol. 132. Freiburg/Schweiz: Universitätsverlag, 1994.

Matthews, Peter. *The Concise Oxford Dictionary of Linguistics.* Oxford: Oxford University Press, 1997.

Mayes, A. D. H. "Deuteronomy 4 and the Literary Criticism of Deuteronomy." *JBL* 100 (1981): 23–51.

Mays, James L. "The David of the Psalms." *Int* 40 (1986): 143–55.

———. "The Place of the Torah-Psalms in the Psalter." *JBL* 106 (1987): 3–12.

McCann, J. Clinton. *A Theological Introduction to the Books of Psalms: The Psalms as Torah.* Nashville, TN: Abingdon, 1993.

——— ed. *The Shape and Shaping of the Psalter.* JSOTSup, vol. 159. Sheffield: JSOT Press, 1993.

McCarthy, Dennis J. "Covenant and Law in Chronicles-Nehemiah." *CBQ* 44 (1982): 25–44.

McConville, J. G. "Ezra-Nehemiah and the Fulfillment of Prophecy." *VT* 36 (1986): 205–24.

McCready, Wayne. "A Second Torah at Qumran." *Studies in Religion* 14 (1985): 5–15.

McKane, William. *Proverbs.* OTL. Philadelphia: Westminster, 1970.

Meyers, Eric. "The Use of *Tôrah* in Haggai 2:11 and the Role of the Prophet in the Restoration Community." In *The Word of the Lord Shall go Forth: Essays in Honor of David Noel Freedman in Celebration of his Sixtieth Birthday,* ed. Carol L. Meyers and M. O'Connor, 69–76. Winona Lake, IN: Eisenbrauns, 1983.

Micheli, Raphaël. "Emotions as Objects of Argumentative Constructions." *Argumentation* (2008): 1–17.

Millard, Matthias. *Die Komposition des Psalters.* FAT, vol. 9. Tübingen: J. C. B. Mohr, 1994.

———. "Von der Psalmenexegese zur Psalterexegese: Anmerkungen zum Neuansatz von Frank-Lothar Hossfeld und Erich Zenger." *Biblical Interpretation* 4 (1996): 311–28.

Miller, Cynthia. "Patterns of Verbal Ellipsis in Ugaritic Poetry." *UF* 31 (2000): 333–72.

Miller, Patrick D. "Deuteronomy and Psalms: Evoking a Biblical Conversation." *JBL* 118 (1999): 3–18.

———. "The End of the Psalter: A Response to Erich Zenger." *JSOT* 80 (1998): 103–10.

———. "Kingship, Torah Obedience, and Prayer." In *Neue Wege der Psalmenforschung,* ed. Klaus Seybold and Erich Zenger, 127–42. HBS, vol. 1. Freiburg: Herder, 1995.

———. "The Psalter as a Book of Theology." In *Psalms in Community,* ed. Harold W. Attridge and Margot E. Fassler, 87–98. Society of Biblical Literature Symposium Series, vol. 25. Leiden: Brill, 2004.

———. "Trouble and Woe: Interpreting the Biblical Laments." *Interpretation* 37 (1983): 32–45.

Mirsky, Aharon. ספר דברים בדעת מקרא *[Deuteronomy in Da'at Mikra (Hebrew)].* Jerusalem: Mossad HaRav Kook, 2001.

Mitchell, David C. "Lord, Remember David: G. H. Wilson and the Message of the Psalter." *VT* 56 (2006): 526–48.

———. *The Message of the Psalter: An Eschatological Programme in the Book of Psalms.* JSOTSup, vol. 252. Sheffield: Sheffield Academic Press, 1997.

Moran, William. "A Note on Psalm 119:28." *CBQ* 15 (1953): 10.

———. "The Ancient Near Eastern Background of the Love of God in Deuteronomy." *CBQ* 25 (1963): 77–87.

Moriarty, Frederick L. "Word as Power in the Ancient Near East." In *A Light unto My Path: Old Testament Studies in honor of Jacob M. Myers,* ed. Howard N. Bream et al.,

345–62. Gettysburg Theological Studies, vol. 4. Philadelphia: Temple University Press, 1974.

Mowinckel, Sigmund. "Psalms and Wisdom." In *Wisdom in Israel and in the Ancient Near East*, ed. M. Noth and D. W. Thomas. VTSup, vol. 3. Leiden: Brill, 1955.

——. *The Psalms in Israel's Worship*. Translated by D. R. AP-Thomas. New York: Abingdon Press, 1962.

Murphy, Roland E. "A Consideration of the Classification 'Wisdom Psalms'." In *Studies in Ancient Israelite Wisdom*, ed. James L. Crenshaw. The Library of Biblical Studies. New York: Ktav, 1976.

——. "Religious Dimensions of Israelite Wisdom." In *Ancient Israelite Religion: Essays in Honor of Frank Moore Cross*, ed. Patrick D. Miller, 449–58. Philadelphia: Fortress, 1987.

Nagar, Marie A. "The 'Shir Hadash' of Saadiah ben Eliyahu Chouraqui—A Rabbinic Commentary on Psalm 119 with a Glimpse into the Intellectual History of the Jewish Maghreb." Ph.D. diss., City University of New York, 1996.

Najman, Hindy. *Seconding Sinai: the Development of Mosaic Discourse in Second Temple Judaism*. Supplements to the Journal for the Study of Judaism, vol. 77. Leiden: Brill, 2003.

——. "The Symbolic Significance of Writing in Ancient Judaism." In *The Idea of Biblical Interpretation*, ed. Hindy Najman and Judith H. Newman, 139–73. Leiden: Brill, 2004.

Nel, Philip J. "Psalm 19; The Unbearable Lightness of Perfection." *JNWSL* 30 (2004): 103–17.

Newman, Judith H. "The Scripturalization of Prayer in Exilic and Second Temple Judaism." In *Prayers that Cite Scripture*, ed. James L. Kugel, 7–24. Cambridge, MA: Harvard University Press, 2006.

Newsom, Carol A. *The Self as Symbolic Space: Constructing Identity and Community at Qumran*. Studies on the Texts of the Desert of Judah, vol. 52. Leiden: Brill, 2004.

——. "Spying out the Land: A Report from Genology." In *Seeking Out the Wisdom of the Ancients: Essays Offered to Honor Michael V. Fox*, ed. Ronald L. Troxel et al., 437–50. Winona Lake, IN: Eisenbrauns, 2005.

Nicholoson, E. W. *Deuteronomy and Tradition*. Philadelphia: Fortress, 1967.

Nickelsburg, George W. E. "Torah and the Deuteronomic Scheme in the Apocrypha and Pseudepigrapha." In *Das Gesetz im frühen Judentum und im Neuen Testament*, ed. Dieter Sänger and Matthias Konradt, 222–35. Göttingen: Vandenhoeck & Ruprecht, 2006.

Nickelsburg, George W. E. and Michael E. Stone. *Faith and Piety in Early Judaism: Texts and Documents*. Philadelphia: Fortress, 1983.

Niditch, Susan. "The Visionary." In *Ideal Figures in Ancient Judaism: Profiles and Paradigms*, ed. John J. Collins and George W. E. Nickelsburg, 153–80. Chico, CA: Scholars Press, 1980.

Nielsen, Henrik Skov. "The Impersonal Voice in First-Person Narrative Fiction." *Narrative* 12 (2004): 133–50.

Nodder, Marcus. "What is the Relationship between the Different Stanzas of Psalm 119?" *Churchman* 119 (2005): 323–42.

Nogalski, James D. "Intertextuality and the Twelve." In *Forming Prophetic Literature. Essays on Isaiah and the Twelve in Honor of John D. W. Watts*, ed. James W. Watts and Paul House, 102–24. JSOTSup, vol. 235. Sheffield: Sheffield Academic Press, 1996.

Noonan, Michael. "Complementation." In *Complex Constructions*. Vol. 2, *Language Typology and Syntactic Description*, ed. Timothy Shopen, 42–140. Cambridge: Cambridge University Press, 1985.

Noth, Martin. *The Deuteronomistic History*. JSOTSup vol. 15. Sheffield: JSOT Press, 1981.

———. *Die Gesetze im Pentateuch. Ihre Voraussetzungen und ihr Sinn.* Schriften der Königsberger Gelehrten Gesellschaft, Geisteswissenschaftliche Klasse 17, vol. 2. Halle: M. Niemeyer, 1940.

———. *Überlieferungsgeschichtliche Studien.* Darmstadt: Wissenschaftliche Buchgesellschaft, 1943.

Olyan, Saul M. "Ben Sira's Relationship to the Priesthood." *HTR* 80 (1987): 261–86.

O'Connell, Matthew J. "The Concept of Commandment in the Old Testament." *Theological Studies* 21 (1960): 351–403.

O'Connor, M. *Hebrew Verse Structure.* Winona Lake, IN: Eisenbrauns, 1980.

Östborn, G. *Tôra in Old Testament: A Semantic Study.* Lund: Llakan Ohlssons, 1945.

Otto, Eckart. "Das Deuteronomistische Geschichtswerk im Enneateuch. Zu einem Buch von Erik Aurelius." *ZAR* 11 (2005): 323–345.

———. *Das Deuteronomium im Pentateuch und Hexateuch. Studien zur Literaturgeschichte von Pentateuch und Hexateuch im Lichte des Deuteronomiumsrahmens.* FAT, vol. 30. Tübingen: Mohr Siebeck, 2000.

———. *Das Deuteronomium. Politische Thologie und Rechtsreform in Juda und Assyrien.* BZAW, vol. 284. Berlin: de Gruyter, 1999.

———. "Das Ende der Toraoffenbarung. Die Funktion der Kolophone Lev 26,46 und 27,34 sowie Num 36,13 in der Rechtshermeneutik des Pentateuch." In *Auf dem Weg zur Endgestalt von Genesis bis II Regum: Festschrift Hans-Christoph Schmitt zum 65. Geburtstag.* BZAW, vol. 370. Berlin: de Gruyter, 2006.

———. "Jeremia und die Tora. Ein nachexilischer Diskurs." In *Tora in der Hebräischen Bibel: Studien zur Redaktionsgeschichte und synchronen Logik diachroner Transformationen.* BZAR 7, 134–82. Wiesbaden: Harrassowitz, 2007.

———. "Vom biblischen Hebraismus der persischen Zeit zum rabbinischen Judaismus in römischer Zeit. Zur Geschichter der spätbiblischen und frühjüdischen Schriftgelehrsamkeit." *ZAR* 10 (2004): 1–49.

Otto, Eckart, ed. *Tora in der Hebräischen Bibel: Studien zur Redaktionsgeschichte und synchronen Logik diachroner Transformationen.* BZAR 7. Wiesbaden: Harrassowitz, 2007.

Perdue, Leo. *Wisdom and Cult: A Critical Analysis of the Views of the Cult in the Wisdom Literatures of Israel and the Ancient Near East.* Missoula, MT: Scholars Press, 1977.

Perlitt, Lothar. "Die Verborgenheit Gottes." In *Probleme biblischer Theologie: Festschrift für Gerhard von Rod zum 70. Geburtstag*, 367–82. Munich: Chr. Kaiser Verlag, 1971.

Perrot, Charles. "The Reading of the Bible in the Ancient Synagogue." In *Mikra: Text, Translation, Reading and Interpretation of the Hebrew Bible in Ancient Judaism and Early Christianity*, ed. Martin Jan Mulder et al., 137–59. Compendia Rerum Iudaicarum ad Novum Testamentum. Assen/Maastricht: Van Gorcum, 1990.

Pietersma, Albert. "The Present State of the Critical Text of the Greek Psalter." In *Der Septuaginta-Psalter und seine Tochterübersetzungen*, ed. Anneli Aejmelaeus und Udo Quast, 12–32. Mitteilungen des Septuaginta-Unternehmens, vol. 24. Göttingen: Vandenhoeck & Ruprecht, 2000.

Pinto, Basil de. "The Torah and the Psalms." *JBL* 86 (1967): 154–74.

Plett, Heinrich F. "Intertextualities." In *Intertextuality*, ed. Heinrich F. Plett, 3–29. Berlin: de Gruyter, 1991.

Ploeg, J. P. M. van der. "Le Psaume 119 et la Sagesse." In *La sagesse de l'Ancien Testament*, ed. Hemchand Gossai, 82–87. Paris: Gembloux, 1979.

Polak, Frank H. "Sociolinguistics and the Judean Speech Community in the Achaemenid Empire." In *Judah and the Judeans in the Persian Period*, ed. Oded Lipschits and Manfred Oeming, 589–628. Winona Lake, IN: Eisenbrauns, 2006.

Polzin, Richard. *Late Biblical Hebrew: Toward an Historical Typology of Biblical Hebrew Prose.* HSM, vol. 12. Missoula, MT: Scholars Press, 1976.

Porten, Gary. "Midrash: Palestinian Jews and the Hebrew Bible in the Greco-Roman Period." In *Religion*, ed. Hildegard Temporini, 103–38. Vol. 19.2, *Aufstieg und Niedergang der römischen Welt*. Berlin: Walter de Gruyter, 1974.

Pyeon, Yohan. *You Have Not Spoken What Is Right About Me: Intertextuality and the Book of Job*. Studies in Biblical Literature, vol. 45. New York: Peter Lang, 2003.

Rad, Gerhard von. *Old Testament Theology*. Translated by D. M. G. Stalker. 2 vols. New York: Harper & Row, 1962.

——. *Studies in Deuteronomy*. Chicago: Regenery, 1953.

——. *Weisheit in Israel*. Neukirchen-Vluyn: Neukirchener, 1970.

——. " 'Righteousness' and 'Life' in the Cultic Language of the Psalms." In *The Form Critical Problem of the Hexateuch and other Essays*. New York: McGraw-Hill, 1966.

Raitt, Thomas M. *A Theology of Exile: Judgment/Deliverance in Jeremiah and Ezekiel*. Philadelphia: Fortress Press, 1977.

Reif, Stefan C. *Judaism and Hebrew Prayer: New Perspectives on Jewish Liturgical History*. Cambridge: Cambridge University Press, 1993.

Reindl, Joseph. *Das Angesicht Gottes im Sprachgebrauch des Alten Testaments*. Erfurter Theologische Studien, vol. 25. Leipzig: St. Benno Verlag, 1970.

Rendtorff, Rolf. "Anfragen an Frank-Lothar Hossfeld und Erich Zenger aufgrund der Lektüre des Beitrages von Mattias Millard." *Biblical Interpretation* 4 (1996): 329–31.

——. "Esra und das Gesetz." *ZAW* 96 (1984): 165–84.

——. "Noch einmal: Esra und das 'Gesetz'." *ZAW* 111 (1999): 89–91.

——. "Die Tora und die Propheten." In *Freiheit und Recht: Festschrift für Frank Crüsemann zum 65. Geburtstag*, ed. Christof Hardmeier, Rainer Kessler, and Andreas Ruwe, 155–61. Gütersloh: Verlagshaus Chr. Kaiser, 2003.

Reynolds, Kent Aaron. "The Answer of Psalm cxix 9." *VT* 58 (2008): 265–69.

——. "The Voice of Infinitives in Biblical Hebrew." *ZAH* (forthcoming).

Ricoeur, Paul. "The Self in the Mirror of Scriptures." In *The Whole and Divided Self. The Bible and Theological Anthropology*, ed. David E. Aune and John McCarthy, 201–20. New York: Crossroad Publishing Company, 1997.

Riedel, W. "Zur Redaktion des Psalters." *ZAW* 19 (1899): 169–72.

Robert, André. "Le Psaume 119 et la sapientaux." *RB* 48 (1939): 5–28.

Rofé, Alexander. "The Piety of the Torah-Disciples at the Winding-Up of the Hebrew Bible." In *Bibel in jüdischer und christlicher Tradition: Festschrift für Johann Maier zum 60. Geburtstag*, ed. Helmut Merklein, 78–85. Frankfurt am Main: Anton Hain, 1993.

Rogerson, J. W. and J. W. McKay. *Psalms 101–150*. The Cambridge Bible Commentary on the New English Bible. Cambridge: The University Press, 1977.

Runeson, Anders. *The Origins of the Synagogue: A Socio-Historical Study*. Coniectanea Biblica, New Testament Series, vol. 37. Stockholm: Almquist & Wiksell International, 2001.

Sabourin, L. *The Psalms: Their Origin and Meaning*. 2 vols. New York: Alba House, 1969.

Safran, Bezalel. "The Problem of Theodicy in the Book of Psalms." *The Yavneh Review* 7 (1969): 63–68.

Sailhamer, John. *Introduction to Old Testament Theology: A Canonical Approach*. Grand Rapids, MI: Zondervan, 1995.

Samely, Alexander. "Between Scripture and its Reworkings: Towards a Classification of Rabbinic Exegesis." *JJS* 42 (1991): 39–67.

——. *Rabbinic Interpretation of Scripture in the Mishnah*. New York: Oxford University Press, 2002.

Sanders, E. P. *Judaism: Practice and Belief 63 B.C.E.–66 C.E.* Philadelphia: Trinity Press International, 1992.

Sanders, James A. *The Dead Sea Psalms Scroll*. Ithaca, NY: Cornell University Press, 1967.

——, ed. *Qumran Cave 11*. DJD 4. Oxford: Clarendon Press, 1965.

——. *Torah and Canon*. 2nd ed. Eugene, OR: Cascade Books, 2005.

Satlow, Michael L. "'And on the Earth You Shall Sleep': *Talmud Torah* and Rabbinic Asceticism." *The Journal of Religion* 83 (2003): 204–25.

Sauer, Georg. "Weisheit und Tora in qumranischer Zeit." In *Weisheit auserhalb der kanonischen Weisheitsschriften*, ed. Bernd Janowski, 107–27. Gütersloh: Chr. Kaiser, 1996.

Schäfer, Peter. "Das 'Dogma' von der mündlichen Tora." In *Studien zur Geschichte und Theologie des rabbinischen Judentums*, 153–97. AGJU, vol. 15. Leiden: Brill, 1978.

Schildenberger, Johannes. "Das Psalmenpaar 111 und 112." *Erbe und Auftrag* 56 (1980): 203–7.

Schmitt, Hans-Christoph. *Arbeitsbuch zum Alten Testament*. Göttingen: Vandenhoeck & Ruprecht, 2005.

Schnabel, Eckhard J. *Law and Wisdom from Ben Sira to Paul*. Wissenschaftliche Untersuchungen zum Neuen Testament, vol. 16. Tübingen: J. C. B. Mohr, 1985.

Schniedewind, William. "Linguistic Ideology in Qumran Hebrew." In *Diggers at the Well*, ed. T. Muraoka and J. F. Elwolde, 245–55. Studies on the Texts of the Desert of Judah, vol. 36. Leiden: Brill, 2000.

——. "The Textualization of Torah in Jeremiah 8:8." In *Was ist ein Text? Alttestamentliche, ägyptologische und altorientalistische Perspektiven*, ed. Ludwig Morenz and Stefan Schorch, 93–107. BZAW, vol. 362. Berlin: de Gruyter, 2007.

——. *The Word of God in Transition: From Prophet to Exegete in the Second Temple Period*. JSOTSup, vol. 197. Sheffield: Sheffield Academic Press, 1995.

Schofer, Jonathan Wyn. *The Making of a Sage*. Madison, WI: University of Wisconsin Press, 2005.

——. "The Redaction of Desire: Structure and Editing of Rabbinic Teachings Concerning Yetser." *The Journal of Jewish Thought and Philosophy* 12 (2003): 19–53.

——. "Spiritual Exercises in Rabbinic Culture." *AJS Review* 27 (2003): 203–26.

Scholem, Gershom. "Revelation and Tradition as Religious Categories in Judaism." In *The Messianic Idea in Judaism*, 282–303. New York: Schocken Books, 1971. [translation of: "Offenbarung und Tradition als religiöse Kategorien im Judentum." In *Über einige Grundbegriffe des Judentums*, 90–120. Frankfurt: Suhrkamp Verlag, 1970.]

——. "Three Types of Jewish Piety." *Eranos Jahrbuch* 38 (1969): 331–48.

Schreiner, Josef. "Gottes wirkendes Wort nach dem Alten und Neuen Testament." In *Gegenwärtig in Wort und Sakrament. Eine Hinführung zur Sakramentenlehre*, 11–47. Buchreihe Theologie im Fernkurs, vol. 5. Freiburg: Herder, 1976.

——. "Leben nach der Weisung des Herrn." In *Gesammelte Schriften zur Entstehung und Theologie des Alten Testaments*, ed. Erich Zenger, 379–402. Würzburg: Echter, 1992.

Schuller, Eileen M. "Petitionary Prayer and the Religion of Qumran." In *Religion in the Dead Sea Scrolls*, ed. John J. Collins and Robert A. Kugler, 29–45. Grand Rapids, MI: Eerdmans, 2000.

Schultz, Richard L. *The Search for Quotation: Verbal Parallels in the Prophets*. JSOTSup, vol. 180. Sheffield: Sheffield Academic Press, 1999.

Schunck, Klaus-Dietrich. "Der Alttestamentliche Tora-Begriff." In *Altes Testament und Heiliges Land: gesammelte Studien zum Alten Testament und zur biblischen Landeskunde*, 243–55. Frankfurt am Main: Peter Lang, 1989.

Schwartz, Baruch. "Torah from Zion: Isaiah's Temple Vision (Isaiah 2:1–4)." In *Sanctity of Time and Space in Tradition and Modernity*, 11–26. Jewish and Christian Perspectives Series. Leiden: Brill, 1998.

Scott, R. B. Y. *The Way of Wisdom*. New York: Macmillan, 1971.

Searle, John. *Speech Acts: An Essay in the Philosophy of Language.* Cambridge: Cambridge University Press, 1970.

Seeligmann, I. L. "Indications of Editorial Alteration and Adaptation in the Massoretic Text and the Septuagint." *VT* 11 (1961): 201–21.

——. "Voraussetzungen der Midraschexegese." In *Congress Volume: Copenhagen, 1953,* ed. G. W. Anderson, 150–81. VTSup, vol. 1. Leiden: Brill, 1953.

Seidel, Moshe. "Parallels between Isaiah and Psalms." *Sinai* 38 (1955–56): 149–72, 229–40, 272–80, 335–55 [In Hebrew].

Seybold, Klaus. "David als Psalmsänger in der Bibel. Entstehung einer Symbolfigur." In *König David: biblische Schlüsselfigur und europäische Leitgestalt,* ed. Walter Dietrich and Hubert Herkommer, 145–63. Stuttgart: W. Kohlhammer, 2003.

——. *Die Psalmen.* HAT, vol. 1/15. ed. Matthias Köckert and Rudolf Smend. Tübingen: J. C. B. Mohr, 1996.

——. *Die Wallfahrtspsalmen: Studien zur Entstehungsgeschichte von Psalm 120–134.* Biblisch-Theologische Studien, vol. 35. ed. Ferdinand Hahn et al. Neukirchen-Vluyn: Neukirchener, 1978.

Sheppard, Gerald T. "Wisdom and Torah: The Interpretation of Deuteronomy Underlying Sirach 24:23." In *Biblical and Near Eastern Studies: Essays in Honor of William Sanford LaSor,* ed. Gary A. Tuttle, 166–76. Grand Rapids, MI: Eerdmans, 1978.

——. *Wisdom as a Hermeneutical Construct: A Study in the Sapientializing of the Old Testament.* BZAW, vol. 151. Berlin: de Gruyter, 1980.

Sherwood, S. "Psalm 112—A Royal Wisdom Psalm?" *CBQ* 51 (1989): 50–64.

Shinan, Avigdor, and Yair Zakovitch. "Midrash on Scripture and Midrash within Scripture." *Scripta Hierosolymitana* 31 (1986): 255–77.

Shuger, Debora K. "The Philosophical Foundations of Sacred Rhetoric." In *Rhetorical Invention and Religious Inquiry,* ed. Walter Jost and Wendy Olmstead, 47–64. New Haven, CT: Yale University Press, 2000.

Ska, Jean-Louis. "From History Writing to Library Building: The End of History and the Birth of the Book." In *The Pentateuch as Torah: New Models for Understanding its Promulgation and Acceptance.* ed. Gary N. Knoppers and Bernard M. Levinson, 143–70. Winona Lake, IN: Eisenbrauns, 2007.

——. *Introduction to Reading the Pentateuch.* Winona Lake, IN: Eisenbrauns, 2006.

Skehan, P. W. *Studies in Israelite Poetry and Wisdom.* CBQMS, vol. 1. Washington, D.C.: Catholic Biblical Association, 1971.

Smend, Rudolph. *Die Entstehung des Alten Testaments.* Theologische Wissenschaft: Sammelwerk für Studium und Beruf, vol. 1. Stuttgart: W. Kohlhammer, 1978.

Smith, Mark. "The Levitical Compilation of the Psalter." *ZAW* 103 (1991): 258–63.

Smyth, H. W. *Greek Grammar.* 1916. Revised by Gordon M. Messing. Cambridge, MA: Harvard University Press, 1956.

Snaith, Norman. "A Lamp Unto Our Feet." *Expository Times* 63 (1951): 58–59.

Soll, Will. "Babylonian and Biblical Acrostics." *Bib* 68 (1988): 305–23.

——. "The Israelite Lament: Faith Seeking Understanding." *Quarterly Review* 8 (1988): 77–87.

——. *Psalm 119: Matrix, Form, and Setting.* CBQMS, vol. 23. Washington, D.C.: Catholic Biblical Association, 1991.

——. "The Question of Psalm 119:9." *JBL* 106 (1987): 687–88.

Sommer, Benjamin D. *A Prophet Reads Scripture: Allusion in Isaiah 40–66.* Stanford, CA: Stanford University Press, 1998.

——. "Revelation at Sinai in the Hebrew Bible and in Jewish Theology." *Journal of Religion* 79 (1999): 422–51.

Spieckermann, Hermann. *Heilsgegenwart: Eine Theologie der Psalmen.* FRLANT, vol. 148. Göttingen: Vandenhoeck & Ruprecht, 1989.

——. "Mit der Liebe im Wort: Ein Beitrag zur Theologie des Deuteronomiums." *Liebe und Gebot: Studien zum Deuteronomium: Festschrift zum 70. Geburtstag von Lothar*

Perlitt, ed. Reinhard G. Kratz and Hermann Spieckermann, 190–205. Göttingen: Vandenhoeck & Ruprecht, 2000.

Spinks, D. Christopher. *The Bible and the Crisis of Meaning: Debates on the Theological Interpretation of Scripture*. New York: T & T Clark, 2007.

Stemberger, Günter. "Zum Verständnis der Schrift im rabbinischen Judentum." In *Bibel in jüdischer und christlicher Tradition: Festschrift für Johann Maier zum 60. Geburtstag*, 212–25. Athenäums Monografien, vol. 88. Frankfurt am Main: Anton Hain, 1993.

Stern, Sacha. *Jewish Identity in Early Rabbinic Writings*. Arbeiten zur Geschichte des antiken Judentums und des Urchristentums, vol. 23. Leiden: Brill, 1994.

Steussy, Marti J. *David: Biblical Portraits of Power*. Columbia, SC: University of South Carolina Press, 1999.

Stiebert, Johanna. *The Construction of Shame in the Hebrew Bible: The Prophetic Contribution*. JSOTSup, vol. 346. Sheffield: Sheffield Academic Press, 2002.

Stolz, Fritz. "Zeichen und Wunder: die prophetische Legitimation und ihre Geschichte." *ZThK* 69 (1972): 125–44.

Stone, Michael E. "Ideal Figures and Social Context: Priest and Sage in the Early Second Temple Age." In *Ancient Israelite Religion: Essays in Honor of Frank Moore Cross*, ed. Patrick D. Miller, Paul D. Hanson and S. D. McBride, 575–86. Philadelphia: Fortress, 1987.

Stuhlmueller, C. *Psalms*. 2 vols. Wilmington, DE: Glazier, 1983.

Sweeney, Marvin A. "The Book of Isaiah as Prophetic Torah." In *New Visions of Isaiah*, ed. Roy F. Melugin and Marvin A. Sweeny, 50–67. JSOTSup, vol. 214. Sheffield: Sheffield Academic Press, 1996.

Sweeney, Marvin A. and Ehud Ben Zvi, eds. *The Changing Face of Form Criticism for the Twenty-First Century*. Grand Rapids, MI: Eerdmans, 2003.

Talmon, Shemaryahu. "Heiliges Schrifttum und Kanonische Bücher aus jüdischer Sicht—Überlegungen zur Ausbildung der Größe 'Die Schrift' im Judentum." In *Mitte der Schrift? Ein jüdisch-christliches Gespräch*, ed. Martin Klopfenstein et al., 45–79. Judaica et Christiana, vol. 11. Bern: Peter Lang, 1987.

——. "Pisqah Be'emsaʿ Pasuq and 11Qpsᵃ." *Textus* 5 (1966): 11–21.

——. "Torah as a Concept and Vital Principle in the Hebrew Bible." *Greek Orthodox Theological Review* 24 (1979): 271–89.

——. "TORA—NOMOS—GESETZ: Die Bedeutung des Judentums für die christliche Theologie." In *Lernen in Jerusalem, Lernen mit Israel; Anstöße zur Erneuerung in Theologie und Kirche*, 130–47. Berlin: Institut Kirche und Judentum, 1993.

——. Review of *The Dead Sea Psalms Scrolls and the Book of Psalms*, by Peter S. Flint. *JBL* 118 (1999): 545–47.

Tannert, Werner. "Zum Begriff 'thorah' bei Jeremia und Deuterojesaja." In *Bekenntnis zur Kirche: Festgabe für Ernst Sommerlath zum 70. Geburtstag*, ed. Ernst-Heinz Amberg, 25–32. Berlin: Evangelische Verlagsanstalt, 1960.

Tate, Marvin E. *Psalms 51–100*. Word Biblical Commentary. Dallas, TX: Word, 1990.

Thiselton, Anthony C. "The Supposed Power of Words." *Journal of Theological Studies* 25 (1974): 283–99.

Thomas, Marlin. "Psalms 1 and 112 as a Paradigm for the Comparison of Wisdom Motifs in the Psalms." *JETS* 29 (1986): 15–24.

Tooman, William. "Ezekiel's Radical Challenge to Inviolability." *ZAW* 121 (2009): 498–514.

Tov, Emanuel. *Scribal Practices and Approaches Reflected in the Texts Found in the Judean Desert*. Studies on the Texts of the Desert of Judah, vol. 54. Leiden: Brill, 2004.

Tucker, Gene M. *Form Criticism of the Old Testament*. Guides to Biblical Scholarship. Philadelphia: Fortress Press, 1971.

Tucker, W. Dennis. "Literary Forms in the Wisdom Literature." In *An Introduction to Wisdom Literature and the Psalms*, 155–66. Macon, GA: Mercer University Press, 2000.
——. "Is Shame a Matter of Patronage in the Communal Laments?" *JSOT* 31 (2007): 465–80.
Ulrich, Eugene. "The Dead Sea Scrolls and Their Implications for an Edition of the Septuagint Psalter." In *Der Septuaginta-Psalter und seine Tochterübersetzungen*, ed. Anneli Aejmelaeus und Udo Quast, 323–36. Mitteilungen des Septuaginta-Unternehmens, vol. 24, Göttingen: Vandenhoeck & Ruprecht, 2000.
Urbach, Ephraim E. *The Sages: The World and Wisdom of the Rabbis of the Talmud.* Translated by Israel Abrahams. Cambridge, MA: Harvard University Press, 1987.
Van Leeuwen, Raymond C. "Form Criticism, Wisdom, and Psalm 111–112." In *The Changing Face of Form Criticism for the Twenty-First Century*, ed. Marvin A. Sweeny and Ehud Ben Zvi, 65–84. Grand Rapids, MI: Eerdmans, 2003.
VanderKam, James C. "The Righteousness of Noah." In *Ideal Figures in Ancient Judaism: Profiles and Paradigms*, ed. John J. Collins and George W. E. Nickelsburg, 13–32. Chico, CA: Scholars Press, 1980.
Vermes, Geza. "The Torah is a Light." *VT* 8 (1958): 436–38.
Volkwein, Bruno. "Masoretisches «Zeugnis» oder «Bundesbestimmungen»." *Biblische Zeitschrift* 13 (1969): 18–40.
Wagner, Max. *Die lexikalischen und grammatikalischen Aramaismen im alttestamentlichen Hebräisch.* BZAW, vol. 96. Berlin: Töpelmann, 1966.
Walter, D. M. *The Book of Psalms.* The Old Testament in Syriac according to the Peshitta Version. II.3. Leiden: Brill, 1980.
Waltke, Bruce K. and Michael P. O'Connor. *An Introduction to Biblical Hebrew Syntax.* Winona Lake, IN: Eisenbrauns, 1990.
Waschke, Ernst-Joachim. "David redivivus. Die Hoffnungen auf einen neuen David in der Spätzeit des Alten Testaments." In *König David: biblische Schlüsselfigur und europäische Leitgestalt*, ed. Walter Dietrich and Hubert Herkommer, 179–209. Stuttgart: W. Kohlhammer, 2003.
Watson, Wilfred G. E. *Classical Hebrew Poetry: A Guide to its Techniques.* JSOTSup, vol. 26. Sheffield: Sheffield Academic Press, 1984.
Weeks, Stuart. "Wisdom Psalms." In *Temple and Worship in Biblical Israel*, ed. John Day, 292–307. Library of Hebrew Bible/Old Testament Studies, vol. 422. London: T & T Clark, 2005.
Weinfeld, Moshe. "The Dependence of Deuteronomy upon the Wisdom Literature." In *Yehezkel Kaufmann Jubilee Volume*, ed. Menahem Haran, 89–111. Jerusalem: Magnes Press, 1960.
——. *Deuteronomy 1–11: A New Translation with Introduction and Commentary.* The Anchor Bible, vol. 5. New York: Doubleday, 1991.
——. *Deuteronomy and the Deuteronomic School.* Oxford: Oxford University Press, 1972.
Weiser, Artur. *The Psalms.* Translated by H. Hartwell. OTL. Philadelphia: Westminster, 1962.
Wellhausen, Julius. *The Book of Psalms.* New York: Dodd, Mead, and Co., 1898.
——. *Die Composition des Hexateuchs und der historischen Bücher des alten Testaments.* 4th ed. Berlin: de Gruyter, 1963.
——. *Prolegomena to the History of Ancient Israel.* Gloucester, MA: Peter Smith, 1973.
Wells Jr., Roy D. "'Isaiah' as an Exponent of Torah: Isaiah 56:1–8." In *New Visions of Isaiah*, ed. Roy F. Melugin and Marvin A. Sweeney, 140–55. JSOTSup, vol. 214. Sheffield: Sheffield Academic Press, 1996.
Westbrook, Raymond. "What is the Covenant Code?" In *Theory and Method in Biblical and Cuneiform Law: Revision, Interpretation, and Development*, ed. Bernard M. Levinson, 15–36. JSOTSup, vol. 181. Sheffield: Sheffield Academic Press, 1994.

Westerholm, Stephen. "Torah, Nomos, and Law: A Question of 'Meaning'." *Studies in Religion* 15 (1986): 327–36.

——. "Whence 'the Torah' of Second Temple Judaism." In *Law in Religious Communities in the Roman Period: the Debate of Torah and Nomos in Post-Biblical Judaism and Early Christianity*, 19–43. Studies in Christianity and Judaism, vol. 4. Waterloo, Ontario: Wilfrid Laurier University Press, 1991.

Westermann, Claus. "Die Begriffe für Fragen und Suchen im Alten Testament." *Kerygma und Dogma* 6 (1960): 2–30.

——. *Praise and Lament in the Psalms*. Translated by Keith Crim and Richard N. Soulen. Atlanta, GA: John Knox, 1981.

——. *The Psalms: Structure, Content and Message*. Translated by R. D. Gehrke. Minneapolis, MN: Augsburg, 1980.

——. "Zur Sammlung des Psalters." In *Forschung am alten Testament*, 336–43. Theologische Bücherei, vol. 24. Munich: Kaiser, 1962.

Wevers, John W. "A Study in the Form Criticism of Individual Complaint Psalms." *VT* 6 (1956): 80–96.

Whedbee, J. William. *Isaiah & Wisdom*. Nashville, TN: Abingdon Press, 1971.

Whybray, Roger N. "Psalm 119: Profile of a Psalmist." In *Wisdom, You are my Sister*, ed. Michael L. Barré, 31–43. CBQMS, vol. 29. Washington, D.C.: Catholic Biblical Association, 1997.

——. *Reading the Psalms as a Book*. JSOTSup, vol. 222. Sheffield: Sheffield Academic Press, 1996.

Willi, Thomas. *Die Chronik als Auslegung*. FRLANT, vol. 106. Göttingen: Vandenhoeck & Ruprecht, 1972.

——. *Juda—Jehud—Israel: Studien zum Selbstverständnis des Judentums in persischer Zeit*. FAT, vol. 12. Tübingen: J. C. B. Mohr, 1995.

——. "Thora in den biblischen Chronikbüchern." *Judaica* 36 (1980): 102–5; 148–51.

——. "Torah—Israels Lebensprinzip nach dem Zeugnis des späteren Alten Testaments." In *Meilenstein: Festgabe für Herbert Donner zum 16. Februar 1995*, ed. Herbert Donner et al., 339–48. Ägypten und Altes Testament, vol. 30. Wiesbaden: Harrassowitz, 1995.

Williamson, H. G. M. "The Concept of Israel in Transition." In *The World of Ancient Israel: Sociological, Anthropological, and Political Perspectives*, ed. R. E. Clements, 141–62. Cambridge: Cambridge University Press, 1989.

Willis, J. T. "Psalm 1—An Entity." *ZAW* 91 (1979): 381–401.

Wilson, Gerald. *The Editing of the Hebrew Psalter*. SBL Dissertation Series, vol. 76. Chico, CA: Scholars Press, 1985.

——. "Evidence of Editorial Divisions in the Hebrew Psalter." *VT* 34 (1984): 337–52.

——. "The Shape of the Book of Psalms." *Interpretation* 46 (1992): 129–42.

——. "The Qumran Psalms Manuscripts and the Consecutive Arrangement of Psalms in the Hebrew Psalter." *CBQ* 45 (1983): 377–88.

——. "The Qumran Psalms Scroll Reconsidered: Analysis of the Debate." *CBQ* 45 (1985): 624–42.

——. "The Use of Royal Psalms at the 'Seams' of the Hebrew Psalter." *JSOT* 35 (1986): 85–94.

Winston, David. "Theodicy in Ben Sira and Stoic Philosophy." In *Of Scholars, Savants, and Their Texts: Studies in Philosophy and Religious Thought*, 239–49. New York: Peter Lang, 1989.

Wiseman, D. J. *The Vassal Treaties of Esarhaddon*. London: British School of Archeology, 1958.

Wolf, Hans Walter. "Psalm 1." *EvTh* 9 (1949): 385–94.

Wright, Benjamin G., III. "'Fear the Lord and Honor the Priest': Ben Sira as Defender of the Jerusalem Priesthood." In *The Book of Ben Sira in Modern Research*, ed. Pancratius C. Beentjes, 189–222. Berlin: de Gruyter, 1997.

Wright, Jacob L. *Rebuilding Identity: The Nehemiah-Memoir and its Earliest Readers.* BZAW, vol. 348. Berlin: de Gruyter, 2004.

Yadin, Azzan. "Qol as Hypostasis in the Hebrew Bible." *JBL* 122 (2003): 601–26.

——. *Scripture as Logos: Rabbi Ishmael and the Origins of Midrash.* Philadelphia: University of Pennsylvania Press, 2004.

Zahavi, Dan. *Subjectivity and Selfhood: Investigating the First-person Perspective.* Cambridge, MA: MIT Press, 2005.

Zakovitch, Yair. "Juxtapositionen im Buch der Psalmen («Tehillim»)." In *Das Manna Fällt auch Heute Noch*, ed. Frank-Lothar Hossfeld and Ludger Schwienhorst-Schönberger, 660–73. HBS, vol. 44, Freiburg: Herder, 2004.

Zenger, Erich. "Daß alles Fleisch den Namen seiner Heiligung segne." *Biblische Zeitschrift* 41 (1997): 1–27.

——. "The Composition and Theology of the Fifth Book of Psalms." *JSOT* 80 (1998): 77–102. Originally published as "Komposition und Theologie des 5. Psalmenbuchs 107–145." *Biblische Notizen* 82 (1996): 97–116.

——. "Dimensionen der Tora-Weisheit in der Psalmenkomposition Ps 111–112." In *Die Weisheit—Ursprünge und Rezeption; Festschrift für Karl Löning zum 65. Geburtstag*, 37–58. Münster: Aschendorff, 2003.

——. "JHWH als Lehrer des Volks und der Einzelnen im Psalter." In *Religiöses Lernen in der biblischen, frühjüdischen und frühchristlichen Überlieferung*, 47–67. Tübingen: Mohr Siebeck, 2005.

——. "Der Psalter als Wegweiser und Wegbegleiter: Ps 1–2 als Proömium des Psalmenbuchs." In *Sie wandern von Kraft zu Kraft: Aufbrüche, Wege, Begegnungen—Festgabe für Bischof Reinhard Lettman*, ed. A. Angenendt, et al., 29–47. Kevelaer: Buzon and Bercker, 1993.

——. "Die späte Weisheit und das Gesetz." In *Literatur und Religion des Frühjudentums*, ed. Johann Maier and Josef Schreiner, 43–56. Würzburg: Echter, 1973.

——. "Torafrömmigkeit: Beobachtungen zum poetischen und theologischen Profil von Psalm 119." In *Freiheit und Recht: Festschrift für Frank Crüsemann zum 65. Geburtstag*, ed. Christof Hardmeier, Rainer Kessler, and Andreas Ruwe, 380–96. Gütersloh: Verlagshaus Chr. Kaiser, 2003.

Zimmerli, Walther. "Jahwes Wort bei Deuterojesaja." *VT* 32 (1982): 104–24.

——. *Der Mensch und seine Hoffnung im Alten Testament.* Göttingen: Vandenhoeck & Ruprecht, 1968. Translated as *Man and His Hope in the Old Testament* (London: SCM, 1971).

——. "Zwillingspsalmen." In *Wort, Lied und Gottesspruch*, ed. J. Schreiner, 105–13. Forschung zur Bibel, vol. 2. Würzburg: Echter, 1972.

INDEX OF REFERENCES

AUTHOR INDEX

SUBJECT INDEX

SUPPLEMENTS TO VETUS TESTAMENTUM

88. BARRICK, W. Boyd. *The King and the Cemeteries.* Toward a New Understanding of Josiah's Reform. 2002. ISBN 90 04 12171 4
89. FRANKEL, D. *The Murmuring Stories of the Priestly School.* A Retrieval of Ancient Sacerdotal Lore. 2002. ISBN 90 04 12368 7
90. FRYDRYCH, T. *Living under the Sun.* Examination of Proverbs and Qoheleth. 2002. ISBN 90 04 12315 6
91. KESSEL, J. *The Book of Haggai.* Prophecy and Society in Early Persian Yehud. 2002. ISBN 90 04 12368 7
92. LEMAIRE, A. (ed.). *Congress Volume, Basel 2001.* 2002. ISBN 90 04 12680 5
93. RENDTORFF, R. and R.A. KUGLER (eds.). *The Book of Leviticus.* Composition and Re ception. 2003. ISBN 90 04 12634 1
94. PAUL, S.M., R.A. KRAFT, L.H. SCHIFFMAN and W.W. FIELDS (eds.). *Emanuel.* Studies in Hebrew Bible, Septuagint, and Dead Sea Scrolls in Honor of Emanuel Tov. 2003. ISBN 90 04 13007 1
95. VOS, J.C. DE. *Das Los Judas.* Über Entstehung und Ziele der Landbeschreibung in Josua 15. ISBN 90 04 12953 7
96. LEHNART, B. *Prophet und König im Nordreich Israel.* Studien zur sogenannten vor klassischen Prophetie im Nordreich Israel anhand der Samuel-, Elija- und Elischa-Überlieferungen. 2003. ISBN 90 04 13237 6
97. LO, A. *Job 28 as Rhetoric.* An Analysis of Job 28 in the Context of Job 22-31. 2003. ISBN 90 04 13320 8
98. TRUDINGER, P.L. *The Psalms of the Tamid Service.* A Liturgical Text from the Second Temple. 2004. ISBN 90 04 12968 5
99. FLINT, P.W. and P.D. MILLER, JR. (eds.) with the assistance of A. Brunell. *The Book of Psalms.* Composition and Reception. 2004. ISBN 90 04 13842 8
100. WEINFELD, M. *The Place of the Law in the Religion of Ancient Israel.* 2004. ISBN 90 04 13749 1
101. FLINT, P.W., J.C. VANDERKAM and E. TOV. (eds.) *Studies in the Hebrew Bible, Qum-ran, and the Septuagint.* Essays Presented to Eugene Ulrich on the Occasion of his Sixty-Fifth Birthday. 2004. ISBN 90 04 13738 6
102. MEER, M.N. VAN DER. *Formation and Reformulation.* The Redaction of the Book of Joshua in the Light of the Oldest Textual Witnesses. 2004. ISBN 90 04 13125 6
103. BERMAN, J.A. *Narrative Analogy in the Hebrew Bible.* Battle Stories and Their Equi-valent Non-battle Narratives. 2004. ISBN 90 04 13119 1
104. KEULEN, P.S.F. VAN. *Two Versions of the Solomon Narrative.* An Inquiry into the Relationship between MT 1 Kgs. 2-11 and LXX 3 Reg. 2-11. 2004. ISBN 90 04 13895 1
105. MARX, A. *Les systèmes sacrificiels de l'Ancien Testament.* Forms et fonctions du culte sacrificiel à Yhwh. 2005. ISBN 90 04 14286 X
106. ASSIS, E. *Self-Interest or Communal Interest.* An Ideology of Leadership in the Gideon, Abimelech and Jephthah Narritives (Judg 6-12). 2005. ISBN 90 04 14354 8
107. WEISS, A.L. *Figurative Language in Biblical Prose Narrative.* Metaphor in the Book of Samuel. 2006. ISBN 90 04 14837 X
108. WAGNER, T. *Gottes Herrschaft.* Eine Analyse der Denkschrift (Jes 6, 1-9,6). 2006. ISBN 90 04 14912 0
109. LEMAIRE, A. (ed.). *Congress Volume Leiden 2004.* 2006. ISBN 90 04 14913 9
110. GOLDMAN, Y.A.P., A. van der Kooij and R.D. Weis (eds.). *Sôfer Mahîr.* Essays in Honour of Adrian Schenker Offered by Editors of *Biblia Hebraica Quinta.* 2006. ISBN 90 04 15016 1

111. WONG, G.T.K. *Compositional Strategy of the Book of Judges*. An Inductive, Rhetorical Study. 2006. ISBN 90 04 15086 2

112. HØYLAND LAVIK, M. *A People Tall and Smooth-Skinned*. The Rhetoric of Isaiah 18. 2006. ISBN 90 04 15434 5

113. REZETKO, R., T.H. LIM and W.B. AUCKER (eds.). *Reflection and Refraction*. Studies in Biblical Historiography in Honour of A. Graeme Auld. 2006. ISBN 90 04 14512 5

114. SMITH, M.S. and W.T. PITARD. *The Ugaritic Baal Cycle*. Volume II. Introduction with Text, Translation and Commentary of KTU/CAT 1.3–1.4. 2009. ISBN 978 90 04 15348 6

115. BERGSMA, J.S. *The Jubilee from Leviticus to Qumran*. A History of Interpretation. 2006. ISBN-13 978 90 04 15299 1. ISBN-10 90 04 15299 7

116. GOFF, M.J. *Discerning Wisdom*. The Sapiential Literature of the Dead Sea Scrolls. 2006. ISBN-13 978 90 04 14749 2. ISBN-10 90 04 14749 7

117. DE JONG, M.J. *Isaiah among the Ancient Near Eastern Prophets*. A Comparative Study of the Earliest Stages of the Isaiah Tradition and the Neo-Assyrian Prophecies. 2007. ISBN 978 90 04 16161 0

118. FORTI, T.L. *Animal Imagery in the Book of Proverbs*. 2007. ISBN 978 90 04 16287 7

119. PINÇON, B. *L'énigme du bonheur*. Étude sur le sujet du bien dans le livre de Qohélet. 2008. ISBN 978 90 04 16717 9

120. ZIEGLER, Y. *Promises to Keep*. The Oath in Biblical Narrative. 2008. ISBN 978 90 04 16843 5

121. VILLANUEVA, F.G. *The 'Uncertainty of a Hearing'*. A Study of the Sudden Change of Mood in the Psalms of Lament. 2008. ISBN 978 90 04 16847 3

122. CRANE, A.S. *Israel's Restoration*. A Textual-Comparative Exploration of Ezekiel 36–39. 2008. ISBN 978 90 04 16962 3

123. MIRGUET, F. *La représentation du divin dans les récits du Pentateuque*. Médiations syntaxiques et narratives. 2009. ISBN 978 90 04 17051 3

124. RUITEN, J. VAN and J.C. VOS DE (eds.). *The Land of Israel in Bible, History, and Theology*. Studies in Honour of Ed Noort. 2009. ISBN 978 90 04 17515 0

125. EVANS, P.S. *The Invasion of Sennacherib in the Book of Kings*. A Source-Critical and Rhetorical Study of 2 Kings 18-19. 2009. ISBN 978 90 04 17596 9

126. GLENNY, W.E. *Finding Meaning in the Text*. Translation Technique and Theology in the Septuagint of Amos. 2009. ISBN 978 90 04 17638 6

127. COOK, J. (ed.). *Septuagint and Reception*. Essays prepared for the Association for the Study of the Septuagint in South Africa. 2009. ISBN 978 90 04 17725 3

128. KARTVEIT, M. *The Origin of the Samaritans*. 2009. ISBN 978 90 04 17819 9

129. LEMAIRE, A., B. HALPERN and M.J. ADAMS (eds.). *The Books of Kings*. Sources, Composition, Historiography and Reception. 2010. ISBN 978 90 04 17729 1

130. GALIL, G., M. GELLER and A. MILLARD (eds.). *Homeland and Exile*. Biblical and Ancient Near Eastern Studies in Honour of Bustenay Oded. 2009. ISBN 978 90 04 17889 2

131. ANTHONIOZ, S. *L'eau, enjeux politiques et théologiques, de Sumer à la Bible*. 2009. ISBN 978 90 04 17898 4

132. HUGO, P. and A. SCHENKER (eds.). *Archaeology of the Books of Samuel*. The Entangling of theTextual and Literary History. 2010. ISBN 978 90 04 17957 8

133. LEMAIRE, A. (ed.). *Congress Volume Ljubljana*. 2007. 2010. ISBN 978 90 04 17977 6

134. ULRICH, E. (ed.). *The Biblical Qumran Scrolls*. Transcriptions and Textual Variants. 2010. ISBN 978 90 04 18038 3

135. DELL, K.J., G. DAVIES and Y. VON KOH (eds.). *Genesis, Isaiah and Psalms*. A Festschrift to honour Professor John Emerton for his eightieth birthday. 2010. ISBN 978 90 04 18231 8

136. GOOD, R. *The Septuagint's Translation of the Hebrew Verbal System in Chronicles*. 2010. ISBN 978 90 04 15158 1

137. REYNOLDS, K.A. *Torah as Teacher*. The Exemplary Torah Student in Psalm 119. 2010. ISBN 978 90 04 18268 4